P9-CLI-620

PRESIDENTIAL SELECTION

PRESIDENTIAL SELECTION

Alexander Heard and Michael Nelson, Editors

DUKE UNIVERSITY PRESS   DURHAM 1987

© 1987 Duke University Press
All rights reserved
Printed in the United States of America
on acid-free paper ∞
Library of Congress Cataloging-in-Publication Data
Presidential selection.
Includes index.
1. Presidents—United States—Election. I. Heard,
Alexander. II. Nelson, Michael.
JK524.P69 1987   324.973   87-9164
ISBN 0-8223-0750-2
ISBN 0-8223-0785-5 (pbk.)

To our children

Stephen	Michael
Christopher	Sam
Frank	
Connie	

Contents

Preface

The way Americans choose their presidents has been studied exhaustively. Scholars and journalists have created an enormous and important literature addressing campaign finance, nominating procedures, the mass media, electoral participation, and other significant aspects of the subject. But the literature on presidential selection is also remarkably self-contained. Most studies of how Americans choose their presidents are simply that, studies of how Americans choose their presidents.

In this collection of thirteen original essays we have not neglected traditional concerns. But we also have tried to incorporate three important themes into the study of presidential selection. First, what are the international implications of the U.S. presidential selection process? How does the process affect other nations? Does it enhance or diminish the ability of the United States to deal effectively with the rest of the world? Second, how do changing characteristics of the presidential selection process affect the shaping of public policies, and vice versa? How, for example, have changes in citizen participation, campaign technologies, and campaign finance laws altered the balance of political power among important institutions and interests? How might changes in communications policy modify television's role in presidential campaigns? The third theme, made especially timely by the bicentennial of the Constitution, is the influence of the Constitution on presidential selection. What are the effects of the constitutionally prescribed qualifications for the presidency? What provisions does the Constitution make for unusual circumstances, for selecting presidents outside the normal electoral channels, and with what effects?

This book had its origins in an invitation to study the presidential selection process that was extended to Alexander Heard by the Alfred P. Sloan Foundation. To assist in that undertaking, prominent scholars from the United States and elsewhere were commissioned to write papers. The topics were carefully defined, individually and in relation to each other, to fill lacunae, but also to provide a well-integrated, comprehensive treatment of presidential selection.

As the papers came in during 1983 and 1984, it became clear that although they had not been commissioned for purposes of publication, a large proportion could with relative ease be revised into publishable form. Grouped together, they would make a collection of quality, timeliness, and unusual scope. In 1984 Heard invited Michael Nelson to serve as coeditor of the book that was now planned. Since then, with Nelson's guidance, the authors have revised their papers extensively to incorporate not only editorial suggestions but more recent events, such as the 1984 election and the temporary transfer of power from President Ronald Reagan to Vice President George Bush in July 1985.

We have many people to thank in addition to the Sloan Foundation and the authors. The study of presidential selection for which the papers were commissioned was conducted in the Vanderbilt Institute for Public Policy Studies, of which Erwin C. Hargrove was director during most of the work and Clifford S. Russell at the end. Lottie M. Strupp, Assistant Director for Administration of the Institute, gave cheerful and essential support all along the way. Scarlett G. Graham and Kay L. Hancock, associates of Heard, contributed decisively in defining the original twenty-four topics on which scholars were commissioned to write; Graham compiled the index. Nanette B. Fancher and Wanda Uselton, administrative assistants, and Thomas A. Underwood, research assistant, helped at important stages. The work was done in facilities made available by Vanderbilt University.

Alexander Heard
Michael Nelson

1   Change and Stability in Choosing Presidents

ALEXANDER HEARD AND MICHAEL NELSON

For two decades politically active Americans have been preoccupied with proposals to change the way they choose their presidents. Substantial change actually has occurred. Actions taken by the parties radically modified the means of nominating candidates; offical actions by government spread the suffrage and altered campaign funding; and informal campaign practices evolved, some quickly and others gradually.

These essays address the significance of four recent and important trends in the presidential selection process and one continuing concern.

1. Changes have occurred in the world context in which American government is conducted.
2. The pools of volunteers who dominate American politics—voters, contributors, political activists, aspiring candidates, and office-holders—have been changing.
3. The structure and technologies of presidential campaigns also have been changing, as reflected recently in opinion sampling, campaign coordination and organization, and political finance.
4. Innovations in the mass media have always affected political processes, but never more so than recently.
5. The presidency can become vacant between elections under many different circumstances. There is much disagreement about these

possibilities and the potential consequences if any of them should arise.

The concerns, analyses, and proposals that appear here reflect the important attention that scholars are giving to the way Americans choose their presidents.

A New World Context

American presidential selection usually is studied as part of the unique set of circumstances, historical conditions, and traditions that constitute the United States. Comparisons are drawn between the present and previous eras. Is the modern system of primaries and caucuses, for example, more or less democratic, more or less effective, more or less legitimate, than when national party conventions dominated the nominating process? Assessments of the influence of party organizations, the mass media, interest groups, financial contributors, issues activists, and others ordinarily accept the traditional contours of American politics as fixed. Similarly, when proposals are made to reform presidential selection, often through changes in the constitutionally prescribed structure of the government, the normal frame of reference is past practice in the United States.

Our interest here is not to propose a new constitutional system. But we do wish to explore whether Americans can benefit from considering the effect of present selection procedures on American international relations, and also whether they can learn anything applicable to the United States from practices for choosing political leaders that are followed in other nations.

The issues, interests, and ambitions that animate American presidential elections are primarily domestic, but the consequences are at least as important to the world as to the nation. On the great issues of war and peace, Ralf Dahrendorf observes in his essay on "Presidential Selection and Continuity in Foreign Policy" that it is the president of the United States who is largely responsible for "whether the world lives in a climate of tension or of détente, of arms race or of disarmament talks." Similarly, Ernest May, in "Changing International Stakes in Presidential Selection," suggests that much of the international economy is dependent on presidential policies that, although vitally important to people outside the United States, are not controlled by them.

Both Dahrendorf and May discover obstacles to the responsible exercise of American military and financial power in presidential selection practices. Dahrendorf finds a potent tension between the imperatives of becoming president and those of being president: "Candidates for president are chosen and elected primarily for domestic reasons, yet once elected their most consequential responsibilities are in the international field." Electoral pressures may move a candidate to endorse a protectionist trade policy or to attack international agreements that offend certain groups—even at the risk of alienating allies and making all nations question the reliability of the United States as an actor in world affairs. "During the early primaries in particular," writes May, candidates "are often put questions by zealots who want to test the degree of commitment to their particular cause." Democrats in 1984, for example, outdid each other in pledging their fealty to such policies as a proposed "nuclear freeze" and the transfer of the U.S. embassy in Israel from Tel Aviv to Jerusalem. "Such performances make many Americans nervous," May observes. "Understandably, they make foreigners even more so."

Dahrendorf also regards the sheer volatility of presidential politics as unsettling in its international consequences. Because "the role of the presidency is supreme" in foreign policymaking, new presidents can bring rapid and dramatic changes in policy that are disturbing to others. Dahrendorf characterizes as "staggering" and "unbelievable" the dramatic swings in policy that have occurred in recent years. Control of the presidency has passed from Richard Nixon and his "cynical geopolitics" to Jimmy Carter's "moralism of a good partner," and then to Ronald Reagan's "new patriotism of a combination of missionary isolationism and crude power motives."

Yet Dahrendorf and May, despite full sensitivity to the difficulties to which the presidential selection process contributes, each find it, on balance, to be healthy. Prudence is the quality that foreigners most desire in American presidents, according to May, and prudence is what American voters have given them. "Most of the time, the nominating process [has] winnowed out just about everyone whose approach was not careful, prudent, and risk-minimizing," he argues. "In instances in any way exceptional, the voters nearly always chose the more prudent-seeming candidate when the general election came around." Especially in the nuclear age, adds Dahrendorf, this desire for prudence has bound Americans and foreigners together, forging "an ultimate and unbreakable link between domestic and international affairs."

May, too, finds solace for the international community. "The American public that cares about foreign publics is very large and diverse, and it has been growing," he argues. Ethnic loyalties have always moved many Americans to political action in behalf of their ancestral homelands. But nowadays other influences are at work, and in a less sectarian way: the internationalization of American business, widespread foreign travel, and the broadening effects of higher education.

Although Dahrendorf and May, in their pleas for an international perspective on American presidential selection, are concerned about the interests of foreigners in the relationship between the selection process and the world, an American stake pervades this relationship as well. Presidents deal with the leaders of other nations on a host of economic and security issues. To the extent that their prior careers prepare or fail to prepare them for this task, the national interest presumably will prosper or suffer accordingly.

Richard Rose's study of the career backgrounds of post-World War II leaders, and contenders for leadership, in the United States, Great Britain, France, and West Germany, suggests a degree of pessimism. The title of his essay, "Learning to Govern or Learning to Campaign?," poses a question seemingly answered: in Western Europe the former, in the United States, the latter.

Rose finds that of the fourteen people who have been nominated by the two major political parties as candidates for president of the United States since 1945, almost all have been experienced electoral politicians, but only three (Dwight Eisenhower, Adlai Stevenson, and Richard Nixon) could claim "significant prior knowledge" of national security issues. Still worse, no president in the postwar era has had any direct prior experience with economic policy, either in government or the private sector. In contrast, Rose shows that European prime ministers are much more likely to have spent time as ministers of foreign affairs, economic affairs, or both. Even if they have not, they typically have served in cabinets at whose meetings international issues were discussed frequently.

The differences Rose uncovers, more than anything else, manifest more fundamental and important differences between the American system and the parliamentary systems of Western Europe. Almost every aspect of politics and government in Western Europe is more institutionalized than in the United States—distinct party identities as compared to diffuse ones, unitary national governments in contrast to the three-branch, three-tiered American federal system, a mass media more constrained by law and custom than in a First Amendment society, and more. Conspicuously, the highly patterned, structured leadership selection processes of European democracies contrast sharply to the fluid, comparatively free-form set of activities by which American presidents are chosen.

Because the American presidential selection process is both complex and loosely structured, particular elements in it are much more likely to affect the overall character of leadership selection than in European countries. Campaign finance regulations, media practices, polling, and other details of electoral campaigning normally are not very influential in shaping and channeling political conflict in Western Europe. Americans, however, are required to expend great effort considering such matters. Not only does the fluidity and complexity of the process make the details consequential, but so does the great latitude for unintended consequences that arises from that fluidity and complexity because of the number of interconnections between the many elements of the process.

Volunteer Democracy: Voters and Candidates

The periodic encounters of two sets of volunteers are the essence of American democratic elections: voters seeking leadership and candidates wanting to supply it. The formal and informal rules that govern those voluntary efforts are important aspects of the presidential selection process that merit attention. To understand what kinds of people voluntarily seek office, and what kinds vote, is of great consequence.

Voters—in particular, the laws and procedures that govern their participation in elections—are Gary Orren's concern in "The Linkage of Policy to Participation." Orren finds American voters distinctive in some significant respects. In other democratic nations, citizens vote at a high rate. Moreover, nonvoters do not differ substantially in their social characteristics from voters. In the United States, neither of these conditions obtains. Voter turnout in recent presidential elections typically has been 50 to 60 percent, and nonvoters are disproportionately poor, nonwhite, and less educated. Orren argues that such an unrepresentative electorate poses an organic issue in a system that relies on the electoral process to foster legitimacy, representation, and civic education. Even worse, the gap between the voting rates of high-status and low-status citizens has been widening in recent elections and nonvoting soon may become habitual for large numbers of people.

For American voters, participation in elections is almost entirely voluntary. Would-be presidential candidates not only must decide to seek their party's nomination, but face the important additional challenge of attaining the label "serious." What kinds of candidates succeed? Michael Nelson approaches this question in "Who Vies for President?" in the manner of Sherlock Holmes solving a case: "Eliminate the impossible and whatever is left, however improbable, is the answer."

The Constitution bars some people from consideration on the basis of age, nationality at birth, and length of residency. Although the reasons for these constitutional provisions may be archaic, and their effects sometimes unsettling (Henry Kissinger, born in Germany, could not have served as president even if, as secretary of state, the line of succession had reached him), the main constraints on would-be candidates for president are in the hearts and minds of voters. Nelson shows that, historically, the electorate's operative list of qualifications for the presidency has removed from consideration women, nonwhites, non-Christians, and bachelors. It also has stipulated that candidates have recent, prominent governmental experience if they are to be taken seriously, which in recent years has meant service as senator, governor, or vice president. But, Nelson indicates, other standards and prejudices that were important to voters in earlier periods, such as Protestantism, have been altered or abandoned, and changes in the current list may be occurring as well.

If Nelson's main concern is for the influence of the U.S. Constitution and American culture on presidential candidates, John Aldrich's is for the varying rules and procedures that the Democratic and

Republican parties have used to stucture nominations for president. In "Methods and Actors: The Relationship of Processes to Candidates," Aldrich asks whether changes in party rules that have occurred during four historical eras since 1872 (the most recent beginning after the 1968 election) have altered the kinds of candidates selected by the parties and, later, by the voters. In important respects, having mainly to do with the personal and political backgrounds of candidates, changes in rules apparently have made little difference. On the other hand, rule changes, especially more recent ones, have affected the kinds of campaigns candidates must wage to be successful, and therefore the political skills required of them. For example, "the need for public support induces a bias in the system that favors those who can best use the technology of public campaigning and who can invest the most and longest effort in campaigning."

Modern Campaign Elites

The number and representativeness of the voters who take part in selecting a country's leadership, and the quality of the candidates who are chosen, are important but not exclusive measures of the process. Also significant is how particular aspects of it shape political conflict in the larger system, affect the political agenda, and magnify or diminish the influence of various participants. Three essays give attention to, respectively, the actions of pollsters, party politicians, and interest groups as intermediaries between voters and candidates. Again, the comparison with Western European democracies is instructive. The British political scientist Dennis Kavanagh has observed that "in recent years candidate and issue factors have become much more important than political parties in deciding elections in the United States. We talk in Western Europe about a volatile electorate, but it is on a much smaller scale than has occurred in the United States. . . . [O]ne reason for this change in the United States is called the 'new politics'. . . . the mass media, advertising, opinion polls, public relations."

James Beniger and Robert Giuffra treat political pollsters as a new campaign elite in their essay, "Public Opinion Polling: Command and Control in Presidential Campaigns." The growing importance of polls in American politics is demonstrated, they show, by the fact that presidential candidates in recent elections have employed five different kinds of polls—benchmark, follow-up, panel, tracking, and focus—at nine different stages of the campaign—from deciding to run to monitoring daily fluctuations in opinion during the weeks before election day. The influence of pollsters has risen sharply: candidates use their interpretations of public opinion to help mold both the style and substance of campaigns. Inevitably, successful presidential candidates now maintain a close relationship with their pollsters while in office.

Part of the pollsters' appeal is the aura of certainty that surrounds their analyses. "Unlike the typical presidential adviser," Beniger and Giuffra write, "the pollster has the added advantage of being able to support his advice with seemingly objective quantitative data." The effects on governance may be profound. As presidents try to cater to public opinion, they may neglect their responsibility to lead by shaping public opinion with independent policies. Ironically, such a strategy may contain the seeds of its own failure. Beniger and Giuffra portray Jimmy Carter as a president whom the public regarded as vacillating because he "continually shifted positions in response to changes in Patrick Caddell's polls." In contrast, Ronald Reagan's success can be explained largely by his persistence in offering an unchanging set of appeals.

To the extent that modern polling has made candidates more self-reliant and their pollsters more important in the presidential selection process, traditional party politicians are correspondingly weaker. The role of parties in presidential campaigns also has been diminished, Herb Asher argues in "The Three Campaigns for President," by campaign finance legislation enacted by Congress during the 1970s. Such legislation "created a situation in which three possible campaigns could be conducted simultaneously for the presidency —the candidate-dominated campaign, the party-directed effort, and a set of activities sponsored by concerned citizens and organizations independent of the candidate and party." But even this listing overrepresents the parties' influence because the candidate-centered campaign heavily influences the other two. A system that elevates the influence of candidates distorts governance and weakens the parties, Asher argues: the main concern of the candidate-centered effort with its many campaign specialists is for the short-term objective of winning and not the long-term goal of governing.

Xandra Kayden observes in "Regulating Campaign Finances: Consequences for Interests and Institutions" that the balance of power among interest groups in society has been affected by the recent campaign finance laws, not just the relative importance of candidates and parties. Public financing and effective restrictions on the size of campaign contributions, for example, have reduced the influence of big business in presidential campaigns while increasing that of organizations whose members are aroused by controversial moral issues. Disagreeing with some other authors in this volume, Kayden argues that the national party organizations have been strengthened in recent years by campaign finance legislation because of the unique services they can provide presidential candidates in a highly regulated system. She also sees a measure of stability and continuity developing in the campaign process in the form of professional campaign consulting organizations.

Such disagreement among the experts is not surprising. Clearly, new campaign rules and technologies, and the new or altered campaign elites they have produced, have transformed the presidential selection process profoundly. But the precise delineation and assessment of this transformation are not likely until time allows a longer and better informed perspective.

Changing Communications

The mass media, like pollsters, party politicians, and interest groups, are important in modern presidential election campaigns. Indeed, so pervasive have the media become in presidential selection that both political practitioners and political analysts have found it difficult to delineate the functions, importance, and proper place of media politics. The chapters by James David Barber, "Presidential Politics and the Myth of Conciliation: The Case of 1980," and Thomas Patterson, "Television and Presidential Politics," are two efforts to understand some of these issues.

Barber's essay extends to the 1980 election the theory of the mass media and presidential politics that he first propounded in his 1980 book, *The Pulse of Politics*. The theory holds that the rise of various forms of national media in the twentieth century, notably newspapers, magazines, radio, and television, has caused presidential elections to be dominated by the theme of "conflict" in one election, "conscience" in the next, and "conciliation" in the next, in an ever-recurring cycle. In 1980 the pulsebeat produced a conciliating election, one in which "the public appetite [is] for solace and ease, unity and friendship." In harmony with this mood, Barber argues, candidate Reagan offered voters a vision of America that was more myth than reality. The mass media, far from bringing him to terms on substantive matters, contributed to this "drift to fiction."

Barber's concern for mass public mood swings in presidential elections is not surprising, given the fluid, loosely structured American political system. Neither is the importance he logically attaches to the detailed activities of a campaign elite that in European settings is minor, the media. Patterson, like Barber, is concerned mainly with how well the voters are served by presidential elections campaigns; like Barber, he regards the nexus between candidates and the media as crucial for this concern.

Given the weakness of American political parties, the needs of the electorate in presidential elections can be met, Patterson argues, only if candidates can get their messages across on television and broadcasters can supplement those messages with objective reporting based on facts and opinions independently obtained. Assessing recent research on television's coverage of presidential campaigns, Patterson concludes that broadcasters can perform their function adequately through news programs. But, by granting insufficient access, those same broadcasters have obstructed candidates' efforts to get their own appeals out. Voters are left puzzled about what the issues of the election really are.

Special Succession to the Presidency

The Constitution figures remotely in most scholarly treatments of presidential selection. The electoral college, whose methods of functioning are spelled out in Article 2 and the Twelfth Amendment, is now regarded not as a decisionmaking body but as a mirror or magnifier of the popular vote. The two-term limit on presidential tenure imposed by the Twenty-second Amendment is of obvious importance, but only when an incumbent president is sufficiently popular, vigorous, and ambitious to desire a third term.

The essays of this volume have directed attention to the comparatively free-form character of American politics. But the rules and procedures ordained in the Constitution are worth a closer look. In fact, the Constitution shapes the selection process in a variety of subtle as well as obvious ways. Although, for example, the electoral college does not elect the president in the way the framers intended, its requirement that a candidate must receive a majority of the electoral votes to win has contributed to the creation and endurance of a two-party system. Its allocation of votes to states has ensured that when third parties are formed, those that are regionally based will fare better than those whose support is thinly spread across the nation. And its encouragement of bloc voting by states heightens the importance of the large, competitive states. Most important, perhaps, the electoral college's status separate from Congress allows presidents to claim an independent national mandate.

If, in ordinary times, the influence of the Constitution on the manner of presidential selection is subtle, its influence in extraordinary circumstances is direct and controlling. Indeed, the Constitution anticipates and provides for as many as a dozen contingencies that would require "unusual" presidential selection, that is, selection by a method other than the normal one in which presidents gain office by winning a majority of the electoral votes. Articles I and II and amendments Twelve, Twenty, and Twenty-five, taken together, not only anticipate the possibility that no president will receive an electoral vote majority, but also provide for presidential selection in the event of the president's—and in some cases the president-elect's—death, resignation, conviction for impeachment, or disability. The Twenty-fifth Amendment also provides against the possibility that the vice presidency, whose incumbent is successor to the presidency in all constitutional cases of unusual selection, is unoccupied in time of crisis.

In "Presidential Selection and Succession in Special Situations," Allan Sindler examines several provisions of law and Constitution that pertain to unusual selection. Sorting out the underlying issues, he finds widespread agreement with the longstanding belief that presidential vacancies should be filled by succession rather than special election, preferably succession by the vice president. Sindler applies two criteria to existing and proposed succession arrangements: first, do they assure that the presidency will be occupied by a member of the departed president's party?; and second, do they assure that potential successors will be people selected for their present offices by the departed president?

The American Way

When Europeans discuss electoral reform, they usually concentrate on basic questions. They ask, for example, whether proportional representation or a system of single-member districts with a winner-take-all rule is best. Only such basic possibilities really affect political activity in the highly institutionalized European democracies. In the relatively free-form American political system, proposals to change the manner of selection usually—and appropriately—are at the level of minor detail. Unlike in Europe, political reformers in the United States do not often feel the need to resort to massive institutional change to cope with the ills they diagnose.

The proposed reforms in these essays were not designed as an integrated set of recommendations. Yet they share in common the quality of "institutional tinkering." Thomas Patterson, for example, offers a detailed proposal to set aside network television time during the four weeks prior to a presidential election for a series of evening broadcasts in which the candidates could speak directly to the voters; journalists could question the candidates; and the candidates could debate each other. Such a proposal, Patterson argues, "asks neither candidates nor broadcasters to compromise their respective advocacy and scrutiny functions. Instead, it combines those functions in a complementary way that would enable candidates to present their agendas and broadcasters to assess them."

Richard Rose makes a detailed proposal for reform in his essay. Rose, whose ideal nominating process would "balance considerations of intraparty ideological preferences, electoral appeal, and effectiveness in office," suggests that a national presidential primary be held by each party with convention delegates awarded to candidates in proportion to their share of the vote. Ordinarily, Rose predicts, no candidate would win a majority of delegates in the primary, which would restore the convention's role as the true forum for presidential nominations—a much desired outcome, in his opinion. Although Herb Asher and John Aldrich make no specific proposals, their individually expressed preference for enhanced party control of the nominating process is in accord with Rose's.

Gary Orren and Allan Sindler share an ambivalence about the magnitude of electoral reform they desire. Orren would prefer to see voter registration made compulsory, in frank acknowledgment that voting, like taxpaying, is a duty and should be treated as such. Realizing that such a view would run counter to American individualist values, however, Orren instead endorses a variety of proposals to make registration easier and more convenient for potential voters. Sindler, whose preference would be for constitutional amendments that would, for example, eliminate the "faithless elector" problem from presidential elections, nonetheless emphasizes reforms that could be accomplished by the less elaborate process of simple legislation: reconfigure the line of succession to assure that partisan control of the presidency could not change if the office became vacant, and make clear that if the presidential election winner were to die before the electoral college formally cast its vote, the victorious vice presidential candidate would be elected instead. Even these authors' bolder proposals would not fundamentally alter the existing system.

Other contributors make specific suggestions for reform, but only after expressing a broad satisfaction with the current presidential selection process. Michael Nelson applauds recent developments in the mass media and in campaign finance laws that have made it easier for persons who have built successful careers in the private sector to enter electoral politics at a high level, thereby broadening the talent pool from which presidential candidates are drawn. Xandra Kayden also commends the campaign finance laws for, in her view, strengthening the political party organizations. In addition, Nelson concludes that the recent democratization of the nominating process "has contributed to the breakdown of arbitrary barriers [to the presidency] such as religion and age, and seems likely to have this effect on racial and sexual barriers." Condemning remaining barriers to talent, he suggests that the Constitution's two-term limit and its requirement that presidents be natural-born citizens should be repealed.

Finally, from his international perspective, Ernest May judges that, on balance, the American presidential selection process works well. He finds wisdom in the proposal of only minor reforms, those whose purpose would be to lead presidential candidates to inform themselves better about international issues. Dahrendorf also eschews advocating substantial alteration of the process, not only because he thinks "American institutions have worked quite well," but also because the uncertainty of reform makes it impossible "to see how any other process can guarantee the emergence of different persons [as president], let alone a different political stance by those who emerge."

The recommendations of these thirteen independent political analysts for improving the presidential selection process expose two general conclusions. The process is far from perfect; it needs adventitious improvement, not radical change.

2 Presidential Selection and Continuity in Foreign Policy

RALF DAHRENDORF

Three arguments are explored in this chapter. The first is that for-eign policy requires a greater degree of continuity than domestic policy in order to be effective. This has not always been fully recog-nized in the United States. The second argument is that the American tradition in international affairs recently has been transformed by changing international circumstances. After a period of pax Ameri-cana, the world order has become one of fragmentation and uncer-tainty, a circumstance that both increases and dissipates American power. Third, among U.S. foreign policymakers, the presidency has a supremely strong position. But in view of the electoral and the decisionmaking process, this strength serves to aggravate the weak-nesses of American foreign policy.

Continuity in Foreign Policy

Continuity, consensus, and nonpartisanship are popular notions, even though they are at variance with the assumptions of the demo-cratic process. Most people like unity, but our constitutions know better, given our divergent interests and changing aspirations. Par-ties, competition, diversity—and as a consequence discontinuity and change—are the lifeblood of liberty. Such continuity as exists is based on agreement on the rules of the game; it is provided by the constitutional framework within which the democratic process takes place. Discontinuity is contained by the due process of politics.

But foreign policy differs from most domestic policies. In the conduct of foreign policy significantly more continuity is necessary. The reason is simple: if foreign policy is to be more than an empty set of announcements, it must become an effective pattern of action. In order to be effective, it has to be credible; in order to be credible, it has to be predictable; and in order to be predictable, it must be carried on with consistency over considerable periods of time.

In a different context it would be intriguing to speculate why this should be so. Several possibilities come to mind. One is, as it were, the "nature of the beast." The foreign policy of a state is by definition an expression of its perceived interest as a total entity (its national interest), and not merely that of particular groups, sections, or classes. The directions of foreign policy must of necessity be determined by deeper currents of substance and style than can find expression in any single election. In practical terms this means that any democratic government must combine, in its foreign policy, partisan interest with the desire to impress on others that it is acting on behalf of the country. Others must not be allowed to try to "sit out" a particular government, hoping that the next one will soon undo what the present one is planning. If only for this reason, there is almost always a good case to be made for bipartisan foreign policy.

The existence of "others"—other states, other actors—is important in another sense as well. The recipients of foreign policy do not always share the specific volatilities of the domestic electorate. They react more slowly and more gradually. When they notice new signals, their initial reaction is often one of bewilderment, even anxiety. The international political system moves in longer waves than any domestic system.

Acceptability abroad is certainly not the only criterion of success for foreign policy. In any case, a superpower can to some extent impose its will on allies and adversaries alike. But whatever the other criteria one employs to judge success, including the defense of national interest, they all lead back to the need for continuity, and the price of discontinuity. It would appear that the United States has paid this price on several occasions, and in several ways. Three examples may serve to advance the argument as well as illustrate it.

Narrow Interests and Wider Ramifications

Sometimes foreign policy decisions are comprehensible in terms of immediate interest, but have ramifications that far outweigh such an interest. Two recent American examples are the sudden termination of U.S. participation in the final stages of the Law of the Seas conference, and its withdrawal from the United Nations Organization for Education, Science and Culture (UNESCO).

In both cases the U.S. position is at first glance quite comprehensible. It is based on certain clear, if narrow, interests and convictions. In the case of the law of the seas, there was the desire of American firms to explore the sea bed in other parts of the world without impediments or restrictions. There was also the plausible political point that to set up a new international authority would not only be costly, but would prevent the effective operation of market forces. In the case of UNESCO it has been demonstrated that a disproportionate share of its budget is spent on central administration rather than on projects in the field. Moreover, the organization had ceased to promote cultural freedom, and had become increasingly a politicized body in which resolutions were passed contrary to the interests of the United States.

To such objections a more general suspicion sometimes was added: that the United States really did not need these international organizations and arrangements to achieve its own objectives. Developments with regard to the laws of the seas will to some extent take place in any case, so it does not matter whether the treaty is signed and ratified. As for UNESCO, it appeared to some to be simply an expensive luxury.

This, however, is where the conflict between narrow interests and wider ramifications comes into play. To act on the narrow rationality of the case, and on its apparent lack of importance, is to ignore certain wider, but predictable ramifications of these decisions. First, the obvious: if certain acts are not very important, why annoy others? It was clear to everyone concerned that many actors—countries, but also individuals, American and otherwise—had a stake in the Law of the Seas Conference and in UNESCO. Indeed, to create a certain stir was one of the intentions of the negative U.S. decisions. But why should that be worth doing if the issue is of only modest importance?

It is not difficult to see the political answer to such questions: there are domestic constituencies—protectionist, inward-looking, conservative—that are pleased by acts of international defiance.

Does this matter? It is not too farfetched to claim that in the minds of the alert public all over the world, if not in the analyses of governments, American attitudes to the law of the seas or UNESCO are extrapolated into other international arenas. There is at least a lingering suspicion in many people's minds that a country that is cavalier in its approach to some international arrangements is perhaps not quite as serious as it claims when it comes to negotiating a reduction in arms, or anything else for that matter. However genuine U.S. protestations to the contrary may be, the impression persists. When this happens, the preference for immediate interests becomes an obstacle to substantive decisions of foreign policy. A minor discontinuity stands in the way of major continuities.

The Shocks of Change

The most important single change in post–World War II American foreign policy may well have been the set of decisions announced on August 15, 1971. On that day, President Richard Nixon and Treasury Secretary John Connally suspended the convertibility of the dollar into gold and imposed a surtax on imports. These measures were accompanied by statements from the president and Secretary Connally which argued that the United States has the same right as any other country to put its own interests first. In view of the serious decline in international monetary reserves and the threats to its competitive position, the president argued, the United States' ability to guarantee its security was in jeopardy. The issue may sound technical, but it meant that the United States was putting the postwar system of stable exchange rates guaranteed by the dollar, and of free trade guaranteed by American policy, on notice. The existing system had guaranteed the free world, and perhaps the rest of the world, that there was a reliable yardstick of economic progress. Currencies were pegged to the dollar (which in turn was tied to U.S. gold reserves) and trade followed reliable rules. Thus the shock of change was enormous. What Secretary Connally described as "fair" rather than "free trade" in fact meant a return to the economic war of all against all after two decades in which rules binding on all were upheld by American power, and American responsibility.

Perhaps, the "Nixon shocks" (as they soon came to be called in Japan) were not even regarded by the administration as foreign policy decisions. Certainly, much of the preparatory work had been done in the Treasury Department. The then under secretary, Paul Volcker, had toured the world ceaselessly trying to persuade others to do something about the disequilibria of trade and money. Everyone knew that serious problems existed in the United States. Moreover, Volcker's attempts at civilized persuasion had largely failed, so that a certain impatience in Washington was understandable.

But this is only part of the story. Here, we are concerned with three foreign policy implications of the August 15 decisions, all of continuing relevance in the 1980s. First, the United States declared to the world that it no longer believed in the usefulness of the international system that it had been instrumental in building after World War II. Henceforth, the United States would prefer the foreign policy of states to the creation of mutually binding rules. Second, therefore, the United States preferred an international system that was governed by crude and often short-term interests to one in which such interests were subordinated to medium-term considerations of stability. Third, the United States demonstrated its intention to communicate with the rest of the world by fiat rather than by negotiation. It showed impatience with inconclusive processes of consultation, and a readiness to go it alone.

Clearly, these are overstatements with regard both to American intentions and the effects of the measures of August 15, 1971. So far as intentions are concerned, the State Department clearly had not changed its internationalist approach. More important, there are indications that the president himself was a bit shocked by the effects of his measures on the world outside. Ensuing negotiations soon led to the abolition of the surtax on imports, and when President Nixon hailed the agreement to continue international consultation on parity changes (the Smithsonian Agreement of December 1971) as "historical," he clearly hoped it would undo some of the damage from August. In fact, it did not. The international monetary system has never again been the same; as far as trade is concerned, America's partners will rightly remain on the alert.

Thus, the events of August 15, 1971, had a lasting effect on the way the United States is regarded in the conduct of international affairs. An element of unpredictability now surrounds the world's perception of American foreign policy. It is widely felt that one never quite knows what may happen next. One element of this perception has to do with American skepticism toward international arrangements and institutions. The deeper questions concern the relationship between power and responsibility in the minds of those who are in charge of American foreign policy. The rest of the world, including America's allies, recognizes that it is going to be affected by American decisions in which it is not going to be involved beforehand. But although the United States is by far the most powerful nation in the world and can force all others to live with the consequences of its actions, it cannot expect stable alliances to last while it is acting in a unilateral, narrowly national-interested manner.

No doubt American decisionmakers recently have weighed all this: we are passing through a phase in which Soviet policy is geared at least in part to exploiting differences within the alliance, and also one in which the American budget deficit and its consequences make some sort of super-1971 all but inevitable in the near future. They obviously do not find the price too high—and who in Europe is to argue with them? But the point remains that if discontinuities in foreign policy take the form of shocks to the rest of the world, it becomes that much more difficult to build stable and predictable relationships.

The Need for Consultation

Other countries are not immune to the temptation to conduct their foreign policy by surprises rather than by evolution. But if smaller powers go their own way without consultation, they immediately feel the consequences. Great Britain's short-lived attempt to uncouple its economy from the world, and France's unilateral introduction in 1986 of visa requirements for citizens of most countries are two among many examples. One major change in foreign policy by a smaller power in the 1970s took a very different form, however: Germany's Ostpolitik, for which the "grand coalition" of 1966–69 laid the groundwork, and which was formally initiated after Willy Brandt's election as federal chancellor in 1969.

In the immediate and narrow sense, Ostpolitik involved a new relationship between the Federal Republic of Germany, the German Democratic Republic, Poland, and the Soviet Union. The conclusion of treaties governing these relationships was therefore the proximate objective of the new policy. But the ramifications of Ostpolitik were clearly wider. For one thing, the new approach to the East raised questions about Berlin, such as, were Berliners to benefit from the new travel possibilities opened up for other Germans? But any question touching on the status of Berlin directly involved the three Western powers, the United States, Britain, and France. Also, recognition of the German Democratic Republic represented a fundamental change in a position that Germany had asked all its friends to uphold; it therefore had to be explained. Above all, it had to be demonstrated that the normalization of relations with the East would not detract from Germany's Western commitment.

All this meant that the conclusion of the treaties was in many ways the simplest and most straightforward part of Ostpolitik. The difficult task was to explain the precise significance of the new policy to friends, allies, and neutrals. An enormous amount of energy and considerable time was expended to do so. At times, the protagonists of the new policy became impatient with this process. But Chancellor Brandt and Foreign Minister Scheel insisted on seeing it through. In retrospect, it can be said that if the Ostpolitik was effective, it was above all because of this seemingly unending process of information, explanation, reasoning, and persuasion.

The example may be exceptional for several reasons, but it is relevant to one of the evergreens in America's relations with the world, and notably with Europe, namely, consultation. In one sense, consultation is, and always has been, a red herring. When people say there has been a lack of consultation, they are merely describing a malaise, not explaining it or offering remedies. The imposition of a surtax on imports would not become palatable if American ambassadors chose to present the case in the capitals beforehand. Lack of consultation thus is not always what it seems to be. In particular, it is not remedied either by declaring a "Year of Europe," as Secretary of State Henry Kissinger did in 1975, or by setting up yet another joint committee or regular meeting.

What is needed to cope with the issues that underlie complaints about lack of consultation is probably two things. The first is regular meetings between those responsible for decisions at all levels, that is, political leaders, parliamentary leaders, administrators, advisers, and communicators. It has sometimes been argued that the retreat of the East Coast foreign policy establishment and the rise of new elites from the South and the West has broken traditional ties across the Atlantic. There is also a certain political reluctance on the part of congressional leaders to be seen traveling abroad too frequently. Nevertheless, a number of unofficial arrangements exist that facilitate informal meetings, and there is still a great deal of travel to and from the United States.

The second, more important need is for foreign policymakers to go out and patiently explain changes in policy to everyone. In providing such explanations, even change will have to be placed in the context of continuity if it is to make sense to others. In other words, "explanation" must mean more than simply telling others that this is what is going to be done and here are the reasons why. Connections must be established with what was done in the past and what is being done in other areas. A new policy must be made plausible to an anxious constituency. At any rate, such is required if one wants to minimize the friction that otherwise would occur and produce a more sophisticated effectiveness than that of sheer power.

The "Nixon shocks," the law of the sea, and Ostpolitik are not random examples, and others could be cited. For example, one day the saga of the Strategic Defense Initiative (sDI) will be written. From the initial "ultimatum" to allies to express their willingness to participate within two months, through the tortuous negotiations of agreements that are virtually devoid of substance, to an as yet unknown destination—this story will confirm the present argument. It is preferable, and to some extent necessary to observe considerable continuity in foreign policy. Tax or welfare reforms may become effective once they have passed all parliamentary and legal hurdles, whether they have been agreed to by large or small majorities, and whether they are reversals or mere adjustments of an existing regime. But foreign policy remains shrouded in uncertainty and surrounded by doubt if it is sprung on others by a new president, or by a president who has discovered a "new way forward."

The Presidency and Foreign Policy

To say that there is insufficient continuity in American foreign policy is not to say that there is no continuity. Any history of the United States would emphasize certain consistent themes, notably those of isolation and intervention, withdrawal, and the attempt to impose moral standards on others. The postwar decades saw the emergence of an international order guaranteed by the United States, a pax Americana. Even if some recent changes cast doubt on the continuity of this condition, American domination remains a fact, and with it the prevalence of American values. Consciously or not, then, the theme of geopolitics has been added to those of isolation and intervention.

Such continuities form the background for any attempt to turn from perceptions of American policy and its setting to those who actually conduct it, from responsibility to those who are responsible. In this chapter, our concern is for the role of the president, the effects of the electoral process, and the relation between domestic pressures and international needs.

The Role of the President

In the making of foreign policy the role of the president is supreme. None of the constraints that operate on the presidency can be regarded as an effective buffer on an individual president's influence, so vacillations and idiosyncrasies of policy are to be expected. American foreign policy is as sensitive to domestic and international pressures as the president is. More than any other field, foreign policy is presidential policy in the United States.

The overstatement of this thesis is almost too obvious to require explication, but it is overstatement that can be substantially defended. Consider first the structure of the foreign policy process. There are, to be sure, several actors other than the president, and they are of evident, if limited importance.

Constitutionally and by tradition, the Senate plays a major part in shaping and, more particularly, in checking foreign policy decisions. For many years now, individual senators have been among the most prominent policymakers in international affairs. Their names are associated with important foreign policy measures, and in some cases, with diplomatic assignments. Since Vietnam, there has been an increase in Senate power. Yet when all is said and done, the Senate is too big, too diffuse, and too distracted by other things, and is not in a constitutional position to initiate major foreign policy decisions.

In addition to the Senate, there is what one might call the foreign policy constituency or, less politely, the foreign policy establishment. It used to consist of public-spirited, widely traveled members of the old Eastern families, mostly professionals and businessmen, who met regularly, were in and out of government, and always were at hand to advise, go on missions, or shape views. With a certain democratization of foreign policymaking in recent years, and a shift of power from the East to the South and West, this group also has changed. In the 1980s it is much less an identifiable establishment than it was in the 1950s and 1960s; it is more diffuse, both geographically and by affiliation. The Council on Foreign Relations no longer represents it fully, but neither does the Georgetown Center for Strategic and International Studies or the Heritage Foundation. The separateness of foreign affairs from most other policies elevates the influence of individuals and groups who rely more on thought and information than on constituency politics. But this influence has to be exercised through those who have power, mainly through the presidency.

There are, of course, pressure groups that wish to advance their special interests through foreign policy. Farmers and the auto industry are two obvious examples of economic lobbies. Ethnic groups also play a large and increasing role. And, in response, the House of Representatives now appears to play a growing part in influencing foreign policy. Once again, though, it is important to note that influence is not power.

In one sense the influence of the State Department on the foreign policy process is obvious. It also is clear that at times it has been a separate and identifiable actor in the policymaking process. Several secretaries of state, some quiet, others flamboyant, have rightly been identified with individual styles and directions in foreign policy. Yet there are major differences between the State Department and the foreign offices of many parliamentary democracies. One is that the State Department is not the main initiator of foreign policy. Another is that it does not serve as a systematic filter for foreign policy decisions that are made at the White House. Finally, the State Department cannot be relied upon to give continuity to foreign policy.

There are subsidiary, yet important reasons for the limited role of the State Department: the absence of an independent electoral base for the secretary of state is one; the stunted opportunity structure of career diplomacy, with plum jobs both at home and abroad going to political appointees, is another. But the main reason is the supreme position of the presidency, that is, of the president himself and his immediate advisers, notably in the National Security Council and its staff.

Consider some of the cases discussed earlier. One is struck immediately by the overriding role of the president. The termination of American participation in the Law of the Seas Conference was announced by President Ronald Reagan immediately after his inauguration in 1981. The decision to pull out of UNESCO was made later, but also suddenly. Moreover, one suspects that in both cases, a domestic constituency was pleased, but the State Department was upset. This was certainly true on August 15, 1971. In all cases the president could have gone either way. There are no clear predictors in the system, nor are there institutional buffers to restrict the president's room for maneuver. As far as the international system is concerned, the president can, within a remarkably wide range of discretion, build or dismantle it.

From any perspective, the changes in foreign policy from Nixon to Carter to Reagan were staggering. The greatest power in the world, within ten years, moved from the internationalism of cynical geopolitics through the moralism of the good partner to the new patriotism of a combination of missionary isolationism and crude power motives.

In the defense field, then, it is no surprise that President Reagan explicitly dissociated himself from the policies of his predecessor. No president can predict entirely or bring about the ratification of important treaties, like SALT II. He may not be able to guarantee that certain weapons systems he regards as important for international as well as national reasons will be financed by Congress. But whether the United States operates from a position of conciliation and negotiation, or from one of strength, if not superiority, is to a large extent a matter for the president to decide. Thus it is in the hands of the American presidency whether the world lives in a climate of tension or détente, of arms race or disarmament talks.

The president of the United States does not, of course, throw dice to determine what position to take. What he does—indeed what he can do—is influenced by the stance he took (successfully) during the election campaign and by his entire political posture. His position also has a great deal to do with the mood of the times, a vague but important notion that includes the prevailing mood of allies and adversaries alike. For example, in view of the exhaustion of earlier initiatives, the repeated succession problems in the Soviet Union, and a certain reversal of trends in public opinion in the free world, the early 1980s was not a very likely period to revive détente. But even so, there remains a considerable range of options to set the tone and initiate real developments that is available to the president at any one time.

In sum, the supreme position of the presidency in foreign policy-making enhances the likelihood of frequent shifts and changes in policy. To be sure, it would be highly misleading to suggest that such vacillations are either random or total. There are constraints on American foreign policy that operate against the declared preferences of any president. President Carter's human rights approach to international relations faltered on the exigencies of geopolitics even before the Iranian hostage crisis. President Reagan's second-term interest in arms control may well have been the result of pressures from home and abroad as much as his own preferences. But these constraints to a very large extent exist outside the institutions and processes of American politics. They are not the result of checks, balances, buffers, or strains toward continuity within the system.

Selection and Election of the President

At least some of the constraints that operate on the presidency in foreign policy are, of course, domestic. The president's general political posture as well as the more specific line he took during his election campaign already have been mentioned. In this connection another institutional thesis warrants discussion: the selection and election of presidents. Candidates for president are chosen and elected primarily for domestic reasons, yet once elected their most consequential responsibilities are in the international field. In these circumstances American presidents are more likely than the leaders of parliamentary democracies to feel constrained by domestic pressures. They must pay a considerable political price for becoming internationalists. Some are prepared to pay this price, at least in their second term.

Once again the overstatement of the thesis is obvious. Some presidential campaigns in recent American history have been overshadowed by international issues. Televised debates between the candidates invariably have included foreign policy matters. Many recent candidates of both parties have publicized the recognition they have received in other countries. They have traveled, had their photographs taken with world leaders, even used their personal standing to do what governments had failed to do, as when the Reverend Jesse Jackson persuaded President Assad of Syria to free an American prisoner. On the other hand, some parliamentary democracies have elected leaders who were quite untried in international affairs. Prime Minister Thatcher of Britain and Chancellor Kohl of Germany provide the most striking recent examples. Above all, some apparently well-trained and well-tried leaders have turned out to be quite inept once elected, even as some rather unlikely men have found their way into the history books for their achievements in international affairs.

When all this is said, it still remains that a presidential election system that is for all intents and purposes direct and popular, favors candidates who relate directly to the major concerns of the electorate. What has been described as the relative separateness of foreign policy is by implication a remoteness from most people's immediate concerns, at least most of the time. Thus, the Henry Cabot Lodges, Averell Harrimans, and Elliott Richardsons were always more unlikely candidates than the Johnsons, Carters, and Reagans. Even the combination of domestic appeal and international flair that characterized John F. Kennedy was very much the exception in American history. Correspondingly, apart from issues of war and peace, and perhaps the translation of ethnic and economic interests into international affairs, election campaigns tend to be dominated by domestic issues. Economic and social policy take precedence over foreign and even defense policy.

In truth, things are not all that different elsewhere. All elections, whatever their international ramifications, are primarily about domestic issues. Yet the peculiarities of the American system are noteworthy. First, there is the role of the president of the United States. If there is any truth to the argument of the preceding section, the presidency brings with it supreme power in U.S. foreign policy. In the present phase of world affairs, it is, moreover, power on behalf of the mightiest country of the world, power to build or destroy in military, economic, and political terms. Nothing in the presidential selection process prepares candidates for this power. Again, this would not be so problematic if there were institutional buffers and balances to guarantee continuity, or at any rate to complicate discontinuity. But there are not. Thus it is possible for a person who has been chosen for his ability to sell the electorate a certain style of leadership and certain domestic promises to move into the White House and find himself confronted with inescapable foreign policy decisions. He may even discover that although it takes time, energy, and frustrating compromises with Congress and special-interest groups to implement domestic programs, foreign policy decisions can be made immediately. Either way, the disjunction between domestic pressures and international needs is evident.

In this regard a glance at electoral behavior is relevant. In 1983 and 1984 several democratic leaders were reelected, notably Kohl, Thatcher, and Reagan. But even their reelections were partly negative decisions. Many voters seemed to have turned against the leader of the opposition; incumbents benefited from weak opponents. More generally, much voting seems to have become negative. What used to be the advantage of office has almost become an electoral disability. In part this is because of the increasing volatility of the electorate. Many traditional allegiances have become loose and situational. In part it is traceable to changes in the socioeconomic climate. Whoever is in power is likely to find it much more difficult to govern now than at a time of continuous economic growth. More people are worse off, or otherwise disgruntled, at the end of almost anyone's tenure of office than at the beginning. The result is frequent changes of government. Reagan to the contrary, this includes the presidency of the United States.

In the light of the dangers of discontinuity, such changes are clearly a serious matter. They inevitably mean that whoever defeats an incumbent does so on the strength of being different. As a result, the temptation for new incumbents to pursue a discontinuous foreign policy becomes even greater than it is already. Thus, the new volatility and the new negativism of the electorate serve to strengthen traditional American volatilities and reduce the effectiveness of foreign policy.

One other mismatch between domestic and international requirements needs to be mentioned. Almost invariably, domestic political pressures operate against involvement and for withdrawal and protection. This is a fortiori the case in a climate in which employers, unions, farmers, and sometimes even traders and consumers have reason to fear for their economic position. Institutionally, it is no more difficult for the American president to stand up to such pressures than it is for the leaders of parliamentary democracies. But politically, such resistance is rather less likely. By selection and election, the president is above all trained to listen to domestic signals. International signals are clearly secondary, and even if perceived they will be more readily discarded. In addition, the president is more exposed than the leaders of parliamentary democracies. His supreme power in foreign affairs also makes him the obvious target of public criticism if his international actions cut across lines of vested interest. This in turn means that the president can only indulge in the separation of foreign from domestic policy to a limited extent. He has to think of trade-offs between domestic and international actions, which is likely to lead him to an anti-internationalist rather than an internationalist position. Finally, issues of international involvement or withdrawal are, constitutionally, the most likely to require assent by other bodies; the president cannot afford to have his policies rejected by the Senate very often. All this makes for what may be called a strain toward protection in the American presidency. It emphasizes the unusual, not to say exceptional nature of presidential internationalism.

It would be wrong to conclude this argument without listing at least some of the countertrends. There is a strong case for arguing that the tendency to elevate domestic interests and concerns in the process of selecting and electing American presidents is mitigated by several significant circumstances. No one elected to the U.S. presidency today can fail to be aware that the fate of the earth is in his hands. Responsibility for nuclear war alone provides an ultimate and unbreakable link between domestic and international affairs. Moreover, the government is organized in such a way that this responsibility is never forgotten. The proximity of the National *Security* Council and the national *security* adviser as presidential instruments of foreign policy tells part of the story. There are other institutional safeguards. Whatever changes in personnel may take place in the departments of State and Defense when a new president is elected, there is also some continuity. More important, new incumbents soon recognize some of the constraints on action, whether they like them or not.

Few postwar presidents can be described as great statesmen in international affairs. (There is not even agreement on who they are.) By almost any standard great mistakes have been made by those responsible for American foreign policy. But not only has there not been a disaster with worldwide ramifications, at no time has there been even the slightest reason for doubt that on the major issues of war and peace, liberty, and human welfare, the United States is a reliable and predictable world power.

As for reforms, this essay offers none. Once or twice in the course of the preceding argument, possible institutional changes have been hinted. For example, continuity of policy and also the explaining of intended changes might be better served if the American foreign service were to become largely professional. A political foreign service may be a convenience for the president, but it is an inconvenience for the credibility and predictability of his policies. In the same context the relationship between the White House and the Senate, and the ways Congress organizes itself for foreign affairs, may be comprehensible to the initiated, but foreign policy also concerns others who are far away. If a presidential promise of aid is rejected by Congress, the foreign policy effect is, to say the least, unfortunate. One wonders whether there are more readily comprehensible procedures than those presently in operation.

However, when it comes to the central issue of this book, the presidency, institutional changes will not remedy practical deficiencies. The United States should not, for example, abandon the system of presidential democracy and embrace that of parliamentary democracy. Nor should there be a foreign affairs test for presidential candidates or the establishment of yet another senior post in the foreign affairs field, or any other constitutional or institutional change in the presidency.

This conclusion will disappoint some, but there are good reasons for it. Most proposals for change are spurious, which is reason for a degree of ironic reticence. More important, however, there is no perfect institutional arrangement. By and large, and despite the doubts voiced explicitly or by implication in this analysis, American institutions have worked well. One may criticize the stances American presidents have taken in international affairs, or, more generally, the kinds of people brought forth by the process of presidential selection and election. But no other process could guarantee the choice of different persons, let alone different political stances among those chosen.

What matters is something less complex, but in the end more effective. It is a lively public debate of international issues that is based on critical analyses of past behavior and a sense of present and future needs. It is, in other words, a development of the climate of informed opinion. If the present essay has made a small contribution to the shaping of such a climate, it has fulfilled even its "institutional" ambitions.

3 Changing International Stakes in Presidential Selection

ERNEST R. MAY

American presidents are chosen by American citizens. Whether delegates to conventions, voters in primaries, or voters in the general elections, everyone with a formal role in the selection process has to be a citizen. Section 441e of Title 2 of the U.S. Code makes it a crime for any foreign national to give money to a candidate, or for an American even to *ask* for a foreigner's money.

Yet many people not eligible to take part in presidential selection have a stake in the outcome. They do not necessarily accept all the pretensions of American presidents or presidential candidates. In 1980, for example, the London *Economist* commented, "President Johnson used to refer to himself as 'leader of the free world.' President Carter seemed to imagine himself such after Afghanistan. Everyone promptly made clear that he was nothing of the sort."[1] But many people in other countries care about the choice of American presidents. Some feel that presidential actions may affect their livelihoods, perhaps even their very survival. Others simply make American presidents their totems—the world's equivalent of the British Commonwealth's queen.

Press coverage is indicative. In Great Britain highbrow newspapers and magazines (such as *The Economist*) say almost as much about American as about British politics. Back in 1952, when the postwar world was beginning to take shape, the London *Spectator* commented on how the American rhythm has become the world's rhythm. While Americans went through the rituals of nomination, election, and postelection transition, said the *Spectator*, people everywhere else had a "sense of vacuum."[2] The closeness of the British watch on American elections is reflected in the *Social Science Index*, an annual guide to periodical literature in the social sciences published in English. For 1976 it listed 106 articles dealing with that year's presidential election. Of these, eighty-two had appeared in British journals. That figure probably says more about the criteria of the *Index* than about the proportion between British and Americans writing on the subject. Still, in absolute terms, eighty-two is a large number.

The attention given to American presidential politics elsewhere in the developed world is illustrated by an issue of *Der Spiegel* reporting on the 1980 U.S. election. A Hamburg weekly that resembles both *Time* and the *New Republic*, *Der Spiegel* is both antimilitaristic and chauvinistically German. It is anything but pro-American. Nevertheless, of sixty-six pages on politics and world affairs in its issue for November 10, 1980, twenty-two—exactly one-third—dealt with the United States. And the editors seemed to assume that their readers had a good deal of background knowledge about the subject. The lead story, for example, told of a conference at the German Foreign Ministry being interrupted so that the permanent under secretary could receive a bulletin on returns from Dixville Notch, New Hampshire, a hamlet long regarded as an election day bellwether. Other stories quoting the chancellor, members of the Bundestag, and figures in the West German business world contained unexplained references to past American elections, to public opinion polls, to people who had unsuccessfully sought nomination, to the electoral college, and to other matters that an American teaching an introductory American government course would not necessarily take for granted as known by American college freshmen. And this was in a year when, in the view of the *New York Times*'s Flora Lewis, European interest in the American presidential election was less than usual.[3] In 1984 a *New York Times* poll taken by telephone in Western Europe found respondents just about as well informed as Americans on the candidates and issues. The majority had clear preferences, with West Germans divided evenly between Ronald Reagan and Walter Mondale but the French three-to-two for Reagan.[4] From the very beginning of the campaign, when Mondale, Gary Hart, and other

Democrats were vying for votes in the Iowa caucuses, mass circulation dailies such as *Le Matin* of Paris and the *Stuttgarter Zeitung* had correspondents on hand. Japanese newspapers had no fewer than twenty.[5]

Neither is extensive press coverage of American presidential campaigns confined to developed countries. In 1960 James Markham surveyed major metropolitan dailies in South American capitals. During that year of the Nixon-Kennedy contest, with, of course, debates about policy toward Cuba and economic aid for the hemisphere prominent in the campaign, he found dailies in Bogotá, Caracas, São Paulo, Montevideo, Buenos Aires, Santiago, and Lima giving U.S. affairs an average of fifty column inches (one-half to three-quarters of a page) every day. In the United States, by contrast —in spite of Fidel Castro—comparable dailies give Latin America an average of two-and-a-half inches a day (about as much as a standard obituary).[6]

A study prepared for the U.S. Information Agency in 1976 reported almost comparable levels of attention to American politics during that election year in newspapers of the Middle East, North Africa, and South Asia.[7] In 1984, just for the fun of it, *Wall Street Journal* correspondents asked taxi drivers in foreign cities their opinions on the American election. While a few drew blanks, the majority heard responses—and supporting arguments—not much different from those to be heard between LaGuardia and Manhattan or LAX and Beverly Hills. In Canton, in the People's Republic of China, for example, a female cab driver said she favored Mondale because his running mate was Geraldine Ferraro. She thought their victory would promote women's liberation everywhere.[8] What better evidence that, at least in symbolism, America's elections are the world's elections?

To this evidence, one can react in at least four different ways. The first is to say "So what?" Foreigners can watch all they please. They are free to root from the sidelines. But the choice of presidents is properly the business only of Americans. Second, one can concede that noncitizens may have legitimate reasons for feeling that they have a stake in presidential selection but argue that the process already takes their interests adequately into account. A third possibility is to say that foreigners have a genuine stake, that the current process does not give them sufficient voice, but that the process ought not or cannot be altered to accommodate them. The costs would outweigh the benefits. A fourth possibility is that the process should and can be altered, at least marginally. I lean toward this last view but can best explain why by first reviewing each of the alternatives.

America for Americans?

"So what?" is not an unreasonable response. Politics almost always spills over national boundaries. Greeks cared a lot about palace rivalries in Persia. Those in one Greek city cared about election outcomes in another. So it has been throughout time. Even when Americans seemed most safely isolated from the rest of the world, they were affected by and concerned about politics elsewhere. Southerners like John C. Calhoun were as much alarmed by the antislavery movement in Britain as by that at home, perhaps more so, for they had less leverage against British critics, and those critics were not so easily dismissed as irresponsible fanatics. Though the influence is clearer in retrospect than it was at the time, political and economic life in the United States was greatly affected by the turns in British politics that resulted in the Reform bills and the repeal of the Corn Laws. The economic historian Peter Temin argues persuasively that ups and downs in the American economy were due more to changes in British policy than to the war between Andrew Jackson and the Bank of the United States; it follows that the electoral fortunes of Jackson and his political heirs were correspondingly affected by what British voters did in their elections.[9]

Nor was the dependent relationship entirely a matter of specifics or entirely American-British. Issues were borrowed. So were styles. It is not easy to explain why the United States acquired colonies and had imperialism as a central campaign issue in 1900 without taking into account British "liberal imperialists" and others across the Atlantic from whom American politicians borrowed concepts and slogans. Nor is it easy to explain the preoccupation of Americans during the Progressive Era with procedural reforms except by referring to seminal books such as Woodrow Wilson's *Congressional Government*, which contrasted American procedures with British, much to the favor of the latter.[10]

American presidential politics has often been affected by foreign politics. Washington's Farewell Address warned against too close a mixing of the two. In different ways, the Federalist Alien and Sedition Acts and Jefferson's isolationism aimed to keep American politics American. The futility of such efforts became apparent after the late 1840s, when tides of immigrants made as much American as British the question of Ireland's future and about as much American as German such subjects as German unity and the place of the Catholic Church in German-speaking Europe. (Anyone who thinks today that candidates in presidential primaries go too far in testifying devotion to Israel should glance back at what presidential hopefuls felt obliged to say about Ireland in the nineteenth century.) From the colonial era down to the present, politics in other countries has influenced American presidential campaigns.

Similarly, American politics has nearly always affected politics elsewhere. Attitudes toward the United States (or at least an imagined United States) have defined some British and European political factions from the time of the American Revolution onward.[11] In 1844 some people in Britain and Europe feared that the election of James K. Polk would mean conflict between the United States and Britain and, as a possible result, disintegration of the balance of power that protected the general peace. In 1852 and again in 1856 many abroad thought that if an American election went one way instead of another, it might bring in American involvement and encouragement of liberal nationalism in Europe, or American participation in the Crimean War, with either development having far-reaching effects. In 1860, oddly, foreign commentators generally downplayed the significance of the four-way race principally involving Stephen A. Douglas and Abraham Lincoln. Most people abroad saw the slavery issue as domestic and likely to be patched up, as in earlier campaigns. Subsequently, they were seldom to underestimate how Europe might be affected by choices among American voters. Bismarck thought for a time that the elections of 1868 or 1872 might result in Germany having an overseas ally against Britain. In 1896 foreign apprehension about William Jennings Bryan, the advocate of free coinage of silver, matched that of conversant Americans.[12] And so it was in quadrennium after quadrennium.

Since elections or political debates elsewhere have often affected American presidential contests, and people elsewhere have almost always seen the American choice of a president as significant for them, what, if anything, distinguishes the present from the past? Is there anything different about the United States, and the present day, to differentiate foreigners' concerns about American presidential races from Americans' concerns about an election in the Federal Republic of Germany or in Japan or Israel, or from foreigners' concerns in 1896 or 1936?

The answer clearly is "yes." The United States is so uniquely a world power, and is now so different from what it was even fifty years ago, that the interest of foreigners in current American elections cannot suitably be compared either with their interest earlier or with the interest of Americans in foreign politics today.

In the first place, the size of the United States is not comparable to any other country, including the Soviet Union. In land space occupied and total population, the United States does have rivals. But in gross product, actual output of goods, resources, and money, numbers of educated or skilled people, laboratories, libraries, museums, and almost every other item measurable, the United States has no peer. Apart from land area and gross population, the Soviet Union comes close in only two categories — ready military strength and top-grade athletes. In economic and cultural life, the runners-up to the United States — and they far behind, at least quantitatively — are West Germany, Japan, France, and Britain. The Soviet Union is a minor leaguer, struggling to stay ahead of South Korea and Taiwan. For people everywhere, whether in the developed West (including Japan), in the socialist world (including mainland China), or in the Third World, the United States is the metropolis. It is also, in Lady Barbara Ward Jackson's memorable phrase, the elephant in the bathtub. It may be, she said, a very kindly elephant. Nevertheless, it can cause others no end of discomfort when it takes it into its head to move.[13]

Second, only partly as a function of size, the United States has a capacity for independent action that, while not unmatched, is rare and has counterparts in few countries with significant resources. In this respect the Soviet Union is comparable. Although members of the Soviet Politburo have to think about possible reactions in satellite and other foreign capitals, they still can decide to do almost anything within their national capabilities. They can stage military invasions, try to subvert other governments, cut economic or other relationships, or drastically reallocate their own resources. They alone share with presidents of the United States the ability to order destruction of much of the planet. The governments of most other powers do not have such latitude. As a practical matter, most other governments cannot even move military forces over any distance without at least acquiescence from the United States. This is equally true for France aiding the Saudis at Mecca or supporting Chad against Libya, for Israel acting at Entebbe, and for Britain retaking the Falklands. Some can cross neighboring frontiers—China those of Vietnam or Iraq those of Iran—but, even then they are aware that the extent of action could be limited if the United States (or the Soviet Union) chose to interfere.

Few nations have latitude for independent economic action comparable to that of the United States. To say that is not to imply that other governments must do as Washington bids. Far from it, as Japan's economic policies prove daily. But the boundaries of possible action are narrower for other nations than for the United States, because American interest rates, American terms of trade, the supply of dollars, and constraints on transportation and communications set by American law and policy are critical determinants beyond the control of people outside the United States (perhaps also beyond the control of Americans themselves). Neither is it quite to say that most seemingly independent nations are in actuality dependencies of the United States, although some surely are. To those nations that live by producing and selling raw materials, American trade policy and business conditions are governing forces. Citizens of those countries or aliens resident within them who are supposed to have knowledge about or influence in the United States become by that very fact part of a ruling elite. Theorists who write of *dependencia* can point to real examples, but unqualified examples are rare. More typical is a nation not wholly of dependent status but rather lacking complete independence. The Federal Republic of Germany, to take a great power as an example, can choose among a wide range of policies. In theory, its government could decide tomorrow to leave NATO, to pursue neutralism, to seek negotiated reunification, to become an independent nuclear power, break with the EEC, attempt autarchy, and so on. In practice, Bonn's range of choices is limited not only by internal forces but also by German awareness of possible immediate consequences if its relationship with the United States were to alter significantly. The consequences would not be U.S. paratroops dropping onto the Rhineland but instead Eurodollars emptying out of accounts in Frankfurt, BMWs piling up dockside in Hamburg, and no

200,000 to 250,000 American tourists renting hotel rooms every year.

Although, in practice, choices by the U.S. government are constrained by awareness of possible effects in West Germany, the American government—an American president—can more easily decide to act in disregard of those effects. In most instances, moreover, American decisions are constrained less by demonstrable realities than by beliefs. Dollars on deposit in West Germany and cancelable American orders for West German goods are matters of fact bearing on a decision made in Bonn. For an American president the deterrent to offending a West German government arises less from German holdings of American shares or awareness of the Volkswagen plant in Pennsylvania or concern about passenger miles for TWA than from a supposition that, if pushed too far, the West Germans might leave the Western Alliance. The Soviets might then gain greater influence in Europe, and the result might someday be a situation of possible peril such as that in 1940. Such beliefs are not necessarily immutable. The extreme example is that of South Vietnam, regarded by Americans one year as vital to their safety and a few years later as a liability. In terms of simple capacity to act independently (not, mercifully, in inclination to do so) the person most nearly similar to a president of the United States is a president of Libya.

The present-day Soviet Union is not only less powerful than the United States in most dimensions, it is organized so as to conduct most of its affairs in isolation from influence by developments elsewhere. Except when they involve war or peace (a big exception), decisions by the Politburo are usually not of much moment beyond their own sphere. The role of the Soviet government in the politics of other countries is relatively formalized. Someone who wants to measure Soviet involvement in another nation's politics can start by counting members of its Communist party. In any case, the organizing theory for the Communist party of the Soviet Union supposes that its leaders know what is best for the world, are the vanguard of revolution, and need discipline only from Marxist-Leninist scripture and the party's own democratic centralism. There is no supposition that nonparty members elsewhere have any right to expect that Soviet decisionmaking will take into account what they think independently about their own best interests.

Americans traditionally have professed beliefs that, unlike those of Marxist-Leninists, offer people elsewhere a basis for supposing that their opinions will count and should count. Broadly speaking, Americans have held individuals to be the best interpreters of their own interests. They also have held that the actions of governments should serve the interests of humankind. From the American Revolution onward, Americans continually have debated how their government could best perform such service. Some were inclined to argue for setting an example for others to imitate, when and as they became able to do so. This was commonly accompanied by opposition to active involvement in international politics. Others favored more active efforts to do good. In the nineteenth century, Henry Clay and leaders of the later "Young America" movement argued for helping others to get American-style governments. By the turn of the century the impulse was more to have the American economy serve the world's needs.

In Woodrow Wilson these tendencies converged. His pronouncements during World War I and at the Paris Peace Conference represented the government of the United States as one committed to helping all humans achieve both freedom and material comfort. The Senate repudiated his promise to make the United States a member of the League of Nations, and some Americans rejected Wilson's image of the role of the United States in the world. Henry Cabot Lodge ridiculed the notion that security for Americans depended on peace in faraway places. A president of the U.S. Chamber of Commerce escaped being completely forgettable in history by saying that he did not think it the responsibility of his countrymen to provide a bottle of milk for every Hottentot. In general, nevertheless, American leaders after World War I held to the position that the United States did what it did for the benefit of the rest of the world as well as for Americans. Even in the most workaday debates about tariff protection for farmers or measures of autarchy to escape from the Depression, few members of Congress were prepared to say that American policies should benefit Americans even if they hurt people elsewhere. No president dared do so.

Since World War II the premise that the American government acts for, or at least should act for, the benefit of the world has gone almost unchallenged. Robert A. Taft and George Wallace are the only obvious contenders for presidential nomination to have even come close to doing so. "Outs" usually have described the policies of "ins" as wrongheaded. The Republicans of 1952 charged Truman with misdi-

recting to a stalemated war in Korea, resources better used for rebuilding not only the domestic economy but also world trade. The Democrats of 1960 attacked the Eisenhower administration for, among other
things, inadequate efforts to improve political, economic, and social
conditions in less-developed lands. Richard Nixon's language in 1968
resembled that of Republicans of 1952. While George McGovern was
widely perceived in 1972 to be championing a new isolationism, he
and his followers insisted indignantly that they were merely calling
for a more prudent and humane approach to bettering conditions all
over the world. Jimmy Carter in 1976 made much of his commitment to human rights. Reagan in 1980 contended that his election
would permit America to achieve the strength—military, economic,
and other—that would enable it to fulfill its global duty. As president, he launched "Project Democracy" partly to persuade people
elsewhere of the essentially benevolent character of the American
system of government. For most of two centuries, certainly for almost
all of the last half century, Americans have given people elsewhere in
the world abundant reason for believing that the American government will be and should be responsive to the interests and concerns
of non-citizens.

Because of the size and power of their country, presidents of the
United States are able in unique degree to act to affect significantly
the lives of people in other countries. Largely for the same reason,
they are relatively free from constraints imposed by other governments. The corollary is that people in other countries cannot expect
their own governments to ensure that their concerns and interests
will be adequately taken into account in the White House. Yet American rhetoric, seemingly sincere and practically uncontradicted, gives
people who are not U.S. citizens justification for expecting that American presidents will act with full regard for them. On balance, both
facts and logic give people who are not U.S. citizens a basis for
believing that the presidential selection process ought to take their
interests and wishes into account.

American Voters as Surrogates for Humankind

What of the hypothesis that foreigners already have a voice in presidential selection? It can be argued, on a theoretical plane, that the
interests of noncitizens are accommodated because citizens apply

the same criteria that noncitizens would apply, could they vote. It can be argued that, as a practical matter, noncitizens can influence presidential selection by means other than casting votes.

The theoretical case hinges on an assumption that American citizens who go to the polls act on behalf of humankind. They are surrogates for non-Americans just as they are surrogates for other Americans who cannot or do not vote—those under eighteen, for example. Earlier, male voters were assumed to act on behalf of females. Still earlier, those with property were assumed to act for those without. Before independence, many Americans accepted the then prevailing British theory of virtual representation. What mattered was the official's belief that he *ought* to act representatively. William Pitt, the earl of Chatham, was no less prime minister for all the subjects of George II because his only formal answerability was to the three voters of Old Sarum. For American presidents it might be contended that what matters is not who originally chooses them but how they see themselves after their election. If they think they are leaders of the free world, they will feel responsible for (and to) people other than those who elected them.

Short of that, it can be argued that, since they all care about the same things, American voters act for foreigners at the same time that they act for themselves. Looking back over the whole of American political history, one is struck by the extent to which, in presidential selection, the electorate has seemed to put a premium on prudence. This has not been invariable. Andrew Jackson was expected to make more mischief than he actually did, and Polk was elected despite his making no secret of being prepared to provoke war —perhaps with Great Britain as well as with Mexico. Most of the time, however, the nominating process has winnowed out just about everyone whose approach was not careful, prudent, and risk-minimizing. In instances in any way exceptional, the voters nearly always chose the more prudent-seeming candidate when the general election came around. Henry Clay, who had something of a gambler's air, failed three times. Horace Greeley was resoundingly defeated by Ulysses Grant. William Jennings Bryan was, like Clay, a three-time loser. In more recent years, Goldwater and McGovern suffered defeats almost comparable to Greeley's. The only arguable exceptions were Theodore Roosevelt in 1904 and Ronald Reagan in 1980. Roosevelt's victory owed much to his having had three years as accidental president in which to demonstrate that he was not the "wild man" Mark Hanna had feared he would be. Reagan's first success was probably due to the extraordinary drop in public esteem for Jimmy Carter, partly as a result of publicity about the hostages in Teheran. By 1984 Reagan benefited not only from his own good luck but from an appearance of having talked a much more radical game than he actually played. In choosing presidents, the American electorate generally attaches very high priority to prudence.

In the nominating process as well as in general elections, Americans also have shown concern for leadership qualities. This was usually secondary to prudence. Witness the parade of nineteenth-century presidents that inspired Lord Bryce in 1884 to entitle one chapter in *The American Commonwealth*, "Why Great Men Are Not Chosen Presidents." Witness more recently French savant Raymond Aron echoing Bryce by writing, "The American political and electoral system makes it inevitable that mediocre Presidents will continue to succeed one another."[14] But desire for a president who would *act* prudently, not just sit prudently, accounts in part for the remarkable proportion of military men to be nominated for or chosen as president. It also accounts in part for the enthusiasm with which the voters returned to office presidents with records of apparent accomplishment: Theodore Roosevelt, Wilson, Franklin D. Roosevelt three times, Truman, Eisenhower, Johnson, Nixon, and Reagan. The citizens who have chosen presidents, it can be argued, have paid attention first to prudence and second to capacity for programmatic action.

In addition, American voters have paid attention to personal character or at least to the appearance of virtue. Some opposition to Aaron Burr stemmed from the feeling that he was morally unfit to succeed Washington and Adams. Clay suffered not only from a reputation for recklessness but also from suspicion concerning some of his business affairs. James G. Blaine suffered likewise. The best evidence is provided by Warren Harding who became, at least until Watergate, the symbol of what Americans did not want in a president. Absent scandals, and Harding's inability to separate himself completely from their authors, his presidency would surely rank as one of noteworthy achievement, for it saw, among other things, the capping of inflation, sharp increases in productivity and employment, amnesty for World War I political prisoners (such as Eugene Debs), re-desegregation of facilities in the District of Columbia (made

"Jim Crow" by Southerners in the Wilson administration), détente with Japan, and large reductions in armaments. But Harding himself seemed impure.

Obviously, outcomes in the presidential selection process are influenced by more than the value preferences of American voters. It is nevertheless only oversimplification, not distortion of truth, to say that an important element has been concern by voters to have presidents who would be prudent, who ideally would also be leaders, and who could serve personally as models for the nation's children. From the beginning to the present, the exemplar has been George Washington.

To the extent that all this holds true, existing presidential selection processes do much to protect the interests of noncitizens, for the latter, if they had a voice, would surely put prudence high among their selection criteria. They want, above all, presidents who will not be reckless in diplomatic and military affairs. Broadly speaking, they also want presidents who will exercise prudent leadership, for they recognize that the capacity of other national leaders to set more than short-term courses is limited.

But this theoretical argument can be carried only so far. At levels of specificity below prudence, leadership, and virtue, the criteria of American voters are not necessarily those that noncitizens would apply. Before 1917 and again in the 1930s, voters used commitment to isolationism as one index of prudence. More often than not, they applauded leadership that, in economic policy, was nationalistic and protectionist. Moreover, American voters, even in very recent years, have attached to personal virtue an importance many foreigners thought terrifyingly out of proportion. Even in countries such as Sweden and India, where editorial commentary about the United States often strikes Americans as sanctimonious, Watergate occasioned little moralizing comparable to that of Americans themselves. In most foreign eyes, Nixon was the president who had forged SALT I and détente and the opening to China. It was hard to understand why a little looseness with the truth should lead to his unseating. To this day, many non-Americans remain incredulous. Occasionally, a visitor from the Soviet Union, Eastern Europe, or mainland China will draw his host into a place presumed to be free of listening devices and ask in a soft voice, "What really happened? How did the hard-line opponents of Nixon's policies contrive the coup that unseated him?" Even foreigners knowledgeable enough to understand why Nixon was taken to the block find it nevertheless disturbing that Americans make their presidents answer to an ethical code that has relatively little to do with the ability to protect and advance the interests of the people whose lives their actions may influence. Given this history, few foreigners are likely to feel satisfied that their interests are in safe hands merely because, at some very general level, American voters choose presidents by the same criteria that they themselves would apply.

Foreign Influence in American Elections

Here intervenes, therefore, the more practical line of argument. The 1980s are not the 1930s. Noncitizens do not have to depend entirely on coincidence between their standards and those of citizens. They have ways of influencing how American voters define prudence, leadership, and virtue.

In the first place, directly or indirectly, many foreigners contribute to shaping American public opinion. Foreign governments, of course, maintain studied official neutrality. The chief exceptions are Israel and the Soviet Union. Israeli governments can come close to endorsing candidates. In 1980, when third-party candidate John Anderson visited Israel, the government did its utmost to help him get favorable publicity at home, and Israeli officials acknowledged privately that they hoped thereby to draw votes away from Jimmy Carter.[15] With much less adroitness, the Soviets have tried from time to time by word or gesture to help one candidate or hurt another. During most of 1984 they handled arms control negotiations in such a way as to help Democrats charge the Reagan administration with making no progress. "We do not understand the American electoral mechanism, and we know that we don't understand it," one high Soviet official said to a *Christian Science Monitor* reporter. "But we certainly won't help Reagan during the election."[16] When the Soviet government did decide to make an appearance of an arms control initiative, Foreign Minister Andrei Gromyko consulted openly and evenhandedly with both President Reagan and his Democratic rival, Mondale.

If governments are formally silent and neutral, however, individual officials are not. Many political officers from foreign embassies and consulates, and members of foreign military, economic, and other missions talk more or less freely with American friends about American politics. Many foreign journalists have friends among American journalists, and thousands of foreigners communicate with Americans traveling abroad—officials, journalists, businessmen, tourists. Americans linked with foreigners, either at home or abroad, are likely to be citizens with some potential for leading opinion within their own circles of acquaintance.

Second, many American citizens are direct advocates for the interests of noncitizens. According to Russell Howe and Sarah Trott, fifteen thousand Americans are employed as foreign affairs lobbyists.[17] Millions of others have in varying degrees some other material link. They service, sell, or even produce foreign automobiles or electronic gadgets or they do business in one way or another with foreign countries. Tens of millions are Americans conscious of ethnic or religious ties with foreign lands. While American Jews strongly concerned about Israel may be the most conspicuous such group, they are by no means alone. Witness the quadrennial trials of platform committees preparing planks on "captive nations": Cyprus, Ireland, the two Chinas, South Africa, and the like.

Some of these advocates are in the U.S. government—or hope to be. Many of the thirty to forty thousand members of the Foreign Service, active and retired, millions in the military services, and many thousands in intelligence organizations have formed attachments to people or places abroad. Some of these officials and ex-officials clearly count as molders of voter opinion. In any case, they compose the memoranda and cables and briefings and speech texts that embody the specific actions presidents take in response to voter opinion. Once in office, a president gets every kind of encouragement, both from the bureaucracy and from his own appointees, to regard himself as responsible for much of the world. Candidates for the presidency get similar encouragement because of the makeup of the public interested in what they say about world affairs and because so many people inside the government (or nearly inside it, as, for example, analysts at the Brookings Institution or the American Enterprise Institute) want to help them voice "right" thoughts.

Finally, independent of personal friendships, economic interests, ethnicity, religion, or official position, large numbers of Americans believe that presidents ought not to speak just for their own national interests. The American public that cares about foreign publics is in fact very large and diverse, and it has been growing. During the isolationist 1930s only one eligible voter in eight had even completed high school; fewer than one in thirty had been to college. By 1980 nine out of ten voters were high school graduates, and one in four had a college degree. Although the education received by many of these voters may have been of dubious quality, the statistics signify that a much larger proportion of the electorate than ever before has been exposed to instruction about history and foreign cultures and international affairs. For many, travel has supplemented schooling. Millions saw Europe and Asia in World War II. Unlike veterans of World War I, most of them came back with happy memories. Jet aircraft, a strong dollar, foreign eagerness for hard currency, and the enterprise of travel agents produced millions more travelers in the postwar years. Not counting many millions who went to Canada or Mexico, the annual number of Americans traveling abroad went above eight million in 1980 and, for the most part, continued climbing thereafter.

Analysts of American public opinion long ago noted that the fraction of the people interested in foreign affairs is small; that, even within that fraction, the large majority copy views from a minority of comparatively widely experienced and well-read "opinion-leaders"; and that the opinion leaders in touch with members of Congress and those in touch with presidents tend to be different. The former are likely to be concerned for the protection of particular American interests while the latter are more likely to be cosmopolitans pursuing broad lines of policy or strategy conceived to be for the larger good.[18]

Trends in education and travel have worked to enlarge the "foreign policy public" and its leadership cohorts. The growth of multinational corporations, the Concorde, and other such developments should have caused the cosmopolitan cohort to grow relatively more rapidly or at least increased the presence of opinion leaders with a broad rather than a purely local or single-company sense of interest elsewhere. Suspicion of excessive nationalism hurt Taft in the 1940s and 1950s, Goldwater in 1964, and McGovern in 1972. It handicapped Reagan in 1980, and he and his handlers were careful to see that it did not do so the next time around. Sanford Ungar comments on the "extraordinary pains" taken by the White House staff to ensure publicity for Reagan's June 1984 tour of Britain, France, and

Ireland, explaining, "Presidential staffers care about Reagan's image in Europe not only because they want him to be popular there, but also because a favorable reputation overseas bounces back across the oceans and enhances the President's ability to present himself at home as an able and well-accepted world leader."[19]

Together with coincidence in general selection criteria, the practical means available for foreigners to influence American elections go a long way toward ensuring that the interests of non-Americans are not ignored or even slighted when Americans pick their presidents. Nevertheless, as indicated earlier, I favor some modest efforts to make this assurance more sure.

Foreign Gold?

The period when foreigners' interests receive least attention is that of the presidential primaries. After the nominating conventions, candidates get CIA briefings that cause them to concentrate at least periodically on foreign affairs. Their trainers prep them on questions that may come up in debates. Challengers of incumbents are under particular pressure to show themselves not at a disadvantage in knowledge or understanding of matters about which presidents might be able to claim expertise. Kennedy in 1960, Carter in 1976, and Reagan in 1980 worked very hard to acquire an appearance of being knowledgeable about military forces, arms control, relations with the Russians, regional security issues, the problems of developing countries, and international finance and trade. Looking back, one may question whether either Carter or Reagan acquired much lasting understanding as a result of these exercises. (Or Kennedy either, for that matter. Arguably, it was only the Bay of Pigs affair that opened his mind to learning.) Nevertheless, every speech, debate, press conference, or unguarded conversation with a reporter on a campaign plane offers a candidate an opportunity to alienate some group concerned with some particular part of the world and, in the process, to raise doubts among influential citizens for whom the overriding question is: Can this man or woman handle the larger global responsibilities of the presidency? Foreign commentators are almost as well positioned as Americans to take advantage of such openings.

Before nomination, however, the questions asked of candidates tend to be more parochial. During the early primaries in particular, they are often questions put by zealots who want to test the degree of commitment to their particular cause. The results do little to reassure foreigners about the intelligence or character of potential presidents. In 1952, although Eisenhower had just come from being NATO commander and Europe's hero, the rhetoric he found necessary to use in order to defeat Taft for the Republican nomination resulted in his fitness for the presidency being questioned by practically every leading periodical from London to Berlin. The majority of foreign publications concluded that Adlai Stevenson's posture was more statesmanlike and that he would therefore win.[20] Foreign observers have since become more sophisticated. They expect to hear nonsense during the primary season, and they do. In 1984, when Democrats competing in the Northeast talked at all about matters of high concern to foreigners, they did so in terms reassuring only to minorities with narrow preoccupations. To a man, they implied willingness to protect dying industries by putting up trade barriers. Each tried to outbid the others, first in wooing "nuclear freeze" proponents and then in pledging, if elected, to transfer the American embassy in Israel from Tel Aviv to Jerusalem. Such performances make many Americans nervous. Understandably, they make foreigners even more so.

There may be no way to make the early competition for nomination anything but auction bidding for special interest groups. It might be possible, however, to increase marginally the amount of attention paid during primary campaigns to broad issues of foreign policy and defense policy.

One imaginable measure would be the introduction of highly visible national security and foreign affairs briefings for all individuals identified as possible contenders. It would be in everyone's interest if all potential presidents actually saw a nuclear weapon, a missile test, a submarine, and an army exercise or if they talked, at least on American soil, with official representatives of a variety of foreign governments. A few days for such a purpose could be found in the slack season around Christmas or New Year's just before the election year. And almost no candidate could refuse if invitations were accompanied by promises of foot after foot of professionally made videotape for use later in the campaign.

A second possibility would be to extend dissemination in the United States of samples of foreign reportage and commentary. Few Americans are aware of how intently foreigners watch American politics. Some public-spirited but determinedly neutral organization, such as the League of Women Voters, could assemble a fairly chosen sample of excerpts or summaries or translations and mail them out during the primary season. Some voters might be influenced by knowledge of how foreign observers rated the candidates. If so, the candidates themselves might feel earlier and greater concern about foreign audiences.

Yet a third approach would open the way for foreigners to become special interest groups to be wooed during the period of presidential primaries. Of course, the election laws could not be amended to give them votes, and it is unthinkable that they could be allowed to send delegations to the conventions. (Imagine a delegate rising to declare, "The People's Republic of China casts its . . . votes for . . . .") But candidates' pronouncements in the early primary season are directed only partly to voters or potential delegates. Much of what they say and do is for the purpose of raising money. And it is not wholly unthinkable that, subject to stringent limitations, people not eligible to vote in American elections might be allowed to make campaign contributions.

While the notion may at first seem shockingly "un-American," four points argue that it is not. First, it would not be a large departure from tradition or custom. No law has ever prevented resident aliens from making campaign contributions. Given the size of the country's immigrant population before the restrictive legislation of the 1920s, many past presidential candidates must have received money from foreign nationals. Since statistical data and historical studies show that most immigrants intended to return to their homelands and that many did so, one can surmise that candidates probably received substantial sums from people with primary loyalties to other governments.[21] As a matter of fact, the current law that forbids campaign contributions by foreigners other than resident aliens dates only from the early 1970s, and it was passed with little debate and, so far as one can tell, with little analysis. Reacting to revelations that the United States had given clandestine aid to opponents of Chile's president, Salvador Allende, Representative Elizabeth Holtzman introduced a bill to make it a crime for Americans to contribute money to foreign campaigns. Before it went to the floor, other members of the House Judiciary Committee added a provision making it reciprocally a crime for foreigners to contribute money to American campaigns.[22]

Until that time, a candidate could have taken money from a for-eigner with no penalty except the risk of unfavorable publicity.

The previous observation on publicity incorporates the second point, for campaign fund-raising among foreigners would surely be severely self-regulating. Candidates and their managers would be fearful of finding themselves accounting for funds from Communist sources or from Libya, the PLO, or an Arab sheikh, or for laundered Mafia dollars. If Congress were to amend the existing law, it might permit only contributions by named individuals, not by PACs, and with a thousand dollar total limit on any individual foreigner's dona-tions; but this probably would not be necessary. The only politically safe money for candidates to receive from foreign sources would consist of comparatively small contributions from ordinary citizens in democratic countries.

Third, permitting foreign contributions to presidential campaigns would not be different in principle from permitting out-of-state con-tributions in senatorial or gubernatorial campaigns or out-of-district contributions in congressional campaigns. Many Americans feel themselves affected by elections in which they cannot participate legally as voters. They register concern by writing checks. So long as laws and regulations minimize the corrupting potentialities in con-tributions, why should foreigners be denied a similar privilege? After all, many of them feel that their lives are at stake.

The fourth and last point is that a change in the law would broaden by a tiny bit the pool in which candidates for nomination could fish for funds. At present, because of existing legislation and provisions concerning federal matching funds, that pool is quite small. Any legitimate increase in its size or diversification of its sources would probably be to the good. Especially because it might contribute to raising the level of language about issues, it is hard to see why candi-dates and their surrogates, in addition to seeking money from partic-ular ethnic or religious groups, gun control advocates or foes, right-to-lifers or pro-choicers, gays and lesbians or anti-gays and lesbians, and the like, should not also be able to hold fund-raisers in towns and villages elsewhere in the world.

I suspect that the suggestion of repealing the ban on campaign contributions by foreigners is not realistic. While the logical argu-ments may be strong, visceral misgivings are likely to prevail. In any case, it is hard to imagine any representative or senator thinking it worthwhile to pursue the objective. If there are realistic possibilities for marginally enhancing foreigners' roles and confidence in our presidential selection process, they probably lie in early, fully videotaped, systematic candidate briefings and more publicity in the United States for foreign commentary about the primaries.

These are modest suggestions. None is offered in expectation of its having much effect. What is likely to have more effect is simply for Americans to be more conscious that, when they choose presidents, they serve not only themselves; in some sense, they act as trustees for humankind. And it is neither in their interest nor that of humankind for the presidential selection process to be seen abroad as former German chancellor Helmut Schmidt is alleged to have characterized it in 1980—as one to determine which "provincial buffoon" will next be responsible for the world's well-being.

4 Learning to Govern or Learning to Campaign?

RICHARD ROSE

Democratic leaders need to combine two skills: responsiveness to the electorate and effectiveness in government. Responsiveness to the electorate is necessary because governors hold office by the consent of the governed. Effectiveness in office is desirable too; leaders who cannot achieve at least some of what they propose disappoint themselves as well as those who vote for them. The road to the White House puts a premium upon a politician learning to respond to popular sentiment on the campaign trail. By contrast, equally democratic parliamentary systems in Europe give priority to learning to govern.

The constitutional requirements for election to the presidency are formal; they say nothing about a president's qualifications for doing the job effectively. There is an enormous gulf between becoming president, a task that takes years of campaigning, and being president, a job that allows an incumbent only a short learning period before being assessed a success or failure in the instant judgment world of Washington politics.

No one will be elected president who has not learned how to campaign for office; the arduousness of the nomination and election process sees to that. The forms of the contemporary nominating process, which were occasioned by internal party pressures, such as the Democratic party convention battle of 1968, and by external pressures, such as the publicity national television now gives to early state primaries, has made campaigning far more important in the 1980s than it was a generation or more ago. No sooner was President Ronald Reagan inaugurated for a second term than his would-be successors started campaigning to succeed to his job in 1989. In 1985 an ambitious Congressman Jack Kemp touched base in twenty-four states, and Congressman Richard Gephardt in thirty.[1]

Campaigning is very different from governing. The effect of forcing ambitious politicians to concentrate upon incessant campaigning is to distract attention from learning what it takes to govern. Only after the winning candidate reaches the White House does he have time to think about the problems of governing. Success in an election is a necessary condition for sitting in the Oval Office, but it does not guarantee success in that office. The job looks more difficult from inside the White House than it does from the vantage point of the Iowa caucus. In default of being able to come to grips with government, a president may retreat into campaigning, as Jimmy Carter did during his midterm slump in 1978. But a Rose Garden strategy that emphasizes looking presidential is no substitute for being presidential.

By contrast with a U.S. president, a European prime minister usually is not installed in office after months or years of campaigning in the electorate. Instead, a prime minister takes office by gaining the confidence of the dominant party or coalition of parties in parliament. If an American president must communicate well with the people through the pseudo-intimate medium of television, a prime minister, by contrast, must communicate effectively only in the actual intimacy of parliament. The American primary system requires a presidential candidate to build a personal campaign organization to campaign as a lone wolf; a prime minister must win the confidence of party leaders. Once elected, a president is tempted to use television to appeal over the heads of Congress; a prime minister is directly accountable to the majority in parliament. A prime minister heads a cabinet team; a president surrounds himself with advisers and helpers who depend upon him personally yet cannot do the president's unique job.

Comparing the selection of the president with the route by which politicians become leaders in Britain, France and Germany provides an empirical basis for evaluating the American presidential selection process against the standard of experience elsewhere. The customary way to evaluate the president's capacity to govern is by comparing the performances of different incumbents in office. The trouble with this approach is that exceptional circumstances affect many presidents, as in the departures of John F. Kennedy and Richard Nixon from office. Moreover, three of the eight postwar presidents—Harry Truman, Lyndon B. Johnson, and Gerald Ford—did not enter the White House by campaigning, but by moving up from the unimportant office of vice president. The characteristic method of evaluating performance on television—dissecting the personality of the president—is inadequate to explain performance in office. With all its faults, the personality of the president is relatively constant, whereas the popularity and effectiveness of the president fluctuate greatly.

Although comparison with other countries avoids the assumption that whatever is American must be best, it need not imply that European practices should or could offer a quick fix for Washington's problems. European leaders have their difficulties, and no political institution can readily or surely be transferred from one national environment to another. At a minimum, comparison can add to our understanding of the strengths and weaknesses of the route to the White House.

Tasks of Leadership

The tasks that a president or prime minister must undertake are relatively few, but large in their implications.[2] For ease of exposition, they can be listed separately, but it is the nature of the job that, as a White House staffer once put it, "Everything happens at once—and before 9 A.M." Executive leadership tasks are interdependent. Success or failure in one field, such as maintaining popularity in opinion polls, will affect performance in another field, such as mobilizing legislative support.[3] At a sufficiently high level of generalization, the tasks of a president and a prime minister have a great deal in common: both are concerned with the mood of the electorate and the majority party and both bear responsibility for how their countries are governed. But, institutionally, the positions are different.

Two tasks of presidents and prime ministers—sustaining popular support and party management—are directly related to success in campaigning for office. Three—leading the nation's legislature, preserving national security, and managing the economy—affect how the nation's chief politician succeeds on the job.

Sustaining Popular Support

Winning a series of primary ballots and a national election provides prima facie evidence that a president is good at garnering votes. Once in office, a president must seek popular support in very different circumstances from those of the campaign trail; he not only has the aura of office but also the responsibility for the shortcomings of government. To deal with these problems an incoming president usually recruits the White House staff from the campaign staff, because a major presidential priority is to campaign incessantly for popular support, both as preparation for a reelection campaign, and, incidentally, to boost his standing with Congress.

By comparison, a prime minister is more immediately beholden to party opinion, especially in parliament. Winning elections is desirable, but not necessary. In the coalition systems that are widespread in Europe, the choice of a prime minister is determined by interparty bargaining, not by popular vote.[4] In every parliamentary system it is possible to change prime ministers during the life of a parliament without a general election. Only in France does the president depend upon popular votes for office. However, a seven-year term provides substantial relief from immediate anxieties about reelection. In Britain the autonomy of the prime minister from the public opinion polls is shown by the fact that the party in office has normally run behind the opposition on the monthly Gallup poll, without reducing the effectiveness of party government.[5]

Managing the Party

To paraphrase Ring Lardner, the president would grab the reins of party leadership, only "he ain't got no party." Although a president runs on a party ticket, he does not see himself as dependent upon the party for election. In this respect, a president differs fundamentally from a prime minister, who becomes party leader by the vote of a party caucus, not a popular primary. To win election, a presidential candidate must secure support from a significant proportion of independents, and even some who identify with the opposing party.[6] Democrats consistently lead Republicans in party identification, but Republicans have won six of the nine presidential contests since 1952. Contemporary presidential candidates no longer rely upon the party to organize electoral support; they rely instead upon a personal following sustained by a national network of personally loyal staff.

Managing the Legislature

Both president and prime minister must deal with elected legislators, but they do so from fundamentally different positions. A prime minister is a member of parliament before becoming prime minister, and normally continues to be one during the term of office. Attendance at meetings of parliament keeps a prime minister in touch with sentiment in the party, and among opponents as well. In seeking support for government measures, the endorsement of party leaders in the cabinet virtually guarantees success in parliament.

The president wants what Congress has: authority to enact laws and to appropriate money. Because of the integration that is achieved by party government, a prime minister may take parliament's support as assured; no president can do this. From breakfast meetings to late night telephone calls, a president must always work at congressional relations. The arts of dealing with Congress are not difficult to master: thousands of congressional staffers have acquired them. But they do demand knowledge of the institution, knowledge that is gained most readily by previous experience in Congress. Yet the selection process does not require such experience of a president.

In policy terms a president is continuously concerned with questions of national security and problems of the economy. Peace and prosperity are likely to be major themes in campaigning, but the way issues are treated in an election tends to have very little substantive content.

National Security

Upon entering office a newly elected president inherits a formidable staff system to brief him about global problems, providing updates on an almost hourly basis. There is no assurance in the electoral process that the newly elected president will have a frame of reference into which he can fit all the information that is required to be an expert on Europe, the Middle East, Asia, Latin America, and Africa, as well as on the complexities of arms systems. The most and the least that the campaign can do is test a candidate for obvious ignorance.

In smaller European democracies prime ministers do not need much specialized knowledge of national security issues, for these issues are decided at summit meetings that do not involve heads of small national governments. In Britain, France, and Germany, heads of government are involved in frequent meetings in the European Community, in world summits, and in a flow of international discussion. Because the issues that are of immediate concern to European governments usually are less than global in import, they are more likely to be amenable to influence by national leaders, usually finance ministers and foreign secretaries.[7] To the extent that experience as foreign secretary or finance minister is a stepping stone to the prime ministership, a national head of government may have dealt previously with foreign affairs for years.

Economic Policy

The institutions of American government do not make it possible to manage the economy as many economic theories propose. There is no central decisionmaker in Washington; Congress and the Federal Reserve Board each plan an independent role in decisions. State and local governments independently determine much public expenditure. The fragmentation of institutions that are nominally under the president's authority is symbolized by the existence of the Troika (the Treasury Department, the Council of Economic Advisers, and the Office of Management and Budget) and the Quadriad (the Troika plus the Federal Reserve Board). Institutional hobbling of the presidency is reinforced by the rhetoric of private enterprise. Given free enterprise norms, presidential candidates are discouraged from developing plans to manage the economy, or from thinking in terms of a positive government strategy for the economy.[8]

By contrast, every European prime minister is expected to see that the government provides positive direction to the economy. Socialists are committed to planning, and most non-socialists accept a *dirigiste* role for government. Even the would-be free enterprise Thatcher government in Britain is conscious that it needs an explicit and coherent strategy to influence the economy. A prime minister will have far more resources to influence the economy than are available to a president and often some experience serving in the treasury as well. Cabinet membership of any kind gives a potential prime minister an opportunity to listen to economic issues being discussed in government.

The Previous Experience of Presidents and Prime Ministers

Comparing the prior experience of American, British, German, and French leaders will identify the extent to which the above requirements for directing government are actually met. Prior experience in elective public office is prima facie evidence of skill in mobilizing public opinion. Prior experience in the national legislature will develop skill in negotiating intra- and interparty support. Substantive knowledge of national security policy and of economic policy can best be obtained by holding a post in a government department that is responsible for these problems.

United States

The common attribute of the fourteen Americans who have been nominated for president by the Democratic or Republican parties since 1945 is that nearly every one has had prior experience in running for major office, either at the congressional or gubernatorial level (table 4.1). Dwight D. Eisenhower, a career military official, was the sole exception. Campaigning for office gives politicians a sense of how to sustain popular support.

The majority of presidential candidates had prior experience in Washington, usually in Congress, before running for the top job. Nine candidates had served in Congress, averaging nine years there. This is ample time to learn how to handle congressional relations from the inside, and also to develop a legislator's view of the federal bureaucracy. Two other candidates had worked in the executive branch, thus learning how the federal government looks from the departments rather than from the White House. Familiarity with Washington is the rule among presidential candidates. Two exceptions —Reagan and Carter—each held his first Washington job as president, and Thomas E. Dewey ran for the White House with experience only in New York state politics.

Six candidates and five presidents have had a unique view of the presidency by serving as vice president. In two cases, those of Harry S. Truman and Gerald R. Ford, the experience was too brief

Table 4.1 The Political Experience of U.S. Presidential Candidates since 1945.

| | *Program* | | | *Office* | |
	National security	Economy (years)	Congress	Other federal	State and local
Harry Truman*	o	o	10	1 VP	12 local
Thomas Dewey	o	o	o	o	2 governor; 7 legal
Dwight Eisenhower*	35 Army, NATO	o	o	o	o
Adlai Stevenson	6 Navy, State	o	o	1 agri- culture	4 governor
Richard Nixon*	o	o	6	8 VP	o
John Kennedy*	o	o	13	o	o
Barry Goldwater	o	o	12	o	4 city council
Lyndon Johnson*	o	o	25	3 VP	o
Hubert Humphrey	o	o	16	4 VP	4 mayor, 2 official
George McGovern	2 Food for Peace	o	14	o	o
Gerald Ford*	o	o	25	1 VP	o
Jimmy Carter*	7 career Navy	o	o	o	4 governor, 4 state senate
Ronald Reagan*	o	o	o	o	8 governor
Walter Mondale	o	o	12	4 VP	4 state attorney- general
Median	o	o	11	0.5	4
(Average)	(4)	(o)	(9)	(2)	(3)

*President.

to be significant, and for Lyndon B. Johnson, Hubert H. Humphrey and Walter Mondale, the vice presidency was much less formative than congressional experience. Only Richard Nixon could regard being vice president as his principal formative political experience prior to the presidency. The ambiguous position of the vice president, who is so closely identified with the president that it is difficult for him to act as an independent presidential personality, is hardly a satisfactory preparation for the presidency. Nor have presidents found their time as vice president to be of major benefit in handling the job at the top.

In terms of familiarity with Washington, then, eleven of the fourteen presidential candidates could claim to know the city and its ways well, although for most this meant the view from the Hill. Only Eisenhower, who as a ranking general dealt with elected political leaders at the highest level, and Adlai Stevenson, a lawyer in the departments of Agriculture, Navy, and State, could claim great familiarity with the executive branch. Prior experience in local government or at a state house cannot be reckoned to prepare one for the White House, for a mayor or governor is not responsible for the national economy or national security. In economic affairs, state and local officials react to national trends. In national security, a mayor or governor gains no experience.

The shortcoming in most presidential candidates' experience concerns the major substantive issues of government. No president in the postwar era has had any direct involvement with economic policymaking and, unlike secretaries of the Treasury, presidents also have lacked private sector economic experience. A president's experience with the Treasury, the Federal Reserve Board, and the Council of Economic Advisers begins after reaching the White House. Congressional experience looking at particular appropriation lines in the budget without considering macroeconomic issues is arguably counterproductive for economic policymaking. The Joint Economic Committee of Congress now offers a chance for a representative or senator to learn about economic affairs, but no legislator has yet used it as a springboard to the White House.

National security issues are also usually new to presidential candidates. Only three candidates could claim significant prior knowledge before running for the White House. Ironically, Eisenhower had more experience—in the Army, in the politics of the Allied invasion of Europe, and subsequently at NATO—than any elected official. Stevenson was in the Navy Department and the State Department during World War II. Exceptionally, Nixon was able to use his time as vice president to learn how the national security apparatus works and to represent America abroad. But for the great majority of presidential candidates, prior service in the armed forces, with its worm's eye view of the military, was the main experience of national security. The exigencies of building a career in Congress or a state capital and keeping in touch with the electorate at home inhibit work abroad or extensive foreign travel—except as a carefully calculated part of campaigning for a presidential nomination.

Britain

The British system contrasts markedly with America in the experience of its national leaders. Membership in the House of Commons is a sine qua non for entry to the prime ministership; on average, a prime minister has been a member of Parliament for twenty-five years before being made a party leader (table 4.2). Anyone who becomes prime minister will have had decades of experience in party management within Parliament, and will have won the confidence of colleagues there. Election to the party leadership is exclusively in the hands of members of Parliament in the Conservative party, and has been dominated by M.P.s in the Labour party. Management of the party inside and outside the legislature is second nature to a British prime minister.

The British system is an apprenticeship system; a potential prime minister will have substantial experience in the executive branch of government.[9] After years as an ordinary M.P., a politician commences a career in government by receiving a junior ministerial post and gradually works up the ladder to a senior post in a minor department, then a senior post in a major department as the final stage before being elected party leader. The making of a prime minister is a matter of decades, not months. Before being named party leader, an average M.P. has spent twelve years as a minister. In addition, four party leaders—Hugh Gaitskell, Harold Wilson, Edward Heath, and James Callaghan—had been civil servants before running for elective office, which further broadened their knowledge of the workings of the executive branch of British government.

British prime ministers have a great advantage over incoming American presidents in their knowledge of substantive issues. Seven of the eleven postwar party leaders have served in defense or diplomatic ministries and, in four cases, in both. Those who were experienced in foreign affairs spent an average of eight years as a responsible minister; five—Sir Winston Churchill, Sir Anthony Eden, Harold Macmillan, Sir Alec Douglas-Home, and Callaghan—had been foreign secretary or defence secretary or both.

A prospective prime minister is also likely to have had experience in economic affairs. Seven of the eleven party leaders had been economic ministers, including four—Churchill, Macmillan, Gaitskell, and Callaghan—who had been chancellor of the Exchequer. The average time in office in an economic ministry for those who served

Table 4.2   The Political Experience of Major Party Leaders in Britain since 1945.

	National security	Economy	Total as minister[a] (years)	Other Parliament	Central	Local
Clement Attlee*	2	0	8	23	0	8
Winston Churchill[b]*	15	5	22	39	0	0
Anthony Eden*	21	0	21	32	0	0
Harold Macmillan*	4	4	11	31	0	0
Hugh Gaitskell	0	6	6	10	5	0
Harold Wilson*	0	4	6	18	5	0
Sir Alec Douglas-Home*	9	0	16	32[c]	0	0
Edward Heath*	3	2	13	15	1	0
James Callaghan*	3	3	12	31	11	0
Margaret Thatcher*	0	0	7	15	0	0
Michael Foot	0	2	5	30	0	0
Median	3	2	11	30	0	0
(Average)	(5)	(2)	(12)	(25)	(2)	(1)

[a] All ministerial posts, whether in cabinet or not.
[b] Experience as of first becoming prime minister in 1940.
[c] Includes service in House of Lords.
*Prime Minister.

there was four years (five if the relevant wartime experience of Wilson and Gaitskell is also included).

The contrast between the experience of British and American leaders is extreme. Whatever changes occur in American presidential politics, they are unlikely to produce presidents with the substantive knowledge of policy that British prime ministers have. British leaders differ from each other only in the degree of their expertise. At the top are three individuals—Churchill, Macmillan, and Callaghan—who held both the chancellorship of the Exchequer and major national security posts before becoming party leader. Margaret Thatcher was less experienced dealing with economic and national security issues before becoming prime minister, but her inexperience was relative, not absolute. Prior to being elected party leader in 1975, she already had served fifteen years in Parliament, and seven years as a minister. She was familiar with Whitehall's ways before getting the top job there. The leader of the Labour party who was elected after its 1983 election debacle, Neil Kinnock, was chosen

Table 4.3   The Political Experience of Major Party Leaders in Germany since 1949.

	National security	Economy	Total Ministry
Konrad Adenauer	(1 internee)	0	0
Kurt Schumacher	(11 internee)	0	0
Erich Ollenauer	(13 exile)	0	0
Willy Brandt	(12 exile)	0	0
Ludwig Erhard	0	14	14
Kurt George Kiesinger	0	0	0
Rainer Barzel	1	0	1
Franz Josef Strauss	10	3	13
Helmut Schmidt	3	2	6
Hans-Jochen Vogel	0	0	9
Helmut Kohl	0	0	0
Median[c]	0	0	6
(Average)	(2)	(3)	(6)

Numbers in parentheses indicate experience previous to 1945.
[a] Of which nine years as leader of the CDU parliamentary party.
[b] Of which two years as leader of the SDP parliamentary party.

because he had no experience in government, although he had been in Parliament for thirteen years. His lack of experience has been a handicap in parliamentary confrontations with Thatcher. Significantly, the leader of the Social Democratic party, David Owen, has been more effective than Kinnock in Parliament and in opinion polls, drawing upon the skills and knowledge he acquired during eight years as a minister, including two as foreign secretary.

The Federal Republic of Germany

Although the basis for generalization about the political careers of German leaders is weaker than for Britain and France because of the interruption by the Third Reich, the overall pattern is sufficiently clear to provide an instructive comparison with leadership in the American system.

The modal career pattern of a would-be German chancellor includes substantial experience at both the federal level in Bonn and at the *Land* (state) or local (*stadt*) level (table 4.3). Of the seven leaders who have come forward since Ludwig Erhard, six have had a substantial career in Bonn. The median leader has spent fourteen years in the Bundestag, the elected lower house of the federal Parliament. In five

| Parliament | | Land | | Local |
Bundestag	Bundesrat	Executive	Parliament	government
(1)	—	o	(14)	(28)
(3)	—	o	(7)	o
4	o	o	o	o
8	4	4	11	o
14	o	o	o	o
9	8	8	6	o
15[a]	o	o	o	o
31	o	o	o	o
18[b]	o	4	4	o
9	1	o	2	12
0	13	13	17	o
14	o	o	2	o
(14)	(3)	(4)	(4)	(2)

[c] Excluding Adenauer, Schumacher, Ollenauer, and Brandt, whose careers substantially preceded the foundation of the Bundesrepublik.

cases politicians have held a significant office, either as a minister in a major department or as the leader of their parliamentary party, a position that puts an individual very close to the chancellor.

German politicians have used the structure of the federal system to expand their experience both in government at the ground level and in federal politics in Bonn. Leaders of the *laender* are ex officio members of the Bundesrat, the nonelected upper chamber of the federal Parliament. The two chancellors who lacked any ministerial experience in Bonn—K. G. Kiesinger and Helmut Kohl—each were familiar with power in Bonn by virtue of sitting in the Bundesrat as representatives of the *Laender* of which they were *Ministerpraesident*. Willy Brandt built his postwar political career on the foundations of his activity as mayor of Berlin, H. J. Vogel achieved recognition as mayor of Munich, and Franz Josef Strauss was party leader of the csu in Bavaria. Konrad Adenauer's first political experience was in the city government of Cologne in the Kaiser's pre-1914 Reich.

The German system stands midway between the American and British in the experience that party leaders gain in dealing with major substantive issues. The first chancellors of the federal republic each had a very intense socialization into national security affairs, being raised under a succession of regimes, and interned or exiled. Of the seven most recent party leaders, three have held portfolios concerned with defense or East Germany and three with finance, including one (Strauss) who held both. This shows a higher level of firsthand exposure to substantive problems than in the United States, particularly when one considers that five of seven party leaders have been members of national cabinets in which security and economic issues often dominate the agenda. German politicians devote less time to becoming experts in national affairs than do their British counterparts, investing more effort instead in the complex network of intergovernmental relations through which public policies are delivered.[10]

France

The Fifth Republic illustrates another way that an individual can get to the top, by demonstrating technocratic brilliance as a civil servant and then as a minister dealing with economic or foreign affairs. From 1958 to 1981 the French presidency was always occupied by a person who was well versed in either national security policy or economic affairs (table 4.4). Since the establishment of the Fifth Republic in 1958, twelve men have been president or prime minister. Of these only three—Jacques Chaban-Delmas, François Mitterrand, and Pierre Mauroy—could be said to have followed conventional political careers as that term would be used in Washington today. President Mitterrand is atypical in having been excluded from office for more than two decades until his victory at the 1981 election. But he was elected to the Assembly of the Fourth Republic in 1946 and held a series of ministerial portfolios until the creation of the Fifth Republic by General Charles de Gaulle in 1958.

The characteristic political leader of the Fifth Republic is a technocrat, initially recruited into the civil service through highly competitive examinations and training at *École Nationale d'Administration* (ENA).[11] Like British civil servants, these *enarques* are able to gain political experience at a young age. But unlike Britons, they are then able to accept ministerial appointments from the party in power. Such moves are facilitated by the fact that membership in the Assembly is not required for a ministerial appointment; indeed, an Assembly member must resign upon taking a ministerial job. Chirac, Barre, Giscard d'Estaing, and Fabius rose from the civil service into ministerial appointments in economic affairs. Messmer in foreign affairs, and Couve de Murville was experienced in both. In addition,

Table 4.4   Political Experience of Presidents and Prime Ministers in the French Fifth Republic.

Leader	Ministries National security	Economy	Total Minister	Civil servant	Assembly	Local[a]
Charles de Gaulle President 1958–69	35	0	5	30	0	0
Michel Debre PM 1959–62	0	0	1	9	10	0
Georges Pompidou PM 1962–68 President 1968–74 (6 years as Prime Minister)	0	0	0	0	0	0
Couve de Murville PM 1968–69	min: 10 cs: 8	cs: 10	10	28	0	0
Jacques Chaban-Delmas PM 1969–72	min: 1	0	1	2	23	22
Pierre Messmer PM 1972–74	min: 11 cs: 15		0	13	15	0
Jacques Chirac PM 1974–76; 1986	0	min: 4 cs: 5	7	8	7	4
Valéry Giscard d'Estaing President 1974–81	0	min: 12 cs: 2	14	4	2	0
Raymond Barre PM 1976–81	min: 5	min: 1 cs: 11	6	11	0	0
François Mitterrand President 1981–	min: 7	0	7	2	35	0
Pierre Mauroy PM 1981–84	4	0	0	0	8	14
Laurent Fabius PM 1984–86	0	min: 3 cs: 4	3	7	3	0
Median	5	0	4	7	5	0
(Average)	8	4	4	10	9	4

[a] Omitting symbolic posts in small communes in a constituency.
min = minister; cs = civil servant.

Michel Debre, de Gaulle's first prime minister, had been a civil servant prior to his appointment, and Georges Pompidou was exceptionally well qualified in economic policy because of experience in banking. De Gaulle began his career as a technocrat, too; he was trained as a regular army officer and, like Eisenhower, gained political recognition in World War II.

Notwithstanding many differences, the French system of recruiting political leaders bears similarities to the American system. Just as Washington abounds with young men and women who are special assistants to senior officials in the executive branch, so Paris is full of ambitious young civil servants who have moved into a minister's cabinet, a post more nearly resembling the office of the secretary in Washington than anything found in Whitehall. The fierce competition for ENA means that those who succeed in their training will enter the strategically most important ministries, including attachment to the prime minister or the president's office. Just as a Washingtonian makes a breakthrough by securing a presidential appointment, so a French civil servant arrives when asked to go on leave from the civil service to take a ministerial post, a procedure fully consistent with French law and the law of many continental European countries.

A French leader differs from an American president in not having devoted years to campaigning. Instead he can devote those years to governing. It is possible for someone to become prime minister of France without ever having run for elective office, relying instead on the patronage of the president. A French president or prime minister is more likely to have been involved with economic or foreign policy as a civil servant than to have been an elected member of the National Assembly. An ambitious young politician in France makes straight for Paris and an appointive post in the bureaucracy.

Summary

Of the skills that a president or prime minister would find useful to give direction to government, an American president is likely to enter office with only one: the ability to mobilize popular support. The American system makes campaign skills not only the be-all of the presidency, but also threatens to make it the end-all. A president takes campaign staff into the White House with him, and at the first sign of opposition from Congress may prefer to appeal to the people through the media rather than face up to the facts of government.[12] Even a president who has formerly served in Congress will have problems managing a legislature that has not elected him.

By contrast, prime ministers normally enter office with a demonstrated capacity to deal with substantive economic problems, international issues, or both. Even a political leader who has not been a foreign secretary or treasury minister will have had ample opportunity to observe the interplay of domestic and foreign policy by sitting in cabinet. Leaders are doubly experienced in national government, having served as ministers and as members of the national Parliament, or as civil servants in the case of the French. Prime ministers will have excellent credentials as leaders of both parliamentary and extraparliamentary parties.

Noteworthy differences exist between British prime ministers, German *Bundeskanzlers*, and French leaders, but the similarities are more striking. A parliamentary system is much more likely than the American system to produce a leader experienced in dealing with the substantive problems of government.

Implications for Change

By comparison with leaders of major European nations, an American president normally has had far more experience campaigning for office, and far less experience governing. The European system of strong parties and recruitment from parliament emphasizes an apprenticeship in office; in contrast, the American system is a contest in which the competition is for votes, not for success in government.

The winner in the campaign for the White House is pitchforked into the presidency—ready or not. At the time of taking office, European leaders are at an advantage, for they usually have had far more experience in foreign policy, economic policy, and the points of intersection between the two. This does not guarantee that their policies will be successful, but it does mean that their countries are led by politicians who are experienced in dealing with issues of the highest national priority.

In the United States the president's lack of experience in economic policy could be considered an advantage by proponents of laissez-faire economy. In the words of two experienced academics and Washington officials, George Shultz and Kenneth Dam: "Leadership is often equated with doing something and patience equated with indecision. Indeed, one of the most difficult problems for economic policy is finding ways to do nothing."[13] But noninterventionism was more feasible in the days of Calvin Coolidge than today, when the federal government's taxing, spending, and borrowing policies all have a significant influence on the American—and the world—economy. Moreover, a president concerned about his long-term popularity with the electorate will want to make the economy successful, given the electoral effects of economic conditions.[14]

The case for a laissez-faire presidency does not apply at all to foreign affairs. The president speaks for the country as a whole in dealing with foreign nations, and also is commander-in-chief of the armed forces. The breadth and depth of America's global commitments make it impossible for a president not to be actively involved in foreign policy. For that reason, foreign policy is usually prominent in campaigning. However, a president who travels abroad simply in hope of gaining votes from ethnic groups will get an unrealistic picture of the world. Promises made to one's own electorate are difficult to deliver when they require cooperation from the governments of other countries.

While cross-country campaigning is a good test of a president's relative popularity, it is not a good introduction to being president. Admittedly, campaigning—and even more, victory—strengthens the president's hand with his party and Congress. But incessant campaigning tends to distract attention from the substantive problems of governing. The question that must be faced is: What changes, if any, in the selection process would better prepare an incoming president for the problems of government.[15]

By comparison with the selection of a prime minister, the distinctive feature of the American process is that a would-be presidential candidate is self-employed. Instead of being the product of a winnowing process within a party, in which professional politicians assess a variety of candidates over the years, in Parliament and out, a presidential hopeful is an independent entrepreneur. A candidate must build a personal campaign organization, raise money, and project a positive image to the electorate. In parliament an ambitious politician is tested by leading one party against another, but to secure nomination in the presidential race a candidate first must run against fellow partisans. The length of the campaign trail to the White House is virtually unknown in Europe, and it imposes a high cost in turning a potential president's attention away from questions of effective government.

An alternative to the choice of presidential candidates by primary ballot or legislative caucus is a third possibility: selection by party convention. Party conventions can pick leaders in parliamentary systems as well as presidential systems. The pool of potential leaders is not confined to the national capital. In Germany the Christian Democratic Union (CDU) has twice gone to the *land* level for chancellors. In Canada the Liberals picked Pierre Trudeau as party leader and prime minister in 1968, only three years after he entered Parliament.[16]

The convention choice of a candidate can balance considerations of intraparty ideological preferences, electoral appeal, and effectiveness in office.[17] If the party leans too far in one direction, then defeat will follow, as in the CDU setback in Germany in 1980 under Strauss, or the British Labour debacle in 1983 under Michael Foot. However a party convention is constituted, the important point is that its members are likely to be better informed and better able to judge the campaigning *and* governing qualities of candidates than is the average voter in an American primary. Ironically, the convention system for nominating leaders was once the American custom, and it has been downgraded only in recent decades. The interesting question is whether there are ways in which its importance could be increased.

A minimal way to reduce the burden of campaigning would be to shorten the primary season. This could be done by introducing a national primary, or a series of regional primaries, held within a four to eight week period in the spring of the presidential year. A national primary has considerable justification in theory, for it would not overweigh the judgment of a handful of voters in Iowa and New Hampshire. It also would give each person with a vote for the presidency a chance to vote for a party's choice of candidate.

If a primary did no more than shorten the time in which members of one party fight each other and lengthen the period in which one party standard-bearer fights the other, it would serve a positive purpose. It also would concentrate more attention on how the country should be governed, a different question from how the party should be led. Finally, it would reduce the costly effects—both political and economic—of lengthy primary campaigns.

A more interesting feature of a national primary is that it could become a means of reinstituting the convention choice of the presidential candidate. If convention delegates were elected in every state on the same date and state delegates were awarded approximately in proportion to each candidate's share of the vote, then a national primary would determine the party nominee only under certain limiting conditions. If no serious challenger to an incumbent president was on the ballot, the primary would ratify what was taken for granted. In contested races it would give a majority of convention votes only to a candidate who dominated the field. In practice, presidential primary contests usually involve a field of three or more candidates, none of whom is likely to win more than half the vote.

A national primary would not reduce the representativeness of the party's candidate. If more than half the primary voters favored one candidate, that candidate would be the nominee. It would protect the representative process when voters were divided three or more ways, with no one person preferred by a majority. It would enable delegates representing a majority of the party's voters to determine the party's nominee—and to do it through the normal process of representation.

The old convention system could be subject to two very different types of criticism. The first is that it was unrepresentative of the party's voters, since it was composed of delegates chosen by party caucuses. The second criticism is that the convention involved bargaining between delegates. The latter criticism could be applied to most American institutions, most notably Congress, where bargaining is the only way politicians can reach a stable majority decision. But the criticism of unrepresentativeness could not be applied to a convention whose delegates were directly elected in a national primary.[18]

A popularly elected convention is likely to be criticized because it is representative. A three- or five-way division of national opinion appears, superficially, less clear-cut than the emergence of a candidate whose majority is "manufactured" by snowballing a few primary victories. In a nation with an electorate as diverse as the United States, and with two parties competing for heterogeneous coalitions of supporters, it would be surprising not to find a number of serious candidates for the presidency within each party. If Democratic or Republican voters divided three or more ways in their support for prospective presidential candidates, then the convention would be divided into three or more blocs, with none likely to have the majority needed for nomination.

A convention whose delegates divided their support among several candidates would not be incoherent: it would be an assembly under pressure to aggregate preferences, a classic problem of representative democracy. In doing so, delegates could judge the relative importance of each candidate's stands on issues, popular appeal to the national electorate, and likelihood of being an effective president. Straightforward rules could be adopted to eliminate the candidate with the least votes on each ballot, and to permit withdrawals, in order to ensure that the convention could nominate a candidate without undue delay.

There is no reason for a party convention to choose a personable incompetent or an unelectable academic. In a country of 225 million people, it should be possible to find two candidates who each combine the ability to campaign successfully with the ability to be effective in office. The most a change of rules can do is alter the bias of the system in favor of one or another attribute. If European systems may sometimes be criticized for giving too much weight to the party caucus and too little to popular preferences, there is no doubt about the bias in the American system today: it gives too much weight to learning to campaign, and too little to learning to govern.

5 The Linkage of Policy to Participation

GARY R. ORREN

Elections are the great public ceremonies of American life. We elect beauty queens and all-star teams, presidents and coroners. Popular demands for a greater voice in political affairs emerged earlier and have been met more fully in this nation than in any other. Because of the steady extension of the franchise, increases in the number of public officials who are elected, and expanding citizen involvement in the selection of party nominees, the United States is the most democratic country in the world.

But if the health of a democracy can be measured by the level of popular participation in its electoral system, ours is ailing. Compared to other democracies, voter turnout in the United States has been low for a long time, and has been getting lower. In 1980 and 1984, almost two eligible citizens stayed home for every one who voted for Ronald Reagan.

The Problem

Should we lament the low and declining voting rate in America? Many observers believe that it is nothing to worry about. Those complacent about low turnouts can be divided into two main schools: one applauds the decline and the other simply shrugs. The first claims that nonvoting is a sign, perhaps a requirement, of a healthy democracy. The second maintains that turnout makes little difference in electoral outcomes.

Adherents of the first school offer several reasons for welcoming low political participation. First, they claim that since nonvoters generally hold democratic values less dear than voters do, their abstention prevents the dilution of democracy. Low participation, it is argued, usually bodes well for democracy, since it indicates general satisfaction with the political system. Extremely high participation —especially a sudden upsurge—often reflects social conflict and discontent, which, in turn, can threaten democratic institutions.[1]

The second school holds that low political participation is neither curse nor blessing.[2] Nonvoting does not diminish the representativeness of our political system because nonvoters' preferences for candidates and policies mirror those of voters. Indeed, the evidence suggests that the final outcomes of most presidential elections probably would not have changed if nonvoters had gone to the polls.[3] Nor should low turnouts cause concern for our civic health since nonvoters are just as likely as voters to feel both the obligation to vote and a sense of political efficacy. Finally, the proponents of this perspective contend that nonvoting does no more violence to democratic principles than it does to political practice. The right to abstain is as essential to democracy as the franchise itself.

There is a more extreme variant of this second view that nonvoting makes little difference. That is the view that voting itself makes little difference. For some advocates of participatory democracy, nonvoting is far less troubling than the challenge of getting citizens deeply engaged in self-government. Benjamin Barber has argued that although balloting has the aura of democracy—indeed, Americans think that democracy means voting—it is a minimalist or "thin" expression of citizenship. In fact, choosing representatives in elections, according to Barber, encourages privatism and passivity, which are incompatible with a true democratic ideal. Only when citizens seek a higher ideal—deliberating, sharing, and engaging with each other in such forums as neighborhood assemblies, town meetings, national service programs, and citizens' courts—do they really participate. Against this vision of "strong democracy," declining turnout at the polls seems largely irrelevant.[4]

The premise guiding this chapter rejects both these schools of thought, arguing instead that low levels of political participation are neither beneficial nor benign, and certainly not irrelevant. The details of the argument emerge throughout the chapter. But anticipating some of those details now, the core of the thesis turns on the functions that are served by voting in a democracy.

Elections satisfy several purposes, but three stand out as particularly important. The first is to create a government with enough legitimacy and authority to govern. In the United States the authority to enact or alter laws resides with the people, who delegate this authority to officials through elections. The government's legitimacy derives not from divine right or the power of the sword, but specifically and exclusively from the fact of election. Thus a criterion for judging a democratic system is how many people vote; democracy is diluted if only a small fraction of the citizenry participates. Graham Allison put the central question succinctly at a conference on voter participation: "When half of the people drop out, what does this imply about the legitimacy of a democratic government that —according to its own Declaration of Independence—'derives its just powers from the consent of the governed'?"[5] Those who minimize the importance of low turnout generally either are silent on the legitimacy issue or argue that those who refrain from voting are satisfied with the functioning of government and are happy to leave well enough alone. George Will has suggested, for example, that nonvoting is a "form of passive consent."[6] But as Seymour Martin Lipset pointed out many years ago, such an explanation is not altogether plausible, and recent evidence, as we shall see, confirms his conclusion.[7]

A second function of democratic elections is to ensure that the government responds to the people and fairly represents their interests. The desire to be elected and reelected directs representatives' attention to the needs and hopes of the electorate. While the legitimacy issue is decided by the magnitude of the vote, questions about government responsiveness turn on the composition of the electorate. The criterion here is who votes, that is, how representative the electorate is of the public as a whole. If particular groups tend not to vote, their needs are apt to be ignored, for voting is the primary mechanism for assuring that government attends to the views and values of the governed. Further, as the number of participating citizens shrinks, the views of political activists are enhanced. Thus in the absence of a highly mobilized electorate, we would expect special interest groups to exercise greater influence over public policy. The evidence demonstrates that the active electorate is not a representative sample of the entire voting age population. The disparity between the voting rates of upper and lower status groups is large and increasing. Whether voters and nonvoters also differ in their political attitudes and preferences is much less clear, since the data are meager and inconclusive.[8]

Of course, the question is not only whether voters and nonvoters hold different opinions, but also how likely it is that their respective concerns will appear on the public agenda. Policy agendas are usually set not by the public directly, but rather by political leaders in anticipation of voter response. If leaders know that a particular group does not turn out at the polls, they often assume that the group and its needs can be safely ignored. The differential treatment of Southern blacks before and after they began to vote in large numbers is a case in point. Public officials are more responsive to citizens who are politically active.[9]

This second function of democratic elections, to serve as barometers of popular sentiment so that government can properly respond to public needs, is crucial. But it is not their sole purpose. If it were, we could replace elections with public opinion surveys. Large random samples would more conveniently and more accurately reveal public preferences. Yet no matter how representative such surveys might be, they would do little to advance the first function of elections, fostering legitimacy, and even less to advance the third.

In addition to conferring legitimacy and assuring that the government is responsive to public needs, democratic elections serve a more elusive, but no less important, third function. Elections are a primary mechanism for civic education and allegiance, for improving the democratic character of citizens, and for making citizens feel they belong to a political community. The question here is not how many or who votes but the quality of the electorate. This ancient Greek notion, which reverses the causal arrows of social science that typically point from subjective feelings of efficacy to political action, is that political participation can encourage citizens to feel more empowered, to become better informed, and to acquire a sense of membership. These feelings, in turn, foster higher levels of participation. Unfortunately, the last two decades have witnessed a steady erosion in the civic attitudes of Americans; feelings of civic duty, political efficacy, political trust, and attachment to the political system have waned.

The American electoral system falls short of the democratic ideal in all three criteria: how many vote, who votes, and the quality of the voters. Voter turnout in the United States is the lowest of any advanced industrial democracy, and continues to decline. The electorate is unrepresentative because voters come disproportionately from the more advantaged groups in the country. And in recent years American citizens have increasingly lost the civic attitudes that are the hallmarks of a thriving democracy.

Voter Turnout

The history of the franchise in America is a history of its expansion.[10] But the franchise only grants the right to vote; not all choose to exercise that right. Figure 5.1 traces the turnout rate in presidential elections from 1824 to 1984.[11] It is helpful to divide this history into four distinct periods: an era of high turnout from 1840 to 1896, a steep drop in voter turnout beginning in 1900, a modest resurgence from 1928 to 1960, and our current era of declining turnout.[12]

The high-water mark of the post–World War I era was 1960, when turnout reached 64 percent. The voting rate fell almost ten percentage points between 1960 and 1980, marking the longest period of steadily declining turnout in American history.[13] As Figure 5.1 shows, this decline has been gradual for the most part. The main exception is the three point drop between 1968 and 1972, which was largely caused by the poor showing among newly enfranchised citizens aged eighteen to twenty. The 1980 turnout rate of 54.3 percent, while less than one percent lower than the 1976 level, represented the lowest turnout since 1948. Four years later, despite an unprecedented investment of money, time, and people to register voters and mobilize them on election day, despite the strikingly clear ideological differences between the two major presidential candidates, and despite the maturing of the baby boom generation, voter turnout increased by less than one percentage point. The 1980 and 1984 elections were two of the four elections since 1828 that registered the lowest voter turnout outside the South.[14]

Turnout falls because fewer of those who are eligible register, or because fewer of those who are registered vote, or both. Low registration tends to reflect long-term factors like low levels of education or an ingrained lack of interest in politics. Low turnout among the

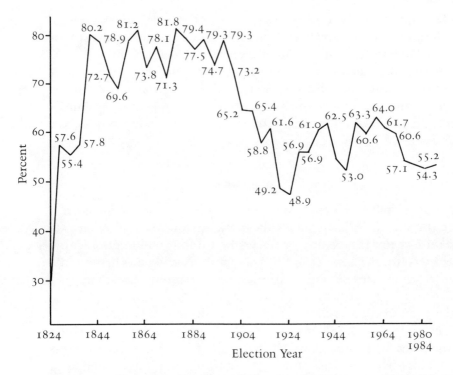

Figure 5.1   Turnout in Presidential Elections by Percentage of Eligible Voters 1824–1984. *Source*: The figures for 1824–1968 are taken from U.S. Bureau of Census, *Historical Statistics of the United States, Colonial Times to 1970*, Bicentennial edition, pt. 2, Washington, D.C., 1975, pp. 1071–72 (from unpublished data supplied by Walter Dean Burnham). Figures for 1972–1984 are from private correspondence with Professor Burnham.

registered usually reflects short-term factors like unhappiness with the choices offered in a particular election.

Figure 5.2 shows, for the period since 1960, the percentage of those eligible who registered and the percentage of those registered who voted. The numbers are telling. From 1960 to 1968 registration held fairly steady, with about three-fourths of the population registered to vote, while turnout among the registered fell. During the next eight years registration dropped nearly five percentage points. The sharp drop-off in turnout between 1968 and 1972 suggests that a number of short-term factors coalesced in 1972, most obviously dissatisfaction with the government's Vietnam policy and a general lack of enthusiasm for either presidential candidate. This was, moreover, the period when eighteen to twenty year olds were added to the voting rolls.

The steep drop in turnout from 1960 to 1972 and the even more extended decline in registration from 1964 to 1980 raise the question of whether the short-term withdrawal from politics that developed in the late 1960s was deepening into a long-term disaffection for the democratic process. The events of 1984 temporarily clouded the picture. Massive partisan and nonpartisan registration efforts added some 12 million names to the voter rolls, and the portion of adults registered to vote climbed more than three percentage points, the first such increase since 1964. At the same time, however, the turnout rate among registered voters fell nearly three points in 1984.

Whatever its ultimate cause, the result of the quarter-century decline in turnout and registration is a shrunken electorate. More than 75 million eligible voters—the largest number in any presidential election—declined to cast ballots in 1984. Voting rates in many of the largest states, including New York, California, and Texas, fell below the national average. In every presidential election since 1920 the nonvoters have outnumbered those who voted for the winner.

A number of commentators have tried to soften these statistics by noting that although turnout in American general elections is com-

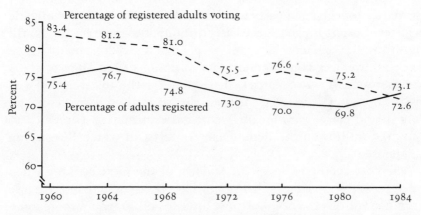

Figure 5.2 Registration and Turnout: Presidential Elections, 1960–1984. *Source*: Committee for the Study of the American Electorate, "Non-Voter Study, '84–'85," Washington, D.C., January, 1985. Voting-age population estimates are from the Census Bureau; official vote counts and actual registration figures are from the secretaries of state and registrars of the fifty states and the District of Columbia. If registration figures were not available for a state, the national average was used to estimate state registration.

paratively low, America runs far ahead of every other democracy in the number of its citizens who participate in selecting the major party nominees by voting in presidential primaries. Undoubtedly, primary voting does represent an important additional mode of participation that needs to be added to any final balance sheet: in 1984, for example, 24.5 million people voted in the Democratic and Republican primaries, 26 percent of the number who eventually cast ballots in November.

Just how substantial is primary turnout? And has it increased or decreased in recent years? To answer such questions is fraught with complications. The raw number of primary voters has increased substantially—from 11.2 million in 1960 to 24.5 million in 1984 —largely because the number of primaries has skyrocketed from sixteen to thirty in the same period. As a percentage of the voting age population, the turnout in presidential primaries is considerably lower than in general elections, even lower than in off-year congressional elections. In 1976, in states that held presidential primaries, only 28 percent of the voting age population turned out to vote. In 1980 the participation rate was 25 percent. When assessing turnout in primaries, however, many scholars have argued that the full voting age population is an inaccurate base, since many states restrict their primaries to registered party members. When the number of eligible registered voters is used as the base, turnout does increase, but is still quite low: 43 percent in 1976, 37 percent in 1980. Finally, these national averages conceal enormous variations from state to state, and between the two parties, depending on the institutional and political context. In 1984, for example, 18 million voters cast ballots in the close, hard-fought Democratic primaries, compared to only 6.5 million in the Republican contests, in which Reagan ran unopposed.

The post-1960 boycott of the polls is all the more striking when one considers the factors that might have been expected to increase turnout. Politics has become more intense and, arguably, more interesting since the Eisenhower years. The public is, on average, better off materially and better educated; and higher-status, educated citizens are more likely to vote. Finally, many barriers between the citizen and the polls—literacy tests, extended residency requirements, and the polls tax—have been eliminated. In short, the expansion of the franchise and the dismantling of barriers against its exercise have broadened the opportunity to vote, yet only a bare majority now take advantage of that opportunity.

Who Votes?

Certain types of citizens are more likely than others to vote. Thus the electorate is not only small in relation to the citizenry, it also is unrepresentative of it. Traditionally, the groups considered to be socially and economically disadvantaged display the lowest voting rates. Women vote less than men; poor people vote less than rich people; minorities vote less than whites; the poorly educated vote less than the better educated. Some of this is changing, some not.

Race

Reforms in the past two decades have done much to reverse the nineteenth-century disenfranchisement of Southern blacks. Barriers to voting have been lowered and campaigns have been launched to register black voters. As a result, there has been a sharp rise in black registration in the South. But blacks still vote less than whites, although racial differences have shrunk considerably (see figure 5.3).[15] Nationally, the gap between whites and blacks has hovered around twelve percentage points since 1964. It narrowed to ten points in 1980, and to less than six points in 1984.[16] From 1964 to 1980 there were two distinct voting patterns, a Southern and a Northern pattern (figure 5.4). During those years, black turnout fell sharply in the North but rose in the South. However, in 1984 black voting increased substantially in both regions.

The continuing black-white gap is largely explained by the fact that, race aside, blacks belong disproportionately to other groups that display low turnout: they are less educated on average and are more apt to have low-status jobs. Indeed, when the influence of such social and economic considerations is taken into account, blacks are at least as politically active as whites, and perhaps more so.[17] It is noteworthy, moreover, that the crucial hurdle appears to be registration; once registered, blacks are about as likely to vote as whites. In both the 1980 and 1984 presidential elections, turnout among registered blacks was 84 percent, compared with 88 percent among registered whites.

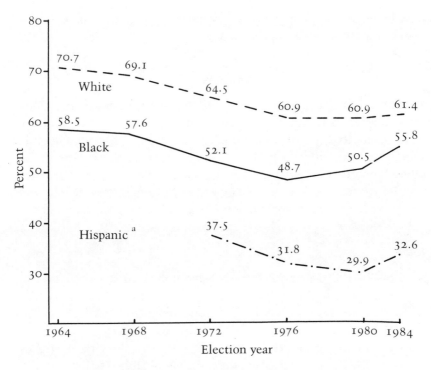

Figure 5.3   Voter Turnout in Presidential Elections by Race, 1964–1984.
[a] Hispanic figures not available for 1964 and 1968.

Data for other minority groups are harder to come by and necessarily less complete. Certainly turnout among Hispanic Americans is low and has been declining. The Hispanic turnout rate is about half the average for other whites.[18] The explanation here, as for blacks, turns in part on low social and economic status. But in this case one also must consider language barriers, as well as the fact that many Hispanics have only recently become citizens. Newly enfranchised voters only gradually master the mechanics of registration and acquire the habit of going to the polls on election day. Again, as with blacks, registration is the hurdle. Among registered Hispanics, turnout is 82 percent, not much different from other groups.

Region

In contrast with the national pattern of declining voter participation, turnout rates in the South have risen over the last two decades.

Southern turnout increased by ten percentage points from 1960 to 1984 while Northern turnout dropped sixteen points, shrinking what had been a thirty-point difference to a gap of only four points between the two regions (see figure 5.5).[19] It is worth noting that, while much of the Southern increase is due to a sharp rise in black participation following the Voting Rights Act and other civil rights reforms, white turnout also rose. Indeed, in absolute terms whites outnumbered blacks by a 7 to 2 margin among newly registered Southern

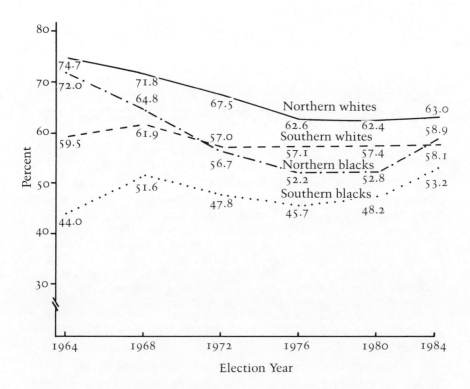

Figure 5.4 Voter Turnout in Presidential Elections by Region and Race, 1964–1984. *Sources*: U.S. Bureau of the Census, *Voter Participation in the National Election of November 1964*, series P-20, no. 143; *Voting and Registration in the Election of November 1968*, series P-20, no. 192; *Voting and Registration in the Election of 1972*, series P-20, no. 250; *Voting and Registration in the Election of 1976*, series P-20, no. 322; *Voting and Registration in the Election of 1980*, series P-20, no. 370; *Voting and Registration in the Election of 1984*, series P-20, no. 397.

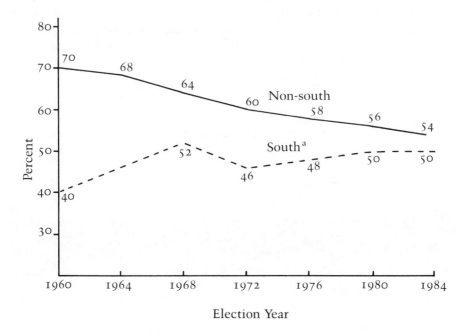

Figure 5.5   Voter Turnout in Presidential Elections by Region, 1960–1980.
[a] South includes Alabama, Arkansas, Florida, Georgia, Louisiana, Missis-
sippi, North Carolina, South Carolina, Tennessee, and Virginia. *Sources*:
Based on actual vote returns and voting age population statistics compiled
by the Elections Research Center, Washington, D.C., in *America Votes* and
the U.S. Bureau of the Census. The data for 1960 to 1980 are reported by
Harold W. Stanley, "The Political Impact of Electoral Mobilization: The
South and Universal Suffrage, 1952–1980" (paper delivered at the annual
meeting of the American Political Science Association, New York, 1981), p. 2.
The data for 1984 are taken from the U.S. Bureau of the Census, *Statistical
Abstract of the United States: 1986*, 106th ed. (Washington, D.C., 1985).

voters between 1960 and 1976.[20] This countertrend in the South
qualifies—and, by providing contrast, emphasizes—the pattern of
decline throughout the rest of the country.

Gender

Women have dramatically improved their showing at the polls. The
turnout rate for women was around 40 percent in the 1920s; by 1964
it had reached 67 percent, only five percentage points lower than the

rate for men (see figure 5.6). Moreover, while turnout rates for both men and women have fallen since 1964, the decline for women has been less, and women are now more likely to vote than are men.[21] The slight increase in turnout from 1980 to 1984 was caused entirely by more voting by women.

Age

The relationship between age and turnout helps explain why voting rates have been declining. The probability of voting is generally assumed to rise from a low level in early adult life, reach a plateau in middle age, and decline again as maturity gives way to old age. Figure 5.7 generally supports this view. Turnout for the youngest category of voters is consistently lower than for other age groups, falling as low as 40 percent in 1980 and 1984. Indeed, according to the data reported in figure 5.7, the decline from 1976 to 1984 was entirely the result of the fall-off among the youngest voters. The ratification of the Twenty-sixth Amendment in 1971, and the coming of age of the postwar

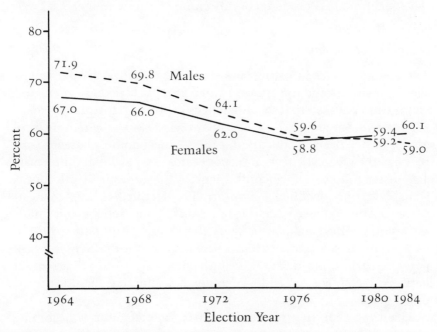

Figure 5.6   Voter Turnout in Presidential Elections by Sex, 1964–1984. *Sources*: Same as for figure 5.4.

baby boom generation, have sharply raised the proportion of the electorate that belongs to this low-turnout age group. At the same time, the proportion of citizens over sixty-five years old—another low-turnout category—also has been growing. Overall, the changing age composition of the electorate probably accounts for at least 25 percent of the post-1960 fall in turnout.[22]

This same set of relationships, however, also offers some encouraging signs for future turnout rates. First, the baby boom generation is growing older and, since voting increases with age, turnout likely will rise. Second, older Americans are voting more than historical trends would predict. Figure 5.7 shows that turnout for voters over sixty-five fell only slightly prior to 1976, and increased by three percentage points in 1980 and nearly three more in 1984. Indeed, the turnout rate for the elderly has been higher than the rate for citizens between the ages of twenty-five and forty-four in the last four presidential elections. We can expect the elderly's turnout to continue rising, moreover, as the generation of politically inactive women that now dominates the senior population passes from the scene, and as the educational attainments of this group continue to increase.

Socioeconomic Status

The major changes in voting laws since the Civil War have involved the extension of the franchise to three groups: blacks, women, and youth. We have seen that the differences in voting rates among racial, gender, and age groups have been narrowing. But when comparing groups on the basis of education—the socioeconomic characteristic that has the greatest effect on turnout rates—we see that differences are, instead, actually widening (figure 5.8). Turnout at all educational levels has declined since 1964. The decline has been greatest, however, among those who have not finished high school, and smallest among college graduates. Thus the turnout gap between these two groups has increased from twenty-six to thirty-six percentage points. Much, if not most, of the differences in turnout that remain between racial, gender, and age groups is a function of educational differences.

Taken together, the figures show that the electorate is becoming more representative of the population at large in some respects, and less representative in others. The voting gap between men and women has disappeared. The gap between blacks and whites persists, but

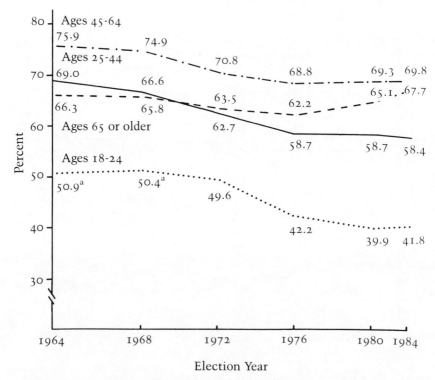

Figure 5.7   Voter Turnout in Presidential Elections by Age, 1964–1984.
[a] Includes only ages 21–24.

has narrowed considerably, as has the larger gap between Hispanics and other citizens. The age gap remains, but its significance is shrinking. But the differences in voting rates between the educated and the less educated, between those with high-status and low-status jobs, and between the rich and the poor remain, and indeed even have widened.

A Cross-National Perspective

One set of benchmarks for evaluating voter participation in the United States is the performance of other democracies. Table 5.1 compares the average turnout in post–World War II elections in nineteen democratic nations. The United States ranks last, with an average turnout rate, 58.5 percent, that is well below the average for the other nations. The second column of table 5.1 displays trends in turnout rates during this period. There is no consistent pattern here; turnout in

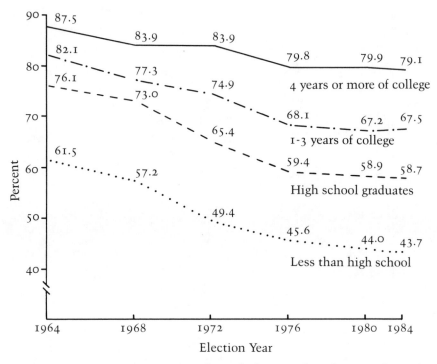

Figure 5.8 Voter Turnout in Presidential Elections by Educational Level, 1964–1984. *Sources*: Same as for figure 5.4.

some countries has declined as much as or more than in the United States, while turnout rates in other countries have increased.

One note of caution is in order: turnout for the United States is measured as a percentage of eligible adults (age eighteen and over); turnout for the other nations is based on registered adults. The distinction is less crucial than it may first appear, since registration is close to universal in many European countries. To illustrate, one study recalculated voter turnout for recent elections in other democracies by using the voting age population as the base rather than the traditional measure of the registered population. The average decline for the nations listed in table 5.1 was only 3.6 percentage points, and only Australia (−11.4) and New Zealand (−10.5) registered drops greater than ten points. More important, even after this recalculation, the United States continued to rank very low, surpassing only Switzerland.[23]

Others, however, have argued that much of the discrepancy between the United States and other democratic nations is an arithmetic

Table 5.1   Postwar Voter Turnout in Nineteen Democracies

Country	Average turnout since 1945[a] (percent)	Postwar trend[b]
Australia	95.4	−0.125
Netherlands[c]		
1948–1967	94.7	+0.183
1971–1981	84.4	+2.850
Austria	94.2	−0.413
Italy	92.6	−0.214
Belgium	92.5	+0.057
New Zealand	90.4	−1.114
West Germany	86.9	+0.468
Denmark	85.8	+0.375
Sweden	84.9	+1.798
Israel	81.4	+0.114
Norway	80.8	+0.486
France	79.3	+0.512
Finland	79.0	−0.013
United Kingdom	76.9	−0.980
Canada	76.5	−0.030
Ireland	74.7	+0.337
Japan	73.1	−0.162
Switzerland	64.5	−3.205
United States[d]	58.5	−1.475
Overall Average	81.0	−0.253

[a] Except for the United States, turnout is defined as votes cast as a percentage of registered voters. The figure for the United States is a percentage of the voting age population. Figures are based on national elections held between 1945 and 1981.

[b] The postwar trend was determined by calculating the slope of the line that best "fits" the turnout data over time. The slope is a measure of the change in turnout per election. For example, Australia has experienced a .125 percentage point decline in turnout per election during the postwar era. Because of unusually low turnout in many nations immediately after World War II, the first election held in each nation after the war was not included in the trend calculation.

[c] The Netherlands eliminated compulsory voting after the 1967 election.

[d] Figures are for presidential elections. The data for all other nations are based on elections for the lower house of the national legislature.

Sources: The first column (average turnout) is from Ivor Crewe, "Electoral Participation," in David Butler, Austin Ranney and Howard Penniman, eds., Democracy at the Polls (Washington, D.C.: American Enterprise Institute, 1981), pp. 234–37. The second column (post-war trend) is calculated from turnout figures reported in Thomas Mackie and Richard Rose, The International Almanac of Electoral History (New York: Facts on File, 1982) and the European Journal of Political Research.

artifact. When the European denominator—the registered population—is used to calculate turnout in the United States, it ranks in the middle of the twenty-four nations. Some cite this as proof that our turnout problem is grossly overstated. However, this argument misses the point. Dividing by the number of registered citizens mathematically eliminates the major component of the turnout problem in the United States, the 30 percent of the population that is unregistered.

What explains the cross-national pattern? There are several factors, including variations in the nature of political parties and the intensity of group conflict, to be taken up later in this chapter. But two more prosaic legal differences need to be mentioned here to allow an informed appreciation of table 5.1. First, most Western European nations compile voting lists through an administrative census, which makes registration virtually automatic. Those that boast turnout rates consistently above 90 percent have compulsory voting rules. Second, the United States is the only Western democracy that places the entire burden of registration on the individual.

One final comparative point should be made. We have seen how, in the United States, voting rates are related to social status: the better educated, more affluent, and more prestigiously employed are more likely to vote than those on the lower rungs of the socioeconomic ladder. The data suggest that this tendency is unique to the United States; studies of several other countries show no such link between status and voting rates.[24] Figure 5.9 displays the participation rates for four occupational levels in Sweden and the United States. In the United States the gap between voting rates for professionals and managers and for unskilled workers is considerable; in Sweden the gap is almost nonexistent.

These data give at least some reason to suspect that the American electoral system may perform less well than others by two of the criteria cited above—conferring democratic legitimacy and ensuring the effective representation of all citizens' needs and preferences. Fewer citizens take part in American elections than elsewhere and, to that extent, the democratic process receives less support. Those citizens who do vote are less representative of the population as a whole than is the case elsewhere. Of course, any evaluation of the American electoral system must take into account the third criterion, the quality of the electorate. Since the level and depth of citizens' political information typically increase with education, any

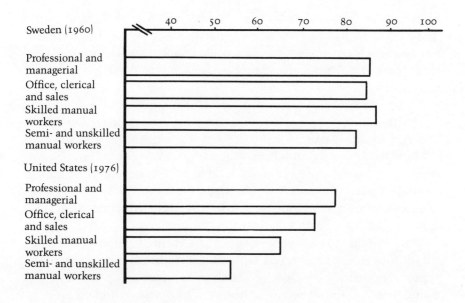

Figure 5.9   Voter Turnout in National Elections in Two Countries by Occupation. *Source*: Samuel P. Huntington and Joan M. Nelson, *No Easy Choice* (Cambridge, Mass.: Harvard University Press, 1976), p. 88.

substantial gain in the representativeness of the electorate probably will dilute the average degree of political knowledge in the voting population. To increase representativeness could pose the dilemma of balancing the "quantity" of political participation against the "quality."

Other Modes of Participation

In their seminal study of political participation, Sidney Verba and Norman Nie divided Americans into six categories according to their political activity. They found that more than a fifth of the adult population does not participate at all, and about the same number limit political activity almost exclusively to voting. Another fifth is active in groups and organizations, while 15 percent are active in campaigns but not in other political efforts. About 4 percent confine their political activity to personally contacting public officials. Finally, slightly more than 10 percent of the population engage in all the various modes of political participation.[25]

There is considerable overlap between some of these categories.

For example, 90 percent of those who are active both in communal groups and in campaigns vote regularly. More important, perhaps, nonvoters seldom engage in other forms of political activity. It is true that "for most Americans voting is the sole act of participation in politics."[26]

As we turn our sights from voting to other modes of political participation, we encounter something of a puzzle. Relatively few Americans participate in politics in ways other than voting — campaigning, communal activity, or individual contacting. Nevertheless, although the United States has the lowest level of voting among Western democracies, it compares favorably with other countries in nonelectoral kinds of political activity. Americans, in fact, have higher participation rates than the citizens of most European nations in political activities other than voting.[27] And, as we shall see, during recent years when U.S. voter turnout was declining, other types of political participation, such as interest group activity and individual contacting, were on the rise. The participation problem in the United States appears to have a distinctly electoral cast to it.[28]

Campaign Activity

The percentage of Americans who participate in political campaigns is low but constant. Figure 5.10 traces the level of citizen involvement in four different campaign activities (contributing money to a campaign, attending a political meeting, wearing a campaign button or displaying a bumper sticker, and working in a campaign) from 1952 to 1984. None of the campaign activities involves a sizable portion of the public. Only button wearing and the displaying of bumper stickers have declined markedly, which is not surprising since campaigns shifted resources during this period to other means of political advertising, such as television. With legislation providing tax incentives for financial contributions to campaigns, the percentage of the public that gives money to candidates appears to have grown slightly. Nevertheless, fewer than one in seven Americans contribute to campaigns. The number of taxpayers earmarking a dollar of their tax liability to the Presidential Campaign Fund was 28 percent in 1980 and 24 percent in 1984.[29] All in all, the number of people engaged in campaigns has remained fairly steady and low.

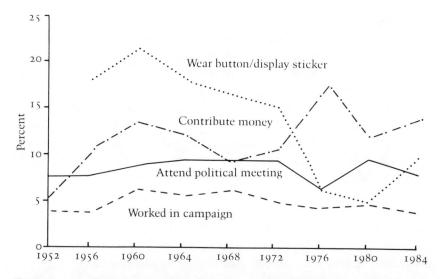

Figure 5.10   Participation of Adults in Campaign Activity, 1952–1984. *Sources*: Warren Miller, Arthur Miller, and Edward Schneider, *American National Election Studies Data Sourcebook, 1952–78* (Cambridge, Mass.: Harvard University Press, 1980), pp. 304–305; National Election Study Codebook, 1980; *American National Election Study 1984: Continuous Monitoring Survey File* (First ICPSR Edition, 1985), pp. 434–37.

Individual Contacting

In contrast with the steady state of campaigning participation and the decline in voter turnout, fragmentary evidence on individual contacting points toward increasing activism. Letter writing to public officials has been on the rise.[30] Since 1960 the mail flow to Congress has doubled, and letters to the White House have quadrupled.[31]

Communal or Interest Group Activity

"In no country in the world," Alexis de Tocqueville observed, "has the principle of association been more successfully used or applied to a greater multitude of objects than in America."[32] Joining groups is an American impulse that stretches back to the earliest days of the republic. Those who closely monitor interest groups, however, have detected a swelling of this kind of activity in recent years. One study characterized this change as a "political revolution" in which "large numbers of citizens are becoming active in an ever-increasing number of protest groups, citizens' organizations, and special interest groups."[33] The growth in the sheer number of groups is only part of the story. The same years have witnessed an increasing centralization of interest group activity in Washington, as well as an expansion in the number of activities in which interest groups engage.[34]

The contrast between voting and interest activity is striking. In one important respect, however, the two domains are alike. Both voting and interest group activity are strongly associated with social status. People of higher status are much more likely to vote or campaign in elections and to be involved in communal or interest group activities as well. As with voting, the tendency for higher-status citizens to participate more in interest groups is even stronger here than in other democratic countries.[35] Finally, not only are individuals with more schooling or higher income more likely to join interest groups in the United States, but the concerns and agendas of national interest groups disproportionately represent business and upper-middle-class interests.[36]

What forces underlie this increase in interest group activity? Interest group formation tends to occur in waves that coincide with periods of increased governmental activism and technological breakthroughs in communication.[37] Accordingly, the growth of government probably has been the most important stimulus to interest group formation since 1960, encouraging the beneficiaries and opponents of new government programs to organize. Groups representing the interests of women, the elderly, consumers, environmentalists, anti-abortionists, and religious conservatives spring immediately to mind. Congressional reforms since 1974, especially the proliferation of subcommittees, which has multiplied the number of decision points in the legislative process, also have heightened interest group activity. The decline of political parties has enhanced the role of interest groups as agents of political intermediation between the public and its elected representatives. Finally, the increasing availability of funds from outside sources, especially private foundations, has helped to foster and sustain interest groups.[38]

A partial answer to the "puzzle of participation"—declining voter turnout accompanied by increases in nonelectoral modes of participation—lies in these governmental and institutional changes. They have encouraged interest group activity while undermining voter turnout. Another clue to the puzzle is the link between voting and other modes of participation. Later we will trace part of the post-1960 decline in voter turnout to a diminished sense of political efficacy in the population. The public's felt need to communicate with and influence its elected representatives, however, has not diminished. If anything, it has soared. Mounds of survey data attest to the recent discontent of the American public. If citizens are no longer expressing their preferences and demands in the ballot box, they are using other forms of political communication to voice their concerns. The skyrocketing of interest group activity and letter writing belies the claim that nonvoting signals "passive consent" in the public.

Voting and interest group activity also share in common a connection to weakened partisan identification and party structures. The decline of party hastens the decline of turnout; interest groups, in turn, have rushed in to fill the void left by diminished parties. Thus, although many who choose not to vote drop out of the system altogether, many others have sought alternative forms of participation.

This chapter began by asking whether declining voter turnout is a serious problem or not. A parallel question could be raised about interest groups: does the apparent growth of group activity bode well or ill for the political system? This question already occupies a central place in current political discourse. American society, according to many observers, is rapidly being balkanized into a collection of narrow, special interests that lack any sense of a larger, common good.

There is less reason to be pessimistic about this development than about turnout decline, however. Ironically, the relative absence of interest group ferment in the 1950s caused social scientists to worry that an unorganized, atomized public was vulnerable to demagogic appeals from the right, and led them to urge more group activity as an antidote. Much of today's lamentation comes from ideologues of the left and right, whose real complaint seems to be not the volume of group activity, but its content. Liberals deplore the work of anti-abortionists, religious groups, and corporate lobbyists, and then, in the next breath, applaud the growing militancy of labor, blacks, and women's groups. Conservatives make the same sort of charges, only with a reverse cast of heroes and villains.

Still, such criticisms ought not be dismissed too lightly. The key problem is not that there are too many claimants on government, but that interest group activity is unlikely to represent the full range and proportion of public concerns. As James Q. Wilson and others have shown, groups are most easily organized if they bear concentrated costs or receive concentrated benefits. Groups such as consumers and taxpayers who bear more diffuse costs are much less likely to make their voices heard. Most scholars also have recognized, as noted earlier, that there is a strong class bias to group activity, and that the poor and disadvantaged are much more difficult to organize than wealthy and corporate interests. To put the issue another way, the problem of interest group activity is not that there are too many interest groups, but that elected officials sometimes lack the resources to resist their demands.

The critics rarely provide specific and effective suggestions about how to restrain all this group activity. The two solutions most often discussed are to create a stronger role for political parties and to impose stricter limitations on political action committees (PACs). The latter is an especially complicated and troubling issue. Undue special interest influence needs to be restrained, but this concern must be weighed against an equally important value: the necessity, in a democracy, to allow aggrieved citizens and interests the means and resources to "petition in redress of grievances."

In any event, both of these solutions—strengthening parties and curtailing PACs—redirect our attention to the need for representative and legitimate elections, and thus the problem of declining voter turnout.

From Causes to Policy Reforms

The participation problem in the United States is not an excess of communal or group activity, but insufficient voting. What, if anything, can be done about this?

The data on voter turnout that was presented earlier give cause for both optimism and pessimism. The most encouraging trends are the elimination of the traditional turnout gap between men and women and the anticipated higher voting rates for the youngest and oldest voters. On the other side of the ledger are the widening chasm in participation between high status and low status citizens, and the possibility that a pattern of short-term decisions not to vote in particular elections may be settling into a widespread abdication from politics in general.

Before we can hope to attack the problem we must understand its causes. There is a bulging literature on this subject, but no explanation commands consensus. We shall not rehearse the findings of that research here. Changing demographic characteristics, deteriorating civic attitudes, shifting features of the political environment, and cumbersome legal rules have all been identified as partial causes of declining turnout, although the relative importance of each remains a source of controversy.[39]

Dividing the record of U.S. voter turnout into two time periods may advance the attempt to sort all this out. Figure 5.1 suggests two separate episodes of falling turnout: a twenty percentage point drop between 1896 and 1936,[40] and a ten-point drop between 1960 and 1980. Although many causes account for the downturn in each period, a few can be singled out.

The main causes of turnout decline in the earlier period, 1896 to 1936, were changes in the party system and changes in election rules.[41] These factors, however, cannot explain the decline since 1960. Election laws have been liberalized during this period. The major causes of the post-1960 decline have been the changing age composition of the electorate, an erosion in civic attitudes conducive to voting, and the fading of citizen attachment to political parties.[42]

Failure to draw the distinction between the two periods of decline can be misleading. For example, the question is frequently asked whether deteriorating civic attitudes can be a major cause of declining turnout in the United States when Americans exhibit more support for their political system than Europeans do for theirs and European turnout has not declined.[43] This question confuses the historically low level of turnout in the United States—the result of the drop from 1896 to 1936—with the declining trend since 1960. Political attitudes are not a major cause of the low level of American turnout. Most of the gap between the United States and other democratic nations is attributable to differences in registration procedures and levels of partisanship.[44] However, political attitudes—feelings of alienation, distrust of government, and low political efficacy—have contributed substantially to the decline in voting since 1960.

Can we suggest from this any directions for future policy? Some things can be manipulated more easily than others:

1. To alter the age structure of the population exceeds—at least in a democracy—the authority of policymakers. But that problem

may be solving itself anyway, as the baby-boom children gradually grow older.

2. To restore citizens' faith in their government is not easy, and cannot be accomplished by pious wishes or legislative fiat.[45] But identifying the problem is the first step toward a solution. It may be a platitude to say that citizens will vote if they believe that the government can be trusted to respond to their needs and preferences, and that they will vote if given an attractive choice of candidates. Yet it is a platitude that American leaders would do well to remember.

3. To shore up party identification also is difficult, but perhaps it is more amenable to direct intervention. There are numerous ways to expand the roles that parties play in elections and in governance.[46] Strong parties will mean more voters, both because strong party identifiers are more likely to vote, and because party organizations can help turn out their supporters.

Frankly, then, our capacity to manipulate the main sources of the post-1960 downturn in participation—causes that are rooted in social characteristics, basic attitudes, or fundamental features of the contemporary political environment—is relatively limited. The prospects may be more promising for changing a separate set of factors, those that are part of the legal system. Some commentators argue that since legal rules are demonstrably not responsible for the post-1960 decline in turnout, reforming the rules will not reverse that decline. But this view may follow a sound premise with an unwarranted conclusion: specific rules have not caused turnout to decline recently, but the legal system has been partly responsible for the low level of political participation in the United States. The ten-point drop in turnout rates since 1960 would have been even worse without the liberalization of voting laws that occurred during that period. Further reforms (especially major adjustments) could offset some of the effects cited above and serve to increase political participation.

The debate over structural reforms to increase voter turnout generally covers three main topics: the laws that control the administration of voting on election day, the regulations and procedures that guide media coverage of elections, and the rules that govern the registration of voters. We shall examine each of these in turn.

Making It Easier to Vote

Several reforms to make voting easier have been proposed. Measures to make the dates and hours of elections more convenient include liberalized absentee voting procedures, twenty-four hour voting, and Sunday or holiday voting.

The liberalizing of absentee ballot procedures may be the most promising measure. Americans are exceptionally mobile geographically, and a surprisingly large proportion of people are away from their homes on election day. The 1982 victory of Republican gubernatorial candidate George Deukmejian in California suggests the potential for liberalized absentee voting procedures to boost turnout. Taking advantage of California's liberal absentee voting rules, the Deukmejian campaign sent out almost one million absentee ballot applications to Republicans who usually do not vote; 400,000 were returned. In addition to giving Deukmejian a 113,000 vote victory over his Democratic opponent, the effort increased the number of absentee ballots to 6.5 percent of the total number of votes cast in California—more than twice the rate in 1978.

Proposals for twenty-four hour voting require that all polls nationwide remain open during the same twenty-four hour period. For example, one plan provides for all polling places to open at 3:00 P.M. (EST) on a Sunday and close twenty-four hours later on Monday. The proposal is based on the reasonable assumption that more hours for voting will mean more voters, since any person wanting to vote could find a convenient time. In truth, busy people are more likely to vote, not less, which casts some doubt on the convenience argument.[47] Furthermore, the administrative costs of twenty-four hour voting would be high. One study found that with twenty-four hour voting, election costs for Los Angeles County would rise by as much as 80 percent, with most of the increase going to additional poll workers and tighter ballot security.[48] The question, then, is whether a turnout increase of unpredictable size would be worth the very predictable higher costs.

Forecasting the effects of Sunday voting on turnout is a bit like "stargazing without the benefit of the astronomer's telescope."[49] The only Sunday elections ever held in the United States were municipal elections in Milwaukee and Cleveland. Turnout was below normal in both. In addition, Sunday voting not only would raise religious objections but also would increase costs substantially because of public employee overtime pay and the higher weekend rates associated with transportation and cartage charges. And turnout in countries that hold elections on "days of rest" is comparable to that in countries holding them on workdays. Designating the accustomed Tuesday election day a national holiday, according to one estimate, would cost employers about \$7.5 billion.[50] On balance, the case for Sunday or holiday voting is not particularly compelling.

All in all, reforms to make voting easier could increase turnout somewhat, but there is little evidence to suggest that the gains would be more than marginal, especially when measured against the costs, both financial and political, of adoption and implementation.[51]

The Media

Some observers contend that the most important reforms to increase the voting rate need to be made not in the way elections are conducted, but in the way television conducts itself when covering them. According to recent studies, television conveys, more than most media, a negative or even contemptuous attitude toward candidates that may contribute to the public's increasingly low regard for politicians and elections.[52] One media analyst argues that the recent decline in voter turnout can be partially attributed to television's cynical portrayal of candidates. Reforms to reduce this effect include rotating the reporters who are assigned to candidates, curtailing the practice of giving better coverage to challengers than to frontrunners, and striking a better balance between covering candidate motives and candidate behavior.[53] Of course, we would have to rely on the good intentions of the media to adopt and enforce such reforms.

The quantity of campaign coverage, as well as its quality, is widely believed to influence voter turnout. In the opinion of some, more coverage means more votes by better-informed voters. The Federal Communications Commission, in an effort to promote more televised candidate debates, ruled in 1984 that radio and television stations could sponsor presidential debates without observing the "equal-time rule" of the Federal Communications Act as long as the broadcasters did not favor specific candidates. Whether more debates encourage increased voter turnout, however, is not clear. What is clear is that policymakers can do little to affect either the quality or the quantity of the media's campaign coverage.

Despite their lack of leverage, policymakers have tried for many years to curb the networks' controversial practice of projecting outcomes before the polls close on election night.[54] Election coverage in 1980 rekindled the controversy over early projections. NBC began its evening news broadcast at 7:00 P.M. (EST) by announcing that "Ronald Reagan appears to be headed for a substantial victory," and at 8:15 P.M. it officially called him the winner, three hours before the polls closed in California. Soon other networks' policy of withholding their projected results in a specific state until the polls close in that state fell by the wayside. During the New Jersey gubernatorial race in 1981, ABC attempted to call an election—incorrectly it turned out—two hours before the polls closed. And a League of Women Voters' study found that, in 1982, newscasts projected results in seven states before their polls closed.[55] Throughout the 1984 primary season, in state after state, the networks identified winning candidates with "characterizations" (stopping just short of formal declarations) while the polls were still open.[56] They actually projected the results of the pivotal Iowa caucuses fifteen minutes before the balloting started (by interviewing participants as they entered polling locations). On election night in November the three major networks declared Reagan the winner while voters were still casting ballots in nearly half the states.

The effects of network projections on voting are the subject of sharp debate. Some people claim that projections actually alter the choices of voters. The strong showing of third-party presidential candidates in Alaska and Hawaii in 1980, for example, has been interpreted as the result of impulsive voter reactions to early projections. In truth, there is little evidence that early projections create either underdog or bandwagon effects for candidates. Most observers agree, however, that projections can diminish voter turnout. Anecdotal evidence confirms that early televised announcements have dissuaded potential voters from casting ballots, but this effect is hard to demonstrate statistically and its precise magnitude is disputed.

According to one study, many potential voters who learned of network projections before the polls closed in 1980 decided that voting would be a waste of time. People who heard about Reagan's victory before 6:00 P.M. (EST) were less likely to vote by 6 percent if they lived in the East, by 9 percent if they lived in the South, and by 12 percent if they lived in the Midwest and West.[57] The networks, however, counter that "7 of the 10 states with the highest turnout [in 1980] closed their polls after the NBC projection and that turnout increased in 9 of 13 states in the Pacific and Mountain time zones."[58] What is more certain is that the effect of projections on turnout depends on the public's initial expectations before an election. If a race is expected to be close but the projections indicate a lopsided victory, as in 1980, then turnout may be depressed. If the public anticipates a landslide and projections suggest a close race, turnout could be stimulated.

The future consequences of projections on the electorate may be much larger than their effect on turnout in any particular election. Early projections may, over time, teach voters that their individual votes do not really count. If voters are conditioned by television to view voting primarily as participation in a horse race (a view reinforced by early projections) and not as a way to express preferences on issues or fulfill civic duties, then they will come to devalue the ballot. The public may even come to realize, with enough reminders from the networks, that as a method for determining who wins or loses, the act of voting is, strictly speaking, irrational for a single individual.[59] If so, the vitality of our democratic system will suffer.

Reforms to remedy the problems caused by early projections must contend with two rather daunting constraints. It would be difficult, if not impossible, for government to compel the networks to hold off their projections without violating their First Amendment rights. Moreover, the pressures of commercial television cause the networks to recoil at the idea of voluntarily withholding their projection of a presidential winner. Network executives seek high ratings, which bring higher advertising rates, and they perceive a direct link between the speed of their projections and their share of the viewing audience. Immediately after the Carter-Reagan contest, NBC took out full-page newspaper ads boasting that it had called the election at 5:15 Pacific time. Stated one network executive, "We really believe that the network that projects earliest and most accurately will have a larger share of the news audience for the next year."[60] In addition to the battle for larger audiences, professional pride undoubtedly has much to do with the competition to be the "firstest with the mostest."

Of the many suggested remedies to the early projection problem, three have received most attention. The first is to make exit polls virtually impossible to conduct. The state of Washington enacted legislation in 1983 to prohibit exit polling within three hundred feet of the polls. Similar laws have been passed in more than thirty states. But such laws are difficult to implement—only a handful have been enforced so far—and probably are unconstitutional.[61]

A second plan would have Congress establish simultaneous poll closings nationwide. Because there would be inequities if every state simply closed its polls at the same moment (8:00 P.M. EST is 5:00 P.M. PST), such proposals sometimes also mandate twenty-four hour voting so that each state would have the same number of evening and daylight hours for voting. Not only is such a plan expensive, it would not solve the problem, since the networks still would be able to make early projections based on exit polling.

The third proposal calls for the networks to refrain voluntarily from projecting results before the polls close. For several years the networks have announced—and often honored—a policy of not reporting a state's election results before its polls close. However, this commitment does not prevent early projections in presidential contests that involve fifty states. Because it is possible to garner enough electoral college votes to win from the Eastern states alone—as the 1972, 1980, and 1984 presidential elections illustrate —all three networks declared victors with the polls still open in nearly half the states.

Recently, the proposed solution with the most political momentum behind it combines the second and third plans. On January 17, 1985, the three major broadcasting networks pledged in writing to refrain from predicting election results in any state until its polls had closed. With that pledge in mind, the House of Representatives approved legislation on January 29, 1986, that would establish uniform poll closings nationwide. According to this bill, the polls would close at 9:00 P.M. in the East, 8:00 P.M. in the Midwest, and 7:00 P.M. in the Rocky Mountain time zone. On the West Coast, the polls would close at 7:00 P.m with the end of daylight saving time delayed for two weeks. (Alaska and Hawaii are exempted from the bill.) What action the Senate will take on this bill remains, as of this writing, unclear. The combination of voluntary network restraint and uniform poll closings would eliminate early projections in presidential elections. However, the plan may not increase voter turnout. By not mandating an equal number of evening and daylight hours for voting in each state (as with a twenty-four hour voting provision), the plan actually may reduce the number of voters who show up at the polls.

Many citizens now vote in the last hour of balloting, but the House bill would advance the poll-closing times in eight Western states.

Proposals for voluntary restraint by the media reflect the need to balance two fundamental objectives of a democracy—a free, uncensored press and free, untainted elections. On the one hand, withholding news may undermine the journalistic ethic of providing complete information to the public as soon as it is available. On the other hand, projections may constitute an intrusion into the democratic process than can decrease participation and affect electoral outcomes.[62]

If the networks' past conduct is any indication, the conflict between these two objectives may prove to be irreconcilable. So far they have insisted with utmost piety that the journalistic ethic of not withholding news is inviolate. In fact, experience shows that the imperative to report the news as soon as possible is not an absolute principle. Journalists often intentionally withhold information they think is irrelevant or contrary to the public interest, such as stories about the personal peccadilloes of public officials or news that would harm national security. Driven by obvious competitive pressures and not First Amendment principles, the networks delay the transmission of news to the West for three hours each evening in order to maximize their audience and advertising revenues.

In short, reforming the way the media cover elections is hampered by two barriers. First, the magnitude of the media's effects on turnout remains uncertain. Some suggested remedies, such as those that violate First Amendment rights, are worse than the disease, while others would be difficult to implement for political and administrative reasons. In any case, most of the cures are uncertain antidotes, and the most palatable approach (voluntary restraint) is beyond the reach of elected officials. As in many spheres of public policy, it may be that only a catastrophe—perhaps an early projection that clearly alters the result of a national election—will precipitate enough public outrage to convince the networks to change their behavior.

Registration Reform

The United States, although the most democratic of countries in terms of citizens' rights to political participation, is the democracy that throws up the most imposing obstacles to the exercise of those rights.[63] In recent decades, steps have been taken to ease the burden of registration, including reforms to help blacks in the South, to eliminate excessive residency requirements, to expand the use of deputy registrars, to extend registration hours, and to introduce, in some states, registration by mail and election day registration. Nonetheless, the voter registration rate in the United States declined from 1964 to 1980. In 1984, 27 percent of the electorate, or about 46 million potential voters, was not registered to vote.

Although registration rules have been loosening throughout the country, states still differ substantially in how easy they make it for people to vote. Only four states allow election day registration, and thirty close registration twenty-four days or more before election day. Fewer than half the states permit all voters to use absentee registration forms. Fewer than half offer evening and weekend hours for registration.[64] As noted earlier, American registration procedures differ markedly from those in most democracies, where registration is either compulsory, automatic, or based on an official canvass.[65]

The effort to increase voter registration attracted much attention and consumed much energy in 1984. An extraordinary number of groups, agencies, and ad hoc coalitions organized major voter registration campaigns. The most publicized of these campaigns were those conducted by liberal organizations and targeted at Democratic-leaning constituencies: the Women's Vote Project, Operation Big Vote, and Human SERVE, along with the personal exhortations of the Rev. Jesse Jackson.

Less appreciated is that Republican and conservative groups were equally active in the registration business. During the primary elections, while the Democratic candidates were busy attacking one another, the Reagan campaign took advantage of $10.5 million in public matching funds to fine-tune the Republican national organization. One important element in this effort was a large voter registration drive that used sophisticated marketing technology and computer-generated mailing lists to target its message to areas likely to be responsive to a Republican appeal. The Republicans were assisted in this effort by groups like the American Coalition for Traditional Values, an alliance of conservative religious organizations that claimed to have registered 3.5 million new voters.

When the dust finally settled in November, all this commotion and shouting produced a good deal less change than many had hoped.

As was shown earlier, voter turnout did not decline in 1984 (an important achievement when one remembers that it had fallen in each of the preceding five elections), but the increase was very slight: from 54.3 percent in 1980 to 55.2 percent in 1984.

Regrettably, this result has led some commentators to dismiss registration reform cavalierly.[66] The 1984 election was widely seen as a foregone conclusion; one can only speculate how much turnout would have declined in the absence of such efforts. Indeed, the registration campaigns of 1984 posed a no-win situation for advocates of registration reform. If turnout had gone up substantially, reform opponents undoubtedly would have cited this as evidence that new legislation was unnecessary. When turnout did not increase, they claimed it as proof that little could be done to overcome deep-seated voter apathy.

Many liberals were equally disappointed at the apparent failure of registration campaigns to help Democratic candidates. In part, this was because they ignored the huge registration efforts of Republican and conservative groups. In a more basic sense, however, such Democratic hopes probably were misplaced from the very beginning. As several academic studies have shown, when compared to voters, nonvoters are distinctive because of their greater political independence.[67] They fit solidly into neither political party, but instead go along with the prevailing tides. In 1984 those tides favored Reagan.

The Effects of Registration Laws

To isolate the precise effect of registration rules from the myriad of other factors that influence voter turnout is a challenge. There is little doubt that convenient rules encourage voting and burdensome ones discourage it; the problem is to assess the size of the effect.

Just as registration rules differ significantly from state to state, so does voter turnout, which in 1984 varied from 69 percent in Minnesota to 41 percent in South Carolina. The states with the most convenient registration systems averaged around 66 percent turnout; those with early closings, limited or no absentee registration, and inconvenient hours had turnout rates averaging about fifteen points lower. To be sure, other factors are at play here that confound any explanation that turns solely on registration rules. For example, there is a regional pattern to registration rules; states in the upper Midwest and the West tend to have convenient registration systems, while all but two Southern states are in the least-convenient category. But this pattern is not unbroken, and departures from the regional tendency, like the six-to-ten percentage point disparity in turnout rates between Idaho and Utah (where registration is convenient) and their next-door neighbors Wyoming and Colorado (where it is inconvenient), suggest that the effect of registration rules is substantial.

A sound analysis requires not only a comparison of registration rules and turnout rates, but also a systematic appraisal of how social, attitudinal, and political factors that affect voting rates vary across states. Several studies have tried to do precisely this. One found that more than 70 percent of the variation in turnout across 104 American cities could be explained by variations in the percentage of the population that was registered. A second study concluded that, even after accounting for political and demographic factors, "states which have registration rules which are generally supposed to facilitate turnout do, in fact, tend to have higher rates of voter participation than those which do not." A third found that restrictive registration laws, particularly early closing dates and limited hours for registering, reduce turnout by about 9 percent in the population at large, and by a larger amount among less-educated citizens. Still another study suggested that convenient registration systems could increase turnout by 4 to 7 percent. Finally, a study of twenty democracies that incorporated attitudinal, demographic, and institutional characteristics into its analysis concluded that automatic registration could increase turnout in the United States by as much as 16 percent.[68] Virtually all the analysts, although concurring that social, attitudinal, and political factors are the most potent determinants of voter turnout, argue that altering registration rules and administrative practices can significantly boost participation.

Reform Proposals

A wide range of registration reforms—some purely hypothetical, others already in place in some states or countries—have been proposed at one time or another. The options for reform can be arrayed according to their degree of departure from present practice.

$- - -$ Least change $- - - - - - - - - - - - - - -$ Most change $- - -$

| Piecemeal reforms | Mail registration | Election day registration | Universal voter enrollment |

Piecemeal Reforms

Most proposals for ad hoc, incremental change involve some sort of federal financial incentive to induce the states to adopt specific registration practices. One plan calls for the federal government to pay for more deputy registrars and longer operating hours at the registration offices. Another proposes to pay bonuses to states that register a prescribed percentage—say, 80 percent—of the voting age population. Still another urges block grants to let the states improve their registration systems in any way they see fit. These reforms maintain the tradition of state control over elections; even if federal inducements were fully effective, they would not radically challenge existing practices. But neither, by the same token, can they be expected to sharply increase voter turnout.

Mail Registration

Voters in twenty states and the District of Columbia can register by mail as a supplementary method to traditional in-person registration. These practices, although differing somewhat in particulars, share certain basic advantages. First, they lower the personal cost of registering; the voter is spared not only the need to show up at the registrar's office during specified hours, but also the need to deal with as many rules and deadlines. Second, they lower the costs of administering the registration process, no small consideration in states where the registration costs per person are higher than average.

One major problem with mail registration is that it makes vote fraud easier. One student of these systems has argued that the combination of mail registration and absentee voting complicates radically the detection of fraud.[69] Some states allow organizations, including political parties, to convey the postcard registration forms between officials and voters, which obviously expands the potential for large-scale fraud. It is precisely this sort of organized fraud, of course, and not the odd instance of individual dishonesty, that prompts urgent concern. It also is true that most existing mail registration systems have too short a history to reassure us fully. Still, there is so far no evidence of serious or widespread fraud in the states that allow mail registration. Moreover, in weighing the risk of fraud, it is well to keep in mind that run-of-the-mill, traditional registration systems from time to time have unwittingly accommodated spectacularly fraudulent schemes.

If the case against mail registration is weaker than it first appears, the case for it is not particularly dramatic: the evidence available to date indicates that it has had only modest effect on turnout rates.[70]

Election Day Registration

Four states—Maine, Minnesota, Oregon, and Wisconsin—let voters register on election day. The Carter administration sponsored a bill to mandate election day registration in 1977. The bill reached the House floor but was withdrawn without a vote when it became apparent that Republicans and conservative Democrats would not support it, claiming that it would result in greater vote fraud.

Election day registration, like mail registration, lowers the personal costs of voting. The tasks of voting and registration essentially merge, and voters need not worry about separate sets of deadlines and procedures. Election day registration could go far toward reenfranchising the rising number of Americans who travel regularly and move often. Moreover, most citizens are much more interested in politics toward the end of an election campaign than at the beginning, and many do not decide to register until the closing days of the contest—too late, under the rules now in force in most states.

Election day registration has drawbacks as well. The number and intensity of election day administrative chores increase, although officials should learn to accommodate the greater burden as they become accustomed to the system. A more serious problem may be fraud. The use of false identification could easily go undetected. But again, the potential for fraud exceeds the evidence that serious —especially organized—fraud has actually occurred. At the same time it is worth noting that the four states that currently have election day enrollment are exemplars of "clean" politics.

Election day registration seems to increase turnout somewhat, although the evidence is still scanty. The system was first in place for a presidential election in 1976. In the nation as a whole, turnout fell 1.2 percentage points that year, but in three of the four election day registration states (Maine, Minnesota, and Wisconsin) turnout rose by three to four points. (Oregon's turnout also increased, but by only 0.6 points.) In 1980, when national rates declined again, Maine and Wisconsin continued to show slight gains, although Minnesota's turnout dropped nearly three points. In 1984 the turnout rate climbed in two of the states but fell in the other two. Turnout in midterm elections may be a better measure of the effects of reforms, since midterm contests are typically less strongly determined by short-term or election-specific factors. The four states with election day registration have exceeded the national turnout average in midterm elections since 1962, but their edge over other states generally has increased since each adopted election day registration.

Of course we cannot attribute all—or, perhaps, any—of this increase to election day registration.[71] Other factors were at play at the same time. This illustrates a more general analytic problem: simple "before" and "after" comparisons often do not reveal very much about the specific effects of a reform. For example, is the gubernatorial or Senate race in a state uncertain and exciting one year and lopsided and boring in the next election? If so, this will cloud, and perhaps obscure completely, the results of any reform introduced between the two elections.

Other methodological problems prevent confident appraisals of election day registration rules. Since the four states at issue histori-cally have had high turnout rates, further gains were bound to come harder than in low-turnout states. Similarly, easier registration rules may make a big difference only within a fairly narrow range, say between 50 and 60 percent turnout. Thus we cannot assume that Minnesota's experience is a good predictor of what would happen if South Carolina introduced election day registration. Until a more subtle analysis of the effect of this reform is conducted, the jury must remain out on the precise size of the effect.

Universal Voter Enrollment

The most far-reaching and ambitious reform—short of compulsory voting—would be universal enrollment, in which the government itself would compile the list of eligible voters prior to each election. Canada uses such a system, and offers a particularly relevant model since it shares with the United States the electoral problems of fed-eral systems that are composed of heterogeneous and geographically dispersed citizens. Idaho's registration system is analogous to Cana-da's; county clerks must appoint registrars in every precinct to con-duct door-to-door canvasses.

Many proposals for universal enrollment have been made. While differing on some points—when and for how long voters should be enrolled, which level of government should run the system, and who should pay for it—most call for dividing the United States into districts and sending officials door to door to register all citizens who are eligible and willing to vote. To register by mail or on election day would lower the personal burden of registration, but automatic enrollment essentially would eliminate it. Were universal enrollment to be adopted, fewer citizens would forfeit their vote because of a recent change in residence. More centralized administration could curb problems that are caused by the latitude local registration officials currently enjoy. Such a plan would offer less potential for fraud than would mail or election day registration. Finally, the very process of canvassing would direct citizens' attention to the upcoming election.

There are three main arguments against universal voter enrollment. First, it collides with two potent American political values —individualism and localism. Although enrollment would not be compulsory, it would lose its basis in individual initiative and motivation. Administered canvasses also would centralize a government activity that historically has been under local control. Second, universal enrollment would be expensive, perhaps unjustifiably so; the most often cited cost estimates—which may be wide of the mark either way—range between $50 and $100 million.[72] Third, critics fear that such a system would be an invasion of privacy.

We can only speculate about how much universal enrollment would affect voter turnout, but some hints are offered by the experience of the four states that allow election day registration, of North Dakota (where voters need not register), and of Idaho (where deputy registrars canvass most precincts). Wherever door-to-door canvasses are standard practice, political participation is high. Idaho's turnout rates, for example, have ranged from seven to fifteen percentage points above the national average since 1960.

What Is to Be Done?

Debates over what to do about voter turnout inevitably founder on the challenge of changing public attitudes. Fundamentally, the large-scale abdication of Americans from the polls is an attitudinal problem. Yet, although we can conceive of efforts to combat this—for example, educational and media programs that exhort Americans to accept their civic responsibilities—there is little that policymakers can do in the short-run to resuscitate norms of citizenship. The story, then, is familiar to public officials. The main causes of the problem are difficult to influence through public policy, while the policy tools at hand are only indirectly and imperfectly effective, and promise, at best, unsatisfyingly partial solutions.

The registration reforms discussed above are certainly both unsatisfying and partial. None of the proposals is ideal; each has its own limitations. Piecemeal reforms must be adopted by fifty separate state legislatures and probably would produce negligible increases in turnout. Mail registration raises the specter of vote fraud yet may yield only a modest gain in voting. Election day registration, for all its virtues, invites even more opportunities for fraud, could result in administrative bottlenecks, and, most important, would have a hard time getting through Congress because of sharp partisan opposition. Of all the proposals, universal enrollment is probably the least subject to fraud, but it squarely conflicts with traditional American values and would be the most expensive and difficult to administer.

Hybrid Plan

A preferred scheme might be called a "hybrid" plan. Under this plan, Congress would mandate the liberalization of four registration provisions for all federal elections: closing dates, office hours, absentee rules, and the transfer of certification for movers.[73]

The argument goes like this: Universal enrollment would produce the largest increase in turnout but such a plan will not be adopted in the foreseeable future. It also will be difficult to pass an election day plan, and besides, such a plan has some serious problems. Fortunately, we can derive most of the benefits of an election day plan simply by moving the registration deadline closer to election day (say, one week prior), while avoiding most of its problems by not permitting enrollment on election day itself. By far, the single legal provision with the greatest influence on turnout is the registration closing date. If all the states had closed registration one week before the 1972 election, it is estimated that the national turnout would have been higher by nearly six million voters.[74] More than three-fifths of the states now close registration more than three weeks before election day. Local election officials have resisted moving registration deadlines closer to election day on the grounds that they need more time to compile voting lists and distribute them to the precincts. The advent of computerized registration systems has weakened this long-standing claim and, as one study concluded, most states could operate with a closing date of one or two weeks before the election "without any apparent sacrifice of convenience or procedural safeguards."[75]

The hybrid plan includes three additional provisions. Congress would mandate that registration offices remain open during regular business hours and provide evening and weekend opportunities to register as well. More than 60 percent of the states currently do not provide convenient hours for registration. States also would be required to offer absentee registration to all citizens of voting age. At present, six states do not permit absentee registration in any form and another twenty states limit it to certain groups, such as the military or students. Together these two changes should increase turnout an additional four percentage points.

The final piece of the hybrid plan addresses a growing impediment to voting: geographic mobility. The need of those who are settling in a new home to reestablish voting eligibility deters political participation. A large number of Americans is affected: in 1981, 17 percent of voting age citizens (27 million people) had moved within the previous year and 47 percent within the previous five years. Congress would authorize the Postal Service to send change-of-address forms (routinely submitted by most movers) to each state's chief election official, who would shift the registrations from the old to the new addresses, then cancel the old address registrations. This switching would be done only for intrastate movers (83 percent of movers), who were already registered and thus had demonstrated their qualifications to vote in that state.[76]

The hybrid plan would not require local officials to depart radically from their standard operating procedures, which would minimize bureaucratic resistance to reform. Administrative control of elections would remain in the hands of states and localities, weakening the charge that federally initiated registration reform is a violation of states' rights. This plan also would reduce (although not eliminate) the partisan objections that inevitably surface during policy debates on registration reform. The magnitude of the expected increase in turnout would be less than under a universal or election day plan, but it should be on the order of a gain of ten to fifteen percentage points.

Compulsory Voting

Let us contemplate the possibility of moving one step beyond the hybrid plan. Why not institute compulsory registration? The idea of compulsory voting is of course antithetical to the American creed. To most people the franchise is a right or a privilege, not a legal duty. Citizens cherish the freedom not to vote. But why should registration not be required? Why should it not be a citizen's responsibility to be on the rolls of potential, eligible voters? The original purpose, if not the only purpose, of requiring that voters register at all is to prevent vote fraud—that is, to eliminate multiple voting, and to insure that only residents of the geographic area who are entitled to vote in a particular election are allowed to vote in that election. Compulsory registration may be an even more efficient protection against vote fraud than the current voluntary system.

It is instructive to compare American attitudes toward voting with attitudes toward other public endeavors. Many of the functions of a modern democracy—such as raising armies for the common defense, or money for the common welfare—are subject to what economists call the "free rider" problem. Every member shares in the benefit, whether contributing to its achievement or not. They know, moreover, that in any major endeavor their individual contributions are unlikely to make the difference between success and failure. Each citizen's best option, then, is to decline to contribute. But as large numbers of citizens make these same calculations, voluntarism breaks down and public tasks remain undone. To overcome this free-rider problem we introduce an element of compulsion into taxation and military service. Young men are required to register for the military, although they may volunteer to serve or not (except in times of national emergency, when service is compulsory). Americans are required to register with the government and receive a social security number. The payment of taxes is not left to voluntarism but is compulsory at all times. Our voting system, however, still rests on an ethic of voluntarism.

Conclusion

The nature of particular candidates, campaign issues, and political events—factors largely beyond legal control—will either aggravate or ameliorate the short-term problem of participation in particular elections. We must look to structural reforms, particularly the registration process, to attack the long-term problem, which is the near complete abstention from political life of a large fraction of our citizenry.

Not all registration reforms will pay off. Incremental reforms can have only a limited effect on turnout because they are unlikely to reach the roughly 60 million Americans who are engaged in a long-standing boycott of the polls. Such reforms are unlikely to confront the long-run problem for two reasons. First, they are subject to the "Catch-22"–like dilemma that plagues many attempts to change political attitudes and behavior: those people who are attentive to the reforms already are committed participants, while the nonparticipants who are the targets of the reforms are not listening or watching. Also, incremental reforms do not address the status problem, namely that nonparticipants are predominantly lower status. There is little room left to boost middle class participation—84 percent of college-educated Americans are registered to vote. However, only 54 percent of those who have not graduated from high school are on the rolls. Thus the challenge is not to raise turnout across the board, but to increase it among lower-status citizens, a far more difficult task.

The evidence suggests that ambitious reforms, like universal enrollment, the hybrid plan, or compulsory registration, may significantly increase turnout. But although suggestive, the evidence is still too thin to let us confidently adopt or decline such basic reforms on the basis of the evidence. Even with better data, the decision ultimately depends more on values than on evidence. Those who would encourage greater participation through registration reform must come to terms with distinctively American political values—liberty, antagonism toward government, and individualism.

Democracy is a radical idea that political leaders and thinkers have never fully embraced. At best, support for democracy in the United States has been ambivalent. America is a liberal democracy but, historically, the emphasis was first placed on "liberal." The Constitution framers stressed the principles of individual liberty and

limited government rather than universal suffrage. Only during the
Jacksonian era did the "democratic" urge begin to grow. Reserva-
tions about widespread political participation, however, continued
to linger. Some elements within the Progressive movement sought to
expand democracy through such devices as primaries and referenda,
but other Progressives embraced values of rationality, efficiency, and
scientific management that often were at odds with democratic
values. Between the two world wars, political thinkers of the stature
of Walter Lippmann expressed grave misgivings about democracy.
And as we have already seen, a number of contemporary American
political scientists view mass democracy with considerable distrust.

Would-be reformers face another obstacle. Government and politics have never occupied a central place in the popular American
mind. Not only was the American republic born in a climate of
hostility toward established authority, opposition to strong government has been a reverberating theme throughout our history. Nor
has politics commanded much public acclaim. In many respects,
Americans have always treated politics as sport; it is no accident that
we use athletic metaphors to describe political contests today. In the
nineteenth century, political campaigns, with their brass bands and
torchlight parades, served as public entertainment. But cultural innovations in this century, including the rise of professional sports, created alternative social diversions. Radio and television have been
especially instrumental in steering the public away from community-
oriented social activities, including politics, and to activities that do
not require people to leave the comfort of their homes.

Any proposal to make registration more automatic also must confront the strong individualist ethic in America. Appeals to register
and to vote emphasize collective public virtues such as community,
civic duty, and public trust. However, many Americans still regard
voting as a private right that they alone can decide whether or not to
exercise.

Finally, the franchise never has been seen by Americans as a simple, automatic right of citizenship, but rather as a privilege that
individual citizens must earn by passing tests of worthiness. Current
registration requirements are fairly effective "filters"; they screen
citizens on the basis of motivation. People who register usually take
the next step and vote. If we ease registration rules, we presumably
will be adding less intrinsically motivated citizens to the rolls. In

the economists' language, the marginal return from registration will decline. At some point the cost of increasing political participation will exceed the benefit of the next citizen's vote. Defining that point depends on the values we attach to the gains and losses involved.

The debate over registration reform will be couched—as it always has been—in terms of the potential for fraud, the defense of privacy rights, and the level of public costs. These are surely legitimate concerns. But resolution of the debate ultimately will hinge on more fundamental issues of political values. Is it time to make the vote an unqualified right of citizenship, one so valuable that the government should ease and encourage its use? To do so will require some departure from traditional American ideals. But perhaps it is time to reassess some of those ideals.

6 Who Vies for President?

MICHAEL NELSON

In his 1888 work, *The American Commonwealth*, James Bryce observed:

> Europeans often ask, and Americans do not always explain, how it happens that this great office, the greatest in the world, unless we except the papacy, to which any man can rise by his own merits, is not more frequently filled by great and striking men? In America, which is beyond all other countries the country of a "career open to talents," a country, moreover, in which political life is unusually keen and political ambition widely diffused, it might be expected that the highest place would always be won by a man of brilliant gifts. But since the heroes of the Revolution died out with Jefferson and Adams and Madison some sixty years ago, no person except General Grant has reached the chair whose name would have been remembered had he not been president, and no president except Abraham Lincoln has displayed rare or striking qualities in the chair.[1]

Bryce was not the first person to wonder "Why Great Men Are Not Chosen President." Alexis de Tocqueville puzzled in *Democracy in America*, which was published in 1835, that although the Federalist party had "reckoned on their side almost all the great men whom the war of independence has produced," it soon had become extinct.[2] Nor was Bryce the last. The title of a 1967 article by Steven V. Roberts asks: "Is It Too Late for a Man of Honesty, High Purpose, and

Intelligence to Be Elected President of the United States?" Bemoaning that "at a time when events seem to demand a different alternative," the public was being forced to choose from a "group of politicians," Roberts compiled a preferred list of university, corporation, and foundation presidents, cabinet secretaries, and a Supreme Court justice.[3] Steady declines in voter turnout in almost every presidential election since Roberts's article appeared would suggest that Americans still are dissatisfied with the choices that are offered to them.

As expressions of despair, questions like those posed by Bryce and Roberts may or may not be warranted. They can be addressed in a useful way, however, only if they are phrased analytically and answered empirically. Thus, instead of wondering where are the great presidents of yesteryear, we more usefully might ask: What sorts of people comprise the pool of presidential "eligibles" from which we actually draw our chief executives? Specifically,

1. Who—realistically—can vie for president? The American political system imposes constitutional standards that help to define the pool. It also imposes informal standards of both social and career background that define it even more powerfully. What are these standards? What is their basis? How mutable are they?

2. Who chooses to compete for the presidency? Among those who are regarded as qualified, what prompts some to run and some not?

Who Can Compete?

Constitutional Requirements

In the constitutional theories that prevailed during the late eighteenth century, merely to stipulate that public offices would be filled for fixed terms by vote of a plurality of qualified electors or of state legislators was not considered sufficient to assure the republican character of elections. Constitutional specifications of eligibility also were regarded as necessary to prevent certain types of people even from coming before the voters. Several state constitutions required that the governor meet a minimum property-owning—often land-owning—standard, the idea being that voters should be restricted to choosing among candidates with a substantial economic stake in the community. Some states specified that a profession of Christianity, or even Protestantism, was a minimum legal requirement for election, perhaps in accordance with the common law rule that only Christians could be counted on to swear or affirm a valid oath of office. Age and residency requirements for would-be governors were less common than these others.[4]

The plan of government that the framers wrote at the Federal Convention of 1787 included certain standards of eligibility for the presidency. But it is hard to account for them in terms of any stated constitutional theory. The common state standards were explicitly rejected. James Madison records that when Charles Pinckney of South Carolina moved, after much discussion, that "the President of the US the Judges, and members of the Legislature should be required to swear that they were respectively possessed of a cleared unencumbered Estate to the amount of _____ in the case of the President &c &c," his motion "was rejected by so general a *no*, that the States were not called."[5] As for a religious test, not only was one not proposed, but the delegates promptly agreed "nem:con:" to Pinckney's motion that "no religious test shall ever be required as a qualification to any office or public trust under the authority of the U. States."[6] Indeed, it was not until September 7, ten days before the convention adjourned, that the delegates voted to adopt any eligibility standards for the presidency at all. Without discussion, they approved the September 4 recommendation of the Committee on Postponed Matters that now constitutes paragraph 5 of Article II, Section 1: "No Person except a natural born Citizen, or a Citizen of the United States, at the time of the adoption of this Constitution shall be eligible to that Office who shall not have attained to the Age of thirty five Years, and been fourteen Years a resident within the United States."[7]

Because no debate accompanied the delegates' decision, any explanation of why they chose these citizenship, age, and residency standards as the minimum qualifications for the presidency must be somewhat speculative. But what evidence there is points to short-term political considerations as at least the partial wellspring of each provision. In all cases, qualifications were inserted mainly to solve problems that had developed out of the constitution-writing process itself.

Citizenship. The meaning of "natural born Citizen" is not entirely clear; the term never was used commonly, and since 1795 its existence in American law has been confined to the presidential eligibility clause of the Constitution. But historians agree that its appearance in Article II can be traced to a July 25, 1787, letter that John Jay wrote to George Washington, who was president of the Convention: "Permit me to hint whether it would not be wise and seasonable to provide a strong check to the admission of Foreigners into the administration of our national Government, and to declare expressly that the Command in chief of the American army shall not be given to, nor devolve on, any but a natural born citizen."[8]

Historians also agree that fear that a foreign ruler might someday be imported to reign over the United States prompted Jay's letter, although the precise nature of that sentiment is unclear. The convention debates reveal considerable concern among the delegates about the national loyalties and attachments of legislators, but these were manifested in requirements for length of citizenship, not its origin: seven years a citizen for representatives, nine years for senators. Charles Thach has "little doubt" that Jay personally feared Baron von Steuben, a popular Prussian general who had aided the American cause during the Revolution and who—more to the point —had sympathized with Shays's Rebellion.[9] Cyril Means speculates that Jay instead was responding to a popular rumor that "the Federal Convention (which was sitting behind closed doors) was concocting a monarchical form of government and planning to invite Prince Frederick Augustus, the second son of George III, to accept an American crown."[10] In any event, Washington wrote to Jay on September 2 to thank him for the "hints contained in your letter," and two days later the Committee on Postponed Matters included Jay's suggestion in its recommendation to the delegates.[11]

The committee also specified that anyone who was "a Citizen of the United States at the time of the Adoption of this Constitution" would be eligible to the presidency. This seems to have been done in consideration of certain prominent American leaders, including James Wilson, Alexander Hamilton, and Robert Morris, who had been born abroad. It may have been feared that they would not be regarded as "natural born Citizens," even though they, having been born as British subjects, would seem to have been in the same confusing legal category as most other Americans. (The Constitution did not define citizenship.) Still, according to Edward Corwin, "Wilson, a member of the Committee of Detail, seems to have felt the need of such a clause in his own behalf especially keenly," and it was inserted.[12]

Age. As with the other constitutional qualifications for the presidency, the minimum age requirement of thirty-five years was not presented to the Convention or approved by it until far along in its proceedings. The reason seems to be that as late as August, delegates remained committed to their May decision to accept Madison's proposal for legislative selection of the executive for a single term. Because legislators had been assigned age requirements (twenty-five for members of the House, as voted on June 22; thirty for senators, voted on June 12), there may have seemed no need to stipulate one for the executive they would be choosing.

In late August, however, the Convention abandoned legislative selection in favor of presidential eligibility for reelection. In the delegates' minds, the Constitution could include one provision or the other, but not both. As Max Farrand summarizes their understanding of the issue: "If the executive were to be chosen by the legislature, he must not be eligible for reelection, lest he should court the favor of the legislature in order to secure for himself another term. Accordingly the single term of office should be long. But the possibility of reelection was regarded as the best incentive to faithful performance of duty, and if a short term and reeligibility were accepted, then choice by the legislature was inadvisable."[13] Hastening the Convention's change in policy was its August 24 decision to define legislative selection to mean the House and Senate would choose the president jointly, each member having one vote. This convinced small-state delegates that their interests would be ignored and their people effectively disfranchised.

The task then became to develop a nonlegislative method of presidential selection that would neither invite corruption nor alienate any part of the country. The people, the states, and, among diehards, the legislature all had their champions, but the decision of the Convention to refer the whole issue to the Committee on Postponed Matters is evidence enough that most delegates were looking for some new and creative proposal.

The electoral college, in which presidents were to be selected by electors from each state, was the committee's "jerry-rigged" compromise solution.[14] Curiously the proposal bespoke great suspicion of the "college's" electors. Each was charged to vote for two candidates for president from two different states, lest they vote only for local favorites. To ensure that they would cast both votes seriously, the vice presidency was created as an office for the presidential runner-up.[15]

Suspicion also was directed at the voters, whom delegates presumed would be empowered by the states to choose the electors. That this suspicion underlay the Committee's invention of the presidential age requirement on September 4 is evidenced by Jay's defense of it in *Federalist*, no. 64: "By excluding men under thirty five from the [presidency. . .], it confines the electors to men of whom the people have had time to form a judgment, and with respect to whom they will not be liable to be deceived by those brilliant appearances of genius and patriotism which, like meteors, sometimes mislead as well as dazzle."[16]

Residency. The requirement for a period of residency in the United States seems to have been designed to prevent the importation of a foreign king. From a technical standpoint, the provision is constitutional overkill—did not the "natural born Citizen" requirement take care of that possibility?—but it served two political purposes that were important to the delegates. First, it underscored to the citizenry that soon would be deciding whether to ratify the proposed constitution that the framers took popular fears of foreign rulership seriously. Those fears may have been great, if a "leaked" story to the August 22 *Pennsylvania Gazette* is any indication:

> We are informed that many letters have been written to the members of the Federal Convention from different quarters, respecting the reports idly circulating that it is intended to establish a monarchical government, and to send for [Prince Frederick Augustus] &c &c—to which it has been uniformly answered, "though we cannot, affirmatively, tell you what we are doing, we can, negatively, tell you what we are not doing—we never once thought of a king."[17]

Second, the residency requirement—if taken to mean consecutive years of residency—effectively excluded Tory sympathizers who had fled to England during the Revolution.

The designation of fourteen years as the required length of residency fulfilled both these purposes. That the Convention turned down an alternative proposal of twenty-one years can be explained by a single fact: the fourteen-year requirement excluded none of the delegates, a twenty-one-year requirement would have eliminated three.[18]

Political Origins of Paragraph 5. In all cases, then, short-term political considerations influenced the content—even the existence—of paragraph 5 of Article II, Section 1. The various citizenship and residency requirements were written to assure an anxious public that no foreign king or Tory expatriate would rule them. The age requirement helped smooth the passage of the electoral college proposal among delegates who knew they did not want legislative selection but did not know what they wanted instead. At this late stage of the Convention, the delegates' main purpose was to ease the task of agreeing on a constitution and selling it to a citizenry that they presumed would be somewhat skeptical.

The framers did, of course, give serious attention to the deeper issue of choosing suitable presidents. But they saw that purpose being served by other parts of the Constitution. Presidential selection, whether by legislators or electors (or both in the event of electoral college deadlock) was designed to be selection by peers — personal acquaintances of the candidates who could choose intelligently among them. And even if someone of low character slipped through the net and became president, the possibility of reelection would be a powerful incentive to excellence. Whether motivated by "avarice," "ambition," or "the love of fame," argues Hamilton in *Federalist*, no. 72, a president will behave well in order to secure reelection to the office that allows him to pursue his selfish desire. Finally, Jay points out in *Federalist*, no. 64, "So far as the fear of punishment and disgrace can operate, that motive to good behavior is amply afforded by the article on the subject of impeachments."[19]

Legal Issues. Regardless of their origins or their unimportance to the framers, the citizenship, age, and residency requirements for presidential eligibility remain unaltered in the Constitution; indeed, the Twelfth Amendment, which became part of the Constitution in 1804, pointedly applies them to the vice presidency as well.[20] The requirements also continue to pose thorny and unresolved legal issues. Specifically,

1. Do the age and residency provisions apply to the time of election or inauguration? This depends on whether one takes "eligible" to mean "choosable" or "qualified." The former, which is the logical etymological choice, points to the date of election; the latter, which some state courts have used to interpret their own constitutions, would indicate the inauguration day.[21]

2. Does the residency requirement entail fourteen *consecutive* years of residency prior to the election or inauguration? Some chal-

lenged Herbert Hoover's eligibility to assume office in 1929 on the grounds that much of his time during the preceding fourteen years had been spent living abroad. Hoover's defenders prevailed, but they argued narrowly that he had been a resident throughout this period because he had maintained a legal domicile in the United States.[22]

3. Does the "natural born Citizen" requirement disqualify those who are born of American parents on foreign soil? At various times this has been a live issue: the ranks of such people have included Franklin D. Roosevelt, Jr., Secretary of State Christian Herter, Governor George Romney, and Senator Lowell Weicker, among others.

The category of natural-born citizenship is an archaic one. In the most revealing study of its constitutional meaning to date, Charles Gordon argues that the principle of *jus sanguinis*, "under which nationality could be transmitted by descent at the moment of birth," was more a part of the common law of 1787 than the old doctrine *jus soli*, which determined a person's nationality according to his place of birth. Gordon also cites the Naturalization Act of 1790, which was passed by a Congress that included twenty delegates to the Federal Convention, among them eight of the eleven members of the committee that authored the presidential eligibility clause. The act includes this provision: "And the children of citizens of the United States that may be born beyond the sea, or out of the limits of the United States, shall be considered as natural-born citizens."

Gordon concedes, however, that "the evidence of [constitutional] intent is slender" and that "the picture is clouded by elements of doubt." The 1790 Act was repealed in 1795, although apparently not because of the *jus sanguinis* clause. The Fourteenth Amendment, which became part of the Constitution in 1868, refers to citizens as "all persons born *or* naturalized within the United States" (emphasis added). This means, according to controversial dicta by Justice Horace Gray in the 1898 case of *United States* v. *Kim Ark*, that natural-born citizenship is confined to those born "within the United States and subject to its jurisdiction."[23]

4. Could Congress add to the eligibility requirement by simple legislation? Corwin argues, although not at any length, that it already has done so: "A number of sections of the national Criminal Code contain the provision that anyone convicted under them shall, in addition to other penalties, 'be incapable of holding office under the United States.' . . . It can hardly be questioned that such provis-

ions are capable of excluding an otherwise qualified person from the presidency."[24]

Enduring Effects. Because these are all constitutional gray areas, it seems unlikely that the courts ever would try to thwart the will of the people by ruling as ineligible someone who was born abroad of American parents, thirty-five on inauguration day but not election day, or a resident for less than fourteen consecutive years. Still, as Means points out, messy legal challenges could be filed against such a person at almost any time—before the nominating convention, to prevent his name from appearing on a presidential primary ballot; after election day, to enjoin electors from voting for him; or during the term of office, to nullify his actions as president.[25]

The prohibition on eligibility in the original Constitution that has had the greatest effect is the one that excludes naturalized citizens from the presidency. (The age requirement, although it disqualifies more adults than any other, never has been a source of real frustration, perhaps because it bars no one from the presidency for very long.) The citizenship requirement prevented the Liberal Republicans from nominating the German-born Senator Carl Schurz to oppose U. S. Grant's reelection in 1872, and presently bars from consideration Secretary of State Henry Kissinger, National Security Adviser Zbigniew Brzezinski, Ambassador John Kenneth Galbraith, Secretary of the Treasury W. Michael Blumenthal, and Senator Rudy Boschwitz, among others.

The other politically meaningful constitutional disqualifier is the Twenty-second Amendment, which excludes from election to the presidency anyone who already has been elected twice to the office or who has acted as president for more than one and one-half terms. Short-term political considerations had much to do with the amendment's passage through the Eightieth Congress in 1947. Republicans, who voted unanimously for the two-term limit, seemed determined to prevent another Franklin Roosevelt. Ironically, the first president to whom the new limit applied was Dwight Eisenhower, who understandably described it on several occasions as "not wholly wise."[26]

Short-term politics also seems likely to prompt further change in the Constitution's eligibility provisions, if ever such changes are to occur. In March 1983, for example, Senator Thomas Eagleton introduced a constitutional amendment to replace the natural-born citizenship provision with a requirement for eleven years of citizenship.

His motive was frustration over the ineligibility of investment banker Felix Rohatyn—indeed, his staff referred to the proposal as the "Rohatyn resolution." Not surprisingly, the last spate of such proposals occurred in the early 1970s, when Kissinger's exclusion from consideration frustrated some.[27]

Social Background Criteria

The Constitution's specified qualifications for the presidency, however arbitrary and outdated they may be, are broad. They are so broad, in fact, that by estimate from the 1980 census, approximately 87 million Americans are constitutionally eligible. (More than 5 million adults over thirty-five are ineligible because they are naturalized rather than natural-born. And, of course, two Americans, Richard Nixon and Ronald Reagan, are ineligible under the Twenty-second Amendment.)[28] No one, of course, would pretend that 87 million is a realistic estimate of the pool of plausible candidates for the presidency. As William Keech and Donald Matthews observe, "Ironically, democratic elections are impossible in large polities without eliminating almost everybody before the people decide."[29] The United States, which technically draws its presidents from an unusually large pool, realistically draws it from a very small one.

How many are in this pool? Thomas Cronin estimates offhandedly that "there is an 'on-deck circle' of about fifty individuals in any given presidential year."[30] If the index for inclusion is one-time support from even 1 percent of an individual's fellow partisans in Gallup polls on presidential nomination preference, then the number of plausible candidates has ranged from nine in 1936 to forty-five in 1976, with an average of 22.6 per election for the period 1936–84.[31] (A different index—mention of someone's name as a presidential prospect on a network evening news program—produces a similar figure: an average 27.7 per election from 1968 to 1980.)[32] If one raises the standard for inclusion to 5 percent support in a Gallup poll—still low, considering that the lowest preconvention poll showing for a major party nominee was 12 percent, for Adlai Stevenson in 1952—the size of the pool shrinks by almost half, to 12.5 per election (see table 6.1).

To state that the ranks of possible presidents in a given election are numbered in the low dozens is not very helpful, of course, unless we

Table 6.1   Size of the Pool of Candidates for President, 1936–84.

Gallup Poll: Year	5 percent support or more			1 percent support or more		
	Democrats	Republicans	Total	Democrats	Republicans	Total
1936	1	7	8	1	8	9
1940	2	7	9	7	14	21
1944	4	6	10	9	9	18
1948	6	8	14	16	12	28
1952	14	7	21	20	12	32
1956	5	1	6	13	6	19
1960	9	5	14	12	11	23
1964	2	8	10	7	11	18
1968	5	11	16	5	13	18
1972	9	3	12	17	3	20
1976	11	8	19	31	14	45
1980	6	5	11	9	17	26
1984	7	1	8	16	1	17
Total	81	77	158	163	131	294
Average per election	6.2	5.9	12.2	12.7	10.1	22.6

also know what kinds of people are in those ranks. One way of deducing who plausibly can become president is to look first at those who actually have been president. Table 6.2 lists the social background characteristics of all twentieth-century presidents. (The comparable table for defeated major party candidates—table 6.3—is very similar, as would be a table of nineteenth-century presidents.)[33] By their evidence, it seems that we can tentatively eliminate the following kinds of people from the pool of 87 million: women, blacks and other racial minorities, non-Christians, and the never-married. To be sure, this list understates the exclusivity of the pool of plausible presidential candidates. There are other biases at play that, although less absolute, nonetheless have been confining. As Benjamin Page and Mark Petracca observe, presidents "usually have been white, well-to-do, Protestant males, of indistinct (or Anglo-Saxon) ethnic background; married, with a family; and in their middle fifties or older." Richard Watson and Norman Thomas add that presidential Protestantism has been "generally from a high-status denomination" and that presidents, "including those from modest backgrounds, have generally been well-educated at prestigious private institutions and have tended to practice law prior to their entry into public life."[34]

The roster of plausible candidates in recent elections has conformed to this racial, sexual, marital, and religious profile. This can be seen in table 6.4, which groups together presidential possibilities who met one or another standard of "seriousness" in the 1972, 1976, 1980, or 1984 elections. Of the candidacies that attracted at least 5 percent support in even one Gallup poll in the four years preceding each election, one belonged to a black woman (Representative Shirley Chisholm), three to a bachelor (Governor Jerry Brown), one to a black man (Jesse Jackson), and forty-five (90.0 percent) to white, male, married Christians. There is even less variety among those who crossed only the 1 percent barrier: fifty-five of sixty (91.7 percent) in this category filled the standard prescription entirely. The lowest threshold—mere mention on a television network's evening news program—is biased in favor of frivolous candidates who met the easy ballot requirements for the New Hampshire primary, such as comedian Pat Paulsen, community organizer Ed Coll (only thirty-two years old), and Harold Stassen. Even so, the overwhelming majority fit the mold.

Still, changes in the list of social background criteria may occur. New standards may arise. Not every president has had a college degree, but every one since 1933 has and the nation's ever-growing credentialist mores make it more likely that future presidency-seekers will have to as well. (All seventeen of the 1984 plausibles were at least college educated.) Divorced or widowed single candidates may find it easier to be taken seriously (Reagan broke the remarriage barrier in 1980 with scarcely a mention), but aspirants who never have been married may find it harder. America's distaste for homosexuality and suspicion of bachelors seems to have caused one unmarried candidate to publicize his friendship with a female celebrity just to prove his sexual bona fides.[35]

It also is possible that some existing social criteria will disappear from the list, as others have in recent years. In 1960, Clinton Rossiter published a catalog of "oughts" and "almost certainly musts" for would-be presidents that included the following: "northerner or westerner" (southerners Lyndon Johnson and Jimmy Carter were elected in 1964 and 1976, respectively); "less than sixty-five years old" (Reagan turned sixty-nine in 1980); "more than forty-five years old," "Protestant," "a small town boy," and "a self-made man" (forty-three year-old John Kennedy, a rich urban Catholic, was elected in the year Rossiter wrote); "a lawyer" (four of the five last elected presidents

Table 6.2 Social Background Characteristics of Twentieth-Century Presidents.

	Term	Father's occupation and social class[1]	Age[2]
William McKinley	1897–1901	Ironmonger (middle)	54
Theodore Roosevelt	1901–1909	Businessman (upper)	42
William H. Taft	1909–1913	Lawyer (upper)	51
Woodrow Wilson	1913–1921	Minister (upper)	56
Warren Harding	1921–1923	Doctor (upper)	55
Calvin Coolidge	1923–1929	Storekeeper (middle)	51
Herbert Hoover	1929–1933	Blacksmith (working)	54
Franklin Roosevelt	1933–1945	Businessman (upper)	50
Harry Truman	1945–1953	Small landowner (middle)	61
Dwight Eisenhower	1953–1961	Mechanic (working)	62
John Kennedy	1961–1963	Businessman (upper)	43
Lyndon Johnson	1963–1969	Small landowner (middle)	55
Richard Nixon	1969–1974	Streetcar conductor, grocer (working)	55
Gerald Ford	1974–1977	Paint and lumber business (middle)	61
Jimmy Carter	1977–1981	Small landowner (middle)	52
Ronald Reagan	1981–	Shoe salesman (working)	69

[1]Classification drawn from Richard Watson and Norman Thomas, *The Politics of the Presidency* (New York: John Wiley, 1983), p. 110.

have not been); and so on.[36] The class origins of presidents also have broadened. Twentieth-century presidents from William McKinley to Franklin Roosevelt were, like their nineteenth-century counterparts, predominantly upper class in social background (see table 6.5). Yet of the eight presidents since 1945, only one (Kennedy) was born into an upper-class family; four have come from middle-class homes (Harry Truman, Johnson, Carter, Gerald Ford), and three from the working class (Eisenhower, Nixon, Reagan).[37]

Career Background Criteria

Although each of the social background criteria realistically eliminates tens of millions of people from consideration for the presidency, an additional informal requirement—recent, prominent, governmental experience—defines the pool of presidential possibilities most narrowly of all. A survey of the career backgrounds of all

Marital status	Education	Religion	Home state[3]
Married	Law school	Methodist	Ohio
Married	College	Dutch Reformed	New York
Married	Law school	Unitarian	Ohio
Married	Ph.D.	Presbyterian	New Jersey
Married	Some college	Baptist	Ohio
Married	College	Congregational	Massachusetts
Married	College	Quaker	California
Married	Law school	Episcopal	New York
Married	Some law school	Baptist	Missouri
Married	College	Presbyterian	Kansas
Married	College	Catholic	Massachusetts
Married	College	Disciples	Texas
Married	Law school	Quaker	California
Married	Law school	Episcopal	Michigan
Married	College	Baptist	Georgia
Remarried (Divorced)	College	Disciples	California

[2]At time of selection.
[3]During most important adult years.

twentieth-century presidents (table 6.6) and defeated major party nominees (table 6.7) would seem to exclude all but present or recent vice presidents, governors, senators, representatives, cabinet secretaries, generals, judges, and the like from the list. (Business executive Wendell Willkie, the Republican nominee in 1940, is the sole exception.) Ninety-eight percent of the people who drew 5 percent in the Gallup polls for 1972–84 met the career standard, as did 98.3 percent of those who drew 1 percent.

Recent practice has given an increasingly narrow definition to suitable governmental experience. From 1892 to 1916, Robert Peabody and colleagues report, only 45.0 percent of the contenders for major party presidential nominations were senators, governors, or vice presidents. That share grew steadily, to 60.9 percent (1920–44) and 88.0 percent in the post–World War II period.[38] All but two of the fifteen people who have been elected president in this century last served in one of these three offices before being nominated, and all but one of

Table 6.3 Social Background Characteristics of Twentieth-Century Defeated Major Party Nominees.

	Year of candidacy	Age[1]	Marital status
William J. Bryan	1900,1908	40, 48	Married
Alton Parker	1904	52	Married
Charles E. Hughes	1916	54	Married
James Cox	1920	50	Remarried (divorced)
John Davis	1924	51	Married
Alfred Smith	1928	55	Married
Alfred Landon	1936	49	Married
Wendell Willkie	1940	48	Married
Thomas Dewey	1944, 1948	42, 46	Married
Adlai Stevenson	1952, 1956	52, 56	Divorced
Richard Nixon	1960	47	Married
Barry Goldwater	1964	55	Married
Hubert Humphrey	1968	53	Married
George McGovern	1972	50	Married
Walter Mondale	1984	56	Married

[1] At time of election.

the five vice presidents who succeeded to the office after a presidential death or resignation were former governors or senators. (The three exceptions—Secretary of Commerce Herbert Hoover, General Eisenhower, and House Minority Leader Ford—were all leaders in the prominent governmental institutions in which they served.) Of the seventeen plausibles for 1984, all except Jackson were present or former governors, senators, or vice presidents.

Success in the private sector has been less characteristic of American presidents. Carter, who built a prosperous business; Woodrow Wilson, the president of Princeton University; and Reagan, a successful movie actor, are among the few exceptions. It probably is not so much that the others could not have risen high in public life, but rather that they chose public careers instead. Had they devoted their thirties and forties to business or the professions, they might have found themselves in the position of many who have done exactly that: established in private life, inexperienced in elective politics, and unwilling, perhaps unable, to make the transition.

The explanation for the recent narrowing of the prominent governmental experience criteria to senator, governor, or vice president (the

Education	Religion	Home state[2]
Law school	Presbyterian	Nebraska
Law school	Protestant	New York
Law school	Baptist	New York
Grade school	Episcopal	Ohio
Law school	Presbyterian	West Virginia
Grade school	Catholic	New York
Law school	Methodist	Kansas
Law school	Episcopal	New York
Law school	Episcopal	New York
Law school	Presbyterian	Illinois
Law school	Quaker	California
Some college	Episcopal	Arizona
M.A.	Congregational	Minnesota
Ph.D.	Methodist	South Dakota
Law school	Presbyterian	Minnesota

[2]During most important adult years.

latter usually attained after service as a senator or governor) seems to lie partly in the democratization of the nominating system. When party leaders dominated the process, they were able to range somewhat widely in their choice of nominees. The rise of primaries and open caucuses placed cabinet members, representatives, and other potential candidates at a disadvantage. Unlike senators, governors, and vice presidents, they do not represent large electoral constituencies. Thus, they lack both the electoral base and, more important, the experience at campaigning on a grand scale that modern nominating politics rewards.[39]

Senators and governors. Interesting changes have occurred in this century within the narrow subgroup of senators and governors. The changes have come in two shifts. From 1900 to 1944, five of the eight men who were elected president and five of the nine who were nominated but not elected were chosen by their parties from positions in state government, usually as governor. This was not only a twentieth-century pattern, but one that included the entire post–Civil War era. The 1948 election marked an abrupt shift, however. From then until 1972, all five elected presidents and four of the six defeated major

Table 6.4   Social Background Characteristics of "Plausible" Candidates for President: 1972–84.

Gallup Poll	Social background				Candidates who met all social criteria (percent)
	Racial minorities	Women	Non-Christians	Never married	
5 percent support or more	Shirley Chisholm (1972) Jesse Jackson (1984)	Shirley Chisholm (1972)	—	Jerry Brown (1976, 1980 1984)	90.0
1–4 percent support	Julian Bond (1976) Edward Brooke (1976)	Ella Grasso (1976)	Milton Shapp (1976)	Ralph Nader (1976)	91.7

party nominees were drawn from the federal government. Indeed, every nominee in the final four elections of this period—Kennedy, Nixon, Johnson, Barry Goldwater, Hubert Humphrey, and George McGovern—was either a senator or a vice president who had served most recently in the Senate (see table 6.8). But no sooner had this pattern, its "consistency unmatched at any time in the history of the republic," taken root than a second shift appeared that seemingly undid it.[40] In 1976 and 1980, Carter and Reagan, two ex-governors, were nominated and elected president.

The direction, as well as the abruptness, of the first shift (from state to national) can be accounted for easily. It reflected the seismic changes in American politics generated by the national welfare state that grew out of the depression and the "garrison state" of the post–World War II period. As Peabody and Eve Lubalin described it at the time:

> Governors now appear to be isolated from national policymaking, and their immersion in parochial state concerns is considered more of a liability than an asset. Moreover, the purely adminis- trative aspects of the president's job have contracted in compari- son to presidential responsibility for formulating complex national economic and social policies, conducting American

Table 6.5   Social Class Backgrounds of Presidents.

Social Class	Pre-Twentieth Century		Twentieth Century (1900–45)		Twentieth Century (1945–81)	
	No.	percent	No.	percent	No.	percent
Upper	13	56.5	5	62.5	1	12.5
Middle	3	13.0	2	25.0	4	50.0
Lower	7	30.4	1	12.5	3	37.5

Source: Richard Watson and Norman Thomas, *The Politics of the Presidency* (New York: John Wiley, 1983), p. 110.

foreign affairs, and leading national public opinion . . . . Increasingly, because of the nationalization of American politics and disproportionate media coverage of the president and members of Congress, the latter political officials have become most familiar to the public and provide much of what national and partisan leadership of public opinion now exists.[41]

No such change prefaced the post-1972 events. The experiences of 1976 and 1980, when men of state politics were elected president, instead must be explained largely in terms of the anti-Washington mood that existed among voters in the wake of Vietnam and Watergate. That Carter and Reagan were *former* governors and "unemployed" during the time they were campaigning, however, may indicate something of more lasting significance. As the campaign for the nomination has lengthened, freedom from the responsibilities of office has come to be an advantage to the would-be campaigner. "Those of us who are already in government and public life don't have the time and the resources to run soon enough and early enough to succeed," complained Senate Minority Leader Howard Baker when he abandoned his own campaign for the 1980 Republican nomination.[42] Baker even retired from the Senate in 1984 so that he would be free to campaign for the 1988 nomination if he chose to seek it. Similarly, Walter Mondale foreswore a Senate campaign in 1982 in order to campaign freely for the presidency in 1984, and Senator Gary Hart chose not to run for reelection in 1986 in preparation for a 1988 presidential candidacy.

In truth, underemployment seems to serve a candidate as well as unemployment. All that is needed is time to campaign frequently during the preelection years and steadily during the primaries and caucuses. Former governors have that time; incumbent ones usually

Table 6.6   Career Background Characteristics of Twentieth-Century Presidents.

	Term	Federal				
		Vice president	Cabinet	Other high executive	Senate	House
William McKinley	1897–1901					X
Theodore Roosevelt	1901–1909	X^3		X		
William H. Taft	1909–1913		X^2	X		
Woodrow Wilson	1913–1921					
Warren Harding	1921–1923				X^2	
Calvin Coolidge	1923–1929	X^3				
Herbert Hoover	1929–1933		X^2	X^1		
Franklin Roosevelt	1933–1945			X		
Harry Truman	1945–1953	X^3			X^2	
Dwight Eisenhower	1953–1961					
John Kennedy	1961–1963				X^2	X^1
Lyndon Johnson	1963–1969	X^3			X^2	X
Richard Nixon	1969–1974	X^2			X	X^1
Gerald Ford	1974–1977	X^3				$X^{1,2}$
Jimmy Carter	1977–1981					
Ronald Reagan	1981–					

[1]First government position.
[2]Last government position before election as president or vice president.

do not. Neither do senators who are intent on the business of the Senate, although Senator Alan Cranston managed to function both as Senate Democratic Whip and one of the most active campaigners for his party's 1984 nomination.

Vice Presidents. The vice presidency is an anomalous office in many ways, including its status as a stepping-stone to the presidency. Of the five twentieth-century vice presidents who succeeded to the presidency (Theodore Roosevelt, Calvin Coolidge, Truman, Johnson, and Ford), all subsequently received their party's presidential nomination and all but Ford were elected. (This is in contrast to the nineteenth century, when none of the four vice presidents who became president after a presidential death even were nominated by their parties.) In addition, recent vice presidents have been regarded

| | | State | | | | | |
Judge	Career military	Governor	Lieutenant governor	Legislator	Judge	Local office	Private
		X^2				X^1	Lawyer
		X^2		X^1		X	Lawyer, rancher
X		X			X	X^1	Lawyer
		$X^{1,2}$					Scholar
			X	X^1			Newspaper journalist
		X^2	X	X	X	X^1	Lawyer
							Engineer
		X^2		X^1			Lawyer
						X^1	Small businessman
	$X^{1,2}$						
						X^1	Teacher
							Lawyer
							Lawyer
		X^2		X		X^1	Farmer, small businessman
		$X^{1,2}$					Actor

[3]Succeeded to the presidency on death or resignation of incumbent.

as leading contenders, sometimes heirs apparent, for their party's nomination: Nixon in 1960, Humphrey in 1968, Mondale in 1984, Bush in 1988, even Agnew, for a time, in 1976. Yet it is also true that no incumbent vice president has been elected president since Martin Van Buren in 1836.

The positive aspects of this political portrait of the vice presidency can be accounted for by the greater emphasis recent candidates have placed, in the selection of vice presidential nominees, on experience, ability, and philosophical harmony with the presidential candidate. Winning votes for the presidential candidate is the goal, as it always has been, but voters in the postwar age, aware of how suddenly a vice president may become president and assume the responsibilities of leading a nuclear superpower, care more about a vice presidential

Table 6.7 Career Background Characteristics of Twentieth-Century Defeated Major Party Nominees.[1]

	Year of candidacy	Federal				
		Vice president	Cabinet	Other high executive	Senate	House
William J. Bryan	1900, 1908					X^2
Alton Parker	1904					
Charles E. Hughes	1916			X		
James Cox	1920					X
John Davis	1924			X^2		X
Alfred Smith	1928					
Alfred Landon	1936					
Wendell Willkie	1940					
Thomas Dewey	1944, 1948			X		
Adlai Stevenson	1952, 1956			X		
Richard Nixon	1960	X^2			X	X
Barry Goldwater	1964				X^2	
Hubert Humphrey	1968	X^2			X	
George McGovern	1972			X	X^2	X

[1]Defeated incumbent presidents not included: Taft, 1912; Hoover, 1932; Ford, 1976; Carter, 1980.

candidate's ability to succeed a president ably and faithfully than they care about having all regions of the country or factions of the party represented in the White House. Having picked their running mates on the basis of ability and loyalty, modern presidents are more likely to put them to good use in the administration. Talented to begin with, vice presidents thus gain stature in office: a suitable basis for then claiming their party's presidential nomination.[43]

The vice president turned presidential nominee, however, is in a difficult political situation. Like all contenders for the presidency, the vice president must defend against attacks on his own alleged shortcomings. Yet, unlike the challenger of the other party, the vice president also must defend against all the outgoing president's shortcomings without the compensating advantage of being able to claim credit for the administration's successes.

			State				
Judge	Career military	Governor	Lieutenant governor	Legislator	Judge	Local office	Private
					X[2]	X	Lecturer, journalist
							Lawyer
X[2]		X					Lawyer
		X[2]					Publisher
				X			Lawyer
		X[2]			X	X	
		X[2]					Businessman
							Businessman
		X[2]				X	Lawyer
		X[2]					Lawyer
							Lawyer
						X	Businessman
						X	Businessman
							Scholar

[2]Last government position before nomination.

Mutability of Social and Career Background Criteria

Social Background. Are public attitudes that presently seem to exclude some people from the presidency for reasons of race, religion, or other social background criteria likely to change in the near future? Public opinion surveys on voter prejudice seem encouraging, but perhaps less so than meets the eye. The Gallup poll reported in 1983 that other things being equal, 88 percent of the electorate would be willing to vote for a Jewish candidate for president, up from 82 percent in 1978 and 62 percent in 1958. Seventy-seven percent say they could support a black candidate, the same proportion that was reported in 1978, but double the 38 percent who said they could in 1958.[44] In both cases the figure is substantially higher than the 68 percent who said they could vote for a Catholic in 1959, a year before Kennedy's election. Kennedy's Catholicism, however, also won him many votes from among the quarter of the electorate who were Catholic—indeed, the net effect of religiously prejudiced voting in 1960 may have been favorable to Kennedy. In contrast, a Jewish can-

Table 6.8 Major-Party Presidential Nominees, 1900–1972: Level of Government of Most Recent Office

| | Elected presidents | | Losing major-party nominees (incumbent presidents excluded) | | |
	State	National	State	National	Other
1900–1944	McKinley T. Roosevelt Wilson Coolidge F. Roosevelt	Harding Hoover Taft	Parker Cox Smith Landon Dewey	Bryan Hughes Davis	Willkie
1948–1972	—	Truman Eisenhower Kennedy Johnson Nixon	Dewey Stevenson	Nixon Goldwater Humphrey McGovern	—

didate would have fewer coreligionists and a black fewer racial compatriots to draw upon for prejudiced support to outweigh the prejudiced opposition.

Women are in a more enviable position in this regard—not only has the electorate's tolerance for a female president risen from 52 percent in 1958 to 73 percent in 1978 and 80 percent in 1983, but women make up a majority of the electorate. Curiously, atheists are well-positioned, too. To be sure, voters' expressed willingness to consider electing an atheist as president still is quite low: 42 percent in 1983, up from 40 percent in 1978 and 18 percent in 1958. But unlike women, blacks, and Jews, atheists can profess to be something different from what they are, as some who are in Congress, for example, apparently do.[45]

It is, of course, one thing to observe that conditions are ripe for the breaking down of certain barriers of social background and something else again to predict when that breaking down will occur. Recent history does suggest, however, that barriers to the presidency tend to fall in one of three ways: through facing the issue during a campaign; through the vice presidency; or as an aftermath to an already vanished prejudice.

Facing the issue. No greater obstacle stood between John Kennedy and the presidency in 1960 than relatively widespread public fear of a Roman Catholic president, usually on the grounds that such a president would be beholden to the pope. To blunt the issue's effect, Kennedy faced it squarely. In the midst of a crucial primary campaign, he told a television audience of West Virginians, 95 percent of them Protestant, that:

> When any man stands on the steps of the Capitol and takes the oath of office of President, he is swearing to support the separation of church and state; he puts one hand on the Bible and raises the other hand to God as he takes the oath. And if he breaks his oath, he is not only committing a crime against the Constitution, for which Congress can impeach him—and should impeach him—but he is committing a sin against God. A sin against God, for he has sworn on the Bible.[46]

In September, after winning the nomination, Kennedy appeared before the Greater Houston Ministerial Association and made an equally forthright statement.

In early 1980, Ronald Reagan faced a somewhat different issue —his age. Other nations, including most of the world powers, either ignore advanced age or reward it when selecting their leaders. That this has not been the case in the United States is evidenced by the fact that Reagan, who turned sixty-nine in 1980, was bidding to become the oldest candidate ever to be elected president. Reagan faced the issue less directly than Kennedy, seeking to render it trivial. He did so generally by trying to convey an image of physical vigor, and in particular by organizing his campaign appearances on February 6 into a series of public birthday celebrations in several New Hampshire locations.

Vice presidency. Historically, presidential candidates and their parties frequently have used the vice presidential nomination as a device to reach out to groups for which they have little appeal. This is a relatively safe strategy because hostile voter prejudices seem less likely to be activated by a vice presidential candidate than sympathetic prejudices. Kennedy chose Lyndon Johnson, a southerner, in 1960 for this very reason, and did much better in the South than he otherwise might have.

Once in office, a vice president's race, religion, sex, or—in Johnson's case—regional background is less likely to remain frightening to previously prejudiced voters because the individual's qualities will be more apparent. Familiarity seems to breed contentment in such cases; the share of voters willing to vote for a Catholic jumped from 68 percent to 82 percent right after Kennedy's election, and has been rising steadily ever since. And however tragic the circumstances, should the vice president succeed to the presidency, as Johnson did after Kennedy's assassination in 1963, the waning of prejudice is likely to be quickened.

However probable are the good effects on tolerance of a vice presidency, the opposite also is possible. For example, if a member of a previously excluded group became vice president and behaved in a way that seemed to confirm people's fears, the effect might be to revive and intensify prejudices. (It was Johnson's awareness of this that led him to work so hard to promote the cause of civil rights.) Prejudices also might be reinforced if defeat at the polls were blamed —correctly or incorrectly—on the voters' response to the presence of such a person on the ticket.

Social tolerance. Like southernness and Catholicism, divorce was long considered a barrier to the presidency. Yet Reagan campaigned in 1976 and was elected in 1980 with scarcely a hint that his divorce should be held against him. The reason seems to be that society's tolerance for divorce had grown so great during the 1960s that it no longer was a barrier when candidate Reagan encountered it.

Certainly the democratization of the nominating process will hasten the removal of the religious, racial, and sexual barriers. In the past the caution of old-style party professionals made them slow to recognize changes in popular prejudices until long after they had occurred. "He had to prove to them that he could win," said Theodore Sorenson of Kennedy's campaign for his party's nomination. "And to prove that to them, he'd have to fight hard to make them give it to him, he couldn't negotiate it. . . . So it evolved from the top down that you had to go into the primaries."[47] By their nature, primaries, which are far more important and pervasive now than they were in 1960, register changes in social tolerance almost directly.[48] They also provide a forum in which prejudices can be addressed openly.

What effect did the vice presidential nomination of Representative Geraldine Ferraro in 1984 have on the status of women in presidential politics? The choice of a woman was received well: polls had indicated a growing willingness, even desire, among voters for a female vice president, and Ferraro's nomination gave the Democratic ticket its only surge in the polls in 1984. But Ferraro had serious individual weaknesses that may have hurt on election day: as only a three-term representative, she was underqualified according to modern career criteria, and her family finances became a subject of public controversy during the campaign. Ferraro's political weaknesses, however, were personal, not gender-related, as evidenced by the fact that the ranks of candidates mentioned as presidential or vice presidential possibilities for 1988 included Mayor Diane Feinstein of San Francisco, transportation secretary Elizabeth Dole, former United Nations ambassador Jeane Kirkpatrick, Representative Pat Schroeder, and Supreme Court justice Sandra Day O'Connor.

Career Background. As we saw earlier, recent history has indicated a distinct narrowing of the career criterion of recent prominent governmental experience to three main offices: senator, governor, and vice president. Indeed, it may be more accurate to reduce this list to two: of the ten most recent vice presidents, only Ford and Bush were not senators or governors at the time of their selection. This "rule of two" may distress those who would broaden the presidential talent pool to reincorporate cabinet secretaries, judges, and other political officeholders, as well as leaders from the private sector, but there is some evidence to suggest that it is not rigid. The early roster of candidates for 1988 included an unusual sprinkling of congressmen, such as Jack Kemp and Richard Gephardt, mayors (Feinstein, Tom Bradley), cabinet secretaries (James Baker, Alexander Haig), and private citizens (television evangelist Pat Robertson and Chrysler president Lee Iacocca). This may be coincidence, or it may reflect the wider ranging eye of the television news camera: toward the House, which recently has allowed live and taped coverage of its sessions, and, in the Reagan era of political and governmental decentralization, toward local mayors and state governors, corporate executives, and evangelical preachers.

Underlying the narrowing trend, moreover, is a broadening one that may turn out to be more significant. Firm though the high elective officeholding standard for the presidency may be, it has become steadily easier in the last decade or so to attain such offices. Two closely related reasons account for this: the rapid loss of control by state party organizations of the candidate selection and postnomination processes, and the simultaneous rise in the importance of individual entrepreneurial campaigning through the media. Celebrity status automatically brings mass media exposure to a candidate, which opens up the Senate and statehouse to famous astronauts (senators John Glenn and Harrison Schmitt), athletes (Senator Bill Bradley), actors and television journalists (Governor Ronald Reagan, Senator Jesse Helms, Representative Fred Grandy of "Loveboat" fame), and the like. Or money can buy such exposure in the form of paid advertising, a strategy that is especially suited to wealthy candidates because of the recent mix of campaign finance laws and court decisions that restricts the contributions one can receive from others but not those made to one's own campaign.[49] Several multimillionaires have been able to win major party nominations for governor or senator in recent elections by spending millions of dollars from their own fortunes.

It already has been mentioned that few twentieth-century presidents have had noteworthy careers outside politics. As Watson and Thomas observe, "the career pattern of most American presidents has been to serve in elective public office from an early age until they are elected to the presidency."[50] Close reexamination of data that Joseph Schlesinger compiled on 1,626 major party senatorial and gubernatorial nominees—that is, those who form the pool from which presidents are drawn—reveals that 37.6 percent of them first attained public office during their twenties, and 61.4 percent before they reached age thirty-five.[51] The vast majority of the under-thirty-five group—some 67.2 percent—were lawyers. (In contrast, only 32.2 percent of those who won their first office later in life were lawyers.) The career path to the top of the political ladder, then, traditionally has looked something like figure 6.1a.

It probably is no coincidence, however, that among the few exceptions to the lawyer-career politician rule are the two most recent presidents, farmer-businessman Carter and actor Reagan. Carter- and Reagan-style exceptions may well become as much the rule as the career politician pattern, if recent pools of contenders are any guide: Bradley, Glenn, Hart, Kennedy, Baker, Helms, Percy, Reagan, Brown, and Bumpers won their first political offices at the senatorial or gubernatorial level, and Kemp and Jackson hardly fit the careerist mode. The era of entrepreneurial media politics has so loosened the career background criteria that the life histories of an increasing number of future presidents are likely to include substantial time in the private sector (figure 6.1b).

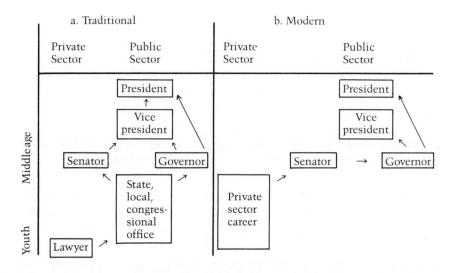

Figure 6.1   Career Paths to the Presidency.

Motivation

The subject of political motivation is so poorly understood that any treatment of the subject must be tentative. In the case of those who enter politics after long careers in the private sector, almost nothing can be said because they only recently have become numerous. (Perhaps the explanation is nothing more than the superior social status that positions such as senator and governor enjoy in American society, higher even than the highest private sector occupations.)[52] And although much has been written about the motivations of career politicians, not much of it is conclusive.

Given these limits, however, we at least may ask, What moves certain career politicians at an advanced stage in their career to mount campaigns for the presidency?

"To win" is only one of several answers to that question. A variety of motives at one time or another have impelled candidates to run for president. In almost every recent election, for example, there has been at least one highly visible candidate whose main purpose has been to promote a cause. Governor George Wallace opposed President Johnson in several 1964 primaries to protest his party's civil rights policies. In 1968, Wallace was joined by Senator Eugene McCarthy, who was running in opposition to American involvement in Vietnam.

Representatives John Ashbrook and Paul McCloskey challenged President Nixon's renomination in 1972, attacking him for being too liberal and too conservative, respectively. Ellen McCormack entered some 1976 Democratic primaries solely in order to advance the "right to life" cause. Jesse Jackson's 1984 candidacy had as its primary purpose the political mobilization of previously unregistered or non-participating blacks so that they could exert more influence in the political process. George McGovern seems to have decided to run in 1984 as a way of pressuring other Democratic contenders to remain true to his brand of liberalism.

It is, of course, hard to sort out issue advocacy from self-promotion —the lure of the spotlight—when judging the motives of such candidates. Clearly, though, self-promotion is the very essence of some candidates whose main purpose is other than to win. Some run in order to position themselves for the vice presidential nomination; others to lay the foundation for a future, more serious campaign for the presidency; and still others for reasons that are purely idiosyncratic.[53]

Ironically, for those whose purpose in becoming a candidate really is to win the presidency, the obstacles to running are highest of all. They also are higher than ever. Woodrow Wilson once looked to a time when "we shall be obliged always to be picking our chief magistrates from among wise and prudent athletes."[54] He was writing in 1908, when the race for the presidency involved active campaigning only during the fall—itself a recent innovation at the time. The road to the party nomination still was one that a candidate strolled rather than ran. If someone wished to be his party's nominee for president, his only recourse was to impress party professionals, who generally would wait until the last possible moment before committing themselves. To announce one's candidacy before the election year or to campaign in primaries were strategies of desperation that betrayed weakness.

The recent history of presidential selection could not be more different. McGovern's successful candidacy for the 1972 Democratic nomination was announced in January 1971. Carter announced in December 1974 for the 1976 nomination. George Bush, a candidate for the Republican nomination in 1980, campaigned 329 days in 1979, at almost nine hundred political events. Alan Cranston announced his candidacy for the 1984 Democratic nomination on

February 2, 1983, Gary Hart on February 17, Walter Mondale on February 21, Reubin Askew on February 23, Ernest Hollings on April 18, and John Glenn on April 18. Jesse Jackson, the last candidate to enter the race, announced on November 3, several days earlier than the announcement of the first candidate to declare in 1968 (George Romney, on November 18, 1967) or in earlier elections. Even these dates are deceptively late; all began hard campaigning virtually as soon as the 1980 results were in.

The main purpose of all this activity has not been to win the support of influential party professionals, but rather to raise money, develop appealing issues, devise shrewd campaign strategies, impress national political reporters, attract competent staff, and build active organizations so that one can win delegates directly in the primaries and caucuses. Quite obviously, this effort takes a great deal of time and energy throughout the interelection period. And even then, the odds of winning are in virtually all cases less than even and, for many would-be candidates, quite long.

Who, then, will run if being president is the only lure? In trying to answer that question, John Aldrich has applied the concept of the "risk taker."[55] A risk taker, according to Aldrich, "is one who is more likely than others to enter hazardous or uncertain situations, i.e., select a risky alternative." If in earlier stages of their careers high-level officeholders have shown a willingness to run for office when there was good reason to think they would lose, one may reasonably expect them to run for president at some point. In Aldrich's operationalization of the term, to have challenged an incumbent officeholder, or to have run in a constituency that during the three most recent elections gave an average 57 percent or more of its votes to the other party, marks one as a risk taker.

Unfortunately, risk taker — so defined — is a somewhat elusive concept. The term connotes the healthy zest for politics and spirit of adventure that is characteristic of James David Barber's active-positive personality type. But as defined by Aldrich, the ranks of risk takers also would include those whose ambition in politics is compulsive in origin and destructive in effect — Barber's active-negative, Harold Lasswell's political man.[56] Indeed, as the presidential campaign continues to lengthen and the investment required for running grows, one may expect a certain proportion of active-positive risk takers to channel their energies into other endeavors. Active-negatives, whose motives in seeking power are irrational and drive them obsessively, are less likely to be deterred.

One can make too much of all this, of course. There are exceptions even to the active personality rule: Reagan's slow-paced approach to the 1980 Republican nomination campaign demonstrated that a relatively passive campaign still can work, at least for someone with Reagan's media skills. Further, although for every would-be president the risks of losing are high, they are not as high in some elections as in others. For example, a senator or governor risks less if he runs for president in a year when he is not up for reelection than in a year when he is. Or, political circumstances simply may change. Mondale withdrew his long shot candidacy for the 1976 Democratic nomination in December, 1974 after deciding that he was not "willing to go through fire" and spend his nights "sleeping in Holiday Inns." Such obstacles seemed less deterring to front-runner Mondale as 1984 approached.

Conclusion

"Is this the best we can do?" asks Thomas Cronin, summarizing a common lament about presidential selection. "With our large and highly educated population, why can't we produce Washingtons, Jeffersons, Franklins, and the like?"[57]

As an expression of despair, questions such as these may or may not be warranted. According to a 1982 ranking by historians, the first half century of our history under the Constitution did produce several presidents who scored in the upper third—Washington (3), Jefferson (5), Jackson (6), and John Adams (14). But although the most recent half century includes Nixon (34), Carter (26), and Ford (23), it also numbers Franklin Roosevelt (2), Truman (8), Eisenhower (9), Johnson (12), and Kennedy (14) in its ranks. No intervening period comes close to matching the present one for presidential quality, if historians' standards of evaluation are any guide.[58]

Nonetheless, the question of whether the American system is as well-suited as it could be to putting forth the ablest people for the presidency is an important one. It is a question to which we will return explicitly after addressing two other, related issues: constitutional reform, and the effects on candidate quality of the modern nominating process.

Constitutional Reform

Jeffrey Tulis has noted the "synoptic character" of the framers' view of government, a view in which many constitutional threads were woven into a common fabric.[59] Tulis chastises modern scholars of American politics for studying political institutions individually rather than synoptically, but the same criticism could be directed at the constitutional reformer who singles out one provision of the Constitution for change without considering its place in the integrated constitutional scheme. The Constitution is not holy writ, never to be changed, but proposals to replace, alter, or add to particular provisions are more likely to serve their intended purpose if they are made in full awareness of why a provision originally was inserted, and what others might be affected.

With regard to the constitutional standards of eligibility for the presidency, there is little evidence to suggest that advocates of the Twenty-second Amendment had the slightest understanding of the great importance the framers attached to the president's eligibility for reelection. Yet the two-term limit stands as the single alteration in the original Constitution's list of presidential qualifications. This becomes ironic when one considers that the Constitutions' other qualifications—those specified in paragraph 5 of Article II, Section 1—were relatively unimportant to any theory of government that the framers may have had. The age, residency, and citizenship requirements, like the electoral college, each were included mainly for the purpose of overcoming some short-term obstacle in the constitution-writing process itself. These, surely, were threads that could have been pulled from the fabric at any time subsequent to the Constitution's ratification without causing any serious unraveling at all. Any or all of them could be struck or, as in Senator Eagleton's proposal, modified while doing no violence to the broader plan of government. When one considers the tangle of legal issues that could arise under the age, residency, and citizenship requirements, the arbitrary exclusion of talented Americans who are naturalized citizens, and the difficulties of presidential succession that would occur if a naturalized Speaker of the House, president pro tempore of the Senate, or secretary of state had to be passed over, there seems no good reason not to repeal or replace this paragraph by constitutional amendment.

Effects of the Modern Nominating Process

Recent writing on presidential selection has been preoccupied with the nominating process in general and the alleged ills of party reform in particular. To many professional political analysts—scholars, journalists, and politicians alike—the old style system of nomination by party leaders seems ever more attractive as a mechanism for selecting able presidential candidates. "In the old way," says David Broder, "whoever wanted to run for president of the United States took a couple of months off from public office in the year of the presidential election and presented his credentials to the leaders of his party, who were elected officials, party officials, leaders of allied interest groups, and bosses in some cases. These people had known the candidate over a period of time and had carefully examined his work."[60] As it happened, the qualities those political peers were looking for were, according to Jeane J. Kirkpatrick, the very qualities that made for good presidents: "the ability to deal with diverse groups, ability to work out compromises, and the ability to impress people who have watched a candidate over many years."[61] And when they decided on someone, Austin Ranney writes, "the delegates would follow their lead and choose him. The coalition of leaders also would see to it that the party's platform would help unite the party and put it in the best possible position to win the election."[62]

There is more nostalgia than history in these and similar accounts: the sepia tone that overlays memories of what Ranney calls the "good old days" obscures the warts.[63] Writing in the late nineteenth century, the high water mark of party organization in this country, Bryce reported in *The American Commonwealth* that party professionals indeed had a talent for choosing electable candidates. But he also felt compelled to explain why great men are not chosen president in terms of that very skill. "It must be remembered that the merits of a President are one thing and those of a candidate another thing . . .," Bryce wrote. "It will be a misfortune to the party, as well as to the country, if the candidate elected should prove a bad president. But it is a greater misfortune to the party that it should be beaten in the impending election, for the evil of losing national patronage will have come four years sooner."[64]

Aside from the mixed record of the old-style system and the inherent impossibility of recapturing the past even if one wanted to, it should be remembered that the democratization of the nominating process has had several good effects on the presidential talent pool. Most important, it has contributed to the breakdown of arbitrary barriers such as religion and age, and seems likely to have this effect on racial and sexual barriers as well. Democratization also has enhanced the importance of media skills for would-be presidents. It may be a lamentable fact that presidents need such skills, but it is a fact nonetheless, and a selection process that did not require them would not be very helpful.

One can note these good effects of democratization without endorsing the lengthened campaign that has accompanied it. The two are, of course, separate phenomena—indeed, one of the main arguments for extending the democratizing tendency to a national primary in late summer of the election year would be to shorten the campaign.[65] Length weeds out those who, perhaps for altogether commendable reasons, are not willing to campaign for four years on the off chance that they will be nominated and elected president. Presumably it does not weed out those whose motive in political life is compulsive. Logically, one would expect the latter to constitute a distressingly larger share of those who are willing to make the race.

A Broader Range of Talent?

The democratization of the nominating process that has accelerated the breakdown of social background barriers to the presidency has had several effects on the system's informal career requirements for recent, prominent governmental experience. It has helped to define those requirements to include only senators, governors, and vice presidents, that is, those who are experienced at large-scale campaigning. But as we have seen, this narrowing effect masks a deeper, broadening one. The breakdown of party control over the nomination process at all levels of the federal system, along with recent changes in the rules that govern campaign finance and the rise of media campaigning, has made it possible for people who have spent most of their lives building reputations or fortunes in the private sector to mount serious campaigns for senator and governor without any prior experience in politics. If elected, they are in a position eventually to compete with career politicians for the presidency.

Both these conditions of modern presidential selection—the requirement for prominent governmental experience and the greater ease with which it can be acquired—are good for the country. It would be foolish to nominate, much less elect, someone devoid of experience in high elective office as president. Presidents need certain skills if they are to lead successfully.[66] Skills of political rhetoric and bargaining seem to be developed best by running for office and serving in government for a period of several years. The same can be said of the subtle but vital capacity to sense the public's willingness to be led in different directions at different paces at different times. Success in the private sector alone speaks well of a person and usually requires some of these skills. But only politics requires all of them. Even management of administration is different in the public sector than in the corporate or academic world.

To say that political experience is essential to presidential success, however, is not to say that a lifetime of such experience is essential. It may not even be altogether desirable. One cannot be but humbled by the roster of Franklins, Jeffersons, and Washingtons that invariably is juxtaposed with subsequent generations of presidential contenders. Nor can one be but struck by a quality that distinguished their careers: an ease of movement between the public and private spheres of life that allowed them to be seasoned by both and ignorant of neither. In this light, the trend toward easier lateral entry into political office at the congressional and gubernatorial levels for those whose lives have been spent primarily in private pursuits is to be applauded for its broadening effects on the talent pool from which presidents are drawn.

7 Methods and Actors: The Relationship of Processes to Candidates

JOHN H. ALDRICH

Reforms of the presidential nomination process, begun in the wake of the tumultuous 1968 campaign, have altered the presidential landscape in many important ways. Critics point to everything from the untidy nature of the new process (it is far too long, complex, enervating, and costly) to the accelerated decline of political parties as consequences of these reforms. But do different kinds of candidates run for nomination under the new rules? If the answer is no, then criticism and proposed new reforms must rest on fundamentally different grounds than those implicit—and often explicit—in the controversy surrounding the post-1968 reforms.

At first blush, the proposition that "changing the rules changes the game" seems straightforward. Virtually all theories of political behavior recognize the importance of institutional arrangements to politics, including the traditional institutionalism of pre–World War II political science, Eastonian and other systems theories, and the "new institutionalism" in rational choice theories. Practically speaking, why would such controversy surround reform efforts if the rules

I would like to thank Cindy Aldrich for her assistance and Alexander Heard and Michael Nelson for their advice, encouragement, and editorial assistance. Much of my thinking on this topic was the product of research made possible by a grant from the National Science Foundation, SOC 76-24218. I remain grateful to them for their support. They share no blame, of course, for the analysis or interpretation reported herein.

did not help some and hurt others? Yet there are equally good reasons to believe that changes in nomination practices over the last century or so have had at most marginal consequences: nomination procedures have been embedded in a two-party system throughout this time, the nomination is but the penultimate step in the selection process, and the ultimate step of popular election may dominate nomination decisions. Thus nomination procedures may be too small a part of the institutional structure that governs presidential elections to matter greatly. Moreover, the choice to run remains a voluntary decision of ambitious politicians, a choice that may be made more in light of who else has emerged as major competitors through the larger political process. The question of whether Edward Kennedy would run in 1972 or in 1976 greatly shaped how (and even if) other aspirants would run. In short, while all might agree that "institutions matter," the arguments may cut either way, depending on whether one views the nomination rules as crucial or as secondary to the need to win the general election.

This chapter begins by developing these theoretical arguments. Then, after reviewing the extant research, the research design and methods of analysis will be discussed. As we will see, the results of historical comparisons suggest that presidential candidates look remarkably similar across four eras with differing nomination procedures. The changes that have emerged appear to be a consequence of changes in the context, the conduct, or both, of electoral politics rather than in the different nomination systems. The historical record that is available for systematic comparison, however, may miss the real consequences of the most recent reforms. In particular, presidential "vitas" may look quite similar over the last century, but the changed requirements of campaign strategy may induce biases that help some who share the proper credentials more than others.

Before turning to the theoretical arguments, an important point should be made. No single rule or process defines any given nomination system. Rather, the rules of nomination are a complex set of procedures, not all of which are reformed at any one time. Thus, for example, we define the current nomination system as having come into existence for the 1972 campaign. The 1972 campaign differed from 1968 in several important respects. The McGovern-Fraser Commission rules were in place for the Democratic party. In response, many states changed their methods of selecting delegates, most notably by the marked increase in the use of primary elections. Moreover, the first of the campaign finance reforms of the 1970s went into effect in early 1972. These numerous changes (and others) mean that we cannot, nor do we attempt to, isolate the effect of any one change.

At the same time, the period 1972–84 (or any other period) was one within which numerous further changes were made. The McGovern-Fraser Commission rules were altered by the Democratic party for 1976, again for 1980, and yet again for 1984. Every election year at least some states and state parties change the rules governing their delegate selection procedures, and often many do. Campaign finance procedures also changed greatly for 1976 and then were modified for 1980 and 1984. Moreover, candidates experiment with the best way to deal with changes—the conventional wisdom about how best to use nomination rules in a campaign changes with time and experience, and candidates are continually innovative in their strategies. In short, no two elections are ever the same in their institutional arrangements or candidate decisionmaking, let alone strategic and historical contexts. Yet we suggest that the four historical periods we analyze show enough similarity within each period and differences across the periods to permit conclusions to be drawn.

Theoretical Arguments

Most theories of political behavior emphasize the importance of the rules that define the system, our primary subject, as well as the motivations, goals, and decisionmaking processes of the actors involved and the historical context and circumstances surrounding their decisions. Let us examine briefly the arguments on both sides of the central proposition, namely that changing the rules changes the game.

Institutional Arrangements

Arguments that the rules changes matter. The numerous critics of the new nomination process have attributed a great variety of consequences to the post-1968 reforms. The delegate selection and financial reforms have democratized the process, it is argued; that is, they have caused the nomination campaign to be conducted in public and to the public. Contenders today seek delegate support at the grass roots level by obtaining mass popular support in primaries and caucuses. They also seek resources, especially money, through a mass public campaign effort, largely because of the legal limits on the size of allowable contributions from groups and individuals and the availability of federal matching funds for small, individual contributions. Of course, it is the need for popular support in primaries and caucuses that creates the need for such large amounts of money and other resources.

Two important consequences flow from these rules. First, there is much less need for, indeed much less value attached to, the building of a coalition of important party leaders and groups. Fragmentation and public competition replace the integrative consequences of party coalition building.[1] Second, the candidates run their public campaigns as individuals. The candidate- or personality-centered campaign differs sharply from the party-centered campaign of years past. Thus, not only could a George McGovern win the Democratic nomination independent of important party figures, but he could do so while pushing them outside national presidential politics, as symbolized by the unseating of Mayor Richard Daley and his Illinois delegation at the 1972 convention.

In more general historical terms it is clear that the structure of nomination campaigns has changed greatly. The earliest period we examine (1876–92) is marked by a strong party system in which overt campaigning by candidates was simply not done. Beginning in 1912 the presidential primary had spread sufficiently to make plausible a strategy of contesting the nomination by "going over the heads of the party to the people." Such a strategy did not work until the post–World War II period, when the public campaigns of John Kennedy in 1960 (in the Wisconsin and West Virginia primaries) and Barry Goldwater in 1964 (through his use of dedicated conservative followers to flood caucuses and win at least one contested primary) actually were necessary ingredients to their victories. And, of course, the public campaigns of Eugene McCarthy and Robert Kennedy in 1968 essentially unseated an incumbent president, made Hubert Humphrey's nomination victory ring hollow in the fall, and led directly to some of the new reforms.

These differences in institutional arrangements clearly affected the kinds of strategies employed by candidates, even those who followed the "old" coalition-building approach. At the very least, old-style candidates often had to fend off public campaigns, as did William Howard Taft in the face of Theodore Roosevelt's challenge in 1912. If strategies change, it is but a short logical step to the conclusion that some people are more effective users of the new strategies than others.

Arguments that the rules do not matter greatly. Two fundamental aspects of presidential nominations have not changed. First, the nominee must stand for election in the fall under rules that, for the most part, have been historically constant. Second, the nominee still must secure the support of a winning coalition of delegates at the nominating convention. Recent reforms have changed only the means of securing delegate support; and even now candidates must convince decisionmakers that, among other things, they are electable. Moreover, except for the 1980 (and possibly 1976) Democratic convention, most delegates have been free, legally, to support whomever they preferred. Thus, this counter argument goes, although the rules changes have affected the strategies of candidates in securing delegate support, the crucial delegate incentives to back someone who is consistent with party principle and can be a winner in the fall have not altered greatly. This suggests that we look briefly at the incentive structure of the nominating process.

The Goals of Actors

The claim that goals have changed. The argument that the incentives of important decisionmakers have fundamentally altered rests on two major claims. The first is that the public is the major audience for candidate appeals today, rather than the party leadership. The second is that this change has altered the incentives of candidates.

It is clear that relatively little decisionmaking about presidential nominations occurs at the convention, whether in smoke-filled rooms or on the convention floor itself. It is hard to imagine William Jennings Bryan's "Cross of Gold" speech securing his nomination today. Indeed, Kennedy's speech at the 1980 Democratic convention appeared to move delegates as much as Bryan's must have, but with no effect on the nomination contest. The majority of delegates run for their seats or are selected for them because they support a particular presidential hopeful. This personal commitment is perhaps as important a binding incentive as any party rule. Thus it is that the public effectively chooses delegates already bound to candidates by principle if not by law.

If the public has replaced party chieftains in influencing delegates' votes at the convention, then we must look at the incentives of the public. It seems reasonable to argue that the public votes in primaries on much the same basis as in general elections. Empirical efforts have emphasized two points. First, the same rule, the Kelly-Mirer "simple act of voting" (i.e., adding up the "plusses" and "minuses" for each candidate and supporting the candidate with the highest "score"), seems to apply as well in primaries as in the general election.[2] If anything, the second point, that the public has less information about candidates in the nomination campaign than in the general election campaign, suggests that their decisions are based even more on their perceptions of the candidates' personal qualities. Scott Keeter and Cliff Zukin, in the most extensive work on primary voting, suggest so by their very title, *Uninformed Choice*.[3] Clearly, party allegiance is irrelevant to structuring voter choice in primaries. Issue voting seems uncommon, perhaps because each party's candidates differ less from each other than do the typical Democrat and Republican in the fall. What is left to voters is their perceptions of the candidates' personalities and leadership capabilities, qualities of individuals rather than partisans.[4] Those who attend caucuses appear to be motivated as much by the goal of picking an attractive leader who can win in the fall as by the typical party leader's concerns with party in its many meanings.[5]

Clearly, candidates' strategic incentives must change in response to the changed system. In particular, candidates must portray themselves as the leaders the public seems to want, rather than as the embodiment of their party and its principles. If the public is disenchanted with the Washington or the party establishment (or both) the candidate who runs against the establishment has an advantage. It is again but a short step to say that a Jimmy Carter could pursue that strategy far more effectively in 1976 than, say, Henry Jackson could.

The counterargument. The counterargument rests on two points. The first is that the need to win the fall election shapes the incentive of party leaders. Thus, whatever else they may want, wise and successful party leaders know that it makes no sense to back a loser. Thus, the public always has determined who the parties nominate. A prime example is Kennedy in 1960. Doubts about electability were the primary obstacle in Kennedy's path. His strategy was to convince party leaders that he was electable, and what better way to do so than to win public support in primaries?

The second point is that the goal of backing winners is not unique to party bosses, but may be found in the public today. At one level, how else can we explain "momentum" in primary campaigns?[6] At another level, one of the best recent studies of caucus and state convention participants has emphasized how important electability appears to them.[7]

Finally, the dominant incentive of candidates is to win nomination and that means, at base, defeating whoever else runs. The strategy for doing so, therefore, may depend more upon who provides the opposition and what qualities, background, skills, and potential they bring to the campaign.

A Note on the Context

No one disagrees that the nature of American politics generally, presidential power, and nomination politics have changed fundamentally in the last one hundred years. We take it for granted, for example, that candidates campaign overtly for nomination. Overt campaigning in the 1880s, however, was regarded as an unseemly display of naked ambition that, by itself, would greatly diminish a contender's hopes. Today, the technology of television, computerization, and the like have altered the levers a candidate can use to appeal for support. This suggests a different interpretation of party reform efforts.

The larger social and political institutions and technologies may be seen as defining a macrosystem within which individual decision-making must operate. As this macrosystem changes, a new equilibrium of individual behavior must be struck. Particular institutions, therefore, have to be refined—even revolutionized—to take the larger realities into account. Thus, for example, the increased importance of the presidency in international and national affairs inevitably heightens public concern about who will be president. Thus, too, the technology of media and the like have opened new strategic opportunities to presidential hopefuls.

In this view party reforms may be seen not as independent variables, but as variables determined in large part by larger sociopolitical and technological changes. For instance, the rise of television, mass mailing, fund-raising capabilities, and public opinion polling may be seen as having defined a context in which candidates can appeal to the public through the mass media more effectively than by trying to run a typical, labor-intensive, highly organized effort with the support of local and state political party organizations. The decline of political parties as effective electoral institutions may be understood, in this sense, as the consequence of these larger social and technological changes. Reform efforts, then, are best regarded as attempts to align political parties to current political realities, not just typical power struggles. Without some change, this argument goes, the political party would be an even less effective vehicle for shaping political campaigns. Parties, in short, may have had to reform to survive in a competitive—and new—political environment.

The Evidence of Others

Most studies of candidates or prospective candidates look at two types of characteristics: their personal and political backgrounds.

Personal Background

The social "constraints" in the nominating process are fairly rigid and hard to change.[8] These include such background or ascriptive characteristics as race, sex, and religion. Over time, of course, these and other constraints change, either with great difficulty (as with religion, and presumably sex and race) or slowly and apparently so uncontroversially as to be unnoticed (such as urban residency and divorce).

Paul David, Ralph Goldman, and Richard Bain examined several social characteristics of nominees and "other contenders" from 1832 to 1956, including geography, age, education, and occupation.[9] Geography is a particularly political phenomenon. They note that "presidential nominations have been increasingly concentrated in a small number of states," especially New York, but that this trend might change, since "more states are becoming pivotal."[10] Thus their view is one in which party decisionmakers choose nominees with a carefully calculating eye to the fall.

They found presidential nominees to be typically between fifty and fifty-four years old, about five years younger than other contenders. This they described as a function of career pattern, anticipating the arguments soon to be made by Joseph Schlesinger about ambition and the political opportunity structure.[11] They (like all others) found education to be relatively high and comparable to the levels of the average senator or governor. Law was the main occupation outside of politics. Other professions from which candidates emerge are generally just that—professional occupations, which provide a rather high social and economic status and serve as the base for entry into politics. In effect, then, presidential candidates and even nominees are about like other high officeholders or serious contenders for high office.

Political Background

Much more research has been done on the nature of the political experience that potential candidates bring to their presidential campaigns. There is, in fact, broad consensus about how to understand that experience. Almost invariably it is based on the application of Schlesinger's theory of ambition and opportunity structure.[12] The evolution of this structure is also well chronicled.[13] Two points are especially notable.

First, as Schlesinger argues, "ambition lies at the heart of politics."[14] Still there are many kinds of, or goals behind, ambition. Schlesinger means primarily ambition for office for its own sake, in particular, ambition for office as a career. Thus he and those who follow him are led naturally to look at career patterns, the "opportunity structure" that describes those patterns, and factors that make it more or less likely that politicians will run for an office.[15] To be sure, this is a useful approach only when the offices studied are career offices rather than part-time avocations, such as at the beginning of the nineteenth century. The approach also would fare less well if there were much "lateral entry" from outside politics, as when Ronald Reagan ran for governor. Yet, as will be seen, there is evidence of at least a truncation of the opportunity structure for presidential candidates.

The second point about Schlesinger's theory is the changing of the opportunity structure over time. As is well chronicled by now, the vice presidency has become more of a stepping stone to presidential nominations, while the cabinet and the House of Representatives have become less important. Another alteration has been the rise of the Senate relative to the governor's office as a source of candidates, although our evidence suggests that the extent of this change is somewhat exaggerated.[16]

Presidential candidates, then, are vice presidents, senators, or governors. The rest of the opportunity structure consists of how one rises to one of these "manifest offices." The "base office" (or first office held as one begins a political career) is either the state legislature or a judicial office like state's attorney. From either base office, one might run directly for governor, or make intermediate stops at the state senate, statewide elective office, or the House. To get to the Senate, one generally runs from the state legislature to the House, then to the Senate (or possibly to governor, then senator). Such longish career patterns seem less common today. There also has been some speculation about the advantages of being "gainfully unemployed" in the new nomination system, in order to free time for constant campaigning.[17]

In sum, what we know about the characteristics of candidates is that the "typical" candidate (especially nominee) comes from the demographic "mainstream" and has demonstrated political career ambitions by climbing to the approximate penultimate step on the opportunity structure.

Prominence

James Beniger points out that, since 1936, standing high in the Gallup poll has been a virtual guarantor of nomination.[18] From 1936 on, James Davis calculates that 61 percent of nominees ranked first in the very first Gallup poll of the campaign, while all nominees but Adlai Stevenson in 1952 were first in the final Gallup poll.[19] Donald Collat and colleagues use candidate standings among delegates during the campaign as another device to predict the eventual nominee.[20] These "predictions" share the belief that "prominence" is a crucial qualification for presidential nomination.[21] One would anticipate that this relationship would be true generally, since prominence gives any nominee an advantage in the general election, but it would be more true, if anything, now that the primary campaign has become so important. However, one also can use the primary campaign to develop that prominence, as did McGovern and Carter.

Limitations

The systematic study of candidates for the presidential nomination has yielded relatively few insights into the kinds of candidates nominated, at least in the sense that someone in the public would anticipate. That is, the public's expectation would be that the answer to the question "Does the method of nomination affect the kinds of candidates who run for and win presidential nomination?" would involve conclusions about leadership qualities, competency, and possibly policy or ideological beliefs. The problem, of course, is that there is too little data about presidential candidates to permit personality profiles of this kind.

Nominations Systems

To study the effects of rules changes, we must look at differing sets of rules. Here, four historical periods are defined on the grounds that they were characterized by a particular type of nomination structure, were of approximately equal duration, and included a roughly equal number of candidacies. Finally, the periods were chosen so as not to cut across the dates usually taken as marking critical or realigning elections.

"Legal" Periods

1972–84. The current nomination system begins in 1972, with the new rules of Democratic nominations established by the McGovern-Fraser Commission and the first federal financing rules.

1952–68. The first comparison period is the one immediately before. We begin with 1952 because it makes a cleaner break with the past than, say, 1948, particularly in terms of candidates. Only Robert Taft and, for other reasons, Richard Russell, predated 1952 as significant national political figures. Thus, for the most part, candidates in this period were products of postwar politics. This period also is one in which primaries are of secondary importance. Only Estes Kefauver in 1952 and possibly Nelson Rockefeller in 1964 could be said to have "gone the primary route" in a serious way until the climactic 1968 campaign. That Kennedy, Humphrey, and possibly Rockefeller in 1960 and Goldwater in 1964 did campaign in primaries before 1968 is rather different than "going the primary route."[22]

For them, primary campaigns would be only one part of a successful candidacy. This period and the most recent one also span the time of television's coverage of nominations.[23]

1912–32. The election of 1912 marks the first time that presidential primaries existed in any number and were used by candidates (in this case, Theodore Roosevelt and Robert LaFollette). The period ends in 1932 because of the New Deal realignment, as well as the demise of competitive nominations and the two-thirds rule for nomination in the Democratic party.

1876–96. The final period lasts from the end of Reconstruction to the 1896 realignment. It is typical of the nineteenth-century era of strong parties. We start with 1876 rather than earlier because by then the two parties were competitive, the full nation was involved, and the period, like the others, spans about twenty years and attracted about forty candidates.

Other Divisions

The four periods can be grouped for analysis in different ways. Most important, of course, are the differing types of nomination procedures. But the first two and last two periods also neatly divide the era of the Depression, television, and high-tech campaigning from the era that preceded these changes. The presidency and national government also have been much more important since 1952 than before 1932. Or, we can think of the first and third periods as ones in which party organization was relatively stronger and the voice of the people comparatively weaker than in the second and fourth periods, in which the primary had an invigorating effect on many campaigns. In short, the various combinations of periods provide rather different perspectives on the nomination system.

The Data Set

Defining the Candidates

The data set consists of candidates for major party nomination from all four periods (see appendix). The definition of who was a candidate was generous, but the procedures employed here were more judgmental than most. Other scholars typically use a rule, such as "received at least x percent of the votes in some presidential ballot at a convention." But any single rule becomes problematic because of the differing nomination systems. Important contenders now may receive no votes at the convention because of their earlier withdrawal from the race. And candidates who do receive votes, especially at more recent conventions, may be rather unimportant, such as a favorite son who did not intend to become a nominee.[24] The list used here comes from reading descriptions of the conventions and campaigns and from checking the convention and primary return records.[25]

Candidates Who Run More than Once

Before turning to the independent variables, there remains the question of how to count people who ran for more than one nomination. The standard rule that others have used is to count each person only once. There are some problems with this decision. First, some candidates transcend periods. This is a particularly serious problem for the most important period division, 1968 to 1972, because candidates such as Humphrey, Reagan, and Nixon are truly important figures in both periods. Second, there are only slight differences in results whether one uses a "persons" data set or a "candidacies" data set. Finally, the candidacies approach, which we adopt in this chapter, permits the study of multiple candidacies per se. This count yielded 155 candidacies over the four nomination periods investigated.

Independent Variables

The independent variables fall into the two usual sets: nonpolitical and political backgrounds. A codebook and data set may be obtained from the author.

Private background. The variables for private background are the standard "facts" on one's life that can be gathered systematically. These include state, age, education, family background, and private career. There were three variables pertaining to the private career. The first was whether the career figured significantly in the individual's biography.[26] The second was whether that career was pursued during the five years before the presidential campaign. The third was the most significant occupation in private life, which may or not have been the most prestigious position ever held. Family background was a judgmentally determined three part ranking of relatively poor, middle class (generously defined), and relatively wealthy, whose purpose was to get at the extremes. Was there a period in which larger proportions of poor or wealthy candidates were common?

Political background. A number of different concerns governed our effort to measure political background. One was to get as full a history of major offices held as possible. For ten offices (all national offices, governor, senator, representative, and judge), the following coding scheme was employed: a zero indicated that the candidate, to that point, had never held that office, a "1" indicated it was the most recently held office, a "2" the second most recently held, etc. A few other offices also were recorded in a simple "yes" or "no" format. The most current office held was recorded more carefully, especially in terms of those not in office at the time of the campaign. Here, the question was the circumstances of leaving. Did they, like Carter, leave the governorship because of constitutional requirements or, like Reagan, "retire" in "favorable" circumstances because of a two-term tradition? Or were they defeated, forced to resign, etc.? There were very few difficult decisions here. Formal electoral defeats for "important" offices were recorded, including whether the candidate later won some subsequent election. Each candidate's age at the time of winning first elective office and the length of time served in "top" offices were gathered. Information about their success in the current campaign was gathered, along with some information about future campaigns.

Finally, some political party information was collected. Did the candidate hold a formal party leadership position such as state or national chair? We also tried to infer from biographical sketches and other sources whether the individual was an important "figure" in state or national party politics, even if holding no formal position. This was a much more common occurrence than holding a titled position. The aggregate figures make sense, but such decisions remain judgmental. Finally, we recorded whether the candidates were ever members of another major party or a minor party prior to the current campaign (by "members" the individual had to have engaged in some observable activity in that party). For the period 1876–96, this meant identifying a number of Whigs turned Republicans.

Data Analysis

Overview

Here a brief description of the data is presented for all four periods. The basic picture is not, of course, much different from that in the data analyzed by others.[27] Unless otherwise noted, the averages reported are medians because of skewed distributions on some variables.

Personal background. The average candidate is fifty-six years old. About three in ten graduated from college, another half either went to graduate school or read the law. Most (80 percent) had another career beside politics, and a third had one in the five years preceding candidacy. Over half were lawyers, about one in seven were involved in a large business. About 16 percent were from a (subjectively estimated) "poor" family, 19 percent from a "rich" family.

Office experience. As table 7.1 shows, around a fourth of all candidacies were by individuals who held no office when they sought the presidency, but only a few had never held political office. Of those not in office when they ran, three-quarters had left office under favorable circumstances. About one-third had lost an election at some point, but most had won again since then.

The typical (whether mean, median, or mode) candidate held two offices prior to his candidacy. He was elected to his first one in his mid-thirties and, if in national office, served eleven and a half years. If we include governors, the average service in office was only nine and a half years.

Many had served at some point in the Senate or governor's office (43 percent each) and nearly as many (37 percent) in the House. Equal proportions were currently governors and senators before running. However, 28 percent of the 155 candidacies were by individuals who were in the House, then in some subsequent office before running for president. This figure is nearly three times the number who ran for president directly from the House.

Nearly a quarter of the candidates had been a state representative at some time in their career, nearly always early in a long career. The median state representative held three further offices before running for president. Thirteen percent of the candidates had been cabinet members (usually at the time they ran), 12 percent had been state

Table 7.1   Office Held at Candidacy and Current or Immediate Past Office of All Presidential Candidates.

	Currently held office (percent)	Current or most recent office (percent)
President	8.4	10.3
Vice President	1.3	3.2
Senator	30.3	33.5
Representative	7.7	9.0
Governor	20.6	29.0
Cabinet	3.9	7.1
Other	1.9	5.2
None	25.8	2.6

$(N = 155)$

senators, another 11 percent had held some statewide office other than governor, while only a trace ever were judges or mayors. (Twelve percent had held some other elective post than these.) By inference, state representative is a much more prominent "base office" than is state's attorney and other state and local offices. This makes the presidency more similar to the Senate, in which state representative is the dominant base office, than to the governor's office, whose base includes other offices.

Most presidential candidates (66 percent) were running for the first time, although 23 percent were running for the second time. Almost as many former vice presidential nominees (13 percent) as former presidential nominees (15 percent) were presidential candidates. Of the 35 percent who ran at least a second time for nomination, a surprisingly high 44 percent were successful.

Party experience. About a quarter of the candidates held a formal position of leadership in their political party, such as state or national chair. An additional third were figures of some note in party circles. About 13 percent had been associated with some other political party prior to their presidential nomination bid, usually a major party (especially the Whig party).

Summary. As noted earlier, these data shed little new light on the nature of presidential candidacies. Possibly the most surprising finding is that most presidential candidates held three or fewer prior offices. Other than that, the typical presidential candidate is as described elsewhere: a mainstream, well-educated man from a middle-class background who held a high-status position in private life, was well into middle age, had about a decade of political experience, and occupied a major elective office when running for presidential nomination, usually one with a strong electoral base.[28] Presidential candidates were involved in partisan politics, often heavily, but were not likely to be formal party leaders. In short, presidential candidates have had presidential "vitaes" or "credentials."

"Serious" candidates. One could object that, as plausible as the above description may be, these credentials are understated. Many more candidates run for nomination than have reasonable chances to win. Perhaps those whose candidacies appear serious possess different (and presumably even stronger) vitaes.

"Serious" is defined post hoc and differently for the four periods, in order to reflect the differing political realities of each period. For 1876–96, a candidate was considered serious if he got more than 20 percent of the vote (the median highest vote received by candidates in this period) on some national convention ballot. In the next period, 1912–32, a candidate is serious if he got at least 17 percent of a roll call (again the median), if he won at least 14 percent of the votes cast in all primaries, or if he won at least two primaries (again, the median for each of these three measures). The comparable three medians for 1952–68 are 17, 2, and 11 and for 1972–80 are 2, 1, and 12. In the first period, 20 of 42 candidacies were judged serious, as were 30 of 40 in the second period, 16 of 32 in the third, and 25 of 41 in the fourth.

What is this more serious group of candidates like? They are virtually the same as the rest. The only differences of any note (and these illustrate how very similar serious candidates are to the rest) are the following: 5 percent more are lawyers, fewer come from poor backgrounds, they are more likely to have multiple candidacies (44 percent to 35 percent), and are about ten percentage points more successful in those future bids (55 percent win compared to 45 percent). (These latter figures hold because 18 percent are incumbent presidents, compared to 11 percent of all the candidacies.) In short, there is very little difference between the more successful and the less successful candidates.

*Did Different Sorts of Candidates Run
in the Different Periods?*

Does the distribution of personal and political characteristics vary
from period to period?

Personal background. No systematic change in the age of candidates occurs over time. Whether serious or not, candidates were
slightly older during the two periods when primaries were most
important (fifty-seven for serious candidates in 1912–32 and 1972–84,
compared to fifty-four and fifty-five for the first and third periods,
respectively). Education levels gradually increased, undoubtedly in
synchrony with, but less extensively than, the general public. The
incidence of candidates from a wealthy background is higher in
nonprimary periods (21 percent and 31 percent for 1876–96 and
1952–68, respectively, compared to 10 percent for 1912–32 and 15
percent for 1972–84). There is a gradual increase in the proportion of
candidates who had no private career but politics, one that is sharper
but more erratic among serious candidates (5 percent to 20 percent
to 31 percent to 24 percent) across the four periods. What may be a
more substantial sign of the growing demands of politics as a career
is the decline in the proportion of candidates who pursued a nonpolitical career not long before a presidential bid. Until 1972 about 35
percent did so within five years of a campaign. Only 24 percent of all
candidates and 20 percent of serious ones have done so since 1972.
Although the percent of candidates currently holding office is lowest
for the most recent period for all candidates, it is highest for serious
candidates. Variation by period, however, is still slight. There has
been a slight broadening of private career background recently to
include educators and others, but the law dominates in all periods.

The most interesting point about state of residence is the gradual
broadening of the base of presidential candidates. Overall, candidates
emerged from thirty-five different states. But before this distribution
can be broken into periods, two factors must be considered: the
differing number of candidacies in each period and the differing number of states. To account for variations, a measure of "geographic
dispersion" was created. This measure contains three elements: the
number of distinct states from which candidates came in a period,
the number of candidacies in a period, and the number of states.
Since the number of states varied within some periods, the number of
states casting electoral votes in the election held at the midpoint of

each period was used. The geographic dispersion of candidacies is the ratio of the number of states that produced candidacies to the number of candidacies times fifty-one divided by the total number of states. So, for example, if all forty-one candidates in the last period had come from distinct states, geographic dispersion would be one (it could approach, but never quite be, zero). The index has increased from .42 in 1876–96 to .48 in 1912–32, then .48 again in 1952–68, and .60 in the last period, 1972–84. What is most interesting is the relatively high concentration of forty-two candidacies from thirteen (of thirty-eight) states in the first period (with Ohio, New York, and Indiana accounting for exactly half of the candidacies) to the forty-one candidacies from twenty-four separate states in the latest period (with only California supplying many candidacies at all). What explains this development? A plausible answer is that candidates run the campaign now, and the candidates' campaigns are national appeals. In the past, state and local party organizations were more important, and therefore the campaign was a coalition building effort, often arranged geographically.

Conclusion.

1. For the most part, there has been no real change in the personal backgrounds of presidential candidates.
2. What changes there have been generally reflect societal changes.
3. There is a hint of the growing importance of choosing politics as a career early in life and sticking with it, but just a hint. If true, this reflects the growing specialization of life generally and the growing importance of government in daily life.
4. Fewer candidates from wealthy families run in the periods in which the primaries are important, but whether this is electoral screening, self selection, or coincidence is unclear. A similar conclusion can be reached about the apparent geographic broadening of candidacies.

Political party career. There is a notable change in the importance of party in the presidential candidate's career. Figure 7.1 presents the relevant data. What is clear is that the change is between the first two periods and the second two periods. Candidates, serious or otherwise, have not been nearly as likely to be involved in party politics since World War II as they were before the New Deal. There is an increase in the most recent period in the incidence of candidate involvement in some other party (17 percent) that makes it comparable to the first period. Whether this is significant is unclear. Reagan is considered a "switcher" and his multiple candidacies inflate that figure.

Conclusion. (a) A Burnham-style decline of parties trend can be seen among presidential candidates.[29] Thus, for instance, candidates are drawn from a wider geographical base and show less involvement in party affairs. These findings also may reflect the influence of television in the two most recent periods, leading to a greater "personalization" of candidates' campaigns. (b) There is no indication, however, that the increased importance of presidential primaries or financial changes caused this decline, since it first was found in 1952–68. Rather, it was caused by changes either in our political system or in the larger society.

Office backgrounds. Table 7.2 provides three sets of figures on candidates' currently held or immediate past offices. Table 7.2 reports on all candidacies, Table 7.3 on "serious" candidacies, and Table 7.4 shows another scholar's findings for four similar periods for actual nominees.[30] Basically, each formulation tells the same story: the increasing importance of the vice presidency and the Senate and the decreasing importance of the House (around 1900) and the cabinet.

There is one interesting twist. Many suggest that the Senate was not an important source of presidential candidates before the adoption of the Seventeenth Amendment made them be directly elected. Since then, however, the Senate has become a very important source, especially for Democratic candidates. The governorship, conversely, is supposed to be somewhat less important today than it once was. In truth, the story is not so simple. First, as the data show, the governorship is a crucial stepping-stone for candidates, serious candidates, and nominees in periods when primaries are important (1912–32 and 1972–84). Second, although the Senate is more important than ever before, it was always an important source of candidacies and serious candidacies, even before the direct election of senators. Senators also are more likely to be repeating candidates, mainly because of the limited tenure of governors.

Differences also exist between the two parties, with a reversal between 1932 and 1952. Table 7.5 reports the proportion of all candidates of the Democratic and Republican parties who most recently were senators or governors before their campaigns. Overall, each party

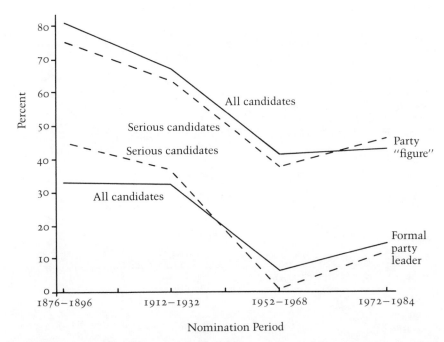

Figure 7.1 Party Role Played by All and by "Serious" Candidates, by Nomination Period.

draws on the two offices about equally, but there are clear partisan changes by period. Before the New Deal, Democrats drew many governors (35 percent and 46 percent in the two periods) but few senators (18 percent and 14 percent, respectively). The Republicans, in contrast, drew many senators but few governors. After World War II the pattern reverses. Half the Democratic candidates are senators, less than one-third governors. Between 1952 and 1968 the Republicans had twice as many governors as senators seeking nomination. Since 1972 there have been too many presidential incumbents seeking the Republican nomination to yield reliable figures about other offices.

Surprisingly, the incidence of "gainfully unemployed" candidates is not unusually high in the 1972–84 period—indeed, of the serious candidates, more are in office in this period than in any other. The conventional perspective reflects the character of the three exceptions (namely Carter, Bush, and Reagan).

Table 7.6 reports the various percentages by period of candidates

Table 7.2   Most Recent Political Office Held, by All Candidates.

Office	Period			
	1876−92	1912−32	1952−68	1972−84
President	11.9%	12.5%	6.3%	9.8%
Vice president	0	0	12.5	2.4
Senator	28.6	25.0	40.6	41.5
Representative	16.7	7.5	0	9.8
Governor	23.8	32.5	34.4	26.8
Cabinet	11.9	12.5	0	2.5
Other	4.8	5.0	3.1	7.3
None	2.4	5.0	3.1	0
Total N	42	40	32	41

Table 7.3   Most Recent Political Office Held, by "Serious" Candidates.

Office	Period			
	1876−92	1912−32	1952−68	1972−84
President	25.0%	16.7%	12.5%	16.0%
Vice president	0	0	12.5	8.0
Senator	25.0	20.0	56.3	36.0
Representative	20.0	3.3	0	8.0
Governor	20.0	36.7	12.5	28.0
Cabinet	5.0	13.3	0	0
Other	0	6.7	0	4.0
None	5.0	3.3	6.3	0
Total N (= 100%)	20	30	16	25

(both all and serious) who did not hold any of the various high offices. There are many bumps and wiggles in the data, but two are potentially significant. First, there is a tendency for serious candidates to come from only the very top offices. Although few candidates of any kind come from an office below governor, this tendency is slightly greater among serious candidates. More significant is the difference between the first two and last two periods in the likelihood of state legislators eventually becoming presidential candidates. About one-third of all candidates in the periods 1876−96 and 1912−32 were former state legislators, compared to one-half as many in 1952−68 and 1972−84. Although the state legislature still may be the "base office" of the political opportunity structure, it appears to be of decreasing importance. Similarly, more than twice as many

Table 7.4   Most Recent Political Office Held, by All Nominees.*

Office	Period			
	1868–1892	1896–1924	1928–1956	1960–80
Vice president becoming president	0%	18.0%	11.0%	50%
Senator	10.0	9.0	0	30
Representative	10.0	9.0	0	0
Governor	40.0	27.0	56.0	20
Federal appointee**	20.0	27.0	11.0	0
Statewide elective	0	9.0	0	0
None	20.0	0	22.0	0
Total N	10	11	9	10

*From James W. Davis, *National Conventions in An Age of Party Reform* (Westport, Conn.: Greenwood Press, 1983), table 9, p. 166, updated by the author to include former vice president Mondale in 1984.
**As nearly as I can ascertain, these are all cabinet officers but Hughes, who was a justice of the U.S. Supreme Court.

Table 7.5   Proportion of Candidates Most Recently Senators or Governors, by Nomination Period.

	Party		Period
	Democrat	Republican	
Senator	17.6%	36.0%	1876–92
Governor	35.3	16.0	
N=	(17)	(25)	
Senator	13.6%	38.9%	1912–32
Governor	45.5	16.7	
N=	(22)	(18)	
Senator	55.6%	21.4%	1952–68
Governor	27.8	42.9	
N=	(18)	(14)	
Senator	50.0%	18.2%	1972–84
Governor	30.0	18.2	
N=	(30)	(11)	
Senator	34.1%	29.6%	Total, All
Governor	33.0	21.1	Four Periods
N=	(91)	(71)	

candidates had held some relatively minor office in the first two periods as in the latter two.

The argument that post-World War II candidates are less likely to have methodically climbed the ladder of offices to the presidency than in earlier periods finds further support in the evidence. Eliminating those who never held elective office, the average (mean) number of offices held by the presidential candidates has declined from 2.8 to 2.4 to 2.0 to 2.1 in the four periods. Of course, this trend cannot be tied to a particular nomination system, but rather to generally declining party vigor or to the growth of national media, much like the decline in party "figures" who run for president.

Contemporary candidates are not less experienced in government than their predecessors. Indeed, the length of service in major offices by candidates is increasing rather than decreasing for candidates. Table 7.8 shows the median years of service first in high national office, then in high national office and as governor for all candidates and serious candidates in the four periods. Again there are bumps and wiggles, but the basic pattern of candidates since World War II holding fewer offices longer than in earlier periods is apparent. Carter, in 1976, is the only nominee far under the period average. Nixon, McGovern, Reagan, and certainly Gerald Ford met or exceeded the average.

Conclusion. By and large, changes in office background and in political and elective experiences cannot be traced explicitly to changes in the nomination rules. Rather, changes in candidacies seem to be brought about by changes in the larger political system. To the extent that nomination systems have any significant effects, they would be traceable to the importance of primaries. (Thus the periods 1876–96 and 1952–68 are more alike, as are 1912–32 and 1972–84.) Notably, serious candidates are much more likely to be (or have been) governor in the primary periods than in the other two periods. Nonetheless, there are some ways, such as the number of prior offices held by candidates, in which the first two periods are more alike and the last two periods more alike.

Campaign experiences. The one (unsurprising) place in which "period effects" are attributable in part to the rules of nomination is in variables related to the current campaign.

First, the candidate in today's system does face a larger field, if contesting in the absence of an incumbent. There was very little

Table 7.6   Percentages of All Presidential Candidates Who Did Not Hold
Other Offices, by Nomination Period.

Office	Period			
	1876−92	1912−32	1952−68	1972−84
Senator	54.8	72.5	43.8	53.7
Representative	50.0	70.0	65.9	65.9
Governor	64.3	47.5	62.5	61.0
Cabinet	83.3	80.0	87.5	97.6
Federal judge	97.6	95.0	100.0	100.0
State judge	97.6	95.0	96.9	95.1
State senator	85.7	87.5	96.9	85.4
State representative	61.9	75.0	90.6	80.5
State-wide office	83.3	87.5	100.0	87.8
Mayor	85.7	97.5	93.8	95.1
Other elected office	85.7	80.0	96.9	92.7

Table 7.7   Percentages of Serious Presidential Candidates Who Did Not
Hold Other Offices, by Nomination Period.

Office	Period			
	1876−92	1912−32	1952−68	1972−84
Senator	65.0	76.7	25.0	52.0
Representative	55.0	73.3	56.3	72.0
Governor	65.0	40.0	87.5	56.0
Cabinet	85.0	80.0	87.5	100.0
Federal judge	100.0	93.3	100.0	100.0
State judge	100.0	93.3	100.0	92.0
State senator	95.0	83.3	93.8	88.0
State representative	70.0	76.7	93.8	80.0
State-wide office	90.0	86.7	100.0	84.0
Mayor	85.0	100.0	93.8	96.0
Other elected office	95.0	83.3	93.8	92.0

change in the average number of candidates seeking nomination
during the first three periods, nor were there party differences. For
the first three periods, the average number of candidates seeking
nomination when an incumbent was not running was 4.4, 3.7, and
3.2 for Republicans; and 3.2, 4.2, and 4.0 for Democrats. In 1980 the

Table 7.8   Median Years Served by Presidential Candidates in High Political Office, by Periods.

Office		Period			
		1876–92	1912–32	1952–68	1972–84
ALL CANDIDATES*					
National office**		11.2	6.0	13.5	14.8
National and gubernatorial		11.5	7.0	10.2	10.6
	N	42	40	32	40
SERIOUS CANDIDATES*					
National office		10.8	5.7	13.6	16.3
National and gubernatorial		8.0	6.8	13.0	14.0
	N	20	30	16	25

*These figures exclude candidates with no years of service.
**"National" offices include president, vice president, Senate, House, cabinet, and Supreme Court.

only nonincumbent nomination contest for Republicans, seven major candidates sought nomination; an average of nine sought nomination in the three Democratic contests.

Second, how contemporary candidates run is quite different. For example, the proportion of twentieth-century candidates who made no primary campaign effort at all was highest (34 percent) in the period 1952–68. The comparable figure for 1912–32 was 25 percent, and for the contemporary period it is essentially zero. The percentage who campaigned in more than a handful of available primaries has increased, from 48 percent in the period 1912–32 and 44 percent in 1952–68, to 61 percent in the contemporary period.

The change from 1876 to 1984 in the typical nominating convention is no less dramatic. The number of convention ballots has dwindled, of course. However, the latest period is the only one in which the primary campaign is a full substitute for the convention. This trend is reflected in the first slow, then substantial, increase in the proportion of candidacies that yielded absolutely no votes at the convention (from 0 percent in 1876–96 to 5.0 percent in 1912–32, and 15.6 percent in 1952–68 to 39.4 percent in 1972–84). The reason, of course, is that candidates who lose in the primaries now withdraw before the convention.

General Conclusions. Three general conclusions seem warranted.

1. With regard to the personal backgrounds and many of the political experiences of presidential candidates, there is almost no significant change over time.
2. Where there are differences in political experience measures, these differences are most pronounced in distinguishing the earlier two periods from the later ones. Such differences must be attributed to causes other than the nomination rules, such as the declining importance of party organizations and the rising importance of media and other modern technologies. These changes reduce the importance of faithful and long service to the party, especially compared to the ability to attract media attention and broad popular support. There are a few differences between the primary periods (1912–32 and 1972–84) and the nonprimary periods, such as the incidence of governors running for president, but these are relatively few and slight. In no case can we find anything that makes the contemporary period unusual or distinctive when it comes to the political backgrounds of presidential candidates.
3. There are, clearly, substantial differences in how candidates run for nomination.

How to interpret these three conclusions? It seems that credentials of background and experience stand almost as necessary conditions for running for president. These conditions transcend nomination systems because, in all periods, the public must be convinced that the party's nominee is a worthy contender for the office. The first step in so convincing the public is to have a presidential "vita." No matter who chooses the nominee, they must be convinced that the candidate has at least a plausible hope of winning the public's support in the fall.

These nearly necessary conditions are not sufficient for a presidential nomination. The sufficient conditions may change from period to period and, therefore, may be affected by the differing rules governing nomination. Because differing rules require differing strategies in different periods, some candidates who meet the necessary conditions of credentials and credibility may have an advantage over others who also satisfy these necessary constraints. The concluding section looks at some of these effects, especially in the contemporary nomination era.

The Effects of Strategic Differences

The evidence indicates that presidential candidates since 1972 differ little from those of earlier eras. Such a conclusion contrasts with many of the criticisms of the current system. Critics claim, in part, that the current system contains biases that produce candidates different from those that would emerge from other nomination processes. It is therefore important to address this issue.

First, we must emphasize that possession of presidential credentials may be necessary for a candidacy to succeed but is a minimal (and insufficient) requirement. Put alternatively, many may possess the necessary experience and background, but only a few actually run or are nominated for president. It may be that the "screen" described in this chapter is a broad one. This point may be reflected in one common criticism of the current system.

This criticism is that the method of nomination does not select great presidential nominees and, perhaps, not even good ones. The first difficulty with this position is that standard lists of the great and the weak presidents include names that are widely distributed across eras. That is, no nominating process generates strong or weak presidents systematically. The second difficulty is that the sets of qualities considered to make good or great presidents are subjective, judgmental, often controversial, and almost always based in part on some qualities that can be judged only in hindsight.[31] Without agreed-upon criteria, no system can be designed to favor those who most nearly qualify, and if presidents can be judged to satisfy the criteria only in hindsight, no system can be designed to do so in advance.

A second (and related) criticism of the current nomination system is that it rewards qualities, skills, and capabilities that may be important for winning elections but may not be very useful for governing once in office. Nelson Polsby, for example, writes of the difference between the old and new nomination systems in terms of coalition building (especially among leaders) and fragmentation.[32] His claim is that older methods of nomination encouraged the candidate to build ties to other leaders in the party. In doing so, the successful candidate would have to develop some of the skills and build some parts of the coalitions needed to enact legislation once in office. The new nomination system encourages candidates to develop personal organizations and to contest against others in the party (hence the fragmentation). It also gives little incentive to the candidate to devote much effort to wooing other leaders. In fact, part of the justification for the Democrats' creation of "superdelegates" for the 1984 nominating convention was to breathe some life into this form of intraparty coalition building.

It seems that the critical concern underlying Polsby's account is not who runs for nomination, but how they run. But this claim, powerful as it is, cannot be that intraparty fragmentation, with consequences for governance, is an inevitable result of the current system. Certainly, Reagan's campaign in 1980 illustrates the lack of inevitability. Nor is it coincidental that the hallmark of Reagan's first-term legislative successes was coalition building in Congress combined with the adroit use of mass media to mobilize popular backing. In other words, successful legislative coalition building may require the kind of public campaigning done in today's nomination system, even if the experience of Carter's administration suggests that building popular support does not, in and of itself, guarantee success at legislative coalition building.

The more general point is that successful presidential governance may best be achieved through a combination of popular mobilization and legislative coalition building. If that is true, then the implications for design of nomination (and election) institutions ought to be based on the search for mechanisms that reward those who are able to do both tasks. Perhaps, for instance, the move to "superdelegates" in the Democratic party was a step in the direction of a system that accentuates the building of both popular support and party leadership support. This is not to advocate any particular method, but to suggest that nomination methods should be designed to advance those qualifications that are thought most important for the president in office rather than the candidate seeking nomination.

Conclusions

In this chapter we have argued two basic points. First, there is a set of nearly necessary conditions concerning personal background and political experience that make a presidential candidate minimally credible to party and public alike. These conditions transcend the four historical eras examined, and thus are not greatly affected by changes in nomination methods. That the conditions are nearly necessary does not mean they are sufficient.

The second conclusion concerns variations in how candidates run for nomination. Here nomination procedures have wrought significant changes in what candidates must do beyond satisfying the minimal conditions. These changes, in turn, have affected the kinds of candidates who benefit from the nomination system. The current need to appeal to the public instead of the party appears to assist candidates who are different from the bulk of their competition, and thus not always at the core of the party's mainstream. The need for public support induces a bias in the system that favors those who can best use the technology of public campaigning and who can invest the most and longest effort in campaigning.

The "problem" with the post-1968 reforms is that they addressed a single set of related problems, how to open up the system to as broad a set of participants—in the public and among presidential aspirants—as possible. The consequence, partly intended and partly unintended, was a rejection of the old coalition-building route and its complete supplanting with a mass, popular campaign. The problem was an overemphasis on one set of skills and strategies. Presidential governance is complex and far from unidimensional. Systems should be designed that reflect, or give incentive to, all aspects of desired behavior. For nomination politics that means a system that maintains the selection of credentialed candidates, that is, those who satisfy minimal demands of qualification; that encourages or assists those skilled in building support in the public; and that encourages or assists candidates who are skilled in the art of persuasion among the other branches of government.

Appendix: Presidential Candidates, by Year of Candidacy

Year	Republican	Democrat
Period One		
1876	James Blaine	Thomas Hendricks
	Benjamin Bristow	Samuel Tilden
	Roscoe Conkling	
	Rutherford B. Hayes	
	Oliver Morton	
1880		
	James Blaine	Thomas Bayard
	James Garfield	Winfield Hancock
	Ulysses S. Grant	Henry Payne
	John Sherman	Samuel Randall

Year	Republican	Democrat
1884		
	Chester A. Arthur	Thomas Bayard
	James Blaine	Grover Cleveland
	George Edmunds	Thomas Hendricks
		Alan Thurman
1888		
	Russel Alger	Grover Cleveland
	William Allison	
	Chauncey Depew	
	Walter Gresham	
	Benjamin Harrison	
	John Sherman	
1892		
	James Blaine	Horace Boies
	Benjamin Harrison	Grover Cleveland
	William McKinley	David Hill
Period Two		
1912		
	Robert LaFollete	Champ Clark
	Theodore Roosevelt	Judson Harmon
	William H. Taft	Oscar Underwood
		Woodrow Wilson
1916		
	Albert Cummins	Woodrow Wilson
	Henry Ford	
	Charles Evans Hughes	
	Elihu Root	
1920		
	Warren G. Harding	James Cox
	Hiram Johnson	Edward Edwards
	Frank Lowden	William McAdoo
	Leonard Wood	A. Mitchell Palmer
		Alfred E. Smith
1924		
	Calvin Coolidge	John Davis
	Hiram Johnson	William McAdoo
		Edwin Meredith
		Samuel Ralston
		Alfred E. Smith
		Oscar Underwood
		Thomas Walsh
1928		
	Herbert Hoover	Alfred E. Smith
	Frank Lowden	

Year	Republican	Democrat
1932		
	Joseph France	John Nance Garner
	Herbert Hoover	William Murray
		Franklin D. Roosevelt
		Alfred E. Smith
Period Three		
1952		
	Dwight D. Eisenhower	Averell Harriman
	Robert Taft	Estes Kefauver
		Adlai Stevenson
1956		
	Dwight D. Eisenhower	Averell Harriman
		Estes Kefauver
		Adlai Stevenson
1960		
	Richard Nixon	Hubert Humphrey
		Lyndon B. Johnson
		John F. Kennedy
		Adlai Stevenson
		Stuart Symington
1964		
	Barry Goldwater	Lyndon B. Johnson
	Henry Cabot Lodge	George Wallace
	Richard Nixon	
	Nelson Rockefeller	
	George Romney	
	William Scranton	
1968		
	Richard Nixon	Hubert Humphrey
	Ronald Reagan	Robert Kennedy
	Nelson Rockefeller	Eugene McCarthy
	George Romney	George McGovern
Period Four		
1972		
	Richard Nixon	Shirley Chisholm
		Hubert Humphrey
		Henry Jackson
		John Lindsay
		George McGovern
		Edmund Muskie
		Terry Sanford
		George Wallace

Year	Republican	Democrat
1976		
	Gerald Ford	Birch Bayh
	Ronald Reagan	Lloyd Bentsen
		Jerry Brown
		Jimmy Carter
		Frank Church
		Fred Harris
		Henry Jackson
		Terry Sanford
		Milton Shapp
		Sargent Shriver
		Morris Udall
		George Wallace
1980		
	John Anderson	Jerry Brown
	Howard Baker	Jimmy Carter
	George Bush	Edward Kennedy
	John Connally	
	Philip Crane	
	Robert Dole	
	Ronald Reagan	
1984		
	Ronald Reagan	Rubin Askew
		Alan Cranston
		John Glenn
		Gary Hart
		Fritz Hollings
		Jesse Jackson
		George McGovern
		Walter Mondale

8 Public Opinion Polling: Command and Control in Presidential Campaigns

JAMES R. BENIGER AND ROBERT J. GIUFFRA, JR.

John F. Kennedy became the first presidential candidate to use polls extensively when, in 1960, he commissioned Louis Harris to examine public opinion in several important primary states. This pioneering effort came a quarter century after George Gallup founded the first continuing scientific polling enterprise for public distribution in the 1936 presidential election. Today, major presidential contenders—including presidents seeking reelection—poll virtually daily throughout the primary and national election campaigns. After Ronald Reagan's first inauguration in January 1981 his pollsters began to question one hundred to two hundred people nightly in an effort to gauge fluctuations in the political preferences of different segments of American society.[1]

Polling has proved increasingly useful to presidential candidates because it helps to reduce the many uncertainties that are inherent in the campaign process. By monitoring the concerns of different blocs of voters, for example, polling can be used to predict which appeals will be most effective and efficient, thereby minimizing diffuse, overlapping, and even counterproductive campaign efforts. As a candidate's uncertainty decreases, his command and control of a campaign can be tightened. In the words of pollster Richard Wirthlin, polling is "the science of ABC—almost being certain."[2]

This chapter reviews the developing use of public opinion polling for the command and control of presidential nomination and election campaigns. Applications of polling to reduce uncertainty in decisionmaking are examined at nine major stages in the campaign process. In roughly chronological order, these campaign stages are (1) deciding to run; (2) raising funds, hiring advisers, and gaining elite support; (3) improving name recognition and image; (4) determining voter concerns; (5) targeting opposition weaknesses; (6) developing media advertising; (7) allocating resources; (8) swaying and holding delegates and selecting a running mate; and (9) tracking the election campaign day by day.

We first review the development of public opinion polling in the command and control of presidential campaigns since the 1930s, then examine how polling is used in each of the nine stages of the campaign. The chapter concludes with a brief consideration of how a candidate's successful use of polling to control a campaign increasingly has become a president's use of polls to control his administration and public presentation.

Polling in the Control of Presidential Campaigns

After George Gallup helped to secure the reputation of scientific polling techniques—at the expense of the *Literary Digest* straw poll—in the 1936 presidential campaign, the newly reelected Franklin D. Roosevelt began to commission surveys to reveal public attitudes about pressing national problems. With the growing likelihood of war in Europe in the late 1930s, Professor Hadley Cantril of Princeton University's psychology department conducted polls that pinpointed housing shortages, determined what goods consumers most needed, and gauged opinion about entering the hostilities. Once the United States had entered World War II, Cantril polled members of the armed forces about everything from their uniforms and equipment, food and entertainment, to their opinions of military discipline and leadership.[3]

In the first postwar presidential race, in 1948, advisers to both major party nominees—President Harry S. Truman and New York governor Thomas E. Dewey—relied upon the public opinion polls of Gallup and others to get a sense of where the race stood. They limited their analyses, however, to basic information regarding the candidates' popularity.[4] Because less than 3 percent of all Americans owned a television set in 1948, President Truman broadcast only a single campaign advertisement.[5]

Four years later, polls became an important adjunct to television advertising. With television sets in 45 percent of the nation's households by 1952, the new medium impressed advisers to General Dwight Eisenhower as a potential means to win votes. In order to counter the general's weak performances on the stump and at press conferences, the Eisenhower campaign hired the advertising agency of Batten, Barton, Durstine and Osborn (BBD&O) to produce forty-nine television and twenty-nine radio spots.[6] Despite George Gallup's prominent setback in the previous election (his poll predicted a Dewey victory), he became the Eisenhower campaign's adviser on polling. Unlike later presidential pollsters, however, Gallup did not conduct surveys for the sole use of the Eisenhower campaign but merely analyzed his national surveys and submitted the results to BBD&O.

Since 1952, candidates have continued to shift away from party-centered campaigns and have tried to mobilize existing blocs of voters —blocs based on socioeconomic factors like age or ethnicity, or on emotionally charged issues like abortion or gun control. By the late 1950s, polling had become an important tool for political candidates, whether for the presidency or for lesser political offices. In 1962, two-thirds of the Senate candidates, three-quarters of the gubernatorial candidates, and one-tenth of the candidates for the House used survey research in their campaigns.[7] Running for reelection to the Senate in 1958, for example, John Kennedy hired Lou Harris to sample opinion in several primary states.[8] According to Theodore White, by November 1960, when Kennedy won the White House, Harris "had polled more people across the country than had ever been done by any other political analyst in American history."[9]

During the 1964 presidential campaign, both President Lyndon B. Johnson and his Republican challenger, Arizona Senator Barry Goldwater, made extensive use of polls. Well before the official start of the campaign, however, both public and private polls indicated that Goldwater had little chance against the then popular president. Thanks to the new use of "image polling"—including semantic differential scales and related perceptual testing—by political pollsters, the reasons for Johnson's wide lead were easy to pinpoint. The most important negative quality attributed to Goldwater seemed to be the widespread perception that he acted "without thinking," a quality the Johnson campaign tried to reinforce in voters' minds by using television commercials that raised the possibility of nuclear war.[10]

In the 1968 campaign Vice President Hubert H. Humphrey hired five separate companies to conduct polls in eighteen states, using the information to determine which states to concentrate on and which groups of voters to target in each.[11] Richard Nixon relied heavily upon the Opinion Research Corporation (ORC), which conducted polls that were used to develop themes, allocate resources, and track the campaign from day to day. The development of Nixon's sophisticated television commercials, as chronicled in *The Selling of the President 1968*,[12] depended on polling for information about the candidate's strengths and weaknesses with voters. For example, the decision to stress Nixon's foreign policy experience came after polls indicated that voters viewed this as an important quality.[13]

In 1972 the poor financial condition of George McGovern's presidential campaign helped to launch the career of pollster Patrick Caddell. With the McGovern campaign treasury lacking the funds to hire a prominent polling firm, campaign manager Gary Hart discovered the talented but inexpensive Caddell, then a senior at Harvard.[14] Based on polls he had taken during the New Hampshire primary campaign, Caddell recommended that McGovern concentrate on the university towns of Hanover and Durham, on the southeastern region (which contained a large number of young families and Boston commuters), and on blue-collar workers.[15] Caddell's strategy seemed to work: McGovern garnered 37.6 percent of the vote, a surprisingly strong second-place finish behind frontrunner Edmund Muskie's 47.8 percent. Guided by Caddell's polls, McGovern eventually beat out the Maine senator and former vice president Humphrey for the Democratic nomination.

When Jimmy Carter decided to seek the Democratic nomination in 1976, he enlisted the aid of the now experienced Caddell. As in the McGovern campaign, Caddell's influence stemmed from his ability to anticipate events. Although the New Hampshire primary in late February would be of obvious importance to Carter's success, Caddell foresaw that the Florida primary, scheduled two weeks later, might be even more critical because it promised to be the first major confrontation between Carter and George Wallace. Caddell found Carter to be strong in northern Florida and weak in southern Florida; Catholics and blacks in the Miami, Orlando, and Palm Beach areas, he suggested, were the groups most likely to be won over to Carter's camp. As a result, Carter stumped the southern part of Florida for sixteen of the twenty-one days he spent in the state; he spent the other five days in central Florida, and did not visit the northern region of the state. The strategy appears to have been sound: Carter defeated Wallace by three percentage points to become the clear favorite for the Democratic nomination, a position he never relinquished.[16]

Partly because of increasing media attention to polls, the 1980 presidential campaign was a rollercoaster ride from beginning to end. In December 1979, polls indicated that Ronald Reagan was the choice of 50 percent of Iowa Republicans, with the remaining support spread among six other presidential hopefuls. Despite past evidence that opinion in state primary polls can be volatile, Reagan strategists concluded from the poll results that their candidate ought to remain above the fray in Iowa. To the surprise of nearly everyone, George Bush won the state's caucuses. Like McGovern in 1972 and Carter in 1976, Bush was transformed overnight to the frontrunner on the strength of a single reversal of a poll-based prediction.

Initial polls in New Hampshire, the scene of the next contest, showed Reagan and Bush virtually tied. Relying on extensive tracking surveys, Richard Wirthlin, the Reagan pollster, discovered that his candidate had particular strength in southern New Hampshire. Based on this information, the Reagan campaign organized a massive get-out-the-vote operation in the region. This drive, combined with his good showing in a Nashua debate, resulted in a convincing twenty-seven percentage point victory for Reagan (50 to 23) and a lead in delegates that he never lost.

In the general election Carter and Reagan mounted the most extensive polling efforts in the history of presidential campaigning. Both sides conducted numerous national polls as well as polls in strategic states. The number of public polls taken also proved to be a record.[17] Like Caddell for President Carter, pollster Richard Wirthlin had major responsibility for developing Reagan's campaign plan. Completed in June 1980, the Reagan "Black Book"—as it came to be known —set forth a series of conditions on which victory depended: expanding Reagan's Republican base to include enough moderates and independents to offset the Democratic edge in registered voters; projecting the image of Reagan as a strong, decisive leader; avoiding self-inflicted blunders; attacking Carter as an ineffective, error-prone leader; and neutralizing any "October surprise" that Carter might stage by using the power of his office to manipulate the nation's attention.[18]

The 1984 campaign brought a continued increase in the numbers of both public and private polls. New applications of polling also emerged to reduce campaign uncertainties and to increase command and control of the nomination and election process. Computers assumed a new importance in polling, with pollsters adopting the rapidly proliferating microcomputer to collect, process, and analyze complex information about voters. This information was tailored to differences rather than to similarities among individuals. One important new computer-based tool, used in conjunction with polls, was the geodemographic targeting system. With the help of census data and specially programmed voter registration lists, geodemographic targeting enabled presidential candidates to pinpoint crucial groups of swing voters.

As Walter Mondale demonstrated in the 1984 Pennsylvania primary, for example, geodemographic targeting increases the efficiency of a campaign's telephone banks and field organization. "Let's say, just for instance, that we're really strong with Eastern Europeans and we're weak with the Irish," Joe Trippi, Mondale's state coordinator said a week before the Pennsylvania primary. "Then come Election Day, we'll telephone the hell out of everybody who lives in a ward where there are a lot of Eastern Europeans and knock on doors and get them to go vote, and maybe we don't bother with the Irish wards."[19]

The technique of targeting campaign communication, pioneered in Lew Lehrman's unsuccessful campaign for governor of New York in 1982, proved to be an important part of the 1984 general election campaign. Richard Wirthlin used polls to determine which groups of voters supported Lehrman (and two years later Reagan), which opposed him, and which were undecided. Mailings then were targeted to particular groups, especially undecided voters, with messages individually tailored to issues in which they were likely to be interested and to support the candidate's position. Major themes, such as Lehrman's stand on the death penalty, were communicated on television; less universally appealing messages—on opponent Mario Cuomo's support for abortion, for example—were communicated through direct mail to Catholics and other carefully selected groups of likely voters.[20] Reagan's 1984 campaign used similarly segmented communication (discussing, for example, the economy) in television spots; targeted mailings hit issues like school prayer.

Another innovative technique the Republicans used in 1984 was PINS (for Political Information Systems). An updated version of the computer simulations that were used by Wirthlin in the 1980 campaign, PINS allowed campaign managers to test their strategies daily through the analysis of polls, census data, economic forecasts, and the assessment of operatives in the field.[21] "Because of the electoral college system, the campaign for the White House is not one race, but fifty-one distinct campaigns which have their own very special characteristics," Reagan adviser Richard Beal noted. "No single political junkie, no matter how experienced, can keep track of the important factors involved in these fifty-one races." The advantage of PINS, according to Grayling Achia, the information specialist who developed the system, was "to give the top Reagan campaign managers timely access to enormous amounts of relevant information, to streamline information so the top command can use it."[22]

Candidates' Uses of Polls at the Major Stages of a Campaign

Any campaign by a major party nominee for the presidency ordinarily will include at least five different types of polls, some conducted before the candidate even has declared his intention to run. First comes a national benchmark or baseline survey to gain general information about the political mood of the nation and its feelings about the candidate and his opponents, information that can be used to formulate the campaign's most general strategy. Normally a benchmark poll includes at least two thousand respondents who are surveyed in considerable detail. In 1976, for example, Richard Wirthlin's benchmark poll for Ronald Reagan consisted of almost a hundred questions that generated 212 separate bits of information about each respondent.[23]

Next comes one or more follow-up surveys. The purposes of these polls, usually based on five to six hundred interviews, are to question voters in greater depth about concerns that were raised in the benchmark survey and to measure the effectiveness of potential campaign themes. Follow-up surveys often are conducted on a state-by-state basis in order to locate pivotal areas for potential shifts in opinion.

The third type of polling, the panel survey, is similar to the follow-up in that it is used to refine campaign strategy. In contrast to follow-ups, however, panel surveys involve reinterviewing respondents to a previous benchmark or follow-up poll, and are used primarily to analyze opinion shifts within various demographic categories. Such information can prove valuable in determining how to allocate resources or whether new appeals to voters may be needed.

In recent years, the fourth type of poll—the tracking poll—has become increasingly important in presidential campaigns. Once tracking was done only during the final weeks of a campaign, as in John Kennedy's 1960 effort. Today, however, the well-financed presidential candidate's polling will consist of almost continuous national tracking, at least from the time of his announcement through the general election. Tracking also will be done, although for briefer periods, in certain states.

Unlike the first four types of polls, a final type—the focus group survey—is not based on random samples. Focus groups usually consist of twenty or fewer individuals, selected nonrandomly to reflect general demographic characteristics like age, gender, party, economic status, or race. Trained discussion leaders ask participants to talk generally about the campaign. The discussion is monitored by the campaign's pollsters, who hope to identify ways they might change opinions about candidates. "Focus groups are impossible to quantify," Patrick Caddell maintains. "Their advantage is that you get insights that go beyond your numbers. You get a linear thinking process that explores all sorts of unexpected dimensions to the campaign."[24]

In combination, the five types of polls can be used to increase command and control of a presidential campaign at each of its major stages. The remainder of this section examines each of these nine stages in roughly the chronological order that important campaign decisions must be made.

Deciding to Run

The decision to enter a presidential campaign may be difficult. Potential candidates often rely upon "trial-heat" polls, which measure their standing against various other potential candidates, to decide whether to enter a race. In this application, however, polls can prove misleading. The volatility of public opinion early in a race, combined with the growing length of campaigns (the 1984 race began almost two years before the general election), make trial-heat polls unreliable. More often than not, such polls reflect name recognition rather than measure a candidate's potential strength.

Despite this well-known bias of early trial-heat polls toward better-known candidates, such polls have caused several presidential contenders to drop out of a race. Michigan Governor George Romney ended his 1968 campaign after polls showed him well behind Richard Nixon in New Hampshire. Senator Lowell Weicker dropped out of the 1980 campaign on May 17, 1979, more than six months before the first caucus or primary, because a poll showed him running third in his home state of Connecticut.[25] Other would-be candidates have decided not to enter the presidential race because of their poor performance in early trial heats. Dale Bumpers of Arkansas, for example, decided not to seek the White House in 1984 on the basis of trial-heat polls showing him with little chance to defeat Walter Mondale.

When Robert F. Kennedy considered entering the 1968 New Hampshire primary against President Johnson, the senator's poll in that state showed 28 percent support for him and 60 percent for the president, a result that discouraged Kennedy.[26] In early March, after Eugene McCarthy's success in New Hampshire and the Tet Offensive in Vietnam had completely altered the political landscape, a national Harris poll gave Kennedy a twenty percentage point lead (52 to 32) over the President. Although Kennedy's advisers claim that polls did not play a role in his decision to run, favorable results from surveys in the upcoming primary states of California, Nebraska, and Indiana must have at least provided secondary reinforcement.[27]

Several other candidates have overlooked poor standings in the early polls and achieved considerable electoral success. In fact, each presidential election since 1968 has produced at least one candidate who has made an unexpectedly strong showing despite poor or even nonexistent support in early polls: McCarthy in 1968, McGovern in 1972, Carter in 1976, Bush in 1980, Hart in 1984. For such candidates, strong showings in Iowa or New Hampshire, small states where they can build grass roots organizations and meet voters on a personal basis, yield enormous publicity that dramatically increases their standing in the national polls. Earlier trial-heat polls that predicted disaster for such dark horses may not have been incorrect at the time they were taken, but could not measure the future bandwagon effect of an early caucus or primary success.

Eugene McCarthy, for example, the first Democrat to challenge President Johnson for renomination in 1968, lacked enthusiasm for polls, a characteristic that dominated the Minnesota senator's entire campaign. McCarthy decided to enter the New Hampshire primary despite polls indicating that such a hawkish state would be "unwinnable" for a liberal, antiwar activist. "If the decision is of major importance," McCarthy later wrote, "poll taking is a waste of time and money."[28] New Hampshire Senator Tom McIntyre predicted that McCarthy would get less than 10 percent of the vote; in fact he received 42.2 percent, a startling showing that eventually led to Johnson's withdrawal from the race. McCarthy's lack of reliance on polls had helped him to avoid one pitfall: to invest in a poll, receive discouraging results, and therefore decide not to run.

Early polls can also unduly discourage well-known candidates; for example, incumbents whose past policies have not been as popular as their future campaign proposals might become. In the 1980 campaign, President Carter rose from thirty percentage points behind Edward Kennedy in October 1979, according to Gallup, to twenty points ahead of the senator only two months later.[29] This dramatic shift occurred not only because latent doubts about Kennedy's character had been aroused by the increased media attention that followed the announcement of his candidacy, but also because the hostage crisis in Iran rallied national sentiment behind the president.

Raising Funds, Hiring Advisers and Gaining Support

Even though early polls have often proven to be unreliable, fundraisers, campaign staffers, and the press nevertheless continue to use them in deciding whether to commit money, time, or attention to a candidate. At the start of a presidential campaign, the so-called smart money goes to the strongest candidate in the public polls. Experienced campaign consultants and staffers usually follow suit. Soon thereafter the press can be expected to write about the poll leader's "well-oiled" campaign organization. This coverage, in turn, generates still more contributions, more paid and volunteer workers, and — in a snowballing effect — still greater free exposure in the mass media. Party and elected officials also follow the polls and tend to gravitate toward the favored candidate.

Walter Mondale's 1984 campaign provides an excellent example of this phenomenon. During the 1983 preprimary season, Mondale, best known of the declared candidates because of his four years as vice president, proved to be the strong favorite in early trial-heat matchups. While many of the other Democrats had trouble raising money, Mondale enjoyed the financial support of most major fund-raisers. Ohio Senator John Glenn, the second choice in most polls, also had considerable success raising funds, especially from more conservative Democrats. The candidacies of Reubin Askew, Alan Cranston, Gary Hart, Jesse Jackson, and George McGovern, however, were dismissed as long shots by most large contributors.

In addition, the most experienced Democratic consultants and staffers joined the Mondale team. The Hart campaign, for its part, had to recruit mostly untested staff. While Mondale's campaign manager, Robert Beckel, was a veteran of the Carter efforts, Hart's manager, Oliver Henkel, the candidate's law school classmate, was a newcomer to presidential campaigning. As the press reported these developments, most analysts conceded the nomination to Mondale long before the first caucus or primary.

The fascination of the American press with polls has not been lost on professional campaigners. In Alan Cranston's bid for the 1984 Democratic party nomination, for example, he hoped to give credibility to his campaign by good showings in preelection year straw polls at various state Democratic dinners and conventions, then use the resulting publicity to increase his standing in the major public polls. This shift in perceived popularity, Cranston believed, would signal party leaders and contributors that he had elevated himself above the other lesser-known candidates.[30] When he failed to place well in the straw polls, little else remained for Cranston to do but to drop out of the race.

Before public financing guaranteed both the Democratic and Republican nominees equal funds in the general election, public polls also played an important role in determining spending levels during this final stage of the campaign. As Leonard Hall, chairman of the Republican National Committee during the Eisenhower administration, put it: "If no one else, politicians and spenders read polls. The big contributors like to know where their man stands and, just like at the two-dollar window, no one likes to put money on a loser."[31]

One of the many reasons given for Hubert Humphrey's 1968 defeat was that his low standing in postconvention Gallup polls made fund-raising difficult. To escape this self-fulfilling prophecy, the Humphrey campaign used available public and private polls to counter Gallup and show that victory was possible.[32] Not surprisingly, the same Gallup poll results provided a financial magnet for the Nixon campaign. "When the polls go good for one, the cash register really rings," Nixon was quoted as saying in 1968.[33]

The much rarer case—of good poll standing actually hurting fund-raising efforts—did seem to occur in the 1972 Democratic primary campaign. When polls showed Edmund Muskie well ahead in New Hampshire, many contributors withheld funds, sensing that more money would not be needed.[34] If true, this may be the exception that proves the rule: to attract the money of big contributors, the commitment of experienced staffers, the time of local volunteers, and the attention of the mass media, high standing in the early trial-heat polls ordinarily is both necessary and sufficient.

Improving Name Recognition and Image

Although early horse race results must be interpreted with caution, the same polls often provide information on a candidate's "image" —including name recognition and perceived attributes, both positive and negative—that can be crucial for a campaign. According to Louis Harris, "Voters tell polltakers things that not even the candidate's best friend would tell him. The polltaker, if he has the courage and tact, is able to tell the candidate. In the course of our wanderings through the political hinterlands, we have had to tell candidates that they were considered spineless, arrogant, stuffed shirts, loudmouths, cold, poor speakers, or just plain unknown."[35]

Until the advent of television, while radio and print remained the chief means of campaign communication, individual qualities like physical appearance, dress and grooming, and projected charisma did not dominate a candidate's public image. Since the early 1950s, however, this "personality" dimension has become increasingly important in national politics.[36] Today, when voters are asked about a candidate, they rarely list specific attributes, but instead cite general qualities like "tough," "exciting" or "visionary." This shift can—to a large extent—be attributed to television. Each night during a presidential campaign, viewers can see and hear the candidates as they move from one media event to the next. Elections no longer seem to be contests between the two parties so much as between rival candidate images.

Information about a candidate's public image, especially in the early polls, often will shape his campaign communications and determine the public perception of the campaign. In 1952, for example, Dwight Eisenhower's organization sought to capitalize on his favorable image with Democratic voters. According to Gallup's polls for the Republicans, most voters viewed the general as a man with the leadership qualities needed to resolve the war in Korea. Few voters knew much about his Democratic opponent, Adlai Stevenson. Not surprisingly, television commercials for Eisenhower stressed his experience in foreign affairs, never mentioning his Republican affiliation.[37]

Candidate image, as gauged by polls, has played an important role in several other presidential elections. In John Kennedy's 1960 campaign, polls identified a strictly personal quality—the senator's Catholic religious beliefs—as an issue that he would need to address. Barry Goldwater's pollster, Thomas Benham, recognized early in 1964 that the charge of extremism would haunt the Republican campaign: "Probably most damaging to Goldwater was public acceptance of the idea that he was 'trigger happy.' . . . One of the most prominent dimensions of the Goldwater image was 'acts without thinking'. This was most seriously translated—with the help of both his Democratic and Republican opposition—into the notion that he would be likely to involve the country in nuclear war."[38] In 1976, after pollster Robert Teeter discovered that voters regarded President Ford as liberal on social issues, the campaign developed a series of television spots depicting Ford as "a solid guy with a typical family."[39]

Polls also can play the beneficial role of encouraging an otherwise cautious leader to make a seemingly courageous decision. Walter Mondale's selection of Geraldine Ferraro as his vice presidential running mate, for example, was made much easier by poll results indicating widespread approval for a woman on the Democratic ticket. Because presidential candidates usually are well known, however, their images rarely can be credibly changed. "If you read a poll which shows that you do not excite the electorate, you cannot meet that problem by trying to become something you are not," political analyst Jeff Greenfield points out. "Instead, it makes sense to look at the attributes you are admired for, or that can reasonably be attributed to you."[40]

Richard Nixon's 1972 campaign well illustrates this strategy. Polls indicated that voters did not view the president as particularly warm or likable. They did see him as a competent manager, however, engaged in the important business of running the country. Rather than attempt to counterbalance this image, Nixon's campaign advertising merely underscored the already existing perception of him. While opponent George McGovern's television spots showed him with his family or in small groups of young people, Nixon's commercials recounted presidential trips to Beijing and Moscow.[41]

Perhaps more than any other president, Ronald Reagan has relied upon image and symbol to win broad popular support. From trips abroad to appearances with singer Michael Jackson and meetings with Olympic medal winners, every presidential action seemed calculated to generate maximum positive publicity. This strategy of positive image making proved so successful that Reagan was able through most of his presidency to maintain high approval ratings despite the unpopularity of many of his policies.

Determining Voter Concerns

According to E. E. Schattschneider, determining which issues to discuss is the most important decision that a presidential candidate can make because "the definition of the alternatives is the supreme instrument of power."[42] For the most part, polls inform this process by helping to determine which issues to emphasize rather than what particular stands to take.[43] Normally, pollsters ask voters to express their own views on the problems of government and also to reply to specific issue questions. The issue positions of demographic groups are then analyzed with particular attention given to the undecided voters and to those who might cross party lines to vote for the candidate. As Louis Harris maintains, "when the electorate is analyzed by the hard-core vote for each candidate and the switchers for each candidate, then indeed, [the pollster] can see which issues are firming up the solid base of a candidate, which are bringing votes over to him, and which are losing him votes."[44]

Identifying natural issues for a presidential candidate usually proves to be a continuing process. Robert Kennedy, for example, emphasized law and order in the 1968 Indiana primary and did not dwell on Vietnam, by far the most critical issue in his campaign against President Johnson. Frank Mankiewicz, a Kennedy campaign strategist, later denied that the strategic shift in emphasis had resulted from a John Kraft poll indicating that blacks supported Kennedy while blue-collar whites remained undecided.[45] In 1972, the McGovern campaign made a similar, but largely unsuccessful attempt to appear more moderate. The Democratic platform committee, for example, purposely left out planks on homosexual rights, abortion, and school busing in order to broaden McGovern's appeal.[46]

This ability of polls to help target appeals on issues may be best illustrated by Jimmy Carter's 1976 nomination campaign. Largely because of Carter's lack of national exposure at the time, Patrick Caddell managed to design a "something for everyone" appeal that could hold together the diverse Democratic coalition. On the one hand, Carter appealed to party conservatives by stressing his support for a balanced budget and a reduced federal bureaucracy. On the other hand, he promised to press for national health insurance, a position that appealed to liberals.[47] Carter's handling of the abortion issue also illustrates his carefully tailored issue appeals: before fundamentalist and Catholic audiences, Carter proclaimed his personal opposition to abortion; to liberals and moderates, he promised support for the pro-choice legal position.

The 1980 Reagan campaign followed a similar strategy of segmenting voter communication. Groups in the original Reagan base — conservatives, self-labeled Republicans, and those with high incomes — were consistently reminded of his support for tax cuts and reduced government. Prime targets for expanding his base — independents, moderates, young voters, and union members — were told of Reagan's record as governor of California concerning education, the environment, and equal rights for women and minorities.[48]

Polls are not infallible in determining issue strategy, of course. If a candidate discusses only the issues that are identified in polls, he may miss crucial opportunities to convert voters on wholly new issues. During the 1976 Reagan primary effort against Gerald Ford, for example, Richard Wirthlin's polls indicated that only 12 percent of the voters cared much about foreign policy.[49] As a result, Reagan concentrated on the economy during the early primaries. After a series of primary losses, Wirthlin overrode his own poll data to urge that Reagan add more definition to his challenge by speaking out on U.S.-Soviet détente and on the Panama Canal treaty, the issues that most sharply distinguished him from Ford but that did not even show up in response to open-ended poll questions.[50] The strategy seemed to work, as Reagan won the North Carolina, Texas, and Indiana primaries in rapid succession.

Targeting Opposition Weaknesses

The rise of negative advertising, which attacks an opponent's character or record, has been fostered by various polling techniques. By enabling media consultants to identify areas of weakness in another candidate, polls aid in the creation of radio and television spots that are designed to reinforce negative feelings already held by voters.

During the 1964 Republican primary campaign, for example, Nelson Rockefeller drew attention to Barry Goldwater's extremely conservative positions on issues because surveys showed that many Republicans who supported the Arizona senator disagreed with him on a number of things: the Nuclear Test Ban Treaty, voluntary Social Security, and the graduated income tax, among others. The so-called "Daisy Spot" television commercial, created by Tony Schwartz for President Johnson's 1964 reelection campaign against Goldwater, developed out of polls indicating voter concern over what the senator might do as president, especially in the use of nuclear weapons.[51]

Four years later, Hubert Humphrey's polls revealed that many voters questioned the ability of vice presidential candidate Spiro Agnew to serve as president. To take advantage of this doubt, the Humphrey campaign created a commercial showing a "Spiro Agnew for Vice President" sign accompanied by a sound track of laughter.[52]

The 1980 presidential campaign again illustrated the ability of polling to uncover voters' negative feelings about an opponent and then to help structure advertising to fit those preconceptions. Polls by Patrick Caddell found that although voters were dissatisfied with President Carter's performance in office, they nevertheless liked him personally, found him honest, and saw him as a good family man. In contrast, Democrats liked Edward Kennedy's positions on issues and considered him a good leader, but the majority questioned his honesty and personal values—the opposite, in short, of their feelings about the president. Based on this research, the Carter campaign decided to include subtle, almost subliminal messages about Kennedy's widely perceived shortcomings in its advertising, as in this television commercial: "You may not always agree with President Carter. But you'll never wonder whether he's telling the truth. It's hard to think of a more useful quality in a president than telling the simple truth. President Carter—for the truth."[53] Although not negative on face, this message evoked the cloud surrounding Kennedy's own honesty—a good illustration of polling applied to the targeting of an opponent's weaknesses.

Developing Media Advertising

Public opinion polling has played a major role in the formulation of presidential candidates' mass media advertising since 1952, when George Gallup became the Eisenhower campaign adviser on polling. Based on Gallup's analyses, Eisenhower chose four themes for his television commercials: government corruption, inflation, taxes, and the war in Korea. The Eisenhower spots were shown only in certain swing areas of the nation, selected on the basis of poll data and past voting patterns. In forty-nine counties in twelve nonsouthern states, the commercials aired continually during the campaign's final three weeks.[54] How much Gallup and BBD&O contributed to ousting the Democratic party from the White House for the first time in twenty years cannot be known. The close relationship of the advertising agency and the pollster to Eisenhower, however, marked the beginning of a new era in the use of polls and television in presidential campaigns.

The modern use of public opinion polling to develop media campaigns involves four basic steps. First, the candidate needs to raise a great deal of money because radio and television time is expensive; public polls often determine the amount of funding that will be available. Second, the candidate's staff and consultants must develop a media strategy based on polling information, issue research, and the like; this includes identifying which voters might be persuaded to support the candidate and how best to reach them. Third, radio and television spots must be produced; focus-group polls can be used to gauge audience responses to each potential spot. Fourth, a specialized time buyer usually will be hired to select programs that maximize the number of people of specified types to be reached for each dollar spent; poll data can determine which groups to target and where and when to air each type of commercial.

The 1980 Reagan campaign provides an excellent example of the interaction of polling with media advertising. Unlike the other Republican candidates, Reagan had enough money to make extensive media buys. To a large extent, this funding advantage resulted from his already strong support in the public polls, which increased his attractiveness to contributors. Reagan's pollster, Richard Wirthlin, developed major themes and identified potentially favorable voter groups for the campaign's media strategists to reach.[55] After Peter Dailey, a Reagan media consultant, produced a series of spots, Wirthlin tested each one using focus-group interviews. As a result of Wirthlin's polling, most of Reagan's advertising used the "talking head" format in which the candidate speaks—without embellishment—directly to the television camera. This choice of format resulted from Wirthlin's finding that swing voters considered Reagan's experience as an actor to be detrimental. As Dailey put it,

> We found that if we presented Reagan as anything but a competent former governor offering solutions, we reinforced that level of perception we wanted to avoid—actor. Because our 40-percent base voters knew and loved the governor, they enjoyed stylized associations—the Statue of Liberty, "God Bless America," waving wheat, farmers around a table, the governor choking up while speaking—but for the 15 percent we were targeting, the slightest hint of that kind of production would have been disastrous, invalidating everything we did.[56]

Wirthlin's tracking polls also provided guidance to the campaign's media buyer, especially information on the media viewing habits of undecided voters in strategic states.

Allocating Resources

One of the most important uses of polls is to help determine how to allocate staff positions, money, and the candidate's time. Because these resources often are severely limited in a presidential campaign, their distribution can prove decisive. Louis Harris, a not disinterested expert, estimates that good polling can change an election by up to four percentage points, a potentially crucial edge considering that many races hover near the fifty-fifty mark.[57]

Early in a presidential effort, polls can be used to determine which state primaries and which voter groups within particular states to target for special attention. Following his victory in the Wisconsin primary in 1972, for example, George McGovern needed to decide which of three states—Michigan, Pennsylvania, or Ohio—would be most promising for a maximum campaign effort. In Michigan, Patrick Caddell's surveys showed that busing would hurt McGovern, while Hubert Humphrey enjoyed considerable strength among organized labor in Pennsylvania. Because of the large number of Ohio voters who distrusted politicians and who seemed to be looking for new leadership, Caddell argued for a big effort in that state: "The situation in Ohio is definitely fluid enough to permit a McGovern victory if sufficient time and resources can be devoted to the Ohio campaign."[58] McGovern's near win in Ohio—with 39.4 percent of the vote to Humphrey's 41.4 percent—further increased Caddell's influence in the campaign. According to Theodore White, Caddell "had been so right for so many months in describing the aimlessness and alienation of American voters that, in the shaping of McGovern's strategy, he reached a status just below that of [campaign manager Gary] Hart."[59]

In 1976, as we have seen, Caddell's polling in Florida helped Jimmy Carter to overcome an early George Wallace lead by concentrating the Georgian's efforts in the state's southeastern cities. Similarly, polls helped Robert Kennedy's 1968 campaign by identifying the potential for a victory in Indiana. The same had been true for John Kennedy and West Virginia in 1960.

During the general election campaign, polls help to determine a candidate's most likely supporters by demographic group and state. Normally presidential candidates attempt to identify the states that are most likely to provide them with the 270 electoral votes needed to gain the White House and then devote most of their resources to these states. Jimmy Carter's 1976 victory over President Ford, for example, was won in Southern and major industrial states.[60]

In 1980, Richard Wirthlin's detailed "Black Book" for Ronald Reagan anticipated a difficult, close race in which, the pollster suggested, his candidate could win with "the easiest, least expensive minimum of 270 electoral votes" by concentrating his efforts in twenty-nine states with 320 electoral votes. Wirthlin also identified those groups most likely to vote for Reagan and to have a high turnout rate: "Older voters are almost twice as likely to turn out as are younger voters . . . the highly educated are two to three times more likely to turn out as the poorly educated. . . . 'Born again' Protestants and 'High Church' Protestants are very likely to vote and vote Republican. . . .

Voters in the Mountain, Pacific, farm-belt and Great Lakes regions constitute almost half the population and also have the highest turnout probability."[61]

The Reagan general election effort had three successive goals. The first, from the close of the primaries through September 7, was to solidify the Republican base. The second, from September 8 until October 16, was to expand the Reagan coalition to include moderates, union members, and urban ethnics. The third, from October 17 until the election, was to increase the turnout of targeted groups.[62] For the most part the allocation of the candidate's time, media placement, and field organization paralleled each of these strategic goals, with the greatest allocations made to the "battleground states" of the Great Lakes during September.[63]

Swaying and Holding Delegates and
Selecting a Running Mate

Even before the general election campaign begins, polling plays a role at the party convention, where it has had two important functions. First, polls may be used to convince delegates to support a candidate in a closely contested nomination struggle, particularly if they show one candidate to be stronger than others against the opposing party's candidate. Second, polls can help the convention's nominee to select a vice presidential running mate.

A number of candidates have attempted to use public polls to secure their party's nomination. Nelson Rockefeller, for example, eventually staked his quest for the 1968 GOP nomination almost totally on poll data. Because he had not entered any primaries, Rockefeller spent some $4 million attempting to convince Republican delegates that he, not Richard Nixon, would be the stronger candidate against the Democrats. One month before the convention, polls by Gallup and Harris indicated that this was likely to be true. The final preconvention Gallup poll, however, fielded two days after former president Eisenhower endorsed Nixon, suggested that a Rockefeller candidacy had no such advantage, thereby ensuring Eisenhower's former vice president the presidential nomination.[64]

Among the Democrats in 1968, Eugene McCarthy followed a strategy similar to that of Rockefeller—with much the same result. Relying on preconvention Gallup polls that showed the Minnesota senator only five percentage points behind Nixon, compared to Vice President Hubert Humphrey's sixteen point deficit, McCarthy supporters tried unsuccessfully to win the support of party leaders like Chicago Mayor Richard Daley.[65]

In 1984, Gary Hart's last hope for the Democratic nomination appeared to be polls showing him stronger than Mondale against President Reagan. "Only one thing is going to influence my vote," California Democratic Chairman Peter Kelley said, "and that's what the preponderance of national polls show. If they show Gary Hart running five to ten points better against Reagan than Mondale, then I'll have to give serious thought to voting for Hart."[66]

Beginning in 1960 both Democratic and Republican nominees also have used polls to help select the running mate most likely to help their chances in the general election. To a large extent, John Kennedy chose Texas senator Lyndon Johnson to share the 1960 Democratic ticket because Louis Harris's polls indicated that Texas would be a crucial swing state. Eight years later, Richard Nixon's campaign conducted a series of trial-heat polls to test the relative advantages of various running mates. Unfortunately for Nixon, the candidate who helped the most, Nelson Rockefeller, declined the second spot. During the 1972 McGovern campaign, polls by Caddell indicated that the addition of Edward Kennedy to the ticket would narrow President Nixon's lead over the South Dakota senator from fourteen points to four; no other prospective vice presidential candidate helped the ticket at all. McGovern selected Thomas Eagleton, an ill-fated choice because of past emotional instability, only after Kennedy and various others declined the second spot on the ticket.[67]

During the last three presidential elections, polls have become increasingly important in the selection of vice presidential candidates. In 1976, President Ford chose Robert Dole of Kansas and Jimmy Carter picked Walter Mondale of Minnesota, both, in part, because polls indicated that the midwestern farm-belt states would be crucial and closely contested. After chances evaporated for a Reagan-Ford "dream ticket" in 1980, Reagan turned to moderate George Bush both in an attempt to win support from moderates and independents, and because Bush added foreign policy credentials that polls indicated would best complement Reagan's experience in state office.[68] In 1984, as noted earlier, polls encouraged Mondale's choice of a female running mate.

Tracking the Election Campaign

In Ronald Reagan's 1970 gubernatorial campaign in California, Richard Wirthlin introduced the technique of "tracking"—or continual surveying—to the repertoire of political polling. "Tracking a campaign allows you to watch it almost the same way you watch a movie," Wirthlin has said. "This system enables [you] not only to pinpoint clusters of potentially favorable voters and to identify the opposition, but also to gauge trends in individual cities, states, and regions."[69]

Even before tracking became widespread, pollsters conducted increasingly numerous surveys during presidential campaigns to measure progress and assess strategy. In 1960, for example, after Louis Harris had identified the so-called "religious question," he used repeated polls to chart the success of John Kennedy's attempts to resolve the issue. The 1968 Nixon campaign used frequent state-by-state polls to allocate resources and monitor gains and losses.[70]

Patrick Caddell conducted polls to measure changes in public opinion throughout Jimmy Carter's successful 1976 campaign. This research enabled Caddell to advise his candidate, for example, when voters began to believe charges that he was "waffling" on the issues.[71] Later Caddell used tracking polls to identify shifts among important groups of voters. On September 9, for example, when poll readings showed Carter running poorly among conservative, blue-collar, Catholic, big-city ethnics, Caddell recommended a week of travel in large Eastern cities to attempt to reverse this decline, a strategy that apparently worked.[72]

To a large extent the success of Ronald Reagan's 1980 general election campaign can be attributed to Richard Wirthlin's tracking polls. Taking advantage of a $1.4 million research budget, Wirthlin monitored shifts in public opinion almost daily. Tracking polls served to pinpoint Carter's strengths and weaknesses. Evolving "voter anticipation" readings gave direction to the campaign's communications. When Wirthlin discovered positive perceptions of Reagan, the campaign sought to reinforce them in both the candidate's speeches and in advertising. When Wirthlin discovered negative perceptions, campaign communications tried to correct them. He also pioneered the use of "simulation modeling" programs to gauge the effects of "what if" scenarios. The Reagan campaign was concerned, in particular, about the possible effects of a negotiated release of the American hostages in Iran just before the election.[73]

For the first six weeks of the 1980 campaign Reagan's advisers held fast to Wirthlin's strategy of emphasizing positives, even though their candidate, in the words of David Chagall, was "champing at the bit to attack." The first negative commercials did not air until October 10, after tracking indicated that voters had become familiar with Reagan and his record.[74] As Wirthlin explains, "A lot of people were not aware of the credibility and knowledge Ronald Reagan had. About 40 percent said they knew very little about him or what he stood for. So we attempted to familiarize the electorate with him. Once that was established, we could go on the thematic element of leadership, especially the economy, and take Jimmy Carter on very directly."[75]

Despite tracking's many apparent successes, not all pollsters praise this technique. Since the number of interviews conducted in each individual mini-poll, as it were, is usually small (often about one hundred), some practitioners assert that the observed change too often results from statistical artifact. "To the extent that these measurements are read as finely-tuned reflections of shifts in voter sentiment," Roll and Cantril argue, "a campaign is naively anticipating information that will not be provided."[76] Although the point is well taken, the volatility of opinion in recent presidential elections forces campaigns to devote at least some attention to tracking change. The danger remains, of course, that important decisions will be made solely on the basis of a "blip" in one daily poll—possibly an artifact —rather than on a meaningful trend.

Adapting Polling from the Candidate's Campaign to the President's Administration

The candidate who successfully applies polling to the command and control of a presidential campaign eventually may find himself in the White House. It seems only logical that he would continue to use polling in the command and control of his administration, and indeed this increasingly has become the case. As early as 1936, as we have seen, President Roosevelt commissioned scientific surveys to reveal public attitudes about pressing national problems. Louis Harris, after what at the time—between 1958 and November 1960—had been the most extensive polling effort in American political history, enjoyed major influence in the Kennedy White House. "Upon his reports, upon his description of the profile of the country's thinking and prejudices as he found them," according to Theodore H. White "were to turn many of John F. Kennedy's major decisions,"[77] including those he was to make throughout his term in office.

President Carter's obsession with polls may have created many of his problems as president. Unlike Ronald Reagan, Carter's successor in the White House, the former Georgia governor had not developed a well-defined ideology during his years in the statehouse. During his four years in the presidency, as a result, Carter continually shifted positions in response to changes in Patrick Caddell's polls.[78]

In retrospect, Caddell's strong influence in the 1976 campaign can be attributed to a number of factors: more primaries than had been held previously, a highly volatile nomination campaign with many Democratic contenders and no overriding national issues, and Carter's own lack of a record in national politics. Each of these factors may be expected to make *any* sophisticated pollster more central to a campaign—to take nothing away from Caddell's own string of apparent successes.

After Carter assumed the presidency, Caddell continued to advise him on matters ranging from the Panama Canal treaty to the state of the nation's "psychic health." Unlike past administration pollsters such as Louis Harris, who reported to a campaign manager or to a White House staff member, Caddell reported directly to the president. For this reason, Caddell must be considered the first survey researcher to exert a new kind of influence on presidential politics, transcending the role of pollster and interpreter of opinion to become a full-fledged White House counselor.

When Caddell identified deep public dissatisfaction with the direction the country was headed, for example, Carter blamed what he termed damage to the "national psyche," which he attempted—in a nationally televised address to the nation—to lay upon a long succession of events: the assassinations of the 1960s, Vietnam, Watergate, the energy crises. In retrospect, what Carter called a "crisis of confidence" probably was the result of his own inability to make substantial progress in solving national problems.

Caddell and Richard Wirthlin demonstrate the growing political influence of presidential pollsters. Increasingly they advise candidates on everything from the states in which to campaign to the issues to dramatize or to ignore. Unlike the typical presidential adviser, the pollster has the added advantage of being able to support his advice with seemingly objective quantitative data. Because poll-sters advise candidates and presidents on so many issues, the question of whether they are qualified to do so inevitably arises. A pollster who is an excellent technician is not necessarily the best person to render opinions in times of world crisis. A related problem is the potential conflict of interest whenever individuals who work for private gain hold positions of public trust. Pollsters are unlikely to manufacture survey results but may occasionally be guilty of with-holding bad news or of inadvertently reporting misleading findings.

The complexity of polling techniques, combined with the considerable potential for error, place a heavy burden on the presidential pollster. Because candidates make major decisions based at least partly on polls, pollsters' sampling techniques, questionnaire designs, and interviewing methods ought to be of the highest quality. The problem of accuracy in polls is not often considered by candidates and their advisers, however. Like reporters and other laymen, politicians often overemphasize the importance of a single survey. The pollster bears the burden of preventing a campaign from falling prey to this tendency.

Many observers assert that the growing importance of polls has resulted in an abdication of leadership by presidential candidates. According to Larry Sabato, politicians have become slaves to public opinion:

In the prepolling era, when public opinion was more obscure, profiles in courage were less risky and more plentiful, but few candidates and public officials are bold enough today to defy the vox populi in such a clearly expressed and well-publicized form as a public opinion poll. As a sad consequence, the trustee officeholder may be nearing extinction, while the pure delegate —little more than a humanoid Qube system—multiplies and flourishes. What is true of the officeholder is even more prevalent among candidates for whom election looms like the sword of Damocles.[79]

Perhaps at the extreme, candidates inflexibly follow the polls. If all candidates were what Sabato calls "humanoid Qube systems," a reference to the computer-based, interactive cable television system that affords instantaneous and continual polling, the differences between the Democratic and Republican parties would not be great.

More often than not, polls act as a check on innovative leadership. On the crucial social security issues, for example, the positions of the two parties are not dramatically different. Both sides pledge to do everything possible to save the present system. President Reagan, an advocate of a voluntary retirement system for much of his political career, is content to support the status quo. To a large extent, such acquiescence results from polls indicating that any other position would be unpopular.

On the positive side, however, polls do help to facilitate communication between leaders and the led. As Roll and Cantril put it:

> Research can help uncover the common ground amid the din of conflicting claims and help leaders find the basis for consensus. It can help elucidate the basic concerns of the people, place into context the topical issues of the moment and alert leaders to what it is in public opinion they had better pay attention to. . . . This all suggests that opinion research—technically competent and sensitive to existing political realities—can enhance the strength of the democratic process.[80]

During the Vietnam era, for example, polls played an important role in keeping President Johnson informed of the growing unpopularity of his military policies. In the absence of continual polling, Johnson would have had a much easier time dismissing the antiwar movement as representing a small group of radicals out of touch with the nation. The same may be said of President Nixon at the height of the Watergate scandal. Without polls indicating that he had lost the public's trust, Nixon may well have tried to stay in office.

Ultimately, then, polling can help to contribute to the stability of a democratic society by ensuring that leaders are never too far out of step with the general public. The danger comes when politicians fail to follow the right course because of the Gallup poll. As Walter Lippmann put it a half century ago,

> The notion that public opinion can and will decide all issues is in appearance very democratic. In practice it undermines and destroys democratic government. For when everybody is supposed to have a judgment about everything, nobody in fact is going to know much about anything. . . . Effective government cannot be conducted by legislators and officials who, when a question is presented, ask themselves first and last not what is

the truth and which is the right and necessary course, but "What does the Gallup Poll say?"[81]

Winston Churchill expressed the same opinion from his position as a national leader.[82] "Nothing is more dangerous than to live in the temperamental atmosphere of the Gallup Poll, always taking one's temperature," Churchill wrote. "There is only one duty, only one safe course, and that is to be right and not to fear to do or say what you believe to be right."

9 The Three Campaigns for President

HERB ASHER

It is common today to assert that the conduct of the presidential campaign has been taken out of the hands of the political party organization and given over to campaign teams whose first loyalty is to the candidate and not to the political party. These campaign teams are portrayed as consisting of personal confidants of the candidate and the media, marketing, polling, and campaign management experts who become the hired guns of the campaign. The modern image of a presidential campaign is best exemplified by Richard Nixon's reelection effort in 1972 and Jimmy Carter's election campaign in 1976. Nixon's 1972 campaign was run by the Committee to Re-elect the President (the now infamous CREEP) and had as its major objective an impressive reelection victory for the president. To accomplish this, the president's Republican affiliation was played down and extensive efforts to aid other Republican candidates on the ticket were avoided, lest potential Democratic and Independent supporters of Nixon be upset. The campaign theme "President Nixon, Now More Than Ever" illustrated very nicely the deemphasis of the party label.

I am grateful to Larry Boyle, formerly Information Specialist at the Federal Election Commission, Thomas B. Edsall of the *Washington Post,* and Russ Hodge of the Ohio Republican Finance Committee for granting me very informative interviews. I would like to thank Larry Boyle further for providing comments on an earlier draft of this chapter; his insights about soft money have proven to be very helpful. Finally, I'd like to thank Kathy Botkin for typing the final version of the manuscript.

Although Nixon's 1972 reelection effort was candidate centered, important roles were played by persons with longstanding ties to the Republican party. In contrast, Carter's successful 1976 effort, particularly in the primaries, was orchestrated by persons with weak or nonexistent ties to the national Democratic party. The campaign's Georgia insiders, headed by Jody Powell, Hamilton Jordan, and Peter Bourne, and aided by pollster Patrick Caddell and media specialist Gerald Rafshoon, designed and implemented a strategy in which the candidate ran explicitly as a Washington outsider during the primary season. Subsequently, Democratic party officials and the state party organizations were incorporated into Carter's general election campaign effort. Nevertheless, it was the Carter team within each state and the Carter national team, not the state party organizations and the Democratic National Committee, that ran the campaign. Despite some shaky, strained relationships among the components of the Carter election effort, the campaign was successful. Yet many observers later wondered whether the outsider theme of the Carter campaign and its disdain for the traditional party apparatus presaged and contributed to the eventual difficulties Carter encountered in governing, even with a Democratic majority in both the House and the Senate.

Dominance of the presidential campaign by candidate loyalists rather than party loyalists is most pronounced during the nomination season when several candidates are seeking their party's nomination. This certainly was exemplified by the battle for the 1984 Democratic nomination in which an initial field of eight legitimate candidates was winnowed down to three after the "Super Tuesday" primaries on March 13—former vice president Walter Mondale, Senator Gary Hart, and the Reverend Jesse Jackson. Although the Mondale campaign certainly enjoyed very close working relations with the Democratic party organization, officials and elected officeholders, it was still a campaign designed first and foremost to nominate Walter Mondale. The Hart and Jackson efforts might be viewed as insurgency, even antiparty campaigns. All three campaigns (but especially those of Mondale and Hart) had their hired guns, who were devoted to the promotion of their preferred nominee with little regard for the general election consequences of their actions. For example, Patrick Caddell was given much credit for getting Hart's campaign on track in early 1984.[1] Yet Caddell earlier had offered his services to Senator John Glenn's campaign in late 1983 and before that had sounded out other potential candidates.[2] According to Martin Schram, antipathy toward Mondale by Caddell, arising from differences going back to the Carter administration, account in part for Caddell's presidential preferences.[3]

These examples from the 1972, 1976, and 1984 elections suggest that the image of the presidential campaign as candidate-centered rather than party-centered has substantial validity, although recent developments may result in an enhanced role for the party, an argument developed later. Hence, our first objective in this essay is to explain the decline of the party and use of the candidate-expert team in presidential politics. One part of this explanation has to do with campaign finance reforms that were adopted in 1974 and subsequently modified by Supreme Court rulings and legislative amendments. In particular, these reforms and a Supreme Court decision that permitted independent expenditures in the presidential campaign created a situation in which three possible campaigns could be conducted simultaneously for president—the candidate-dominated campaign, the party-directed effort, and a set of activities sponsored by concerned citizens and organizations independent of the candidate and the party. Thus, our second objective is to describe the three campaigns and to assess their significance for the political parties in presidential campaigns. In the conclusion, we will consider possible reforms in presidential campaigning, including their consequences, desirability, and likelihood of adoption. We also will address the effects of the three campaigns for president on the prospects for effective government in the United States and the role of the political party in governance.

The Decline of the Party in Presidential Campaigns

In considering why the role of the party in the presidential campaign has declined, one can identify two sets of causes—those that contributed to the decline of parties in general and those more specific to the presidential contest. By definition, anything that weakened the party in general contributed to its lesser significance in presidential campaigns. Thus we will first review briefly some of these broader explanations and then analyze in greater detail those factors unique to the presidential contest.

General Causes of Political Party Decline

Probably the simplest way to explain the decline of parties is to state that many of the functions traditionally performed by party organizations and officials have been taken over by other entities and mechanisms. Many of the services, perquisites, and incentives that were basic resources for party influence no longer exist. Patronage opportunities have been substantially reduced with the rise of civil service, merit systems, and court decisions that make it more difficult to remove public employees from office when changes in the partisan control of government take place. Similarly, the social welfare function of the party in providing services to the needy has been replaced by governmental initiatives and programs. Finally, the ability of the party to award contracts and projects to its supporters has been limited by increased requirements for competitive bidding and careful accounting and auditing procedures.

The party also has been weakened in its candidate recruitment and election functions. Obviously the direct primary lessened the party's role in recruiting candidates and the rise of technological specialists in such areas as polling, media, and direct mail fundraising has reduced its role in those candidates' election campaigns. Today the acquisition of resources and strategic and tactical decisions are largely the prerogative of the candidate and not the party, particularly in contests for more prestigious offices. Assuming the availability of money, the candidate can purchase campaign necessities from private vendors rather than rely on the party (which in most cases probably could not provide these services anyway).

A related phenomenon is the rise of the mass media, especially television, as the major source of campaign communication, particularly for more important offices. The successful use of television requires marketing and production expertise that is more likely to be obtained in the private sector than from the political party. Moreover, the use of television encourages a concentration on the candidate rather than on the philosophy and ideology of the political party. For the candidate with ample financial resources, television permits direct appeals to the voter, regardless of the stance of the party organization.

Finally, three developments in the electorate have contributed to a weakening of the parties. The first is the rise in the proportion of Americans who reject the Democratic and Republican party labels and call themselves independents. Although there is some evidence that this upward trend has leveled off and perhaps even reversed, the proportion of independents is substantially higher today than twenty years ago. For example, a 1964 survey of Americans conducted by the Center for Political Studies classified 23 percent of the respondents as independents; a comparable survey in 1984 placed the proportion of independents at 34 percent. In 1952, 40 percent of the presidential vote was cast by strong party identifiers and only 23 percent by independents; in 1984, 35 percent was cast by strong partisans and 31 percent by independents, with the remaining 34 percent cast by weak party identifiers. Certainly the higher the proportion of the electorate that is composed of independents and weak party identifiers, the freer candidates will feel to circumvent the parties and to fashion appeals that minimize overt partisanship. To the extent that these appeals are candidate-centered, they reinforce the notion of a campaign team devoted to the election of the particular candidate rather than the entire slate of party candidates.

Another development in the electorate is the growing distrust of political institutions and authorities. Although there is evidence that this trend has receded a bit, substantially lower levels of confidence in government and institutions are prevalent today than in the not-too-distant past. One manifestation of this phenomenon is citizens' reactions to political parties and elections as institutions that promote governmental responsiveness. In 1964, 68 percent of Americans believed that elections helped a good deal in making government pay attention to the people, a share that dropped to 43 percent by 1984. In 1964, 44 percent of Americans felt that political parties were important in promoting governmental responsiveness. Only 18 percent held that opinion in 1980. Clearly, if only about one-fifth of Americans believe that parties are important in promoting governmental responsiveness, then candidates have less reason to stress party ties in their campaigns or as an instrument of governance, thereby contributing further to the weakened position of the party.

A final development in the electorate is the rise of single issue interest groups and the tremendous growth in political action committees. According to the *Federal Election Commission Record*, the number of PACs grew from 608 at the beginning of 1975 to 4,009 by the end of 1984 with the greatest increase being in corporate and nonconnected PACs. (The number of labor PACs grew only slightly.)[4]

This is probably both a cause and a consequence of the decline in the political party. That is, political action committees may undermine political parties; however, the weakened condition of the parties themselves promotes the growth of political action committees that can offer candidates resources and services the parties are often incapable of providing. American parties have been viewed as umbrella-like, coalitional entities that include heterogeneous groups, some of which are at loggerheads on particular issues. This diversity has been a source of both strength and potential weakness in the American party system. If the single issue groups continue to gain strength, then the party as a vehicle for contesting elections and promoting public policies will be undermined. In a related vein, the substantial growth in the number of political action committees and the increase in PAC money in politics can threaten the loyalty of candidates to their political party. It is clear that if PACs provide candidates with campaign finances and services independent of and even at cross purposes to the political party, then the party will be weakened further. This is not to argue that PACs automatically work against the well-being of the parties. In recent years the national parties have adapted to the PAC presence in a variety of ways, one being to facilitate the coordinated contributions of multiple PACs to their congressional candidates.

The Decline of the Party in the Presidential Contest

Delegate selection reforms. The presidential selection process has witnessed major reforms since 1970 in the two broad areas of delegate selection and campaign financing, reforms that have contributed to the decline of parties. The delegate selection reforms were partially responsible for the tremendous proliferation of presidential primaries because numerous state Democratic parties believed that compliance with national party rules would be easier to accomplish with a primary system than a caucus-convention system. Primaries also flourished because their democratic and participatory virtues were stressed by political elites and the mass media and because it became clear that primary states were receiving much more coverage than caucus states from the news media. Nelson Polsby makes the interesting point that as the presidential delegate selection contest became the central concern within the states, some state parties chose to separate their state and local nominations from the presidential race so that the latter would not intrude on the former.[5] Once these state and local decisions were divorced from the presidential choice, it became even easier for the states to adopt presidential primaries, with their attendant prestige and media coverage. Although the proliferation of primaries was reversed in 1984, primaries are much more important today in terms of actual delegate selection than they were in the prereform era. And as the 1988 campaign approaches, there is much discussion about the number and timing of primaries, particularly since there will be a regional Southern primary early in the nomination season brought about by the decisions of individual southern states to move their primaries to a common date.

The reliance on primaries has a number of detrimental consequences for the political party. The sequential nature of the primary season, beginning with the New Hampshire contest (and the Iowa precinct caucuses), allows a relatively unknown candidate to emerge from the pack, a candidate who may have little support from party leaders and the party organization. Indeed, some aspirants choose to run as outsiders and even antiparty candidates; the declaration of one's independence from the party chieftains is presented as a major reason to vote for the outsider.

The primaries, in conjunction with the public financing system adopted in 1974, encourage lesser-known candidates with weak ties to the party establishment to enter the fray supported by highly personal coalitions. Moreover, the partial public funding provided during the primary season encourages more candidates to declare their intentions early so that they may qualify for these monies. The abolition of the unit rule for convention delegations and the proportional allocation of delegates in the primaries further encourage candidates to enter each state contest since they are likely to win some delegates even if they do not finish first.

The primary process may favor those candidates who appeal to specific and intense constituencies, often located toward the very liberal or very conservative ends of the political spectrum. Candidates of the center may find it difficult to generate support during the primary season, yet the center may be where the bulk of the party is located and may be the best position to occupy for the general election. Certainly the primary electorate is demographi-

cally unrepresentative, being skewed toward higher status individuals. (How Jesse Jackson's candidacy affected this pattern in 1984 is as
yet unclear, although his presence in the contest obviously stimulated a much higher than normal black turnout.) Moreover, there is
some evidence that these higher-status voters are more supportive of
ideologically extreme candidates.[6] Although caucus participants also
can be energized by a particular issue or a charismatic candidate, the
typical caucus vote has more of an organizational basis to it, whether
in the political party or in labor unions or various social groups.

The delegate selection reforms adopted by the Democrats in 1972
reflected a negative view about the role of elected leaders and party
officials. The power of the state parties to appoint delegates was
limited; elected officials were forced either to contest for delegate
slots or stay at home during the national party convention. State
parties also were required to meet certain conditions designed to
foster participation by rank and file Democrats and demographic
"representativeness" in the delegations ultimately selected, even if
that meant undermining the party elites. Since the early and
mid-1970s, the Democrats have taken a number of steps in the other
direction to insure the participation of party leaders at the nominating conventions. For example, for their 1984 convention, the Democrats created the status of "super-delegate" for prominent party
leaders.

In 1986 the Democratic National Committee approved recommendations from the party's Fairness Commission (established to
review the conduct of the 1984 campaign and to make recommendations for 1988) that would increase from 60 to 80 percent the
proportion of Democratic House and Senate members who will
automatically be named as unpledged delegates to the 1988 Democratic convention. Also approved was a recommendation that all
Democratic governors and all members of the Democratic National
Committee be awarded seats as unpledged delegates to the convention. Hence more than one-fourth of the delegate positions at the
1988 convention have been reserved for elected officials and party
leaders. Additional party leaders and officials will attend the convention through their selection as delegates in the caucuses and
primaries. Nevertheless, even with these pro-party changes, the delegate selection system still emphasizes rank and file participation.
Under this system it is the mass media rather than the political

party that interpret the results, handicap the race, determine the viability of candidates, and ultimately pronounce victory and defeat.[7] Given the prominence of the mass media, it is no wonder that primary campaigns are aimed at the newspaper reporters, the television commentators, and the readers and viewers at home. Under the current system, candidates need to convince the media elite and the voters first; party officials are of lesser importance.

Campaign finance reforms. The campaign finance reforms put into place in 1974 and subsequently modified also have been cited as causes of the decline of the political party, although the 1979 amendments to the Federal Election Campaign Act (discussed later) portend a greater role for state and local parties in the presidential campaign. It is argued that the strict spending limits in the general election have severely curtailed party-related campaign activities by the presidential nominees. (An even stronger case can be made that the limitations on party activities in congressional elections invite more extensive participation by PACs, but such races are not our concern here.) Candidates are forced to spend more than half of their limited funds on television and related production costs, leaving little money for the paraphernalia of campaigns. Storefront campaign headquarters are much less common; electoral teamwork among the national, state, and local candidates is diminished because of the reporting requirements imposed by the campaign finance laws. The very fact that the public financing goes directly to the candidates weakens the parties.

For candidates who receive partial public funding during the primary season, the possible financial penalties and negative publicity that would arise from blatantly violating the individual state and overall spending ceilings encourage a highly centralized and nationalized campaign apparatus in which the state plays a limited role. Indeed, once a state's primary or caucus has occurred, the campaign apparatus within that state usually is disbanded, only to be revived should the candidate win the nomination. In a similar vein, the general election spending ceiling for candidates who receive public financing requires a centralized organization to coordinate a fifty state campaign, both so that spending does not exceed the legally allowed amount and so that ineffective expenditures by state and local personnel are not charged against the candidate's overall spending limit. (The specifics of these spending limits are presented in the section on the candidate-centered campaign.)

There are three other aspects of the campaign financing laws (and court rulings and subsequent amendments) that bode ill or well for the party's role in the presidential campaign. First, the contribution limits established by the 1974 law allow greater donations to be made to party committees, thereby presumably providing an advantage to the party. (Again, some would argue that any limit on political party money in any contest simply encourages candidates to seek out other sources of funding such as PACS.) However, this advantage was more than offset by the Supreme Court decision in the case of *Buckley* v. *Valeo*, which struck down the prohibition on independent expenditures by individuals in the presidential campaign as an unconstitutional infringement on freedom of speech. Hence, if independent expenditures continue to grow substantially, the party will be even less significant in the presidential race (and the intent of the campaign finance reforms seriously undermined). Independent expenditures are discussed in greater detail in the next section.

Finally, there was one development in 1979 that presaged a major role for the political party in the presidential campaign of 1984 and years beyond. Amendments adopted in 1979 provided that state and local political party committees could participate in the presidential campaign in a prescribed set of volunteer-related activities—registration and get-out-the-vote drives, literature distribution, and the like. The intent of these amendments was to narrow the widening separation between the presidential campaign and the state and local party committees brought about by the spending limits that publicly funded presidential candidates had to obey in the general election. These allowable state and local activities were classified as exempt, meaning that they did not count against the general election spending limits. Moreover, the amendments made it clear that that portion of the exempt activities that benefited the presidential campaign was to be paid for by funds collected according to the federal campaign finance statutes. As will be discussed later, the 1979 amendments may have created a significant opportunity for wealthy individuals, corporations, and labor unions to undermine the campaign finance reforms of the 1970s.

The Three Campaigns for President

The campaign finance reforms adopted in 1974, the Supreme Court rejection of the ban on independent expenditures by individuals in the 1976 case of *Buckley* v. *Valeo,* and the 1979 amendment that permits state party involvement in aspects of the presidential contest have created the opportunity for three campaigns for the presidency to be waged—the candidate-centered activities, the independent expenditures by individuals and groups supporting particular candidates, and political party efforts. (The 1985 Supreme Court ruling in the case of *FEC* v. *National Conservative Political Action Committee* will further encourage independent expenditures in presidential campaigns. In this case, the Court extended its *Buckley* v. *Valeo* decision by declaring that political action committees can spend unlimited amounts independently on behalf of candidates.) In this section each of these campaigns will be described and assessed in terms of its sources of financial support. Emphasis will be on the 1980 presidential contest (for which ample data are available) and on the 1984 race, in which the party and independent campaigns were particularly prominent.

The Candidate-Centered Campaign

The presidential contest today is dominated by teams of specialists and loyalists whose first obligation is to the candidate and not to the political party of which that candidate is a leader. Funding for the candidate-centered campaign comes mainly from the two main parts of the campaign finance system established in 1974—partial public funding during the primary season and practically full public funding during the general election.

With respect to the primary season, the campaign finance reforms of 1974 set a spending limit of $10 million for the 1976 campaign, a figure that was to be adjusted for inflation in succeeding elections. (Hence, the limit for 1980 was $14.7 million and for 1984 $20.2 million.) The 1974 law enabled candidates to spend an additional 20 percent to defray the costs of fund-raising. A 1976 amendment exempted from the overall spending limits the legal and accounting costs incurred in complying with the campaign finance laws.

In order to be eligible for public funding during the primary season, candidates first had to raise on their own a total of $100,000 from twenty or more states in contributions of $250 or less. In 1980, candidates who met these conditions were eligible for matching public funds for each dollar collected from private contributions up to a total of $7.35 million; in 1984 the matching public funds could total

$10.1 million. Only the first $250 of any private contribution was eligible for matching funds. A candidate who received a $250 contribution from each of four individuals would receive $1,000 in matching funds, while a candidate who received a $1,000 contribution from an individual (the maximum allowed by law) would receive only $250 in public matching funds. Thus, of the $20.2 million that candidates could spend in the 1984 prenomination contest, as much as half could come from public funds. Candidates could choose to reject public funds; in that case, they would not be bound by any expenditure limits, but still could not accept individual contributions greater than $1,000. Since the campaign finance reforms were adopted in 1974, only one major contender—Republican John Connally in 1980—has chosen to reject public funding. All other serious contenders have accepted public monies, often racing to qualify first and thereby receive positive media coverage about the progress of the campaign.

In addition to the overall spending limit, candidates are subject to spending limits for each state's delegate selection contest. The 1974 limit was $200,000 per state or sixteen cents per eligible voter, whichever was greater; this ceiling is adjusted for inflation at each election so that in 1984 the figures were $404,000 per state or 32.3 cents per voter. Significantly, the total of the fifty state spending ceilings far exceeds the overall spending limit. In 1980 the overall limit was $20.2 million (plus 20 percent for fund-raising), but the sum of the separate state ceilings was approximately $60.2 million. Therefore candidates had to allocate their resources very carefully and sometimes played games to meet the technical requirements of the law. For example, given the importance of the New Hampshire primary, candidates want to spend the full amount allowed in that state ($294,000 in 1980 and $404,000 in 1984) and then some. One way to accomplish this is to purchase time on Boston television stations (which reach New Hampshire) and charge these costs against the Massachusetts spending ceiling. New Hampshire campaign workers sometimes stay overnight in neighboring Vermont or Massachusetts so that their lodging costs will not count against the New Hampshire ceiling. The FEC and many presidential candidates have urged Congress to eliminate the state-by-state spending limitations in presidential primaries; FEC Chairman John McGarry has referred to them as an "absolute nightmare."[8]

A more important consequence of the overall limit and the individual state ceilings is that they may encourage "independent" expenditures on behalf of a candidate who faces financial difficulties. For example, Ronald Reagan in 1980 and Walter Mondale in 1984 spent heavily at the beginning of the primary season, which left relatively little money for the later primaries. Allegedly independent expenditures were provided to both candidates to help them overcome their money problems, although in Mondale's case this effort was terminated when publicity made it a political albatross for the candidate.

The Democratic and Republican candidates for president also receive public funds for the general election campaign. The amount set in the 1974 law was $20 million per candidate with an inflation adjustment at each successive election. Thus the amount for 1976 was $21.8 million, for 1980 $29.4 million, and for 1984 $40.4 million. Candidates may reject general election public funding; if so, they are not subject to the general election expenditure limits, but are subject to contribution limits. If candidates accept public money, then they cannot collect private contributions except to help offset the costs of complying with the finance laws. In every election since the 1974 law was passed, both major party nominees have accepted public funding, which might make it seem that the funding of the general election campaign for the major party nominees is very straightforward. But the campaign finance laws also permit coordinated political party expenditures, exempt expenditures by state and local party committees, and allegedly independent expenditures, all of which increase the general election costs substantially. These opportunities for additional spending (some would call them loopholes) will be discussed shortly.

Minor party candidates are eligible for public financing in the general election only if their party received at least 5 percent of the popular vote in the last election. The amount of money given to minor party candidates is proportional to their vote strength. In 1980 the Federal Elections Commission ruled that John Anderson's independent candidacy would be treated as a minor party effort, thereby making Anderson eligible for $4.2 million in public funds *after* the 1980 election and also in 1984, had he run. For a new minor party to qualify for postelection funding in 1988, it must be on the ballot in at least ten states, receive at least 5 percent of the popular vote and provide assurances to the FEC prior to the election that it will comply with the campaign finance laws.[9] Clearly the public financing provisions favor the major party candidates, although a wealthy minor party candidate ineligible for public funds could spend an unlimited amount from a personal fortune.

The patterns of spending of public funds in the 1980 general election illustrate very nicely the media emphasis of the campaign and the importance of the technological specialist to the candidate's campaign team. According to Herbert Alexander, the bulk of the public money received by Carter and Reagan went into their media efforts.[10] About $20.5 million (almost 70 percent of Carter's $29.4 million public subsidy) went to the media, with $15.8 million devoted to television, $2.6 million to radio advertisements, and $2.1 million to print advertising and media production costs.[11] Responsibility for the media campaign rested with Carter loyalists Gerald Rafshoon and Patrick Caddell, both of whom had been a part of Carter's campaign team since he first sought the 1976 Democratic nomination. The Reagan spending patterns were similar, with $16.8 million spent on media advertising and production costs and more than $1 million for polling done by Richard Wirthlin's Decision-Making Information, which remained the White House pollster.[12] Although it appears that less money was spent on media for Reagan than for Carter, this is misleading because it does not include the coordinated political party effort and the independent expenditures for Reagan, which will be discussed shortly.

There is one additional way that would-be presidential aspirants can promote their candidacies and that is to set up a political action committee. Alexander notes that four candidates for the 1980 Republican nomination—Reagan, Bush, Connally, and Senator Robert Dole —established political action committees long before their formal candidacies began.[13] The ostensible purpose of these PACs was to raise and spend money on behalf of candidates for other offices and party committees, thereby enabling the aspiring nominees to win favors from party leaders.

The most prominent of these presidential PACs was Reagan's Citizens for the Republic, which was created to help elect conservative Republican candidates. But such a PAC also could be used to promote Reagan's 1980 chances.[14] For example, in 1977–78, Citizens for the Republic spent $4.5 million, including $590,000 in contributions to federal, state, and local candidates and party organizations.[15] The PAC maintained a full-time staff, produced a monthly newsletter with a circulation of 40,000, and in the process of raising funds developed a mailing list of more than 300,000 contributors. Clearly these activities promoted Reagan as well as the recipients of his PAC's support. Moreover, the presidential PACs allowed the candidates to travel around the country giving speeches and attracting media coverage without their travel costs counting against the spending limits that would apply once they made an actual declaration of candidacy.[16]

After the 1980 election a number of potential Democratic candidates set up PACs, including Walter Mondale, Edward Kennedy, Ernest Hollings and Morris Udall, most of which became defunct. According to Maxwell Glen, Mondale established a PAC (the Committee for the Future of America) in 1981 to promote his 1984 presidential prospects.[17] Mondale's PAC raised $2.1 million in 1981–82, yet only $137,000 was contributed to federal candidates; most of the money was used to build mailing lists and pay for Mondale's political operations.[18] More important, according to Elizabeth Drew, three Republican legislators with presidential aspirations—senators Robert Dole and Howard Baker and Representative Jack Kemp—created their own PACs in the early 1980s even though their likely earliest shot at the nomination would be not in 1984 but 1988.[19] The Kemp PAC—the Campaign for Prosperity—gave $197,000 in 1984 to 109 federal candidates plus assorted contributions to other party and candidate committees.

Because it appears that would-be presidential nominees view the creation of their own PACs as advantageous to their presidential ambitions, we might expect the continued growth of such PACs as a way to get around the expenditure limits that constrain declared candidates for president. Certainly the available evidence indicates that candidates' PACs will play an important role in the 1988 campaign. Five potential 1988 Republican aspirants—Bush, Kemp, Dole, Baker, and Pat Robertson—established PACs. By the end of 1985 they had raised more than $5.5 million, although less than 7 percent of that money went to other Republican candidates or organizations.[20] Most of the money went for activities (newsletters, travel, political advisers, literature, etc.) that would promote a presidential candidacy in its early stages. This raised a legal question of whether these PACs were simply a way to skirt the campaign finance laws.

The issue came to a head in early 1986 when the legal staff of the FEC challenged plans by Bush's PAC (the Fund for America's Future) to spend money to recruit candidates for Michigan's 1986 precinct delegate caucuses. Most observers viewed the Michigan precinct elections as integral to the 1988 nomination because they were the first step in a three-part process to choose the delegates to the 1988 Republican convention.[21] Hence, the FEC staff argued that the fund's outlays were tantamount to presidential campaign expenditures and must be counted as contributions to the Bush campaign. In a controversial ruling, the FEC commissioners rejected the staff recommendation, arguing that the fund's spending was for the party and not the candidate. Should this ruling stand, candidate-centered PACs probably will be highly prominent in the presidential campaign and another loophole will be available for candidates to spend substantially more money in seeking the nomination than current law was designed to permit.

The Political Party Campaign

Until 1979 the national party's role in the presidential general election campaign was very simple: the 1974 reforms allowed each party to spend two cents per voting age citizen on behalf of its presidential nominee, an amount adjusted for inflation. In 1980, the parties' spending limit was about $4.6 million, a figure that increased to $6.9 million for the 1984 election. These national party expenditures on behalf of the presidential ticket do not constitute a separate independent campaign; indeed, the FEC formally labels this activity coordinated party expenditures. According to the FEC *Record*, these expenditures

> count neither as contributions to the candidate nor as expenditures by the candidate or the candidate's authorized committee. The party committee may coordinate the expenditures with the candidate's campaign, but the party committee—not the candidate—must report them. . . . Moreover, the party committee or organization must actually make the expenditure. . . . In the Presidential elections, only the national committee may make coordinated expenditures on behalf of the party's Presidential nominee, although any agent, including a state or local party committee, may be designated by the national committee to make Presidential coordinated expenditures. . . . If the national committee designates a state or subordinate party committee to

make these expenditures, the national committee nevertheless remains responsible for ensuring that the limit is not exceeded.[22]

In 1980, according to Alexander, the Republican National Committee (RNC) spent $4.5 million of the $4.6 million it was entitled to spend on the presidential campaign, most of the money being disbursed in coordination with the Reagan-Bush Committee.[23] Among the major expenditures were $1.1 million for advertising, $1 million for travel, $808,000 for direct mail, and $564,000 for polling. This $4.5 million represented only a small part of the spending done by the Republican National Committee that may have benefited the Reagan-Bush ticket in 1980. For example, the RNC spent over $1 million to stimulate Republican turnout in the general election (Commitment '80), yet only $27,000 of that money was charged against the $4.6 million it could spend on coordinated party expenditures.[24] The RNC, in conjunction with the Republican House and Senate campaign committees, also spent $9.5 million on a media campaign that encouraged viewers to "Vote Republican, For a Change."[25] None of this money was allocated against the $4.6 million, the rationale being that the activity promoted the entire party ticket and not a specific candidate. Yet certainly the Republican presidential nominee profited from the party's media campaign.

The Democratic National Committee (DNC) was not able to raise the full $4.6 million in 1980, and spent only $4 million, of which only $3.4 million was spent before the general election, primarily on media and polling. Unlike the Republican national campaign committees (national, House, and Senate), the Democratic national campaign committees spent little additional money that directly or indirectly benefited the presidential ticket. This was simply because the Republican committees were far more successful in fund-raising than were the comparable Democratic committees. For example, the various Republican national committees spent about $132 million in 1979–80 compared to only about $19 million for the Democratic committees. The Republican National Committee and the Democratic National Committee raised similar amounts (about $10 million) from major contributors and fund-raising events, but the RNC reaped almost ten times more than its Democratic counterpart in direct mail and telephone solicitation—about $40 million to $4 million.[26]

The disparity between the parties in fund-raising ability continues. According to the FEC *Record*, during 1981–82 Republican party committees at the national, state, and local levels spent more than five times as much as their Democratic counterparts ($214 million v. $40 million), contributed three times more money to congressional candidates ($5.6 million v. $1.8 million), and made special coordinated party expenditures for congressional candidates that were four times larger ($14.3 million v. $3.3 million).[27] Examining only the three major national committees of each party, Thomas Edsall reported that the Republicans outraised the Democrats by $191.1 million to $31.7 million in 1981–82 and by $246.1 million to $58.8 million in 1983–84.[28] Although the ratio of Republican to Democratic fund-raising has declined, the absolute difference remains large. Clearly, the Democrats have some catching up to do, particularly in the area of direct mail fund-raising. It is likely that the Republicans will maintain a sizable advantage in this area since the pool of citizens to which it directs its mail solicitations is more prosperous, more ideologically homogeneous, and hence more willing to give.

The Republican party's superior fund-raising performance and its concomitant ability to do more for its presidential candidates (as well as its congressional candidates) do not undermine the spirit of the campaign finance laws for a number of reasons. First, political party participation generally is valued, if for no other reason than to minimize PAC influence. Second, the vast majority of the monies raised by the Republicans comes from relatively small individual contributions, a form of public participation that should be encouraged by a campaign financing system. But there is another disparity between the parties that could threaten the presidential campaign financing system—the presence of "soft money." Moreover, even if the Democratic and Republican Parties had equal ability to raise soft money, these dollars still might be harmful to the letter and spirit of the campaign finance reforms.

In 1979, in response to complaints that the campaign finance laws unintentionally restricted state and local party activity, Congress passed amendments that would encourage grass roots party-building and facilitate state and local party involvement in the presidential contest. Prior to the enactment of these amendments, a local get-out-the-vote drive could not mention the presidential candidate, lest part of the cost of that activity be charged against the presidential election expenditure limit; for the same reason, volunteer activities also were constrained.

The 1979 amendments allowed state and local party committees to spend an unlimited amount of money on campaign paraphernalia —bumper stickers, pins, banners, yard signs, buttons, etc.—if these materials were used for volunteer activities on behalf of a candidate. Party committees also were permitted to spend unlimited sums on volunteer-based voter registrations and get-out-the-vote drives. In both cases the costs of these activities would be considered exempt—that is, they would not count against the general election expenditure limit. The portion of these activities that benefited federal candidates had to be paid for by funds raised in compliance with the laws governing contributions to federal candidates. This meant that monies from corporations, labor unions, and foreign nationals were prohibited. However, that part of these activities that aided state and local candidates could be paid for by monies collected under state and local campaign finance laws, which in many cases allowed unlimited contributions from individuals as well as contributions from corporations and labor unions. The final restriction was that funds could not be transferred from the national party committees to pay for these activities; instead the state and local committees were to do their own fund-raising.

Thus did "soft money" enter the presidential campaign. Essentially soft money is money not subject to federal regulation. It is money collected from individuals, unions, and corporations, typically by state and local party committees, and used by those committees to pay for the state and local part of the campaign activities that are encouraged by the 1979 amendments. Although the national party is prohibited from transferring funds to state parties, it does play a prominent role in assisting the state and local committees to raise these monies. Thus, the Reagan-Bush soft money effort in 1980 raised between ten and fifteen million dollars, which far outstripped the Democratic total.[29] In the months before the 1984 election, both parties talked in terms of $20 million soft money programs that would channel contributions from private donors into state and local party committees.

Reactions to the introduction of soft money into the presidential campaign have been mixed. Herbert Alexander calls the organizational spending by state and local parties "a notable development."[30] He argues that the coordination of national, state, and party committees "obviously helps strengthen the parties" and points to an analysis that recommends removing all limits on state and local party activity in presidential and congressional elections.

Elizabeth Drew, in contrast, believes that the soft money loophole destroys much of the campaign finance system and threatens to corrupt electoral politics.[31] She asserts that although the national parties have taken on the task of raising and distributing the soft money, the money itself is collected under state rather than national law, which means that the only limits on the amounts of such money being spent in states are imposed by the states themselves.[32] And, Drew notes, twenty-eight states permit corporate contributions, forty-one states allow labor contributions, and twenty-five states impose no limitations whatsoever on individual contributions.[33] Hence, she concludes, monies from corporate and union treasuries have found their way into the presidential campaign, as have the sizable contributions from wealthy individuals that characterized the prereform days. Further, state financing restrictions that do exist are largely irrelevant because funds can be shifted from one state to another. Drew cites the example of how the Republican National Committee treated Texas and Missouri in 1980.[34] Missouri allowed corporate contributions in its own elections; Texas did not. Neither state limited individual contributions. Hence, money raised from individuals in Missouri might be sent to Texas, while Texas corporate money would be sent to Missouri and other states that permitted corporate contributions. This activity was coordinated at the highest levels of the Republican National Committee and candidates Reagan and Bush were actively involved in raising the soft money, even though their general election campaign was financed by public funding.[35]

Drew's pessimistic conclusions are in error on one major point —monies spent for exempt political party activities in the presidential campaign must be permissible monies, that is, funds collected according to the federal (and not the state) campaign finance laws. Corporate and labor contributions as well as individual contributions above $1,000 and committee contributions above $5,000 cannot be used to pay for that portion of the exempt activities that is assignable to federal contests. Separate state, local, and federal accounts, each with their own sources of money, must be maintained.

However, as John Noble argues, the establishment of state and local accounts by federally regulated political committees can lead to abuses.[36] These state and local accounts are not covered by federal disclosure laws and limitations, since the monies therein presumably go only to state and local races. But as Noble points out:

> these funds find their way into the federal election process by virtue of federal regulations permitting the allocation of part of the state and local funds to the operating expenses of the affiliated, federally regulated political committee. Without effective oversight of the allocation process, and there is none, the affiliated committee is afforded substantial discretion in the determination of an appropriate allocation formula.[37]

The problem becomes one of allocating costs among the federal and the state and local committees, a process in which much discretion is involved. The FEC has issued a number of advisory opinions on allocation mechanisms and has approved a variety of methods. Typically, the FEC requires that federal candidates be assigned a higher share of the costs than their numbers on the ballot would indicate. The basic point, however, is that there is great flexibility in making these allocation decisions, which raises the possibility that some of the costs of exempt activities on behalf of the presidential candidate might wind up being paid for by federally impermissible monies collected under state statutes.[38]

Alexander's sanguine reaction and Drew's worried response to the soft money developments may both be justified. Greater state and local party involvement in the presidential contest and greater national, state, and local party coordination may be achieved at the expense of gutting the campaign finance laws and creating an "anything goes" system. Certainly the response by lawyers, accountants, and politicians to the campaign finance laws ever since their inception has been to circumvent them—legally. A cottage industry has developed to probe the boundaries and limits of the law.

In 1984 both parties planned to raise large amounts of soft money. In a series of fascinating articles, *Washington Post* reporter Thomas Edsall detailed some of these activities.[39] The executive director of the Democratic National Committee hoped to raise $18 million in soft money for the general election.[40] Edsall noted that the Reagan reelection campaign put into place a team similar in structure and personnel to that used in the 1980 soft money endeavor.[41] Moreover, many state Republican parties planned to spend sizable amounts in 1984 on party-building activities and campaign paraphernalia. In

California, according to Edsall, the state party planned to spend $10.5 million on registration, absentee ballots, get-out-the-vote drives, and related activities.[42] About 30 percent of this amount would come from a federal account that contained no union and corporate contributions; the rest would come from a state account with no restrictions on it. Ohio Republicans hoped for a budget of $2.8 million in 1984 with three separate budget accounts.[43]

Hence, although the presidential candidates were restricted in 1984 to a public subsidy of $40.4 million and $6.9 million in coordinated party expenditures in the general election, and were not allowed to raise any private monies for their own campaigns (except for compliance costs), the total amount spent on behalf of each major party nominee was far in excess of this amount. In addition to the soft money, there is one other major source of funds coming into the presidential contest—independent expenditures. Although the final figures are not yet available, it appears that soft money and independent expenditures in 1984 provided a monetary advantage to the Republican presidential ticket despite a substantial increase in labor spending on behalf of the Democratic candidates.[44]

The Independent Campaign

According to a Federal Election Commission publication, "The FEC and the Federal Campaign Finance Law,"[45] an independent expenditure is "one made for a communication which expressly advocates the election or defeat of a clearly identified candidate and which is not made with any direct or indirect cooperation, consent, request or suggestion or consultation involving a candidate or his/her authorized committee or agent."[46] In an analysis of campaign finance laws, Jo Freeman points out that the cooperation mentioned in this definition is presumed to exist when an expenditure is made "based on information about the candidate's plans, projects or needs provided to the expending person by the candidate, or by the candidate's agents, with a view toward having an expenditure made."[47]

The problems inherent in determining whether an expenditure is truly independent are illustrated in the following hypothetical example. Imagine a presidential candidate in the general election who allows a privately commissioned voter preference poll in an important state to be leaked. This poll information is reported by the press and some citizens then choose to spend money independently on behalf of the candidate in that state. Would such an expenditure be independent? Or would it be considered coordinated with the candidate's effort and therefore inappropriate? Presumably, in order to judge such an expenditure as being "not independent," one would have to demonstrate that the candidate or the campaign organization leaked the data with the intent of generating independent expenditures. Because this is obviously a very difficult proposition to prove, one can see how large amounts of inappropriate independent expenditures may be entering the presidential campaign. Indeed, this example is not hypothetical but real, according to Elizabeth Drew.[48] Drew interviewed Paul Dietrich,[49] head of the Fund for a Conservative Majority, which spent two million dollars independently in 1980 during the primaries and the general election to help Reagan. Dietrich asserted, "There is no way to enforce independence as long as there is a press corps giving us information and as long as one group puts out information and gets it to the others."[50] As Drew observes, because there is a close-knit community of pollsters and consultants, information about where independent expenditures might be made most helpfully is readily available.[51]

Although the bulk of independent expenditures in the 1976 and 1980 presidential contests were made during the general election, independent expenditures also occur during the primary season and even earlier. One example of independent expenditures that occurred very early in the 1980 presidential election was the large number of committees organized in 1979 with the avowed purpose of drafting Senator Edward Kennedy to be the Democratic nominee for president. According to Alexander, when Kennedy announced his candidacy in November 1979, more than seventy draft-Kennedy committees already existed in thirty-eight states, with total expenditures by these committees of more than $500,000.[52] The Carter campaign committee filed a complaint with the FEC about these committees. The FEC's response was challenged in court and ultimately a U.S. appeals court ruled that under the Supreme Court's *Buckley* v. *Valeo* decision, the draft committees were not political committees and therefore not subject to the contribution and expenditure limits that apply to candidate committees. Because the draft committees were viewed as not supporting a candidate in the legal sense of the term, and because these committees were operating without the authorization of the candidate, they were therefore free to make independent expenditures on behalf of Kennedy.[53] Hence, the skillful use of draft committees may provide another method to circumvent spending limits in the future; such expenditures will not count against the individual state ceilings and the overall spending limit during the nomination contest.

Independent spending also has occurred during the primary season, the largest amount being the $1.6 million spent on Reagan's behalf in 1980, more than half coming from the Fund for a Conservative Majority.[54] According to Alexander, some of these independent expenditures came at critical times for the Reagan campaign.[55] For example, the Fund for a Conservative Majority spent about $80,000 for Reagan in Texas when the Reagan campaign approached the Texas spending limit.

Probably the most publicized instance of "independent" expenditures occurred in the 1984 Democratic nomination battle. The Mondale campaign organized for an early, decisive victory in the primaries and allocated funds accordingly. Thus, when the nomination contest between Mondale, Hart, and Jackson became a prolonged one, efforts were made to inject some independent monies into the Mondale campaign. The recipients were teams of delegate candidates running as Mondale supporters to the Democratic convention.[56] And even though the Mondale campaign rejected any PAC contributions, the delegate candidate committees did accept PAC money, primarily from labor unions.

Initially, Mondale disclaimed any control over these delegate committees, asserting that they were truly independent activities whose spending should not be charged against the spending ceilings imposed on the candidate. However, this claim quickly came under attack by the news media and by Mondale's Democratic opponents. For example, *Washington Post* reporters George Lardner and David Hoffman[57] wrote that FEC reports showed sustantial "apparent coordination between supposedly independent Mondale delegate committees around the country and Walter F. Mondale's national campaign organization. . ."[58] According to the reports, workers from the national Mondale organization were being shifted to the payrolls of the delegate committees in states that were about to hold their primaries and caucuses. In addition, Thomas Edsall reported that Mondale finance director Tim Finchem explicitly expressed support for the delegate committees, and that David Ifshin, legal counsel to the Mondale campaign, provided advice about how to form delegate fund-raising committees to Mondale delegates throughout the country.[59]

In late April of 1984, responding to the sharp political attacks from his Democratic opponents and from the press, Mondale directed that the delegate committees cease operations. Even after this announcement, Mondale received harsh criticism from Gary Hart, who called upon Mondale to return all the monies spent by the delegate committees. In early April, Hart had filed a formal complaint with the FEC. Preliminary estimates were that about 132 delegate committees had been created with a total spending of about $400,000.[60] This entire episode illustrates an enduring fact about the campaign finance reforms: candidates and their lawyers and accountants are constantly seeking ways to get around the laws. That the Mondale effort backfired into negative publicity for the candidate may have the beneficial effect of making future candidates more wary of such activities.

About one month after the November 1984 election the FEC accepted a conciliation agreement with the Mondale campaign that required the campaign to pay $18,500 in civil penalties and to return $379,640 in excess contributions to the U.S. Treasury. In return, the FEC agreed to forgo any further legal action against the Mondale campaign and its individual and labor union supporters.[61]

This settlement offended many observers as having avoided the basic issues. Herbert Alexander wrote: "The settlement is pointedly inconclusive. It goes to the brink of declaring the Mondale campaign at fault, yet stops short of finding fault. . . . The settlement is inappropriate whether the Mondale campaign broke the law or not. If the law was broken, the penalties were far too light. . . . Conversely, the commission should not have extracted any penalties from the Mondale campaign at all if the law was not broken."[62] The more important point is that the FEC is often politically and administratively incapable of providing prompt and definitive decisions about alleged violations of the campaign finance laws. Hence, negative publicity is more likely than FEC penalties to be an effective deterrent to end runs around the campaign finance laws.

The largest independent expenditures occurred in the 1980 and 1984 general elections and most of these independent monies went to support the Reagan campaigns. Alexander reported that more than

$10 million of independent spending was made for Reagan in 1980, compared to less than $30,000 for the Carter campaign.[63] The preliminary totals for 1984 show $15.3 million in independent expenditures for Reagan compared to slightly more than $600,000 for Mondale. These figures represent a dramatic increase from the 1976 election. If the growth rate and the party disparity in independent expenditures continue, it is clear that the intent of the campaign finance laws that both parties have similar financial resources during the general election will be undermined. And a recent Supreme Court decision (discussed below) suggests that independent expenditures will continue to rise. One caveat about the magnitude of independent monies is that a substantial proportion of the funds raised by organizations are used to defray the costs of fund-raising and thus are never spent on behalf of the candidate.

Most of the independent expenditures for Reagan in 1980 and 1984 came from conservative PACs rather than wealthy individuals. There was a provision in the finance laws that limited PACs to $1,000 in independent expenditures, but it was suspended when its constitutionality came under attack. Hence, PACs could spend independently without limit in 1980. Ultimately the Supreme Court deadlocked 4–4 on this provision, which led the FEC to try to restore the $1,000 limitation. When two conservative PACs—the National Conservative Political Action Committee and the Fund for a Conservative Majority—stated that they would try to spend large amounts of money on behalf of Reagan in 1984, the FEC and the Democratic party brought suit in lower court to prevent such expenditures. The lower court ruled against the FEC and the Democrats, noting that the *Buckley* v. *Valeo* reasoning that allowed unlimited independent expenditures by individuals was also appropriate to the situation of PACs. The Supreme Court agreed to review this lower court ruling but rejected a plea by the Democratic party to issue its decision by July 1984. Finally, in March 1985, the Supreme Court by a 7–2 vote struck down the $1,000 limit on independent expenditures by PACs for publicly funded presidential candidates. As in *Buckley* v. *Valeo*, the Court ruled that such limitations infringed upon the freedom of speech and association guaranteed by the First Amendment. Thus, the current status of the campaign finance laws is that unlimited independent expenditures by individuals and PACs are permissible in the presidential contest. But this, of course, begs the earlier question of whether most independent expenditures are truly independent.

Conclusion

Three campaigns for the presidency were conducted in 1980 and 1984. The distinctiveness of these campaigns arose mainly from those provisions of the campaign finance laws and court rulings that permit separate sources of money for candidates, party, and independent efforts. The three campaigns were not independent of each other; indeed, they probably were well coordinated. Certainly, the candidate-centered and the political party campaigns were closely linked, and I would argue that the bulk of the independent expenditures were effectively coordinated with them, given the widespread availability of information about where independent expenditures would be most helpful to a candidate. It may be that small-scale, individual spending is truly independent, but the sizable, committee-based independent expenditures are more realistically viewed as coordinated spending.

Of the three campaigns, only one is working as intended by law — the candidate-centered general election campaign, which is funded primarily by public subsidies given to both major party nominees. A portion of the party-centered effort — the coordinated party expenditures — also works as intended. But some of the state and local party expenditures for exempt activities under the 1979 amendments may have circumvented at the least the spirit of the campaign finance laws. And, of course, the independent general election campaign, originally prohibited by the 1974 campaign finance law, was given life by the 1976 and 1985 Supreme Court rulings.

Thus the three campaigns exist at the expense of weakened campaign finance reforms. As discussed earlier, the 1979 amendments encouraging state and local party activity may allow sizable contributions from wealthy individuals and corporations and unions to reenter presidential campaigns if the allocation among state and federal expenses and the use of impermissible funds to pay for these expenses is not monitored carefully by the FEC. The independent expenditures permitted by court rulings also allow big dollars to enter the presidential contest, which undermines the reformist goals of achieving financial parity between the parties, limiting overall spending, and eliminating the major donor from presidential campaigns. Spending in the 1984 general election far exceeded the basic $40.4 million subsidy to each major party candidate. The only parts of the campaign finance laws that seem to be working as intended are the limits on contributions to committees and the disclosure of contributions. Yet the latter may be made more problematic if the 1979 provisions result in monies being raised in certain states and spent in others, thereby making it more difficult to trace the sources of contributions.

If one accepts the argument that the three campaigns for president are coordinated to varying degrees and are not independent, where does the major responsibility for coordination lie? The answer is clear—in the candidate-centered campaign. It is the candidate's team of pollsters, media experts, and the like that plays the major role in directing expenditures in strategically effective ways. Thus, even as we see more party involvement in the presidential contest, especially during the general election, it is unlikely that the party will exercise more influence in the choice of the presidential nominee.

One can envision reforms in the area of campaign finance that would strengthen the parties, such as giving public funding to the parties, which then would distribute these monies to the candidates. However, because the interests of few representatives and senators, particularly those with presidential aspirations, are served by a stronger party system, this seems to be an extremely remote possibility. A weakened party system provides more maneuvering room for the political entrepreneur. If the Supreme Court would reverse the *Buckley* v. *Valeo* and the *FEC* v. *National Conservative Political Action Committee et al.* decisions in light of the tremendous growth of independent expenditures and, more important, in response to the growing evidence that only a very small proportion of such expenditures is truly independent, another loophole would be closed. For its part, Congress might reconsider the 1979 amendments fostering state and local party activity, although this seems unlikely so long as the Republican party is better able to exploit these provisions and maintains control of the White House.

One also can propose reforms in the delegate selection process that would enhance the role of the party organization and party leaders in the selection of presidential nominees and would concomitantly reduce the intrusiveness of the mass media, the undue

influence of Iowa and New Hampshire, and the incentives for candidates to run against the party in seeking the nomination. One reform
that has received wide public discussion is the establishment of a set
of regional primaries. But although such a system might reduce the
substantial influence of Iowa and New Hampshire and make life
more humane for candidates, it seems unlikely to strengthen
significantly the party's role in the presidential selection process.
Another change that might enhance party influence is to increase
further the proportion of convention delegates who are officially
uncommitted and who are elected officeholders or party officials. If
33 or 40 or 50 percent of the delegates to the national nominating
convention were senators, representatives, governors, state party
chairs, state legislators, and the like, then it is unlikely that the
primaries and caucuses would be decisive unless one candidate virtually swept these contests. Certainly, a higher proportion of uncommitted, "party" delegates raises the possibility that the primaries
and caucuses would play more of an advisory role to the nominating
conventions rather than the determining role they currently are
playing. Moreover, with additional party delegates, a greater opportunity for peer review of would-be presidents would exist. Presidential
candidates would have to do more to convince their party peers by
the persuasiveness of their leadership skills and policy positions,
skillful bargaining and promises of important perquisites, or both.
And perhaps through this peer review process, the interests of the
political party itself might be promoted.

Although these reforms would not substantially affect the conduct of the campaign, they would enhance the ability of the victorious candidate to govern effectively. After all, while the three campaigns for president are of interest in their own right, it is the outcome
of these campaigns that is the bottom line. Many observers argue
that the various delegate selection and campaign finance reforms
have created a system that rewards the skillful campaigner, but provides few tests of a presidential aspirant's ability to govern. Moreover,
the process is so long and drawn out that it places heavy burdens on
incumbent officeholders who aspire to the presidency. The decision
by Howard Baker not to seek reelection in 1984 so that he could vie
for the Republican nomination in 1988 reflects the harsh political
reality that it would be more advantageous to run for president as a
former U.S. senator than as the incumbent Senate majority leader.
Baker's decision is a sad commentary on a selection system that

drags on for years and may, simply by its duration, weed out many potentially excellent presidents. It is more than coincidence that Carter in 1976, Reagan in 1980, and Mondale in 1984 all won their parties' presidential nominations as former, not current officeholders.

The lengthy presidential campaign insures that presidential politics will always be in season and that, as a result, presidential honeymoons are likely to be shorter and presidential lame duck status achieved earlier in a second term. Political commentators have long observed that presidents must in most instances achieve their major accomplishments shortly after their election or reelection. But today it appears that the window of presidential opportunity is shrinking still further as presidential politics continually pervades the political scene. Speculation about the 1988 election and the post-Reagan era became rampant on election night in 1984 and intensified after the 1986 midterm elections. If the media and politicians are constantly looking toward the next election, the power base of the president is eroded and governing is made more difficult.

As discussed earlier, the oft-reformed campaign finance laws and delegate selection procedures have promoted a candidate-centered presidential campaign that relies heavily on hired guns from the world of marketing, polling, direct mail fund-raising, and the like. Some hired guns bring to their political endeavors a win-at-any-cost attitude that makes the campaign primarily a candidate promotion effort; the classical idea of democratic theory that a campaign is a process of citizenry education on the major public issues simply is overwhelmed by the hoopla and hype. Even though the classical image of campaigns may be unrealistic and unattainable, it is important to remember that campaigns characterized by a clear discussion of issues may facilitate subsequent governing by the victorious candidate—assuming that the candidate who addresses the issues directly can win. Certainly the candidate who presents policy proposals before the election and then is victorious will have a better chance of seeing them enacted than the winning nominee who springs new proposals on a surprised citizenry and Congress after the election. There are many reasons why elections cannot be interpreted as mandates for particular public policies. But to the extent that elections entail informed choices by an educated citizenry, the capacity to govern after the election will be enhanced.

The candidate-centered campaign also may weaken the political party and the prospects for governing when the victorious candidate is either unwilling or unable to expand the election coalition to include broader elements of the party in a governing coalition. As mentioned earlier, many of Jimmy Carter's initial problems as president were attributed to his inability to move beyond the close circle of Georgia intimates who were instrumental to his electoral success. In a related vein, the very process of winning the presidential nomination by means of a candidate-centered effort may so divide a party that its November prospects are diminished and its coalitional base threatened. And even if victory is achieved in November, the political party may emerge from the process in a precarious condition.

One may ask: Why worry about the health of the political party? Why should one care whether the candidate-centered campaign contributes to the weakening of the political party? Are not parties becoming increasingly irrelevant and outmoded institutions?

Many scholars have talked about the functions that political parties perform for the American political system. There is disagreement about some of these functions and how well the party performs them, but there is little doubt that the parties play an important role in the governing process by recruiting candidates, organizing and expressing programmatic concerns, and providing linkages across and among levels of government in our highly fragmented political system. Through these and other activities, the parties promote responsiveness and accountability in government.

Political parties are in no immediate danger of extinction. Their activities are too central to the political system to witness any sudden demise. Moreover, parties enjoy substantial protection in election laws and there is increasing evidence that the parties are learning how to respond to the new technological environment of campaigns and elections. Nevertheless, one still must express concern for the parties in light of a presidential selection process in which the candidate-centered campaign is dominant, the independent expenditures campaign is likely to grow in importance, and the party effort remains the weakest of the three. If parties were simply organizations for electing candidates, then their future would be of lesser concern, since other organizations (such as political action committees) could just as effectively use current technology and contest elections. But parties do much more and it is for this reason that the way we conduct presidential (and other) elections raises significant public issues about governance in the United States.

10 Regulating Campaign Finance: Consequences for Interests and Institutions

XANDRA KAYDEN

The 1970s was a decade of major change in the structure of American politics. One of the most significant elements of that change was the passage of the Federal Election Campaign Act (FECA). Originally enacted in 1971, the law was amended several times during the decade and was the subject of a Supreme Court ruling. By 1980 the law was clear, as was the fact that it had changed the relationships between interests and candidates, and between candidates and parties. The presidential selection process, which prompted passage of the law in the first place, was most affected, but the effects of the law reached far beyond the presidency, to Congress and to state and local politics. The law, along with other factors such as the developing technology of communication, has been instrumental in rebuilding the major parties and in giving greater weight to centralization and professionalism in politics. It appears to have nationalized interest group activity at the expense of the interests of local constituencies.

This chapter will explore the development of campaign finance reform: its causes, objectives, and consequences. It will consider the new balance of power between the participants in the political process. Some interests, such as business, have lost influence at the presidential level but increased their participation and influence in Congress. Membership organizations that can provide volunteers to help win caucuses and primaries have gained influence. Organizations that can make appeals on "hot" moral issues also have benefited, although thus far they have had more success in setting the tone of the political debate than in affecting the outcome of the presidential selection process. They may have more influence in elections with less visibility.

The practices of some of the new groups—practices born of new campaign technologies such as direct mail fund-raising and independent spending—are beginning to affect the behavior of older groups. Many of the newer participants in political financing, small donors brought in because of their concern about social and moral issues, may be less committed to the system than their "fat cat" predecessors, and thus a less stable influence in the process. The net result of these competing forces may not be known for some time.

Throughout this essay the analysis will be based on the structures of the law: contribution and expenditure limits, independent expenditures, and public financing. The new rules have created a new game. Our concern is with the game and how each participant (the candidates' campaign organizations, the parties, and the interest groups) plays its chips and moves about the board. Our knowledge is based on the disclosure provisions of the law. These give us insight into the process, but we still are limited by what the players are willing to say, the threat of law notwithstanding. If there are serious abuses of the law, we cannot identify them. On the other hand, if money is not spent publicly and in a way that makes a difference in the outcome of an election, it may not matter. The law relies upon the players to comply, and whether we believe they do or do not probably depends upon the confidence we place in the political system as a whole. I tend to believe they do comply.

The History of the Law

Most campaign legislation has been directed first against the powerful interests of big business and secondarily at the corruption of elected officials. Recent efforts have also been concerned with the amount of money spent in campaigns, but it is not clear whether this is a critical problem for the democratic process or even whether it can be effectively curtailed, given the increased costs of communication, reliance on professionals, and so on. Considering that it is the officials themselves who must enact the legislation, reform usually does not occur unless there have been major scandals, or unless established interests fear a change, as when the rise of machines (and the immigrant populations that fueled them) occurred during the Progressive Era.

The history of campaign finance legislation began with the passage of the Tillman Act in 1907. It prohibited corporate contributions to campaigns, provided some measure of disclosure through the filing of reports to both the respective houses of Congress and the General Accounting Office, and established campaign spending limitations.[1] The law was observed more in the breach than in practice and the ways around it became the rules of the game. Reports were filed, but were not available to the public and were kept for only two years. Most campaign communications costs were exempted, such as stationery, postage, printing, and telephones. Primary elections were excluded from coverage, even though a large portion of the country consisted of single party states where winning the primary was tantamount to election. The Progressive movement was more successful in controlling power when it attacked the political parties by instituting primaries and nonpartisan elections at the local level and by enacting office, rather than party ballots. Campaigns themselves are temporary and there is no second chance. If the rules do not fit the needs of politicians who are contesting elections, experience suggests that the rules will be bent until they do. Any complaints —after the election—are generally academic exercises.

Although there were other attempts at reform in the middle years of the century (the Hatch Act in 1940 limited the influence of incumbency, and the Taft-Hartley Act in 1947 extended the contributions prohibitions to organized labor), it was not until the passage of the FECA in 1971 that the new age of reform began.

The first major step in modern reform grew out of the election of John F. Kennedy to the presidency in 1960. It reflected, in part, the new president's concern with the cost of campaigning (tremendously increased by the use of paid television advertising) and the sense that only a rich man could afford to run. Kennedy established a commission, which suggested that a matching funds program (wherein public funds are provided to candidates in direct proportion to the amounts they raise from private sources) be established for presidential elections. President Lyndon B. Johnson expressed interest in electoral reform but did not submit legislation in time for action before Congress adjourned. The Ashmore-Goodell bill followed in the mid-1960s, after the censure of Senator Thomas Dodd of Connecticut for using campaign funds for personal purposes in 1966. It called for the creation of a Federal Election Commission, which would receive, process, and make public all campaign reports filed by all candidates in federal elections. A weakened version passed the Senate in 1967, but the House failed to act on it.[2]

Throughout the 1960s measures were offered and occasionally passed into law, although none ever saw the light of practice. Senator Russell Long of Louisiana, chairman of the Senate Finance Committee, sponsored a bill that called for a subsidy for presidential elections to be funneled through the national parties. The bill passed, but it was voted "inoperative" the next year, partly out of fear of giving too much power to the political bosses, particularly the national party chairmen, who could, it was felt, exert undue influence in the selection of presidential candidates.[3]

Coinciding with the legislative proposals were academic studies, one sponsored by the Twentieth Century Fund on the costs of campaigning, with special attention to the media, and another by the Campaign Finance Group at Harvard, which argued that the United States did not spend enough on elections. There were lobbying efforts led by the National Committee for an Effective Congress and later by Common Cause. The Citizens Research Foundation began the important task of gathering data about elections and publishing comprehensive studies of campaign costs.

Modern Reform

Throughout the 1970s, campaign finance legislation was passed and amended and ruled upon by the Supreme Court. This legislation has changed American politics as much as the reforms of the Progressive Era. Although the motivations for enacting reform were often the same as those in the past (mainly fear of official corruption and of the influence exercised by business) the methods used were more subtle and the consequences often were unintended.

Campaign finance reform became a reality with the passage of two bills in 1971: the Federal Election Campaign Act and the Revenue Act, which provided either tax credits or tax deductions for citizens' contributions to political campaigns, and a tax checkoff system to help finance the presidential election. The dollar checkoff system, although controversial at the time, provided the revenue for subsidies to presidential candidates. Subsidies went directly to the candidates from the Federal Election Commission, instead of to the parties as proposed originally in the Long bill. The checkoff's use by voters increased steadily until 1984, although it is by no means universal. It rose from 7 percent in 1972 to 27 percent in 1980, dropping to 23 percent in 1984, amounting to $13.5 million for the primary period in 1984 and $24.2 million during the general election, for a total of $35.4 million.[4] Unlike several states that have a check add-on system, the federal dollar is taken from the assessed tax and does not add to the taxpayer's burden.

The original Federal Election Campaign Act of 1971, which passed into law in January of 1972, had the following major provisions.

Contribution limits. Although subsequent amendments were much more severe, the original law focused on the amount candidates or their families could contribute to their own campaigns ($50,000 for president and vice president, $35,000 for the Senate, and $25,000 for a member of the House of Representatives). The Supreme Court voided this provision in *Buckley* v. *Valeo* in 1976, except as it applied to a presidential candidate receiving public funds (who could spend up to $50,000). The law now sets no limit on a candidate's personal contribution to the campaign. It does, however, limit almost everyone else: individuals are allowed to contribute a maximum of $1,000, and political action committees $5,000 per candidate. Political parties also can make contributions to the candidates, usually limited to two cents per voter, but there are a number of other services they can provide candidates at, or below, cost, which frequently makes them the largest single donor to a campaign.

Spending limits. The law placed a ceiling on the amount of money that could be spent for media by federal candidates in all elections. This feature, too, was altered, first by the 1974 amendments and then by the Court in *Buckley*. The limits that currently exist are placed on candidates receiving public funds in presidential campaigns, and on parties.

Oversight. The law called for the clerk of the House and the secretary of the Senate to oversee elections to their respective bodies by handling reports and disclosure, and for the comptroller general to oversee the presidential candidates and other miscellaneous committees. The 1974 amendments then created the Federal Election Commission (FEC) to assume these responsibilities.

Disclosure. The law required that duplicate reports be filed in

Washington and with the secretaries of state or comparable officers within each state in order to inform voters about campaign funding. In addition, candidates and political committees were required to report total expenditures, as well as the names, addresses, occupations, and principal places of business of each of their contributors. Each expenditure over $100 also was to be reported, including salaries and personal services. The 1979 amendments later raised the reporting threshold to $200, but otherwise the provision has remained intact and has become one of the most important elements of modern reform.

The law also called for public reports to the FEC on a quarterly basis, more frequently during election cycles. The 1974 amendments changed the dates of the reports, but the exercise remains and has encouraged the centralization of campaigning.

The 1974 Amendments

The 1971 law was passed largely in response to a growing concern about the money required to win an election in the television age. The Watergate scandals that stemmed from the 1972 presidential campaign gave new impetus to the perennial reformist theme of curbing the power of large donors and the rapaciousness of some of those who would seek their support. The 1974 amendments were, according to one observer, "the most sweeping set of campaign finance law changes ever adopted in the United States, if not the world."[5] Among their features were the following.

Contribution limits. Individuals were limited to contributions of $1,000 to any candidate in any election (primary, runoff, and general). There was a cumulative contribution limit of $25,000 per calendar year for any individual, which includes contributions to candidates, political committees, and parties. The amendments retained the candidate self-contribution limitations (struck in 1976 by the Court), and limited to $1,000 the amount an individual could spend independent of the campaign to influence an election (also struck by the Court).

Political action committees (PACS) were limited to contributions of $5,000 per election, but no cumulative limit was set on their contributions. Political parties were limited in their expenditures on behalf of candidates in general elections to $10,000 in House elections and $20,000, or two cents per voter, in Senate elections, which-ever was greater. Parties also were allowed to spend two cents per voter in presidential elections. In primary elections, the parties were limited to $5,000 and treated as any other committee. At the time, neither party had much money to spend and the limitations were somewhat academic. More recently, the parties have turned out to be far more influential in campaigns because they raise money and can provide services, and because the limitations are more severe on other participants.

Public financing. A matching contributions system was established in which a presidential candidate would qualify for federal funds by raising $5,000 in donations of $250 or less in twenty states. During the primary season, the government would match donations of $250 and less as long as the candidate won 10 percent of the vote in every other primary entered. (A candidate who loses eligibility can be reinstated by winning 20 percent of the vote in a subsequent pri-mary.) This provision, combined with the contribution limit on indi-viduals, shifted the focus of political fund-raising away from the proverbial fat cat toward the small donor, who could be reached largely through direct mail campaigns. It has had a major effect on political participation and rhetoric in America.

The two major parties received flat grants for the nominating con-ventions; thereafter, nominees who chose to accept public financing were required to forgo private contributions during the general elec-tion. In 1984 the presidential candidates each received $40 million.

The Federal Election Commission. The new law created an inde-pendent, bipartisan commission of six members, to be chosen by the Speaker of the House, the president pro tempore of the Senate, and the president. Under *Buckley*, this provision was changed to require that all appointments be made by the president (because of the sepa-ration of powers required by the Constitution). The commission was given responsibility for administering the law, a task made easier by tighter reporting requirements and the required creation of one cen-tral committee per campaign, through which all contributions and expenditures were to be reported.[6]

Watergate notwithstanding, the passage of the 1974 amendments was not without controversy. Wayne Hays, who chaired the House Administration Committee, which was responsible for the legisla-tion, was a strong opponent of public financing. He stalled the bill for more than a year. Because House members come up for reelection so frequently, they tend to be wary of all electoral reforms, and these were bound to be far-reaching. The Nixon administration also forwarded legislation, but its proposals met with little support, some believing that they were designed for failure, given the president's difficulties in the last election. It was, in fact, just a few hours before Nixon resigned that the House passed the FECA on August 8, 1974. The Senate, which had passed another bill the year before while waiting for House action, had included public financing of congressional election in its version, but acceded to the House and dropped that section. The bill was signed by President Gerald R. Ford on October 15, 1974, and went into effect on January 1, 1975.[7]

Challenge in the Courts: Buckley v. Valeo

Controversy did not end with the passage of the law. A wide-ranging coalition of opponents formed that spanned the political spectrum from right to left. During the legislative process, Senator James L. Buckley, a conservative Republican, introduced an amendment to the law that allowed any eligible voter to bring suit challenging the constitutionality of the FECA. The most important issue involved the First Amendment right to freedom of speech, but other constitutional questions concerned rights of association and equal protection. A few days after the law went into effect, Buckley, whose coalition included Eugene McCarthy and Stewart Mott from the liberal wing of the Democratic party, brought suit against the secretary of the Senate (Francis R. Valeo), the clerk of the House, the attorney general, the FEC, Common Cause, the Center for Public Financing of Elections, and the League of Women Voters. Slightly more than a year later, on January 30, 1976, the Supreme Court issued its ruling.

The central issue of the case was the relationship between money and free speech, or as Herbert Alexander described it: "Is an expenditure for speech substantially the same thing as speech itself, because the expenditure is necessary to reach large audiences by the purchase of air time or space in print media?"[8] The Court voided the limits on independent expenditures and on what candidates could spend of their own money on their own campaigns (with the exception of presidential candidates who accept public financing). It upheld the other contribution limits on the grounds that they were only marginal constraints on contributors but did serve to lessen the influence of large donors—an acceptable policy preference. The Court also upheld the disclosure provisions, the public financing scheme for presidential elections, and the notion of a bipartisan commission. It did not accept the role of Congress in appointing the FEC commissioners, however, which forced Congress to rewrite the law. The 111 days it took to do so left a hiatus in the functioning of the commission and the law in the midst of the 1976 election campaign.[9]

The Court recognized three matters of public interest as its reasons for accepting the disclosure provisions of the law as they applied to candidates: (1) providing voters information on the sources and uses of campaign funds; (2) the deterrence of corruption, or the appearance of corruption, by revealing large contributions; and (3) enforcing contribution limits. The Court did not require such disclosure from associational interests lest it inhibit their First Amendment rights: to disclose some groups' membership might deter people from belonging. It also gave greater weight to the First Amendment than to the equal protection clause of the Fourteenth Amendment when it rejected the limitations on candidates' personal contributions, on spending ceilings that might aid incumbents over challengers (because incumbents are more likely to have higher name recognition than challengers, who must therefore spend more to become equally known), or on candidates with support from wealthy interests, who are more likely to have access to disposable income than candidates without such support.[10]

Although there is constant litigation in the courts regarding the law, and some cases have come as far as the Supreme Court, no ruling has yet been as comprehensive as *Buckley* in its effect on reform efforts and the electoral process in general.

No one was entirely pleased with the outcome of *Buckley*. Richard Smolka, citing Chief Justice Warren Burger's separate opinion, noted that the Court

> by "dissecting the Act" failed to recognize that the whole is greater than the sum of its parts. Burger argued that Congress had intended to regulate all aspects of federal campaign finance, but what remains after today's holdings leaves no more than a shadow of what Congress contemplated. I question whether the residue leaves a workable program. . . . The more the courts look at the law, the less they see that can pass constitutional muster.

And what is left may not be sufficient to achieve the primary objective of the law in the first place—to limit the influence or apparent influence of money in campaigns, thereby reducing the likelihood of corruption of elected officials.[11]

The Later Amendments: 1976 and 1979

Congress continued to legislate after the *Buckley* decision. It concentrated more on the Federal Election Commission than on the substance of reform, although it did make some changes. It established annual limits on individual contributions of $20,000 to parties and $5,000 to other political committees; established limits on PAC contributions to parties of $15,000; limited presidential candidates who accept public funds to $50,000 of their own money (as provided for in the original 1971 act, but struck by the Court when it voided limits on congressional candidates); limited corporate PACs to solicitations from stockholders and executive and administrative personnel and their families (in response to an FEC decision deemed favorable to corporations, known as the SunPac Decision, which labor strongly opposed); and increased the amount Senate campaign committees could contribute from $5,000 to $17,500 per election.[12]

Because the FEC had been in existence for several years, the law was rewritten with a view toward "correcting" its behavior. All six commissioners were required to be appointed by the president and confirmed by the Senate, although Congress retains a great deal of interest in the selection of the commission, which is the closest thing to an oversight agency on the legislators themselves. The discretionary powers of the commission were substantially curtailed, especially in the area of advisory opinions, upon which the FEC had relied heavily in the early years, rather than trying to formulate regulations to effect compliance with the law. Because the law was expected to have a profound influence on the political process, the FEC had sought to avoid making broad policy through regulations and instead preferred taking up each question individually.[13]

There was relatively little scandal in the 1976 election, although uncertainty about the law—made more critical for presidential candidates who were depending on the matching funds the commission was slow to dispense because of the hiatus created by the Supreme

Court ruling—complicated the work of campaign planners. In retrospect, it turns out that the effects of the law were relatively moderate on candidates for other offices and on state and local parties, largely because they ignored it and the confusion was great enough for their lack of compliance to get by.[14]

The 1979 amendments grew out of experience in the 1978 elections when the law was fully enforced for the first time. As regulations were formulated and ironed out, and as individuals and organizations —to say nothing of professionals in law and accounting—discovered what was and was not possible, the body of reform began to take shape. "Unintended consequences" were identified and fine-tuning began under the guidance of Frank Thompson, the new chairman of the House Administration Committee.

Fear of corruption and undue influence, and the power of the FEC were less important concerns in 1979 than was the influence of the law on the political process as a whole. Organized labor worried about the growth of corporate PACs. The number of corporate and trade association PACs had increased dramatically, especially after the SunPac decision clarified how corporations could establish PACs. This was partly because the Republican National Committee and other pro-business groups made it a priority to organize corporate PACs, and partly because they began to learn from each other. Labor saw itself in danger of being vastly outnumbered since unions could not proliferate. A number of observers were concerned about the disadvantage the political parties seemed to suffer because of the law, especially at the local level. Fears also were expressed about the growing professionalism and centralization that campaigns required in order to meet the law's reporting standards. And since money was more visible because of disclosure, there was ongoing concern about the costs of elections. Independent expenditures, which bothered campaign professionals from the beginning even though there were relatively few of them in the first two election cycles under the law, were thought to be a wild card in the political arena. This fear would grow, although solutions have remained elusive.

The 1979 amendments simplified many of the law's procedures and absolved many of the small participants from reporting requirements. State and local party restrictions were eased when it became clear that the burden of maintaining separate accounts was widening the division between each party's local and federal candidates. A congressional candidate attending a pancake breakfast held by the county party—and attended by other party candidates for local and state office—created a nightmare for accountants who had to allocate the proportionate benefits and costs between the federal and state candidates. Spending limits were adjusted in some areas and clarified in others. The FEC practice of random audits was restricted, with at least some indication of significant violation now required, and although there was some discussion of extending public financing to congressional elections, the issue was not considered in the legislation lest it jeopardize the noncontroversial problems that Congress wanted to resolve.[15]

Campaign Reform in Practice: The Presidential Experience

The reforms of the 1970s have succeeded because of their ability to measure the income and expenditures of campaigns. They would not have been possible in a less technologically sophisticated age. Their implementation, however, has increased reliance on technology in politics, and along with it the growth of political professionals (especially in law and accounting) and centralization. Another consequence of the law and the growing role of technology has been the rise of some interests and the decline of others. All of these developments are seen most clearly at the presidential level because it is the most visible American election, and because it sets the standard for smaller campaigns.

The Campaigns

The most important consequences of the law for the campaigns themselves involve contributions and expenditures limitations in the states during the prenomination phase, and compliance procedures. Public financing—a major feature of the reform that attempted to alleviate the need for candidates to rely on either large donors or their own wealth—has affected fund-raising strategies and fostered the emergence of independent spending. Public financing seems, at this stage, to have had greater influence on the formation and activities of the groups making the expenditures than it has on the outcome of presidential elections, although it may make a greater difference in other elections.

Contribution Limits

An intent of the law was to limit the influence of large donors. From the very beginning, however, the $1,000 contribution limit has been criticized as being too low for presidential elections. Typically, recommendations for change suggest a $3,500 to $10,000 limit, scaled down proportionately at the Senate and House levels. As the argument goes, "You can't buy a senator for $1,000. You couldn't even rent one." The consequences of the low limit include the following:

1. Campaigns must begin earlier to raise "seed money" and establish credibility, making it almost impossible for a late entrant to amass the resources necessary for an effective campaign for the nomination. The experience of Gary Hart in 1984, as a candidate who became a leading contender only after the caucuses and primaries began, also raises the question of whether the limits—and the times of the primaries—allow enough flexibility to mount a major campaign. Having poured most of its resources into the early primaries and caucuses, knowing that in order to win it would have to make a strong showing in the beginning, the Hart campaign had little in funds or energy left to sustain its efforts once the first surge of momentum passed.

2. The emphasis the FECA places on smaller donations for matching purposes, combined with the improved technology in direct mail fund-raising, has strongly influenced the methods campaigns use to raise money. Increasingly, ideological and negative approaches are used, which may hurt the chances of centrist candidates in both parties. Although politicians in other nations have used direct mail solicitations successfully without making negative appeals, that strategy does not seem to work in the United States, where the incentive to make small contributions is presumed to be principally fear or anger.

3. The campaign organization is forced to devote more of its time and resources to raising money, increasing the cost of fund-raising to at least one dollar for every four raised.[16]

4. The new fund-raising strategy and the reporting requirements of the law have so encouraged a centralization of the campaign that local activity has been seriously limited. Still, it is doubtful that the law is the major cause of the decline of grass roots participation in politics.

5. The contribution limitation has not entirely succeeded in tak-

ing the large donor out of presidential politics. Independent expenditures, contributions to political action committees, and contributions to state parties that do not fall under the federal law and are not reported to the FEC, are available and effective alternatives to those seeking influence. In addition, there are other loopholes in the law that have enabled some to make relatively substantial contributions to presidential candidates, including artists who donate their work for sale by the campaign, and individuals who control lists of donors.

The intent of the law was to take the large donor out of politics, and, despite the exceptions, it has been somewhat successful. It has certainly expanded the base of contributors to include the less affluent. It is unlikely that legislation could ever entirely eliminate the participation of those who seek power through money, given the strength of power as a motivation for human behavior. As time goes on, major loopholes have emerged that, although not necessarily venal or harmful to the process, have contravened the intent of the law and certain expectations and understandings about how the political system functions. One of the most ingenious loopholes grew from the recognition that the federal law applies only to federal elections, not to state elections or state political institutions. Since 1980, both parties, but principally the Republicans, have been organizing and directing those who would like to make large contributions to a number of state parties. The contribution is reported in the state in which it is received, but not in the donor's state or in Washington. The only ones who know the aggregate size of the donor's total contribution are the party coordinators and the presidential campaign staff.

Expenditure Limits

For presidential nomination campaigns, the law provides a formula of sixteen cents times the voting age population of a state, or $200,000 (whichever is greater) as the limit for spending in each state. This figure is adjusted to the price index each calendar year, with 1976 as the base year. The total limit is calculated at $10 million, plus an inflation factor, which by 1984 added up to $40.4 million, half of which could come from public funds.[17] The state limits have turned out to be critical in the early primaries and caucuses, especially because Iowa and New Hampshire are states with small populations. Although more of the candidates' problems stem from the proliferation and timing of primaries and caucuses than from the campaign reform law, it has become a fact of political life that campaign staffs resort to "creative accounting" and other artificial methods of behavior to spend as much as they believe they must in order to make a credible showing. Since Massachusetts has a large limit and New Hampshire a low limit, campaign staffers frequently stay in neighboring Massachusetts hotels and make media expenditures there in order to bypass the lower New Hampshire limit. Another tactic is to charge campaign headquarters expenditures to the costs of compliance with the law, which are exempted from the spending limitations.

One of the most obvious features of the presidential selection process is the timing of the primaries and caucuses, a subject of continuing, some would argue eternal, debate in the Democratic party. However the timing issue is resolved from one election to another, any arrangement will favor some kinds of candidates and hinder others, partly because of the rules laid down by the campaign finance law. There does not seem to be a way to lessen the importance of the early events because of the momentum they give to the candidates who win them or come a surprisingly close second. Because of their importance, therefore, campaign managers will do whatever they can to maximize their chances of success.

According to a Campaign Finance Study Group report on the 1980 presidential election, most presidential campaigns reported spending up to 85 percent of the state limit in the early contests, then dropped to 30 to 40 percent in March, and 25 to 30 percent in April.[18] A similar pattern existed in 1976[19] and in 1984, not only because of political need but also because the later states are larger and have higher limits. Although it may be easier to change the law than to reduce the importance of the primaries, the spending limits' effect thus far has been to engender cynicism about compliance among campaign professionals because of the impracticality of the law.

Once the early campaign season is past, candidates pick and choose which primaries to enter to preserve their matching fund eligibility (which requires that they receive 10 percent of the votes cast in at least one of two succeeding primaries they enter) and to enhance their credibility as presidential contenders.[20] Since the larger states yield larger delegations to the nominating conventions, the smaller states now tend to be ignored by the campaigns, at least as measured by campaign expenditures.[21]

Another result of state spending limits is that once a primary is over, campaign headquarters, which are opened about four weeks before the primary, are closed as soon as possible. The staff often will move to the next state, adding to the tendency of campaigns to be run more by professionals (and roving bands of volunteers) and less by local workers.

Whatever the objectives of the state expenditures limits (a more even distribution of campaign spending, a compliance mechanism that will help the FEC oversee spending, or some combination of goals), they have very few supporters. Most view the state limits as an arbitrary, artificial obstacle that does nothing to advance the presidential selection process. They are a problem for frontrunners, who must spend early and everywhere in order to maintain both their organizations and their standing in the eyes of the media. They are also a problem for candidates seeking to emerge from the pack. Although eliminating or at least alleviating state limits is not an especially controversial notion, congressional leaders charged with campaign finance have been hesitant to open up the legislative process again lest opponents of the entire concept of campaign finance regulation use the opportunity to gut the law.

Compliance Procedures

The law calls for periodic reports on campaign income and expenditures. Meeting that requirement—along with the expenditure limitations—has forced presidential campaigns to alter their organizational structures. Local headquarters, which used to "live off the land" by developing many of their own activities, raising their own funds, and generally representing the candidate to those who wanted to get involved, have fallen victim to the candidates' need to centralize and to keep strict controls over both fund-raising and campaign spending.

Compliance procedures, particularly during the primary period, are often cited as a cause of centralization in campaigns, because of the level of detail required by the FEC before matching funds are granted. Campaign staffs estimate that from three to seven full-time people are required to fill out the forms.[22] More important, the roles of accountants, attorneys, and all of the support staff that are associated with fund-raising and reporting have been enhanced because of the compliance, contribution, and expenditure limitations of the law.

Although the work is clearly burdensome, and stories of FEC mishandling are to be found in every campaign, it is clear that modern presidential campaigns are professional enough to handle it. Stories also abound about using compliance expenditures as a cover for other activities whose costs probably would put a campaign over the expenditures limit in the early primaries and caucuses. Still, no major scandals have erupted after three presidential elections under the law. The most typical ruse, as already noted, is to charge campaign headquarters overhead to compliance costs, thereby avoiding the limits because compliance costs are exempt. From the beginning, the staff of the FEC has been praised by campaigns for its efforts to facilitate their work; as the years have gone by, the procedures have been streamlined and made more efficient. The work of the commission may be an extraordinary accomplishment, considering the difficulties of establishing temporary organizations, let alone regulating them.

Independent Expenditures

The fear that independent expenditures generate in the eyes of most political actors and academic observers is probably worse than the actual experience thus far would warrant, but since 1976, when *Buckley* lifted the limits on such spending, campaign managers have forecast dire consequences to the electoral process.[23] As independent spending groups gain experience with the new spending vehicle, they grow more comfortable with it and others follow their lead. Potentially, then, each election will attract more independent spending than the last. In 1980, more than $13.7 million was spent independently to influence the outcome of the presidential election ($2.3 million was spent on congressional elections).[24] Of that, $12.2 million was spent to elect Ronald Reagan.

In 1980, 85 percent of the independent spending for Reagan was done during the general election, a time when contributions to the campaigns were forbidden to candidates who accepted public financing. In 1984, however, only 40 percent of the independent spending was done during the general election; the rest was spent during the primary period and the few weeks before the national convention. The 1984 pattern raises questions about how much independent spending was tied to the prohibition against contributing to publicly financed general election campaigns.[25] It would be difficult under the circumstances to use the contribution prohibition as an argument against extending public financing to congressional elections.

In 1984, $18.5 million was spent independently, $2.5 million of it used to oppose candidates. As in 1980, most of the money was spent in the presidential election, in support of Ronald Reagan ($15.5 million for the president, with $160,000 spent against him). A little more than a half million dollars was spent on behalf of the Democratic nominee, Walter Mondale, and a little less than a half million was spent against him. Again, as in 1980, most of the money was spent by conservative groups, with the top five spending more than $14.5 million. But, as Michael Malbin has pointed out, 85 to 95 percent of that money went into direct mail fund-raising rather than the purchase of media advertising to advocate Reagan's election.[26]

National Conservative Political Action Committee (NCPAC)	$ 9,742,930
Ruff-PAC	1,952,071
Fund for a Conservative Majority	1,552,927
National Congressional Club	789,353
Christian Voice Moral Government Fund	339,863
Total	$14,576,461

Although almost twice as many groups spent independently on behalf of Walter Mondale (forty-nine to twenty-nine for Reagan), the largest donor, the Senior Political Action Committee, gave only $205,090, which was just about matched by the fifteen labor unions that made independent expenditures ($205,578). Among the other interests that spent in the 1984 presidential election were the nuclear freeze movement ($73,000); antiabortion groups, which concentrated more on congressional elections, but spent almost $11,000 on the presidential race; conservation groups; handgun groups; and women's groups. More corporations and trade associations were involved in 1984 than 1980, but the number remained small (fewer than a dozen).

Independent spending increased between 1980 and 1984: $2.6 million more was spent at the presidential level, and $4.5 million was spent at the congressional level—more than double the $2.3 million spent on congressional elections in 1980. If it can be assumed that spending is at its least effective when the visibility of the candidates is greatest, then the increase at the congressional level should be of more concern than that at the presidential level. For all the money that was spent by the New Right groups, few would attribute President Reagan's reelection to their efforts. Of course, it would be hard to prove that such spending determined the outcome of any given congressional election, but the chances are greater there, and still greater at the state legislative level.

Most of the groups that report independent expenditures do not spend great amounts of money. Many of the expenditures are for ads in local newspapers and on local radio and television stations. Literature is also printed independently, but many of these groups just as easily could have made a contribution to a candidate's campaign or to a party, except in the general election of the president.

The concern is about the big spenders, partly because they represent interests that are often controversial and usually spend negatively, and partly because independent expenditures have always been perceived as a loophole in the law and as being in conflict with the spirit of campaign reform. The Supreme Court has repeatedly held that curtailing such spending would be an infringement of freedom of speech. According to Justice William Rehnquist, who wrote the majority opinion in a 1985 case brought by the Federal Election Commission and the Democratic party against the National Conservative Political Action Committee (NCPAC) and the Fund for a Conservative Majority, the *Buckley* decision meant that "preventing corruption and the appearance of corruption are the only legitimate and compelling Government interests thus far identified for restricting campaign finances."[27]

Independent expenditures, according to Rehnquist, are less apt to be of a corrupting nature than contributions made directly to a candidate. The dissenting opinions by Justices Byron White and Thurgood Marshall take issue with equating free speech with money. According to White,

> If the elected members of the legislature, who are surely in the best position to know, conclude that large-scale expenditures are a significant threat to the integrity and fairness of the electoral process, we should not second-guess that judgment. . . . The credulous acceptance of the formal distinction between coordinated and independent expenditures blinks political reality. . . . By striking down one portion of an integrated and comprehensive statute, the Court has once again transformed a coherent regulatory scheme into a nonsensical, loophole-ridden patchwork.[28]

Whether Congress will ever find a way to limit independent expenditures that will pass muster with the Court remains uncertain. A political scandal, a proven electoral effect, and a change in the makeup of the Court may all have to occur before the current law can be altered. The corruption feared by some is not the old-fashioned kind in which a candidate pockets the money and votes quietly in favor of a hidden interest, but rather a corruption of the process itself. In the meantime, if money is equated with speech, Republican nominees appear to have been talking much more loudly than Democratic candidates in the last two presidential elections. With $40.4 million provided in public funds to each major party nominee (and an additional $6.9 million permitted to the national parties to spend), the added $15.6 million of independent expenditures for Reagan was a substantial amount.

If the issue is one of balance, it cannot be measured only by adding up the independent spendings on one side and comparing it to the other. One important reason for the emergence of the groups that engage in such spending was their fear of labor's influence, especially after the Watergate scandals and the loss to the Republican party of many of its professionals. Labor's strength has been its ability to educate union members (for which it spent $4.4 million in the 1984 election, according to FEC data) and to encourage their participation in campaigns. Money is only part of labor's commitment to the Democratic party. There is no estimating the value of the contributions it has made through volunteer participation. Republican fears of labor led directly to the formation of some of the most important New Right groups, including NCPAC, whose first director, Charles Black, was campaign director of the Republican National Committee.

Whether the response of the right balances out the influence of the left is very hard to tell, especially at the presidential level, because of the complexity of all elections and the visibility of presidential elections, which provide most voters with enough information from different sources to make up their own minds. At a superficial level, it appears to be more a question of balancing apples and oranges, since the concerns of one group are not matched directly against those of the other. On the other hand, labor and the New Right provide a constituency base to their respective parties, which cannot be considered irrelevant. Even though labor is essentially proestablishment, and the New Right antiestablishment, each maintains an uneasy alliance with its party, which appears to be the inevitable nature of alliances.

Since money spent at the presidential level cannot be proven to have an effect on the electoral outcome, independent expenditures appear to have been more successul in affecting the tone of the debate and in providing an alternative method of participation for some groups. A presidential election profoundly affects American politics because of the attention it commands from the public, the tone it gives the political process, and the patterns it sets for electoral behavior. Techniques that are pioneered in a presidential election become part of the repertoire of smaller campaigns; the people it brings into politics become party workers, political activists, and government employees for years to come.

Draft Committees

The 1980 election raised another regulatory problem in presidential campaigns: draft committees. This problem is not dissimilar from independent expenditures because there is a thin line between independence and coordination. It also is tied to the issue of state expenditure limits since the spending of draft committees does not count against a candidate's limits.

The complexity of the problem is not difficult to discern: a group of citizens wants to advance the candidacy of someone—Senator Edward Kennedy in the 1980 case—and raises and spends money to prove to him and the rest of the political world that his entrance into the presidential race is both desired and realistic. The draft committee's activities undoubtedly did influence Kennedy's decision to enter the race, but once he made it, how much of their spending should come under his expenditures limitations? If the answer is "none," then candidates could delay decisions until well into the primary election period, allowing draft committees to raise money and advance their interests. In Kennedy's case the first draft committee was organized in May 1979, and he did not officially enter the race until November 7.

Although suits were filed in the federal courts (which held in favor of the committees on the grounds that they do not fall under the current law), Congress did not act to reform the law between the 1980 and 1984 elections. In retrospect, it may be that draft commit-

tees are most likely to appear when an incumbent president is challenged within the party. If that is true, the issue may not arise again
until 1992, by which time Congress may have amended the law.

A problem similar to draft committees arose in the 1984 elections
with the independent funding of delegate slates. The law allows
candidates for their party's nomination to spend on their own behalf,
but Hart charged that Mondale was using his delegates' candidacies
as an alternative to spending on his own campaign. Mondale eventually disbanded his delegate committees and, after the election, the
FEC ordered him to reimburse the Treasury for the money that was
contributed to them in excess of the federal limits.

Parties and Presidential Selection

The two major political parties have grown significantly stronger in
recent years, and the campaign finance law has been a major source
of their resurgence. The limits of their influence notwithstanding,[29]
the campaign finance law has given the parties a major role to play in
the presidential selection process. This role has been critical in
enhancing the parties as institutions in the broader political process.

In 1978 the consensus was that the reforms were hurting the parties:
destroying the grass roots participation that was the mainstay of
parties at the local level; and giving new weight to interest groups,
which were seen as a direct threat to the role and influence of the
parties. The complexity of the law—its requirements for separate
accounts, allocations between federal and state and local candidates,
the virtual elimination of local fund-raising activities, and the need
to treat corporate contributions (legal in some states but illegal
under the federal law) separately—discouraged participation by local
parties in federal campaigns. Because federal and particularly presidential campaigns are so important to the local political process as
recruitment devices for party activists, the reforms thus were thought
to have a serious chilling effect on party life. Party strength, as measured by voter identification, voting participation, and local activity
was going down.

In 1978 and 1979, Congress moved to ease some of the burdens on
the parties. A postal subsidy was passed that enabled the parties to
communicate through the mail at the same cost enjoyed by many of
the interest groups that qualified as tax-exempt organizations. Both

national and state and local parties were authorized to spend more money on behalf of their candidates, particularly on volunteer activities at the local level, and the recordkeeping requirements on parties were eased.

Party Decline

The parties had been in serious trouble for a long time. The reforms of the Progressive Era were designed to limit the influence of party organizations and were successful: the primary, nonpartisan elections, and the adoption of the Australian ballot all cut seriously into the principal functions of political parties. The New Deal undercut the material incentives local parties used to maintain themselves through the enactment of the Social Security Act and the multitude of government programs to help the disadvantaged. The crisis faced by the nation in the 1930s, and the subsequent party realignment, camouflaged the parties' internal weakness because they created a generation of strong party identifiers that was largely polarized around the policies and personality of President Franklin D. Roosevelt.

By the 1960s a new generation had grown up without strong emotional ties to the parties, and without believing that the parties had much of a role to play in politics. New issues, such as civil rights and Vietnam, arose and divided the nation. From the mid-1960s into the 1980s, interests became more strident and controversial and the parties did not have the internal organizational strength to curb them or to bring them into a consensual coalition. Candidates and interests seemed to go their own ways; confidence in the political system declined.

The campaign finance law came about in response to the social and political pressures of the period. At the same time that Congress was trying to bring credibility back to the political process in general, and to presidential elections in particular, the parties, too, were embarked upon reform. The Democrats concentrated on participation and opening their ranks, the Republicans on rebuilding their national organization with professional skills and financial support from a broad base of small donors. The efforts of both parties, particularly the Republicans, and the new campaign rules began to bear fruit by the late 1970s.

The critical issue for the parties was to regain control of their organizations and their traditional influence over nominations, resources, and public policy. To a large degree they have succeeded: both major parties have highly professional, well-financed national organizations and are reaching down to support strong state party organizations. Although the Republicans are well ahead of the Democrats in developing their resources, the Democrats have been gaining ground steadily and have not been seriously outspent in most elections.

Party Rebirth

The campaign finance law has been pivotal in the recent emergence of the national political parties as strong participants in the political process, in some respects stronger participants than they have ever been. The major elements of the rebirth that stem from the law are contribution limitations to campaigns by individuals and groups; expenditure limits in the presidential race; the need for centralization and recordkeeping; the repertoire of services that only the parties can provide because of the law and because of their resources as permanent political organizations; and a loophole in the federal law that has provided an incentive to contribute to state parties.

Contribution limits. The $1,000 limit on individual contributions and $5,000 limit on groups has left the political party as the largest single donor to all federal campaigns, with its allocation of two cents per voter. In the last several elections, only the Republican party has been able to spend to the maximum, but the Democrats are catching up and as time goes on, all candidates are coming to expect more from their party.

Although the parties play a relatively minor role during the primaries, they are the only other participants allowed to spend money during the general election for a nominee who accepts public financing (as each has done since the law's enactment). Since nonparty contributions are forbidden to the candidates, unless a prospective donor gives to a group promising to make independent expenditures, the only remaining vehicle for giving is the party.

The law imposes a $20,000 limit on individual contributions to the national parties. This is included in the $25,000 limit on what one can give in all federal elections in a year. But there are other ways of giving to the party that are not covered by the law. Such "soft money" is coming to play an increasingly important role for those who want to give large sums. Among the more popular conduits are funds for buildings (hence the new Democratic headquarters in Washington, which comes only a few years after a major Republican construction effort), and contributions to state parties that are coordinated by the presidential campaign or the national party. In 1980 the Republicans raised $9 million and the Democrats $4 million this way.

Soft money clearly subverts the intent of the law to disclose who is contributing, but it is not illegal. As already noted, a donor in Texas can give up to the maximum allowable contribution to ten, twenty, or even fifty state parties, and the donations will be reported only in the states to which they were made (assuming the state has a disclosure law). Only the national party and the presidential campaign will know the value of the entire contribution.

Soft money going to the parties is used for state party overhead, voter registration, and get-out-the-vote efforts, and acts as a kind of mortar binding the state parties to the national party and presidential campaign. The latter achievement may seem superfluous to one who assumes that a state party would automatically share the constituency of its national nominee, but there is an inherent conflict between state and local parties on one side, and the national presidential effort on the other.

The main objective of the state party is to elect state and local candidates; the main objective of the national party and presidential campaign is to elect a president. Candidates for one level of office can have a different constituency than candidates for another. Voter registration efforts directed toward the presidential campaign may hurt a gubernatorial candidate (an experience seen frequently during the 1972 campaign of George McGovern, for example). Other conflicts often arise because the campaign period requires coordination between separate organizations, each with its own players and priorities. People in one organization frequently do not know people in the other, to say nothing of rival factions within state parties. There also are cultural differences between the young professionals who staff the national offices and the typically older volunteers who hold positions in the state and local parties. As one Washington worker put it, "It is the difference between the three-piece wool suiter and the polyester crowd."

Expenditure limits. During the general election, the law limits the candidates to the public money the government provides ($40 million apiece in the 1984 election). In addition, the national parties are provided funds for their nominating conventions and are permitted to raise and spend a limited amount during the general election ($6.9 million in 1984, although the Democrats could muster only $2.8 million). State and local parties also are permitted to raise and spend for volunteer activities; this provision—designed to restore the party grass roots—has become a major vehicle for party activity during the presidential race. Labor unions and other groups such as the Moral Majority are also active in voter registration and get-out-the-vote work, hence their greater value to both the campaigns and the parties compared to nonmembership organizations. In theory, and occasionally in practice, such groups can become competitive with the parties, but on the whole their activities are coordinated with the party (see table 10.1).

Resources. The financial strength of the national committees (particularly, the Republican National Committee) has been the ability to develop a host of services they can make available to their candidates. During the 1984 general election the Democrats spent money on media, postage, printing, travel, fund-raising, and support of state committees and of voter registration and get-out-the-vote efforts (including $85,000 paid to the Rainbow Coalition). The Republican National Committee reported similar spending, but also included phone banks, polling, telephone surveys, computer services, keypunching, equipment rental, consulting charges, and rent.[30]

The money raised and spent by the national committees, particularly by the RNC, accomplished more for their candidates than the dollar amounts might suggest. Most research expenditures are exempt from campaign finance limitations. Although campaign research on issues used to be an activity designed more to occupy volunteers than to generate significant information for the campaign, it has become important in recent years because of the application of market research techniques and the capacity to retain and retrieve vast amounts of information.

The value of party-sponsored research is greater to candidates for offices below the presidency, but is not irrelevant to presidential campaigns. Toward the end of the 1984 campaign, for example, the Democrats could not afford to track the effects of their advertising, and this, the Republicans believe, affected the outcome of the campaign.

The Presidency and the Interests

If controlling the interests has been historically the basis of political reform, the best that campaign finance laws can be said to have done is to monitor them. Perhaps that is all that can be done. Although the media tend to concentrate on the behavior of special interests in each election, the entire subject may be likened to the problem of crime: we cannot know for certain whether crime has gone up, or whether the increase is in the reporting. The campaign finance law has made a significant contribution to American political life through its disclosure provisions. For the first time the behavior of groups and their relationships to candidates can be traced and measured. To some, the amounts of money involved are scandalous, to others the openness of the process is a decided improvement over what went on before.[31] For our purposes, however, the discussion of interests and the presidency will be about whether or not there has been a shift in the balance of power among the interests, and whether the new balance benefits, threatens, or has any effect at all on the political process as a whole.

The greatest role of the interests in the 1984 election occurred in the prenomination phase of the election when contributions were raised from individuals and groups (although the proportion of funds coming from the PACS was very small, largely because PAC money is not matched by the government). Presumably many of those who sent money did so because of the candidates' positions on the issues that were of concern to the contributors, and were encouraged to do so by the candidates and the organizations to which the contributors belonged.

The other important role of the interests was in providing volunteer support for the candidates in the primary and caucus states. In view of the expenditure limits, volunteers who can be mobilized and directed to voter registration and get-out-the-vote efforts may be critical in a close election with a crowded field of candidates. Among the interests that played such roles were organized labor on behalf of Mondale; black church leaders on behalf of Jesse Jackson and later Mondale; the Moral Majority in reaction to the registration of blacks

Table 10.1 Total income of candidates and other spenders* (in millions of dollars)

	Campaign	PAC	Communication	Independent expenditures	Party
Askew	$ 3.2	$.001			
Cranston	8.0	.3			
Glenn	14.1	.3			
Hart	23.2	.005	($ .0007)**	($ .041)	
Hollings	2.8	.2			
Jackson	10.4	.03	.002		
McGovern	3.0	.013		(.0009)	
Mondale	81.6	.122	4.4	.8	2.8
			(.6)	(.5)	
Reagan	74.1	.528	.17	15.7	6.9
			(.045)	(.4)	

*These figures include the candidate committees (including the $40.4 million provided Mondale and Reagan for the general election), communication costs by other organizations, independent expenditures and national party spending. PAC figures are included in the candidates' committees and are not additional funds.
**Figures in parentheses are spending against the candidate.
Source: Drawn from data supplied by the FEC, run April 5, 1985. The author is grateful for the assistance of Michael Dickerson of the Public Records Division.

in the South; and to a lesser extent, groups on both sides of the abortion issue.

What is interesting about the particular mix of groups is that they do not represent an even balance of issues (with the exception of the abortion issue). Labor's main opponent is business, not religious fundamentalism. Business, for its part, although still predominantly Republican in registration and cultural allegiance, has become less important in the party's presidential coalition, and while becoming more important in Congress, is clearly divided and less partisan in its giving strategy, favoring incumbents above all. Business interests have never demonstrated an ability to turn out volunteers, which the prenomination campaign requires. Business also suffers because the campaign finance law places a premium on individual over interest group money. In contrast, other interests—principally organized labor and the New Right—contribute both volunteers and a great amount of independent spending: about $15 million each in 1984. Another possible reason for the deflection of business money to Congress is the trend toward deregulation policy, which has left much of the agenda that business is concerned about to the legislature rather than the executive branch of government.

It is, of course, somewhat simplistic to suggest that labor balances against business, or fundamentalists stand against social liberals, and that these divisions represent the sum total of political cleavage in the nation. What these groups do represent are the coalitions that each party has gathered under its umbrella in order to win elections. Their views are important to the parties, but administrations that come into office with their support do not always repay them with programmatic action. The New Right, particularly, probably plays a greater role in promoting issues for direct mail solicitations by the parties than it does in legislation.

It may be that labor has greater strength in the Democratic party than the New Right has with the Republicans because it is an older and thus more accepted part of the Democratic coalition, and because labor contributes directly to candidates. The New Right, while able to balance labor spending in the presidential campaign, has less influence with individual members of Congress because it spends independently of their campaigns, and is essentially antiestablishment. Richard Viguerie, the leading direct mail solicitor of the New Right, has said that the Republican party had no room for both a Jacob Javits and a Jesse Helms, and has encouraged his supporters to take over a local party if its leaders did not seem compatible with New Right conservatism. To suggest that this attitude might offend party regulars may be something of an understatement. Of the money the New Right spends at the presidential level, there is very little evidence that it seriously affects the outcome of the election.

One cannot be certain that contributing to a campaign directly carries greater weight with the candidate than making an independent expenditure on his behalf (or against his opponent). One can say, on the basis of almost a decade's worth of experience, that independent spending remains controversial and campaign managers frequently try to discourage it. In view of the near-doubling of such spending at the congressional level in 1984, however, and the increase in the number of groups making such expenditures, independent spending may become part of the accepted fabric of political participation. In 1986 the New Right was all but absent, while the American Medical Association PAC (AMPAC) led the list of independent spenders. What happens in the long run will depend on the political content of our elections: how divisive the issues; how vituperative the debate.

One of the strongest arguments against independent spending

relates to the methods the ideological groups use to raise their funds. Direct mail solicitations usually are based on negative appeals: calls to arm against danger. They are appeals to a threatened minority (majorities are less likely to be worried), even if the issue and the sense of danger have to be created in the first place. The use of direct mail solicitations educates recipients and encourages their outrage. It may well expand participation in American politics, but it may do so at the periphery, with those who are less committed to the system and less confident in its institutions. Over time it is possible that these techniques will create a new, divisive, political alignment.

The Costs of Elections

Controlling the amount of money spent in presidential elections has been, if not the primary objective of campaign reform, at least a hope that is expressed during and after every election. In all likelihood it is a concern that will never be met. On one side of the argument is the position usually taken by such groups as the Campaign Finance Study Group that if money buys communication, more money means more communication, and more communication makes for better-informed choices by the electorate. General television advertising by companies rose 18 percent from 1984 to 1985, to a total of $19 billion, with the largest advertiser (Proctor & Gamble) spending $652 million.[32] Compare this to the $301 million that was spent on the presidential campaign in 1984.

On the other side is the argument made recently by Elizabeth Drew, who suggests that "It is not relevant whether every candidate who spends more than his opponent wins. . . . What matters is what the chasing of money does to the candidates, and to the victors' subsequent behavior. . . . The point is what *raising* money, not simply spending it, does to the political process. . ."[33]

Although campaign spending is a broad issue, it is important to recognize that the law has made a profound difference in *how* money is raised, even if it has not significantly altered how *much* money is raised. It is clear that what the candidates raise from individuals is only one part of the picture; parties and PACs are growing into more important conduits for funds than they ever have been.

In an FEC report based on the first eighteen months of the 1983–84 election cycle (pre-general election), PAC spending reached $57 million, a 50 percent increase over the same period in the 1981–82 cycle, and a 128 percent increase over the spending in the entire 1980 presidential election period.[34] By the end of the 1984 election cycle, PAC contributions to congressional candidates reached $104 million, a net increase of 25 percent over the 1982 election and almost double the amount spent in 1980.[35] By the year's end, PAC contributions to Congress weighed in at $135 million, as the interests helped candidates pay off their campaign debts and build up treasuries for the next election. (By then, no one had to guess who would win and who would serve on what committee.)[36]

There is no question that the rising costs of elections are tied to the rising costs of campaign technology (polling, computerized research, recordkeeping, and accounting), of communications (media production and airtime), of transportation, and of the professionalization of politics in general. Elections costs are like the rising costs in health care: we may not require every test or every procedure, but doctors (and campaign managers) are hesitant to omit them. Both candidates and patients face terminal consequences if the right effort is not made.

For presidential candidates, the costs of the election turn on questions of fund-raising and the structure of the law: the contribution limits, spending limits, and public financing. Independent spending, although not insignificant by any means, cannot be calculated by a campaign or attributed to a candidate.

Contribution limits. To the extent that the intent of the law was to shift the emphasis in fund-raising from large to small donors, it has succeeded to a major degree, although not without generating some concern (especially that the individual limits are too low and consequently will engender alternative ways to contribute outside the law). The majority of prenomination contributions (between 55 and 60 percent, which is comparable to congressional elections) continues to come from individuals, and most contributions are less than $500. The Republicans have done much better at raising the greater portion of their funds from small donors, with the average contribution running between $23 and $30 in recent years. In 1980, only 45 percent of Democratic money came from small contributors, compared to 60 percent for Republicans.

The value of small contributors is enhanced by the law, not just because small contributions are matched by the government in presidential campaigns, but because of the methods used to reach them. Direct mail solicitations are centralized, records are easy to maintain, and compliance is neither burdensome nor embarrassing. Unlike the large donor, who expects access to the candidate in return for a contribution, small contributors generally expect nothing but the satisfaction of giving.

Public financing. In 1973, Ralph K. Winter, a member of the Yale Law School faculty and a leading opponent of public financing, argued that contributing to campaigns was an important avenue of political expression that would be narrowed by the regulatory aspects of public financing. Campaign finance laws would have a chilling effect on political activity, would be dangerous (because no fair formula has been devised for allocating the money), and might discourage officeholders from taking stands on controversial issues. It also would force taxpayers into political activity against their will.[37] Herbert Alexander, among others, has argued that public financing in the primaries made possible the candidacy of Jimmy Carter, a little-known regional candidate in 1976, because it had an equalizing effect in lowering the value of large contributors and enhancing the value of small contributors. Similarly, in 1980 public financing helped John Anderson and George Bush, both relatively unknown outside Washington circles.[38]

In 1982 the Campaign Finance Study Group reported that public financing had succeeded in limiting the dependency of presidential candidates on a few large donors, and that it did not hamper the fund-raising abilities of candidates, encourage frivolous candidacies, or impose an artificial parity among those running for office.[39]

In 1980, public funding made up about 40 percent of the money spent in the prenomination and general election campaigns: $103 million of $250 million. Of this, $31.3 million went to prenomination matching contributions (which was 31 percent of the $100 million raised by the candidates), $8.2 million to the major parties for their nominating conventions, and $58.8 million to the major party nominees for the general election. After the election, John Anderson received $4.2 million for winning more than 5 percent of the popular vote.[40] In the 1984 election, $30.9 million was paid out in matching funds, with another $40.4 million going to each of the major party nominees for the general election.[41] In addition, the Republican and Democratic parties received funds to hold the nominating conventions. Again, the amount of public money remained around 40 percent of total expenditures.

Although Professor Winter could not have foreseen the rise of direct mail fund-raising and its base in large numbers of donors, there is no question that the share of American citizens who participate in campaigns by making donations to the candidates, parties, and causes of their choice has increased substantially in the past decade. This increase serves the interest of democracy, even if it occasionally raises the temperature of political debate. The Republican party, for instance, expected to reach one of every four homes through the mails in 1985 to encourage voters to register as Republicans and to make contributions to the party, thus enlarging their base well beyond the three to four million who already make donations to the party.

Campaign Reform and the Public Interest

Although the motivation for campaign reform has been the desire to control undue influence, its broadest goals have been to provide equality of opportunity for those who would enter the electoral system and to ensure an informed and effective choice by the voters. The measure of success would be the freedom and openness of the contest for office. Unfortunately, the rate of incumbent reelection, which has been high at the congressional level since the 1950s, has not been substantially altered. At the presidential level the singularity of each election makes broad conclusions problematic.

The reforms have changed the political landscape, but they have not taken the politics out of the process. Interest groups have been institutionalized through the formal structure of political action committees and may grow stronger in the course of maintaining their organizations; the two major political parties have become stronger at the national level, reversing the flow of influence within the parties from the bottom up to the top down; professionalism has replaced much of the volunteer nature of campaigns; and many political organizations, mainly major direct mail solicitors like the National Conservative Political Action Committee, have become centralized structures that communicate with the local constituencies without benefit of intermediaries. Has all of this altered the democracy? Yes. But we do not know if it has diminished the opportunity to run for office or to make informed choices, at least at the presidential level.

All of the presidential elections that have occurred since the implementation of the law have been without scandals akin to Watergate. Public confidence in the political system has risen according to the polls, but then it was down so low it would be difficult to imagine it not rising. The reforms were doubtless part of the healing process of the post-Vietnam, post-Watergate era, although there are enough loopholes in the law to suggest that the reforms, while necessary, are not sufficient to assure a corruption-free electoral process.

Typically, the goal of regulation is to assure a balance between competing private interests that also serves the public interest. According to Marver Bernstein, the latter part of this goal is the most difficult to achieve because it is usually hard to know what the public interest is, even when Congress is regulating economic activity.[42] How much more difficult that task is when the object to regulate is the drive for power. It is a process that is hard to observe, to say nothing of influence, because it is episodic and its structures and participants are often temporary.

Campaign reform measures money because money is more measurable than power. Money is assumed to be synonymous with power, but that is too simple. The quest for power is assumed to be concerned with economic interests, but neither is that entirely true. Power has an attraction of its own; what is more, politics involves interests of morality and social propriety that are only marginally related to the distribution of goods and services. Much of the hue and cry in recent years has been about the behavior of ideological groups. Their interests are purposive rather than material in nature.

On the other hand, one consequence of campaign reform has been to institutionalize the participants in elections. Campaigns may be temporary, but the supporting players have become a more stable group. Campaign-consulting organizations continue from election to election, and their developing professionalism assures that the individuals involved expect to participate in many campaigns. Professionals look to their peers for approval and care about this as much, or more, than the outcome of any single campaign.

The institutionalization of interest has had another effect on the political landscape: it has shifted the balance of power among the interests. To some extent, that was the intent of the reform, but the result deserves some attention. Big business, which traditionally has been seen as the power to be restrained because it has the largest disposable wealth, has in fact been restrained by the finance regulations at the presidential level. Business has lost ground to those who can turn out committed volunteers at the local level to carry the vote in primaries and caucuses. Business has also lost ground to those who can raise tremendous amounts of money through direct mail solicitations on controversial issues, then spend that money independently. Although a few corporations and trade associations made independent expenditures in 1984, none did so at the presidential level, and most corporate spending was less than $500.[43]

This is not to say that business has entirely lost interest or influence in the race for the presidency. Business PACs contribute more to the campaigns than any other kind of political action committee, but PAC giving in presidential elections is insignificant. There may be other avenues of influence that remain undetected and unreported. Although business has lost ground relative to other interests in presidential politics, it has become more influential in congressional elections, where it now spends more money. This diversion of power ought to be a matter of concern. The lower and less visible the level of office, the more susceptible it is to what can be called undue influence. Disclosure works only if the voting public is aware of who has given what to the candidates. The lower the office, the less likely there will be that awareness.

Conclusion

As Alexander Heard observed at the close of his book on campaign reform, which was written at the beginning of the reform era:

The public habits that comprise campaign practices evolve in response to the total context within which a political system functions. They respond in particular to the expectations of the system held by citizens, expectations that ultimately are rooted in whatever understanding, accurate or inaccurate, there may be in the political system. No fundamental change will be effected in the United States in the process of campaign finance, by legislation or otherwise, without the altered public attitudes and without public recognition of the functions of campaign expenditures, of the propriety of providing them, and of the penalties for not doing so in socially healthy ways.[44]

The campaign reforms enacted in the last decade have altered the political system, and public attitudes also have changed. These are not necessarily synchronized phenomena. Some parts of the political system have changed rapidly and have demonstrated an extraordinary adaptability to the new rules and resources. Perhaps it is in the nature of a democracy to require imbalances and a certain degree of instability so that changes in influence can be reflected in the substance of the system.

Fear of instability, however, has been a dominant theme in the policy of Western nations since World War II, when it was perceived that the instability after World War I paved the way for totalitarian regimes and another world war. That fear has been balanced against the drive for participation and the expansion of democracy, although some would argue that widespread participation is not a necessary condition of a democratic state.[45] Whether they are correct or not, it is a question made critical by campaign finance reform in the United States, which has increased participation at a relatively passive level through contributions, and decreased more active participation among campaign volunteers.

The centralization of many American political institutions —notably the parties—is not inherently bad. In many respects it is a coming of age organizationally for the parties. There are signs that public confidence in the political system is increasing in response to the new party strength: both partisan identification and voter participation levels have stopped declining and actually have risen in the last few years. The rebirth of the parties as strong organizations may well be the first step toward recapturing their historical role in the political process as vehicles for compromise and consensus. If the parties succeed, we need not fear the interests, because in the long run it is the parties that will curb them and build the coalitions for governance upon which representative democracy depends.

11 Presidential Politics and the Myth of Conciliation: The Case of 1980

JAMES DAVID BARBER

A skeptic's defense of democracy begins this side of the idealist's dream of the steady citizen and the visionary leader. Democracy to the skeptic is not a utopia but a set of necessities in support of the opportunity for a decent life—necessities defined and developed over a long and tortuous history perennially interrupted by lapses into chaos and tyranny. A basic necessity is rational discourse. That is difficult enough to sustain among learned, dutiful elites. Among citizenries composed largely of politically ignorant and indifferent masses led by ambitious cynics, keeping the Great Conversation rational is a never-ending challenge. From the "children's crusades" of the thirteenth century down through to modern Nazism and Communism, history demonstrates the inadequacy of religious conviction, intellectual sophistication, and social idealism as guarantors against political madness. Absent concentrated effort, particularly on the part of responsible participants, no automatic guarantee protects the United States from popular insanity.

Rational discourse in support of democracy requires debate and decision by a very wide circle of participants, conducted through media that often subject politics to truncation, distortion, and distraction. In the not-so-distant past, errors could be combatted (if not always defeated) by widespread and varied structures of counsel: the otherwise preoccupied citizen would turn to the politician in the neighborhood or workplace for advice. Parties structured such channels. Now much of that loose-jointed system is gone. Citizens are more and more dependent on journalists, speaking to them through television and the local newspaper, for shaping the nature and content of political discussion.

Historically journalists have contributed significantly to democracy's maladies, fragmenting reality, touting novelty, and reducing argument to linear narrative, for example. But traditionally journalists also have contributed significantly to a strength of democracy: the test of political proposals against facts. If the genius of democracy is pragmatism, the essence of pragmatism is empiricism. Democracy is about what works. Yet, all too easily, political debate can drift away from its factual base, can float out unanchored into a sea of illusion and emotion in which facts are indistinguishable from feelings.

The democratic politician may regard that drift as progress. The reduction of politics to sentiment constitutes a leap away from the elitism of expertise toward the equality of emotion. We vary considerably in the information we possess, but all of us have feelings, and we lay claim to "the right to my opinion." Thus it is little wonder that, as democratization reaches further toward genuine universal suffrage and brushes aside various intermediate political structures, the politics of sentiment appeals to candidates and their media managers and marketing experts.

What sentiments? In *The Pulse of Politics* I argued and tried to demonstrate that three are dominant in presidential election campaigns.[1] The *conflict* theme appeals to the interest that competition typically engenders. The primordial form is the war story—the call to arms, the romance of battle carried over into peaceful politics. Harry Truman's uphill fight in 1948 is illustrative. The *conscience* theme typically is reactive, a call for purity and dignity to counter the corruptions of politics, pejoratively defined. Dwight Eisenhower's 1952 campaign against "Communism, Korea, and Corruption" is an example. The *conciliation* theme appears after too much fighting and preaching have whetted the public appetite for solace and ease, unity and friendship. The classic conciliation election in the twentieth century is 1920, Warren Harding's "return to normalcy." Sometimes politicians and the journalists who interpret them use these sentiments creatively to attract and sustain interest in substantive politics, as devices for getting across the relevant political facts. Too often, however, they cooperate destructively in eluding the factual component, drifting past the historical realities into the realm of fiction where sentiment runs free of empirical restraint.

The drift to fiction in twentieth-century politics has followed all three of these paths. But the conciliation theme is specially suited for this perversion. Conflict directly argues comparison among candidates, which motivates a search for evidence. The conscience election features the invocation of principles, typically including honesty and responsibility. But conciliation offers a general relaxation of tension, including the strain of attention, logic, and civic virtue. Especially in the aftermath of troubled times (such as World War I or the stock market crash of 1929), the temptation to voters to set aside calculation and go on a political vacation is powerful.

That temptation gains force when a candidate appears who offers just such an appeal. It gains all the more force when such a candidate has the rhetorical skill to convey the appropriate sentiment. When other candidates lack either the conciliatory inclination or the skill to seem that way, the expert conciliator is likely to win out, given a reasonably propitious alignment of political forces. Such was clearly the case in 1920.

The Harding Combination

In 1920 the configuration of political power favored the Republicans. President Woodrow Wilson, chief Democrat, had collapsed in the middle of his crusade for the League of Nations, but would not release the reins of power to anyone else in his party. It took the Democrats eight days and forty-four ballots to nominate Governor James M. Cox, like Harding a virtual unknown. Harding, too, was a compromise candidate who, however, had behind him the force of a party hungering for a return to power following the Democratic interruption to their normal hegemony.

National sentiment, what one might call the climate of expectations, also favored a Harding, a conciliator. Only four years previously, Wilson had won reelection as the man who "kept us out of war," only to see "The Great War" come and kill fifty thousand American men. What had felt at first like a reprise of the glorious adventure of the last war—the Spanish-American—turned into an epoch of death, anxiety, and disillusionment. Military peace brought labor war, race riots, a Red scare, soaring inflation (28 percent in 1920), tax raises, and prohibition. More than 500,000 Americans died in the influenza epidemic of 1918–19. The fight for the League split the country, and failed.

Harding thus came onto the presidential scene at just the right time. He had tried his harmonizing rhetoric at the last two Republican conventions, without success. What had been politically inappropriate in 1912 and 1916 fit the bill in 1920.

What Harding had to say was virtually impenetrable to the attentive listener, a melange of obsessively alliterative sloganeering, flag-waving, and appeals for unity. But he looked impressively presidential: tall, solid, florid, and white-haired, with a deep and resonant voice audible in the last row of the hall. With a good deal of practice, Harding had mastered the fashionable gestures of public speaking. Aware that he knew little of the major issues of public policy, Harding nevertheless exuded the confidence, patriotism, and hopefulness people wanted to hear. He won. Before long, his administration collapsed in scandal, registering Harding among historians as the worst president ever, a reputation that survived until the Nixon debacle.

The Analogy of 1980

The election of 1980, which empowered Ronald Reagan, will go down in history as yet another 1920, an election of conciliation. Nineteen eighty was not 1920, Reagan is not Harding. But the situational and personal similarities are too evident to miss. Like Harding, Reagan came on at a time when the opposition party was in disarray. The traumas of the pre-Reagan period (notably inflation and Iran) did not match those of 1916–20, but did comprise a series of important national shocks. The candidates competing with Reagan mistook the mood, stepping away by inclination or ineptness from the conciliation theme. Equally important, Reagan himself, in his character and in his political style, honed over years of practice, could hardly have suited better the opportunity 1980 handed him. What happened in that season and in the years to follow highlights in its contemporary form the ancient problem of the drift to fiction in politics.

Carter: Running as President

Jimmy Carter approached 1980 as a wounded incumbent. Elected in 1976 after a campaign in which both he and President Gerald R. Ford had concentrated on the moralistic themes of conscience politics, Carter's fortunes had declined. The electorate continued to value him highly as a person, but as a president his Gallup approval rating went down below that of Nixon. Part of that decline is no doubt traceable to Carter's awkward relations with the press, particularly his inability to move from lecturing and preaching to the kind of storymaking journalists appreciate. But Carter also suffered a largely negative "professional reputation," as Richard Neustadt defines it, based on a series of mismanaged relationships with leading congressional figures and an apparent reluctance to develop priorities. Probably the overriding cause of his declining popularity between 1977 and 1979 was his failure to break the economic impasse: soaring inflation, rising unemployment, and energy shortages.

In July 1979, recognizing his troubles, Carter assembled a Camp David Domestic Summit, after which he made a national address advocating a new, comprehensive energy program. Some 100,000 favorable letters came in and his approval rating rose eleven percentage points. Then, just as unity and purpose seemed to be developing, Carter suddenly fired four leading members of his cabinet. The impression of incompetence returned.

In the fall of 1979, international crises boosted the president's popular standing, in a familiar pattern. On November 4, 1979, Iranians seized the American embassy in Teheran and captured fifty-two American hostages. "Carter" became "The President" as he protested on behalf of the nation and set to work to free the hostages. Near the end of December, Soviet armed forces invaded Afghanistan. Once again, Carter's unfortunate relations with Congress faded in the public mind and he emerged as the conciliator par excellence, the unifying leader speaking for the whole nation. Publicly he stepped out of political controversy, declaring himself too occupied with international crises to engage in a fight for the Democratic nomination. Behind the scenes, Carter effectively resisted his staff's pressure to conduct a negative campaign, a combative attack on his chief rival, Senator Edward Kennedy. Back in June, Carter had let it be known that if Kennedy ran, he would "whip his ass," a message that neither dissuaded Kennedy nor advanced Carter's reputation. Carter in private did not fail to telephone his friends in the appropriate primary states, to invite politically relevant figures to the White House, to see to the distribution of federal funds to key states, and to time his announcements to political events. But in public, he held to his stance as a statesman above the fray.

The Kennedy Challenge

Senator Kennedy declared his candidacy for the Democratic nomination in November 1979, shortly after the Iranian crisis broke. He, too, got off to a faltering start, beginning with a weak and wandering interview on national television. In the following weeks his speeches came across as vigorous but vague. Then came a classic gaffe, at first unnoticed by the media, soon picked up and headlined across the country. In an interview in San Francisco, after fourteen hours of campaigning, Kennedy said that the Shah of Iran, then America's friend (because deposed by our enemies), had ruled "one of the most violent regimes in the history of mankind" and had "stolen . . . umpteen billions of dollars" from his own people. This basically true statement stimulated candidates across the political spectrum to castigate Kennedy for interfering with President Carter's tireless efforts to secure the release of the hostages.

Kennedy fought on, campaigning day and night in his family's hard-hitting style. In the first contest, the Iowa caucus, Carter defeated him, 59 to 31 percent. Misreading the signs, Kennedy lashed out even more aggressively. At Georgetown University he slammed hard and specifically at Carter's policies and advanced his own definite alternatives. His partisans responded enthusiastically, but his message, delivered by the media to the public at large, fell flat.

The worse he did, the more aggressive he got, growling that "I have only just begun to fight." Kennedy kept up his hard challenge through the primaries. By the time the Democratic convention opened, Kennedy had covered no fewer than 300,000 miles in thirty-nine states and Puerto Rico, Mexico, and the United Nations. At the convention itself, Kennedy combatively led a hopeless charge on the rules binding delegates to vote as instructed in the primaries. He made a strong and popular speech invoking the New Deal and the fervor of the cause, but despite Carter's troubles and his own famous name, Kennedy failed to come through as a plausible alternative. He registered in the politics of 1980 as the first major rejection of a candidate who adopted the conflict mode in a conciliation election.

Rejecting the Republican Battlers

Former governor John Connally of Texas stomped into 1980 like a cowboy at a tea party and was quickly rejected. Early in the season, his media advisers, sensing the national mood, produced commercials showing Connally playing gently with his grandchild. But he soon emerged as the Republicans' most combative candidate. As Senator Strom Thurmond said in welcoming Connally to South Carolina, "I don't know of any man on the political scene today who is more dynamic, more aggressive, and more forceful, who is as tough as this man, and we need a tough man." Connally's performances stimulated applause but few votes. Campaigning for fourteen months and spending some $11 million won him only one vote at the Republican national convention. He faded from the contest.

Other Republican aspirants barely disturbed the political atmosphere. George Bush beat Reagan in the Iowa caucuses by six percentage points after continuous campaigning in a state Reagan did not even visit. In New Hampshire, Reagan and Bush plodded through a televised debate that not even the *Washington Post* found interesting: "GOP Debaters Restate Basic Positions in N.H. Debate" read the headline. A second debate, in Nashua, threatened disorder when five opponents of Reagan showed up, but he managed the confusion gracefully and avuncularly, in an event the *Boston Globe* described as "A Golden Night for Reagan." In the New Hampshire primary three days later, Reagan beat Bush two to one. In Illinois, another debate among Philip Crane, John Anderson, George Bush, and Ronald Reagan turned into another victory for Reagan, the calm and humorous elder of the clan. Anderson and Crane snapped at each other; Bush occasionally interrupted; Reagan basically sat back and let them fight, keeping his cheery and mild aura as he gently condescended to his shrill competitors. He won with nearly half the votes. The press kept up its usual horse race chatter on through the primary session, but in fact there was no serious challenge to Reagan.

Thus, as far as the primary season was concerned, conflict was the loser. Reagan the comforting presence and Carter the steady president in crisis each blanked out their aggressive opponents.

The Lost Cause of Conscience

The conscience theme, traditionally recurrent in presidential politics, had clearly been the dominant theme of 1976 when both Carter and Ford, sensing the pulse of politics, had stressed the need for honesty and decency in Washington. Approaching 1980, some signs indicated a Carter reprise, by naming his energy policy "the moral equivalent of war," perceiving a popular "crisis of confidence," advocating "sacrifice." In a curious thematic reversal, Carter and the Democrats began to appear the cramped and confining Puritans, while Reagan and the Republicans cheerfully called for growth, freedom, and progress, in a rhetoric of expansion. The loose-jointed morality of boosterism was overcoming the tightfisted morality of restriction. As the *Washington Post*'s William Greider put it, the message became "elect Ronald Reagan and let the good times roll." Carter the moralizer faded away early in the campaign of 1980.

John Anderson, Republican representative from Illinois, substituted in 1980 as the exemplar of the conscience theme. Anderson had first emerged in the press as a Republican willing to be quoted against Richard Nixon, as the Watergate crisis gathered. The press discovered him as an apparently hopeless but honest contender. By background, Anderson fit the conscience pattern. A fervent Christian since his conversion at a revival when he was nine, he grew up to run for state's attorney. "I prayed over this initial decision to seek public office," he wrote, "just as I have prayed over every major decision in my life." Later, as a member of Congress, he three times introduced a constitutional amendment declaring that the United States "devoutly recognizes the authority and law of Jesus Christ, Saviour and Ruler of nations, through whom are bestowed the blessings of Almighty God." His moral concerns guided his championing of civil rights, his opposition to the war in Vietnam, and his indignation at the Watergate scandal.

Starting in 1979, Anderson made a sincere try for the Republican presidential nomination, stressing the need for "basic moral courage," and declaring that he wanted to "arouse the conscience and reason of America." He came across in the press and on television as a familiar type: the messianic politician, "running with missionary zeal," a "preachy and abstruse" speaker who "reminds too many people of an angry minister," as *Newsweek* reported. Anderson lost the primary in his home state to Californian Ronald Reagan. He

went on to declare his candidacy for the presidency as an independent. On election day he got fewer than 7 percent of the popular vote
and carried no state.

The most strident voice of conscience politics in 1980 was that of
the Moral Majority, a following of uncertain extent led by the Reverend Jerry Falwell. The movement's genesis and impulse were plain.
Sin was at the root of our problems and government was subsidizing
sin; therefore, government had to be reformed. Politics had long been
an arena in which the religious left was influential—in civil rights
and the peace movement, for example. Now the religious right
—faithful people concerned about crime, drugs, abortion, homosexuality, sex education, and other perceived deviations—would mount
its campaign. But the evidence is that the religious right made little
difference in 1980. The truth seems to be that over the years Americans have become less, not more intolerant. Haynes Johnson, who
has trooped the hustings as much as any professional reporter, found
in 1980 that with respect to race, sex, and other personal matters,
"aside from the vocal single interest groups, you simply don't hear
the kinds of passion about such questions. Where once drugs, sex,
and other trappings of a permissive society were issues during election campaigns, now they are largely absent." Unlike those election
years in which moral concerns topped the political agenda, in 1980
the public in the main found them matters of relative indifference.

Carter's Puritanism, John Anderson's ethical emphasis, and the
querulous challenge of the religious right all fell flat in 1980. What
had seemed a natural agenda-topper in 1976 felt awkwardly out of
place in 1980.

The Decisive Conventions

Neither nominating convention was decisive in terms of its major
function, the choice of a presidential nominee. But at each the winner's performance set the tone of his campaign in a fateful manner.

Just when the story of politics as conflict seemed dead for 1980,
Carter revived it. Having held back his political aggressions for
months, as Kennedy harassed him, Carter chose to demonstrate that
he too could perform as a fighting candidate. His acceptance speech
matched Kennedy's intensity. *Time* reported that, "Perspiration pour-
ing from his face, his voice hoarse, his eyes coldly angry, Carter gave

a shouting stump speech unlike almost any he has delivered before, in content as well as manner. It was a headlong assault on his rival."

The "assault" was mild by the standards of old-time stump politics, a toned down for television translation of Theodore Roosevelt. But Carter and his strategists thought it would be easy to defeat Reagan, on his record, with a negative campaign. Over the years, Reagan had filled the files of his enemies with a remarkably extensive collection of confidently asserted untruths and genially expressed bursts of aggression. Carter's aide Hamilton Jordan advocated hitting Reagan hard on the record, anticipating that "Of all the elections I've been in with Jimmy Carter, this is by far the least difficult." Carter lashed out at Reagan as a "ridiculous" candidate, a man living in a world of "fantasy," a divider at home and a warmonger abroad. As the weeks wore on, Carter occasionally lapsed into hyperbole, suggesting that Reagan was a racist, or wanted war, or would as president divide "black from white, Jew from Christian, North from South, rural from urban." It was a form of rhetoric Carter had never been very good at; his aggressions often sounded shrieky and unconvincing. Worse yet, the press began to point out his "meanness." As Elizabeth Drew explained, "Carter had got across to the public the idea that he was a nice man. When the idea suddenly hit that he might not be such a nice man after all, the public reacted with the sort of disillusionment about which it can be unforgiving." Not until mid-October did Carter and his staff perceive that the attack mode was a failure. In a television interview with Barbara Walters, Carter said that "Some of the issues are just burning with fervor in my mind and in my heart . . . and I get—I have gotten carried away on a couple of occasions." But by then it was too late.

Reagan's convention performance could not have been more contrasting. It too set the tone for his campaign, a tone strongly resonant with that of Warren Harding in 1920 and other conciliators in presidential politics. By the time the Republicans met in Detroit in July, Reagan's nomination was a foregone conclusion. The personal drama of the convention focused momentarily on a bizarre scheme, apparently developed by Henry Kissinger, to get Gerald Ford to take the vice presidential nomination, on the understanding that he and Reagan would share a "co-presidency." That idea quickly collapsed, despite a good deal of television hype, and Reagan, setting aside his doubts, accepted George Bush for the second spot on the ticket.

Programmatic speculation centered on whether or not Reagan would come forth as a reincarnation of Barry Goldwater, whose rightist ideology he had supported in a stirring speech at the 1964 convention.

But Reagan simply transcended these concerns with a classic speech of conciliation, reaching for consensus beyond the disagreements:

> I am very proud of our party tonight. This convention has shown to all America a party united, with positive programs for solving the nation's problems; a party ready to build a new consensus with all those across the land who share a community of values embodied in these words: family, work, neighborhood, peace, and freedom.
>
> I know we have had a quarrel or two in our own party, but only as to the method of attaining a goal. There is no argument about the goal. . . .
>
> More than anything else, I want my candidacy to unify our country, to renew the American spirit and sense of purpose. I want to carry our message to every American, regardless of party affiliation, who is a member of this community of shared values.

The substance of the speech fit nicely with the huge blue banner running across the stage: "TOGETHER—A NEW BEGINNING." Importantly for television, the manner of delivery was even more conciliatory. "The pleasant man might have been talking across the backyard fence or maybe chatting in the kitchen with the kids," said *Newsweek*, "He seemed relaxed and natural. . . . Indeed, the entire speech sounded as though it were delivered off the top of Reagan's head." At the end he asked everyone to join him in silent prayer and then, with "God Bless America," he triggered the applause. *Newsweek* concluded that "The gathering of the Republican tribes in Detroit was in fact mostly remarkable for its make-love-not-war harmonics." The *Washington Post*'s William Greider called the convention "a pivotal event of 1980" in which "the meaning of Republican has changed. In place of the party's old scolding, exclusionary style, there was a new open-armed and confident movement, one that has suppressed the nativist sentiments of its past." Reagan's manager F. Clifton White had told a reporter, "All we're trying to do is keep everybody happy."

The Contrasting Campaigns

Carter continued his attack, quoting Reagan's belligerent statements to paint him as a risky president. But Carter's aggression continued to come across as "mean" in both senses of the word: attacking and petty. Reagan's senior media adviser Stuart Spencer said of Carter, "The harder he gets, the softer we're going to get." When Carter lashed out at Reagan as a divider of "Jews from Christians," Reagan went on network television to say, "I can't be angry. I'm saddened that anyone, particularly someone who had held that position, could intimate such a thing, and I'm not looking for an apology from him. I know who I have to account to for my actions. But I think he owes the country an apology." Again, Reagan's calm and confident manner matched his rhetoric. Accusations that he had changed his positions over the years, confirmed in snippets of videotape, scarcely ruffled his happy demeanor. Nor was he particularly disconcerted when the media took note of his frequent gaffes, demonstrating remarkable lapses in his basic policy information.

Still, the polls were close as the election approached. Reagan's own polls showed that about 44 percent of the people agreed he was "most likely to get us into an unnecessary war," so on Sunday evening, October 19, he went on national television in the manner of Franklin Roosevelt's first Fireside Chat, in the crisis of 1933. Reagan began, "I'd like to speak to you for a few moments now not as a candidate for the presidency but as a citizen, a parent—in fact, a grandparent—who shares with you the deep and abiding hope for peace." Nearly quoting FDR, he said "The only thing the cause of peace has to fear is fear itself." In this talk, he spoke the word "peace" forty-seven times.

Fearing that the president might come up with some "October surprise," such as the release of the hostages or an invasion of Iran, Reagan suddenly accepted a long-standing invitation to debate Carter on October 28, just one week before the election. Broadcast from the Cleveland Music Hall, the debate reached the largest audience in political history, some sixty million families. Reagan began, hardly pausing to notice the question he had been asked, with a comforting thought: "I'm only here to tell you that I believe with all my heart that our first priority must be world peace, and that the use of force is always and only a last resort, when everything else has failed, and then only with regard to national security." The debate continued, with reporters pressing policy questions and Carter cutting hard at Reagan's "ridiculous" plan to cut taxes 10 percent a year over three years. Carter scored point after point. Reagan, in contrast, did not compete, he condescended: "He infused the occasion with a style, a presence, a grandfatherly sense of dignity and kindness that evoked sympathy among millions of Americans who seemed for the first time to understand what kind of a man he really is." As Elizabeth Drew noted, "looking genial is what he does." Jimmy Carter's attempt to paint Ronald Reagan as a dangerous villain failed, not because Reagan had not said dangerous things, but because he did not seem a dangerous man.

As election day approached, Reagan spoke tellingly of the emotion that impels the thirst for conciliation. "Many Americans seem to be wondering, searching, feeling frustrated and perhaps a little afraid," he said. And he set the criterion of decision for 1980 in precisely appropriate terms, not of achievement or principle, but happiness: "Most importantly—quite simply—the basic question of our lives: Are you happier today than when Mr. Carter became president of the United States?"

Conciliation Triumphs

As was to be expected, the postelection polls showed that Reagan had won because the public wanted a change. The turnout rate was the lowest in thirty-two years. About half of the eligible electorate stayed home. Ideology played no markedly significant role. There was no conservative tide—not even a conservative trend. A careful study by Gerald Pomper and colleagues concluded that "There is no evidence that indicated a turn to the right by the nation. Reagan was not elected because of increasing conservativism in the country." "Furthermore," Pomper and his associates reported, "there is no indication that the electorate in 1980 was significantly more conservative on *specific* issues than it had been four years before," and "Overall, there is no reason to accept the election outcome in 1980 as indicating a conservative tide in this country, even though the elected candidate was clearly known and perceived by the electorate as a conservative."[2]

The 1980 Presidential election centered instead on the politics of conciliation. The public made a clear choice between a worried and combative Jimmy Carter and a calm and comforting Ronald Reagan. As Carter adviser Patrick Caddell put it, the election was "a referendum on unhappiness." Reagan's adviser Michael Deaver placed the election exactly in the Harding context: it was "a return to normalcy." As the new administration came in, *Time* sensed that "the U.S. is famished for cheer" after too long a period of feeling "wary, worried, and waiting." Surveys in 1979 had shown 67 percent of the people picking the pollster's alternative that the country was in "deep and serious trouble," 70 percent agreeing that "things are going . . . badly." Regarding the country's future, pessimists had outnumbered optimists by three to one. Confidence in government, business, religion—indeed the whole range of dominant institutions—was far down from the sunny days of the Eisenhower administration. Despite Carter's diagnosis of the problem as some form of alienation or "malaise," the public's troubles were real: inflation and unemployment at home, humiliation at the hands of kidnappers in Iran. Thus again, in reaction to a period of too much conflict and too much moralizing, the American public was ready for relief, for the balm of comforting reassurance. An eighty-four year old delegate to the Republican national convention, Terence Martin, had it right when he observed, "This is what I've been working for since 1920, when I got involved in the Harding campaign. This time, we've got the right man at the right time."

The Pulse of Politics

The election of 1980 confirmed in a clear case the dominance of a single national mood (or "climate of expectations"),[3] that of conciliation, which in varying degrees had dominated the presidential elections of 1908, 1920, 1932, 1944, 1956, and 1968. Following on the clearly conscience-dominated election of 1976, the 1980 election once again indicated the regular sequences of alternating moods —that an election dominated by moral concerns is likely to be followed by a conciliating election. Close analysis of the 1984 campaign and election probably will confirm a revival of the combative, conflict pattern, pointing to 1988 as a return to the conscience pattern once again. These regularities, matters of balance and dominance, not of solo characterization, point to an emotional component in elections of considerable interest to candidates and their managers as well as to scholars of the presidential selection process. For if these rough regularities hold, candidates who fit their rhythm are likely to do better than candidates who contradict them. Such was the case with Jimmy Carter and the others who read 1980 wrongly and with Ronald Reagan who read it as rightly as any president in modern history. The hypothesis is simple: underlying the immediate particularities of presidential campaigns and elections there is a regular (and emotively understandable) mood swing that can contribute significantly to the outcome of the election.

The Drift to Fiction

But there is another, perhaps more fundamental result of the conciliation election, a danger inherent in its reaction against the calculations of politics. That is the drift to fiction. The conciliation election tends to represent a flight from political argument, from the clash of evidence on the one hand and the clash of values on the other. The longing for happiness and harmony can lead the nation away from the realities of politics into territory beyond the reach of the facts. At the extreme, the test of policy is transformed from pragmatism to sentimentality, in which the symbolic and emotional dimension of political discourse overwhelms testing against the historical actualities.

Nineteen eighty called into question whether the nation was losing its capacity to deliberate effectively in choosing a president. The question is neither partisan nor individual. Political science has a weak record in assessing the performance of incumbent presidents; the Reagan administration is no exception. Typical studies of incumbents concentrate on technique and short-term and immediate "effectiveness," postponing for history the far more significant questions of large and deep political consequences. The 1980 case may well illustrate, more clearly than any modern election, how the debate over who should be the next president can degenerate into a theatrical fiction far more concerned with gestures and postures than with serious national alternatives.

Accepting the nominations of their respective conventions, both Carter and Reagan saw the mote in the eye of the other. Reagan insisted that "the Carter Administration lives in the world of make-believe." Carter in turn accused the Reagan team of inhabiting "a world of tinsel and make-believe . . . fantasy America." Both contributed to that drift, although Reagan came to exemplify it. In 1976, Carter had in an important sense run against politics itself—against the calculations by which important new political purposes gather support among the significant actors. Carter tended to reduce politics to technique, on the one hand, and character on the other. The former spreads attention so thinly over a flat agenda of many items and concentrates on such narrow channels of action that the major concerns get little visible definition in public debate. The latter, the reduction to character, can focus so strongly on morals and motives that fact-based calculations fade out. The politically creative contribution of a moralist like Carter is to link the achievement of values to conditions and opportunities in the real world. The pathology of moralism is the drift into a pattern in which praise and blame substitute for effective action.

Reagan exemplified a different political pathology, directly linked to the drift to fiction. In character he is a passive-positive—a president who simultaneously exerts relatively little personal energy and maintains a demeanor of smiling optimism.[4] Like Harding and William Howard Taft, also of that type, Reagan's primary personal motivation in politics is to secure the affection and encouragement of those around him. The passive-positive is essentially an "other-directed" person, in David Riesman's phrase. Reagan through the years developed a remarkable sensitivity to small and larger audiences, learning just how to charm and divert them toward an appreciation of himself. From childhood on he had been attuned to playacting, not only in theaters, but at school, at home, on the playground and beach. As a radio sports announcer and then a Hollywood actor, Reagan operated in a world in which pretending was not considered lying but performing as a professional. "So much of our profession is taken up with pretending," he wrote, "with interpretation of never-never roles, that an actor must spend at least half his waking hours in fantasy." Reagan carried those capacities over into the General Electric lecture circuit, where he quickly discovered that audiences almost never questioned confidently asserted arguments or evidence as long as they found the speaker engaging. The transition to politics was no great leap. Extending his long-honed skills, Reagan expressed simply and convincingly, to a largely indifferent and ill-informed electorate, his anecdotal politics. His cheerful story making and easy eloquence on television made him a natural item of curiosity for modern journalism, much of which found him interesting, if inaccurate. Again and again, responsible journalists took note of some colossal gaffe of Reagan's, some startling revelation of ignorance directly relevant to major policy decisions, only to discover that Reagan's bland reaction was matched by that of readers and viewers. "Like any other speaker," he said, "I'd see something, and I'd say 'Hey, that's great,' and use it." As David Broder put it, "It is apparently President Reagan's belief that words can not only cloak reality but remake it." Reagan demonstrated the possibility that modern political rhetoric can unplug itself from the facts, provided, as in 1980, that the media and the electorate accept plausibility as proof. "Politics is just like show business," Reagan told his aide Stuart Spencer. "You have a hell of an opening, coast for awhile and then have a hell of a close."

Fictional rhetoric similarly escapes the pressure for consistency over time, a pressure that can, of course, stifle rational adaptation. Political calculation depends significantly on the capacity of voters to assess the relationship between intention and performance—a requirement for rationality in the electoral process. In California and in Washington, Reagan's indifference appeared to cancel that check on actions (in economics, defense, foreign policy, etc.) that were markedly contradictory to what he had led voters to expect. The calculability of politics can sustain itself only to the degree that the link between words and actions is steady enough to be discerned and assessed.

Finally, fictional politics sacrifices the requirement of sincerity, that is, the voter's confidence that the politician touts values rooted in his life. Reagan's list of values, for example, advertised "family, work, neighborhood, freedom and peace" as his highest principles —none of which, in fact, had represented strong behavioral commitments on his part in the past. Just as Reagan apparently felt no compunction about acting in his own television commercials without knowledge of or even interest in what his producers gave him to say, so his professed political values remained largely distinct from any personal commitment.

By 1984 the climate of expectations had shifted once again, although the drift to fiction seemed still in train. Reagan fundamentally withdrew from partisan debate in 1984 as had Nixon in 1972, with a similar result: media attention focused strongly on Democratic primary races, in which Walter Mondale was challenged by John Glenn, Jesse Jackson, and Gary Hart. There the usual battle and horse race language predominated. In the general election campaign, Mondale attacked the Reagan deficit, thus concentrating on a concept few voters understood and a threat to economic welfare yet to be experienced. To meet that threat, Mondale called for a rise in taxes, a threat nearly all voters could immediately understand.

But conflict in 1984 did not depend primarily on dramatic issues. To Reagan's eventual advantage, media-dominated politics concentrated on television debates. George Bush and Geraldine Ferraro traded barbs in one, Ferraro lashing out to say, "I almost resent, Vice-President Bush, your patronizing attitude." Two presidential debates formed their own drama. More than 100 million people watched. In the first, Mondale prevailed—surprisingly, given Reagan's stature as a "Great Communicator"—by combining personal geniality with pointed attacks on the president's policies and competence. Reagan appeared confused, ending with a long statistic-ridden ramble, no doubt designed to give the impression that he was well informed. The press declared Mondale the winner. In reaction, the Reagan forces leapt into negative anti-Mondale advertising. But in the second debate, with expectations of Mondale running high, Reagan the media performer came through, discounting attacks on his age with good humor, and stressing his devotion to nuclear disarmament.

Most significant regarding the drift to fiction, however, was that the conflict of 1984 was essentially a conflict of styles. The televised debates provided information on the candidates' issue stands, but such data were almost completely ignored. Instead, the fight was defined in the press as a style show, a comparison based on dramatic effectiveness in a mode of debate no president has to face in office. Image prevailed. The concreteness of empirical conditions gave way to theatrical politics in which facts were reduced to items to be assessed for their contribution to an emotional confrontation. If the contemporary election of conciliation lends itself to sentimentality, the contemporary election of conflict lends itself to theatricality. Both move away from the mundane pragmatism that historically has sustained the rationality of American democracy.[5]

As 1988 approached, Reagan's habitual preference for fiction over fact was repeatedly and dramatically confirmed. With the help of his aides he managed to "spin" a failed summit with the Soviets in 1986 into an image of success. That year revealed a blatant contradiction between the president's forceful rhetoric against deals with terrorists and his secret attempt to ransom hostages by means of an arms sale to the Iranians. His dramatic preelection war on drug use in 1986 was undercut by his proposed cuts in appropriations for the antidrug fight in 1987. Increasingly the contradiction between his public persona as a president in charge and the true situation became ever more evident. As with Nixon in 1974, these presidential lapses from objectivity aroused interest in the critical question: how was it possible, in 1980, for Reagan to be nominated and elected? The resonance between his conciliatory image and the electorate's hunger for a holiday from hard thinking helps to explain how we got onto the course in 1980 that led us to the Reagan second-term presidency.

Had Ronald Reagan not appeared in 1980 to perform as a pied piper of presidential politics, some other experienced modern media man would surely have taken his place. Given the level of public indifference, the complexity of the real issues, and journalism's (and especially television's) new taste for literary rather than empirical stories, not much more time could be expected to pass before either of the parties turned to a professional television figure to run against an amateur. The reduction of politics to sentiment is an ancient threat. And the death of democracy, the ancients understood, results when politicians no longer even aspire to Adlai Stevenson's standard: "Talk sense to the American people."

12 Television and Presidential Politics: A Proposal to Restructure Television Communication in Election Campaigns

THOMAS E. PATTERSON

Presidential election campaigns center on television. The medium's role often is exaggerated, but its importance is obviously substantial. Millions of Americans view the campaign through the network evening newscasts; additional millions see it on morning newscasts, interview programs, and special election telecasts. When news programs do not catch the public's eye, televised political advertising does. Presidential candidates repeatedly present themselves through short commercial messages that intrude on television's entertainment programs.

Television has transformed the candidates' campaigns. The political parties were at the center of election strategy in the early 1900s, and candidates continued in the 1940s and 1950s to assign the party a role nearly as important as that of the media. This strategy was less a testimony to the party's vitality than an indication of how difficult it was to organize a media campaign. The print media, which consisted of a large number of locally based dailies, did not provide an especially suitable foundation for a national campaign. Nor did early television, with its brief newscasts, offer a suitable basis. In the early 1960s, however, network television increased its newscasts to the present thirty-minute format and greatly expanded its news-gathering capacity. Presidential candidates then had a medium tailored to their needs. Because the network audience was national, network news became the center of journalistic coverage of national politics —particularly presidential politics.

Televised political advertising also became a significant part of presidential campaigning in the 1960s. Spending on advertising increased by 300 percent between the 1960 and 1964 elections, a rate of increase that has not since been equaled. Today, televised advertising accounts for the largest share of candidates' spending. Since 1976 the major party candidates in the general election have spent nearly half of their campaign budgets to prepare and buy political ads on television.

Television also provides candidates with special opportunities to reach the voters. The most important of these are the national conventions, which have been televised since 1952, and the general election debates, which were held in 1960, 1976, 1980, and 1984. These events, particularly televised debates in the general election, attract a large and unusually attentive audience. The importance that candidates attach to these televised opportunities is not easily exaggerated. Entering a convention or debate, candidates cease nearly all other activities, concentrating their effort so as to make the best possible impression on the television audience.

The Two Imperatives of Election Television

This chapter will suggest ways of improving television communication during presidential campaigns. The analysis will concentrate on the activities of presidential candidates and television broadcasters, but the interests of the voting public are the ultimate concern. The purpose of the inquiry is to propose a restructuring of the television communication system that will enable the electorate to respond more effectively to the choices it faces in a presidential campaign.

Two imperatives guide the inquiry and recommendations.[1] The first imperative is that presidential candidates must have ample opportunity on television to get their message across to voters. That candidates appear frequently on television does not alone satisfy this requirement. Candidates bear the responsibility to mobilize the electorate during the campaign; one of them will be responsible for governing the nation when the campaign has ended. It is essential, therefore, that candidates have frequent and significant televised opportunities to establish, on their own terms, their views on national policy and leadership.

Election television, however, cannot be entirely within the control of the candidates. Not surprisingly, presidential candidates try to present themselves in one-sided ways, exaggerating their strengths and disguising their weaknesses. A second imperative, therefore, is that television broadcasters must act as the voters' trustees, seeing that neglected aspects of the candidates' records, character, and policies are included in the flow of information. This is not to suggest that broadcasters should act as the political opposition, for this role can be played properly and effectively only by rival candidates, factions, and parties. Neither is it to claim that broadcasters can effectively organize public opinion when candidates are unwilling or unable to do so. Broadcasters can, however, bring hidden facts about the candidates to light, act as a constraint on the candidates' claims, and help the voters to understand the candidates' platforms and abilities.

Some observers may disagree with these imperatives. They may feel, for instance, that presidential candidates cannot be entrusted with the campaign's agenda. After the 1976 campaign, one of America's leading journalists complained:

> If President Ford or Governor Carter had really raised a new issue, or defined an old one in new terms, the press would have been startled into reporting it. In the whole of the campaign, neither Mr. Ford nor Mr. Carter made a single memorable speech, so the press summarized their dreary cliches and the candidates were lucky that the press didn't print the full text of what they said.

Other journalists may share this view, and certainly there are voters who do. Polls indicate that some Americans believe that candidates will say almost anything (or nothing) in order to gain election. Such beliefs, however, are not an adequate basis for broadcast policy in presidential elections. Candidates provide the electorate with its only choices, and if they break faith with the people, the problem will not be solved by restricting their opportunities to communicate with the voters. The conclusion that candidates are untrustworthy, moreover, is unsupported by available evidence. Gerald Pomper's exhaustive study of campaign pledges indicates that winning presidential candidates, once in office, try to fulfill nearly all of their commitments and succeed in fulfilling most of them.[2]

Broadcasters, too, have been criticized in recent elections. Broadcasters are accused of "poisoning the well" by saying repeatedly that candidates are motivated mainly by their desire to win votes rather than by their commitment to particular national policy goals. Whether broadcasters are overly arrogant and cynical, however, is not a basis for undermining their position in the campaign. The news media's responsibility as public trustee can be preserved in practice only by giving reporters the freedom to pursue that responsibility as they see fit.

In accepting the judgment that both broadcasters and candidates must have ample opportunities on television to express their views, the important question becomes: What is the proper balance between the candidates' need to present themselves on their terms and the broadcasters' need to interpret what the candidates are saying? This is a question that, admittedly, has no single answer. There are a variety of communication patterns that would fulfill the requirement, and one searches with difficulty for a basis to narrow the alternatives. Nevertheless, one consideration suggests itself: existing patterns of broadcast communication should be altered only as much as necessary to meet the public's needs. Although radical alternatives are tempting, such proposals should be ignored as impractical. Moreover, existing patterns of communication are only in part a function of broadcast norms and policy. The extraordinary length of American presidential campaigns, for instance, has a substantial influence on the flow of election information. Radical proposals inevitably would fail to account adequately for such factors. On the other hand, a modest proposal for incremental change may find a welcomed place in the existing presidential selection system.

The Broadcasters' Imperative

For broadcasters to fulfill their imperative, they must have frequent and significant opportunities to act as the voters' trustee. In its present form, election broadcasting provides these opportunities. Broadcasters are in a strong position to constrain and evaluate the candidates' claims and to bring neglected aspects of policy and leadership to the electorate's attention. This section will indicate how present conditions fulfill the broadcasters' imperative. The analysis begins with a review of the federal regulations that affect broadcasting and concludes with an evaluation of broadcasters' ability to control election news.

Section 315 and Election News

Broadcasters are not entirely free in their coverage of a presidential campaign. Television editors and reporters operate within a framework of federal regulations, particularly section 315 of the Communications Act and the Fairness Doctrine. Broadcasters contend these regulations violate their First Amendment rights and inhibit their ability to act as the public's trustee. In practice, however, neither section 315 nor the Fairness Doctrine are major constraints on television journalists.

Section 315 requires broadcasters to provide candidates for public office with "equal opportunities." Commonly called the equal time provision, this section stipulates that when broadcasters permit a candidate to "use" a station's facilities, they must provide an equal broadcast opportunity to opposing candidates for the same office. In a 1959 amendment, Congress exempted bona fide news coverage from the equal opportunities provision of section 315. Congress felt the public would be better served if broadcasters were free to exercise their news judgment when reporting on candidates for public office.

Broadcasters accordingly are largely free to decide how much and what kind of regular news coverage each candidate will receive. They may, for instance, interview a political candidate during a scheduled newscast without conducting similar interviews with other candidates for the same office. Such interviews are exempt from the equal opportunities provision even if the station does not routinely invite public figures to appear on its newscasts.[3]

News interview programs such as "Meet the Press" and "Face the Nation" are also exempt from section 315. Congress granted this exemption in 1959 in order to encourage television networks and stations to provide expanded coverage of important political issues and persons. As a result, a broadcaster can invite a candidate to appear on a regularly scheduled news interview program without having to extend this opportunity to opposing candidates. Broadcasters are exempt from section 315 in these cases as long as the "selection of persons to be interviewed and topics to be discussed are based on their newsworthiness."[4] However, the exemption applies only if the broadcaster maintains editorial control of the interview program. If a candidate is allowed to determine the questions that are asked during the program, the broadcaster would not be exempt from section 315.[5]

Broadcasters may alter the format of a regular news interview program and still be exempt from the equal opportunities provision. For instance, the Federal Communications Commission (FCC) will permit stations to lengthen a regularly scheduled interview program or even move it to another time. The FCC regards such changes as news judgments, which are justified by the level of public interest in particular topics or persons.[6]

News documentaries are also exempt if a candidate's appearance is incidental to the subject of the documentary. This FCC ruling came in the case of "Television and Politics," a documentary that examined the use of television by candidates. Although the program included an appearance by a candidate for public office, the FCC ruled that his opponents were not entitled to equal opportunities because the candidate himself was not the subject of the documentary.[7]

Finally, "on-the-spot coverage" of bona fide news events is exempt from section 315. This exemption was provided in 1959 by an act of Congress. Television's coverage of the Democratic and Republican national conventions, for example, carries no equal opportunities obligations to other political parties. Thus, the networks can broadcast in their entirety the acceptance speeches of presidential nominees without providing time to opposing candidates. The FCC has ruled that broadcasters also may interview candidates selectively at a party's convention without violating section 315.[8]

In an important 1975 ruling, known as the Aspen Institute Ruling, the FCC broadened the live coverage exemption to include certain candidate debates and press conferences. Before this FCC decision, televised presidential and vice presidential debates between the Republican and Democratic candidates (but excluding candidates from other parties) could be held only if Congress acted to suspend section 315. In 1975, however, the FCC ruled that debates could be carried live on television if they were bona fide news events. To qualify as such, a debate could neither be sponsored by a broadcasting organization nor use its facilities. Moreover, the debate would have to be carried live and in its entirety, and be televised because of "reasonable journalistic judgment of the newsworthiness of the event."[9] On this basis, the television networks broadcasted general election debates sponsored by the League of Women Voters in 1976, 1980, and 1984.

In *Chisholm* v. *FCC* (1975) a federal court of appeals upheld the

Aspen Institute Ruling. In making its decision the court studied the 1959 deliberations in Congress when the original exemption for live news events was granted. The court noted that although the congressional discussion had made no specific reference to either debates or press conferences, Congress clearly had intended to broaden broadcasters' discretion in their news coverage. The FCC's decision to let broadcasters cover debates and press conferences sponsored by other organizations was, the court ruled, consistent with congressional intent.[10]

In 1976 presidential candidates Eugene McCarthy and Lester Maddox challenged their exclusion from a nationally televised debate between Gerald Ford and Jimmy Carter. The FCC ruled against them, saying it lacked the authority to compel the sponsoring organization to include them, and that broadcasters had acted in good faith in covering a debate from which the two alternative-party challengers were excluded. The FCC also ruled that although Carter and Ford had partial control over the content and format of their debate, this did not, "by itself, exclude coverage of the event" under the equal opportunities provision of section 315.[11]

In 1985 the FCC exempted presidential debates entirely from section 315. They are now regarded as bona fide news events that broadcasters can cover "on-the-spot." A broadcaster now can sponsor and air presidential debates; the one restriction is that the broadcaster cannot turn control of the debate over to the candidates—in other words, the broadcaster must moderate the debate.

A televised appearance by a presidential candidate in a situation other than those mentioned above is considered a "use" by the candidate, and the broadcaster must provide opposing candidates with equal opportunities. The most obvious nonexempt appearance occurs when a broadcaster provides a candidate with free time to be used as the candidate chooses. A broadcaster also cannot arrange a one-time "special" program featuring a candidate without affording the same opportunity to other candidates for the same office. Finally, the FCC has ruled that the news interview exemption applies only to regularly scheduled programs.[12]

Nevertheless, it is apparent that broadcasters have broad discretion in their news coverage of presidential candidates. The major obstacle to expanded election programming has not been legal restrictions on broadcasters but a lack of interest by the broadcasters themselves. Section 315, for example, requires only that "opposing" candidates receive equal broadcasting opportunities. During the nominating phase, this means that only legally qualified candidates within the same party must participate in special broadcasts. The networks have largely ignored the possibilities for political discussion inherent in this aspect of section 315. They have not, for example, regularly conducted televised debates during the presidential nominating campaigns, despite the willingness of major party candidates to participate. For the most part, these debates have been sponsored instead by noncommercial educational stations, which have a significantly smaller audience.

It is often said, unfairly, that commercial broadcasters are concerned only with their profits. On the other hand, the profit motive cannot be dismissed entirely. Nominating debates disrupt profitable entertainment programs, which presumably is why the networks have not covered these events regularly.[13] Economic considerations also may be at the root of the networks' reluctance to create other opportunities allowed by section 315. FCC policy apparently permits a network to invite the Republican and Democratic nominees to appear (perhaps back-to-back) on its Sunday interview program, which could be expanded to an hour (and perhaps even moved to prime time). The networks have not tried to arrange such broadcasts, which would give the public opportunities to view the candidates in what could be particularly revealing situations.

The Fairness Doctrine and Election News

The Fairness Doctrine applies primarily to issues, not candidates. It requires that broadcasters provide "reasonable opportunities" for the presentation of opposing positions on controversial public issues. Under the Fairness Doctrine, broadcasters are obliged to provide substantial coverage of important public disputes. A second obligation is that, when a broadcaster presents one side of such an issue, significant opposing views also must be presented. Broadcasters cannot lawfully ignore significant political opinions that are contrary to their personal beliefs.

Broadcasters have urged the repeal of the Fairness Doctrine, largely on the grounds that it compels them to give time to views they find disagreeable, which they believe infringes on their First Amendment rights, their news judgment, and their responsibility to bring issues before the public.

However, broadcasters are granted considerable discretion in complying with the Fairness Doctrine. It allows them substantial freedom of choice in determining time, format, and speakers. The opposing sides on political issues do not have to be given equal time; each must receive only a "reasonable" amount of time to present its views. If one side's opinion is presented in a news story or editorial, the opposing side does not also have to be broadcast in this way. No one has a right of access; broadcasters can determine for themselves who will speak for each opinion.[14]

The Fairness Doctrine has a special meaning in election campaigns. The FCC has ruled that a significant "issue" in a campaign is the opposing candidates. A broadcaster's failure to cover a "significant" opposing candidate may be regarded as a violation of the Fairness Doctrine. The FCC's position is that broadcasters will cover campaigns thoroughly and that significant opposing candidates will have "reasonable opportunities" to appear in this coverage.[15] This policy does not require broadcasters to give roughly equal news time to the Republican and Democratic presidential candidates in the general election, even though broadcasters sometimes have acted as if they had this obligation. In 1972, for example, Richard Nixon made only seven campaign appearances during the general election, but the networks balanced their coverage of him and George McGovern by reporting on the campaign activities of his surrogates, including Julie Nixon. This practice was legally unnecessary and, in fact, ran counter to the spirit of the Fairness Doctrine.

The FCC has imposed a few specific "fairness" restrictions on election coverage. Broadcasters are not prohibited from endorsing candidates for public office, but when they do, they are required to provide opposing candidates an opportunity to reply.[16] This situation arises when a representative of a station indicates directly or by implication that the station is backing one candidate. In this case the broadcaster must permit the other candidate or a surrogate for the candidate to respond to the editorial. However, if the broadcaster indicates that a surrogate will make the reply, the FCC has ruled that, except in extraordinary circumstances, the choice of who will speak rests with the candidate.[17]

On the whole the FCC's interpretations of the Fairness Doctrine have greatly favored broadcasters. The FCC holds that the Fairness Doctrine was not meant to place tight restrictions on broadcasters, and has argued that they must be given wide discretion in their news judgments. This stated policy has been honored in practice by the FCC. It does not monitor broadcasts to check on compliance with the Fairness Doctrine, responding instead to complaints. The burden of proof is on the complainant.[18] The FCC receives several thousand complaints each year but rejects nearly all of them as not meeting the prima facie criteria for a valid complaint. These criteria are:

1. The complaint must refer to broadcast coverage of a *specific* public issue.
2. The complaint must indicate by time(s) and date(s) when the alleged fairness violation(s) occurred and the nature of the alleged violation(s).
3. The complaint must demonstrate that the issue in question is controversial and of public importance.
4. The complainant must indicate that the station apparently has not provided coverage of opposing views on the issue. (The complainant may do this, for example, by claiming to be a regular viewer and claiming not to have seen coverage of opposing views.)

The small proportion of received complaints (less than 5 percent) that meet these criteria are sent by the FCC to the broadcasters for rebuttal. The broadcasters' rebuttals nearly always satisfy the FCC that a fairness violation has not occurred. Since 1984, in fact, the FCC has directed only one station (WTVH-Syracuse, N.Y.) to broadcast additional programming in order to comply with the Fairness Doctrine. Even then, the broadcaster chose to appeal the FCC's decision to the federal courts.[19]

Coverage of Presidential Campaigns

Broadcasters obviously have substantial freedom under the Fairness Doctrine and section 315, and could reasonably make greater use of it. A presidential campaign, in fact, provides broadcasters with innumerable opportunities to act as the public's trustee. To the extent that they fail to do so, it is largely the result of journalistic norms that lead broadcasters to downplay the substance of election campaigns.

Reporters once served mainly as common carriers, taking their news primarily from candidates' prepared statements. "In the old days," Carl Leubsdorf has noted, "emphasis in election reporting was on what the candidates were saying."[20] Campaign coverage continues to be an outlet for the candidates' appeals. With rare exceptions, every important new statement by a major candidate finds a place in the news. As Timothy Crouse observed, there is even much that the candidates say that is unimportant, or even downright trivial, that the press dutifully reports.[21] Journalists' concern with what Walter Lippmann called the "overt phases of events" also enhances the candidates' control of what the media report.[22] Since the candidates decide what they will say, and where they will say it, they frequently can direct the press's attention to what they want it to see.

Nevertheless, candidates no longer can dictate election news, partly because of the lengthening of modern presidential campaigns. The shorter campaigns of the past enabled candidates to establish the news agenda; whatever they had to say was likely to be fresh news. It is all but impossible, however, for a candidate to control the news for the three hundred or more days of the present campaign. On most days, in fact, reporters are more or less free to base news selections on their own values. And because the media have a daily appetite for stories about the presidential election, reporters are regularly able to portray the campaign in their own terms.

Journalists have a different conception of presidential elections than do candidates. In their coverage of a campaign the media concentrate upon strategic situations, downplaying the national problems, goals, and issues that the candidates are emphasizing. Although journalists consider the campaign to have more than ritual significance, they tend not to view it primarily in terms of the national policy and leadership themes being addressed by the candidates. To journalists the campaign is mainly a competitive "game." "The game," notes Paul Weaver, "takes place against a backdrop of governmental institutions, public problems, policy debates, and the like, but these are noteworthy only insofar as they affect, or are used by, players in pursuit of the game's rewards."[23]

Weaver claims that this journalistic perspective has prevailed in America for more than a century. Not until the campaign reached its present length, however, did reporters have a full opportunity to impress their views on news coverage. In a study of the 1940 election Paul Lazarsfeld, Bernard Berelson, and Hazel Gaudet found that about

50 percent of the election coverage in newspapers was devoted to matters of national policy and leadership. Only 35 percent was concerned with game-related topics, such as winning and losing, strategy, tactics, and logistics.[24] Studies of recent campaigns, however, reveal that the game is now the main subject of election news. In the 1976 campaign, for example, 60 percent of television coverage and 55 percent of newspaper coverage dealt with game-related topics, particularly the candidates' success in the race and their strategies. Only 30 percent of the election news on television, and 35 percent in newspapers, pertained to issues, national problems, leadership concerns, and related topics.[25]

Television's greater emphasis on the game is mainly the result of differences in the styles of broadcasting and newspaper reporting. In the newspaper most election reports are descriptive. They do not have a tight story line and perhaps are best described as strings of related facts that editors can cut almost anywhere in order to fit a story into available space. Nearly always, these strings include verbatim statements by candidates on matters of national policy and leadership.

Television reports, on the other hand, tend to be interpretive in form. Television places greater emphasis on "why" than on "what," attempting to explain rather than to describe. Television's emphasis on interpretation derives from its need for tightly structured stories. To be understood readily by the listening audience stories must be given a clear focus; they cannot be allowed to trail off as a newspaper story does. Further, the average television news story is only ninety seconds long, not long enough for the reporter to tell the news through the words of public officials or with a listing of the facts of an event, as is typically done in the newspaper. The television reporter must assume a more active role, sharply defining and limiting the story so that it can be told in one hundred to two hundred words.

For these reasons, most television news stories are built around themes. Television's "principal need," says Weaver, "is for a clear, continuous narrative line sustained throughout the story—something with a beginning, a middle and an end." Quite unlike the newspaper, television's primary concern is not the facts of an event; it is the theme. On television, notes Weaver, the facts become "the materials with which the chosen theme is illustrated."[26] Description gives way to interpretation.

Consistent with the general tendency of journalists to see the election primarily as a game, the dominant themes of television are the status of the race and the candidates' strategies. This tendency insures that what is said about the election's substance will not stand out as much on television as it does in the newspaper. Facts about what the candidates represent are placed here and there in television reports but frequently serve only a supporting role, acting as background, transitional, or illustrative material for the game-centered narrative.

Fulfillment of the Broadcasters' Imperative

The broadcasting imperative demands more than that broadcasters have sufficient opportunities to discharge their role as public trustee. Whether broadcasters use these opportunities to provide a running commentary on the election game or to assist the electorate in its choice is a secondary issue. Because broadcasters have in the news a powerful means to communicate with the public, there is no compelling need to alter the existing structure of election broadcasting to give them additional opportunities.

Nevertheless, broadcasters should be encouraged to review their election coverage. A presidential campaign is a competitive race for the nation's highest office, an eminently newsworthy topic. But the campaign also affects the direction of national policy and leadership, and broadcasters abdicate their trustee's role in failing to address this aspect of elections more fully.

A recommendation for election news coverage could begin with the simple understanding that presidential campaigns are unusual events. Television news normally is oriented to swift reactions to emerging developments. Broadcasters ordinarily ignore routine activities. Election news is an exception. Although elections consist mainly of repetitious appearances by the candidates, the networks feel compelled to produce daily reports from the campaign trail. Since there is little novelty in what the candidates say and do from day to day, the news gravitates toward the political context of these activities, which may be novel. Is the candidate gaining or losing ground? Trying to win the support of a particular group? Adjusting strategy?

Broadcasters could liberate themselves from this pattern and, in fact, have made some efforts to do so in recent elections. The networks now routinely fit a biographical profile of each major presidential candidate into their news broadcasts at some point. Broadcasters, however, are unwilling to deviate too far from the "here and now" principle of the news. During the 1980 campaign, for example, CBS Evening News at no time provided a retrospective report on Reagan's record as governor of California or as head of the Screen Actors Guild.[27] Broadcasters certainly have the time to prepare such reports if they would choose to do so.

Broadcasters have responded to the criticism that their news programs are lacking in issues by saying that voters are not interested. In a sense, this is correct; the television audience undoubtedly would tune out if election news night after night showed "talking heads" reviewing the candidates' campaign promises. It is also true, however, that viewers do not regard election news in its present format to be particularly interesting or important. Audience research indicates that people tire rather quickly of the largely repetitious reports on campaign activity that currently are directed at them.[28]

The challenge of election news is to find interesting ways of presenting significant information that will help the voters to understand the choices they face. This could include news coverage of many of the same activities now being covered, but accompanied by serious analyses. Much of the present analysis is trivial. To suggest, for instance, that a candidate's speech on agricultural policy is an attempt to win the farm vote hardly deserves to be regarded as analysis; an effort to assess the feasibility and probable effects of the proposed policy would be more thoughtful and perhaps more interesting, as well as more useful, to the electorate. Television news also could include more reports on the candidates' backgrounds, accompanied by analyses of the possible implications for presidential performance.

The prospects for change, however, appear limited. For years now, critics have urged the networks to make their coverage more informative. In the quiet period between presidential campaigns, broadcasters themselves have often vowed to do so. Their good intentions, however, inevitably fade as the next campaign begins. Existing patterns of election reporting are deeply ingrained and reinforced by conventional news standards. As long as journalists are tuned mainly to new developments in the election race, news coverage will continue to stress the candidates' changing strategies and fortunes.

The Candidates' Imperative

The second imperative of election broadcasting is that presidential candidates must have frequent and significant opportunities to present themselves on television in ways they wish to be seen. Candidates are responsible for their campaigns, and one of them will gain the presidency. It is essential, therefore, that candidates be able to communicate their views on national policy and leadership. The principal broadcast opportunities for candidates are provided by television newscasts, televised political advertising, and special telecasts, particularly general election debates. For various reasons these opportunities cannot satisfy the candidates' communications needs.

The great failing of the present system of election broadcasting is that it does not enable candidates to meet their imperative fully. The primary objective of broadcast reform should be to develop additional broadcasting opportunities that will permit candidates to establish their agendas in the voters' minds.

Candidates and Television News

Television news does not provide candidates with sufficient opportunities to communicate their agendas. Broadcasters' emphasis on the election game is only one reason. The issues the candidates stress most heavily are not those reported most frequently in the news. Candidates build their campaigns around both broad policy commitments, such as promises to keep the peace and to control inflation, and specific pledges to the groups and interests aligned with their party. These issues, however, tend not to be the favorites of reporters. The candidates' coalitional appeals are thought to be too narrow to be of general news interest, and their broad appeals are regarded as too vague for easy use. Moreover, these issues usually do not involve the intense conflict that reporters prize in their stories. Pomper's research indicates that only one in ten issue pledges place the candidates in directly opposing positions. Most of the stands they take either overlap with their opponents' positions or appeal to different groups of voters.[29] Finally, the candidates' basic appeals are repetitious, contained in finely tuned stump speeches that are repeated at nearly every campaign stop and before nearly every audience. "When candidates say the same things over and over," says television correspondent Judy Woodruff, "it is not news."

Journalists like clear-cut issues that neatly divide the candidates. Preferably, these issues are also controversial and can be stated simply, usually by reference to a shorthand label, such as "star wars." Often, these issues have relevance only in the context of the campaign. The two most heavily reported issues of the 1976 general election, for example, were not matters of public policy, but gaffes by the candidates—Carter's *Playboy* interview and Ford's remark on Eastern Europe during the second presidential debate. In 1984 another gaffe—Geraldine Ferraro's initial refusal to release her family's tax returns—was covered intensely. Such issues fit the press's conception of "good news"—they are colorful, conflictual, unusual, and sensational.

When campaign issues break, they make the headlines and top the television newscasts. For a week or more they are likely to remain major news stories. This was true of several such issues in 1984, among them Jesse Jackson's reference to Jews as "Hymies" and his association with Muslim leader Louis Farrakhan. When Jackson appeared on NBC's "Meet the Press" in April, he was asked nine straight questions about Farrakhan. Jackson protested: "I want to talk, if I might, about industrial policies to put people back to work, or about African policy, which most of you tend to ignore, or South African oppression. I think that continuing to raise this issue, frankly, is overspending my time."

Michael Robinson's analysis of network evening news coverage during the 1984 general election provides more systematic evidence of the media's concern with clear-cut issues. He found that they accounted for nearly 40 percent of all television news coverage. Included among these issues were George Bush's attempts to define "shame" from several dictionaries and his "kick ass" remark about his debate with Ferraro; Ferraro's finances and her verbal battle with Archbishop John O'Connor; Mondale's controversial meeting with Andrei Gromyko; and Reagan's inaccessibility to the press and his suggestion that the Beirut bombing was somehow Jimmy Carter's fault.[30]

To be sure, candidates do not ignore such issues completely. When an opponent blunders, a candidate exploits it. In general, though, such issues are of secondary interest to candidates, a conclusion supported by Benjamin Page's exhaustive study of campaign issues. He found that each presidential nominee since 1932, including ideologues like Barry Goldwater and George McGovern, stressed general goals and coalition appeals more than specific disputes.[31] Other research has documented the same tendency, while also showing that television journalists tend to downplay such goals and appeals. One comparison of candidates' speeches and election news, for example, revealed a dramatic difference in these communications. General goals and coalition appeals provided 67 percent of the issue content of candidates speeches, but only 26 percent of the issue content on the nightly newscasts.[32] The networks' extraordinary depreciation of goals and appeals is mostly the result of television's preference for subjects that do not require lengthy exposition and appeal to a diverse audience. Even newspapers are sometimes reluctant to make room for the hundreds of words that may be required to present the candidates' broad appeals in a meaningful way. With its preference for action film and brevity, television news seldom makes time for such presentations.

Journalists also have a tendency, as Walter Lippmann noted, to "stylize" issues, a process that reduces issues to catch phrases, which makes them easier and more interesting to report but also distorts them substantially.[33] In the 1984 campaign, for instance, Walter Mondale's appeals to traditional groups within the Democratic coalition made him "the captive of special interests" in press reports, while Gary Hart's tendency to address issues analytically led to the charge: "Where's the beef?" Once attached, such labels are difficult for candidates to shed, working as roadblocks to their efforts to make the electorate aware of their actual positions.

Reporters' concern about what is new and different in the candidates' positions also makes it difficult for candidates to get their messages across. In October 1980, for instance, CBS correspondent Bill Plante enumerated positions that Ronald Reagan had either altered or, more typically, ignored since his nomination. As Plante talked, X's were drawn across Reagan's face to dramatize his apostasy. Plante suggested that Reagan had moved to the political center in order to win the election.

Had Reagan actually changed his policies? The answer, from a reading of Reagan's standard campaign speeches in the fall of 1980, is no. He spoke then mainly of big government, high taxes, and inadequate national defense, the same things he had been attacking for more than fifteen years. His positions were those of a conservative

Republican, not of the centrist that Plante portrayed. The reason he looked so different in Plante's report was that Plante, like other journalists on the campaign trail, concentrated on what was new and different in Reagan's statements, however slight these changes might have been. The first time that a candidate announces his position on an important issue, he can expect television news to report it. After that, the position is no longer newsworthy, but small amendments are.

An effect of this pattern of television reporting is that candidates may appear to voters to be uncommitted to their positions and manipulative of issues. Based on their content analysis of the CBS Evening News's 1980 election coverage, Michael Robinson and Margaret Sheehan concluded that network television presents a negative image of presidential candidates. "Network reporters," they observed, "do seem to want to make the public more aware of the frailties and inadequacies of their elected leadership."[34] Although most news stories were neutral or ambiguous, CBS gave the candidates about three times as much "bad press" as "good press": "CBS, particularly in its coverage of frontrunners, seemed to be turning some motherly advice inside out—the correspondents said something critical or they said nothing at all. . . . Most bad press stories merely chided candidates for contradicting themselves, behaving politically or engaging in symbolism."[35] Robinson and Sheehan estimate that about half of the bad press reports on television came in "closers," the last sentence of a news report that places events in context. These closers often emphasized the self-serving nature of the candidates' campaign appearances and appeals.[36]

Audience research supports the conclusion that the nature of television news confounds the efforts of candidates to use it as a platform. Viewers' perception of the candidates' chances of winning, of campaign events, and of the candidates' campaign styles and strategies are significantly related to what they see on television.[37] Television news exposure also seems to be associated with more negative images of presidential candidates.[38] Frequent exposure to television news, however, is not closely related to voters' understanding of the candidates' policy positions and records, which broadcasters largely downplay.[39]

To change the news simply to serve the candidates' purposes is no answer to the shortcomings of television news. Journalists and candidates have different roles to perform in an election, and the blurring of their responsibilities, which already has progressed to an unhealthy stage in American campaigns, cannot serve either their separate interests or those of voters. Broadcasters could, in Paul Weaver's terms, provide voters a better "window" on the candidates, but cannot responsibly serve as their "platform."[40]

Televised Political Advertising

Televised political advertising offers the candidates a platform, and they use it primarily to communicate the main themes of their campaigns. Because viewers are suspicious of advertising, however, it fails to meet fully the candidates' communication needs.

Most advertising for presidential candidates involves policy appeals, partly on the assumption (probably correct) that voters would be intolerant of commercials that try to sell would-be presidents as if they were soap or cars. Larry Sabato reports that when consultants created some productlike commercials for President Ford's 1976 campaign, test audiences snickered as the ads appeared on the screen.[41] A study of the 1972 campaign found that advertising generally tried to give the voters solid reasons for supporting one candidate instead of the other. These appeals depended largely on issues: the sponsoring candidate attempted to link himself with issue positions that he felt would win him votes and tried to associate his opponent with positions that would cost him votes. Of the political commercials televised during the 1972 general election, 42 percent were primarily issue communications, and another 28 percent contained substantial issue material.[42]

Another study, this one of the 1976 campaign, documented that the candidates' political advertising conformed closely in its issue content to what the candidates were saying in their major speeches. Broad appeals and coalition pledges accounted for 62 percent of the issue material in the candidates' televised commercials, and 67 percent in their campaign speeches. Issues involving clear-cut differences between the candidates, which were so prevalent on television news (74 percent of issue coverage), were a smaller aspect (38 percent) of the candidates' advertising, just as they were a smaller proportion (33 percent) of the candidates' speeches.[43]

Advertising has characteristics that can make it a uniquely powerful form for communicating the candidates' messages. Unlike television news, where the candidates' messages may be obscure, fleeting, and surrounded by competing information, advertising is concentrated. Commercials contain such direct messages that they leave almost no room for misunderstanding, and these messages can be repeated again and again, or at least as frequently as the candidate's budget permits. Audience research indicates that viewers do learn about the candidates' policy positions from exposure to advertising. In fact, available evidence suggests that, in a presidential general election, viewers gain a clearer understanding of the candidates' policies from televised advertising than from television news.[44]

Some critics recommend that the United States adopt the policy of Great Britain, which bans paid advertising. They contend that ads trivialize political discussion, foster electronic demogoguery, and drive up the costs of presidential campaigns. Their recommendation, however, ignores some important facts: most election information, whether in the news or through advertising, flows in bits and pieces; lengthier and more desirable forms of paid broadcasting, such as thirty-minute broadcasts, fail to attract sizable audiences; and most alternative forms of paid communication (for example, direct mail) are more expensive and potentially more devious than televised advertising. Moreover, proposals to ban advertising fail to account for the uniqueness of American politics. Great Britain has strong parties, within and outside of Parliament, and provides free broadcast time to its parties, which can be used by their leaders. The American presidential system rests on weak parties and self-starting candidates, who often need advertising to establish public recognition and distinguish their agendas from those of their opponents.[45]

Advertising, however, cannot fulfill the candidates' imperative. Advertising's problem is its credibility. Because it is purchased by candidates, viewers substantially discount much of what is said in commercials. Advertising lacks the authoritative quality of broadcast news. Viewers are more than twice as likely to question a televised message about a candidate conveyed through advertising than through a newscast.[46] Their assumption, a perfectly reasonable one, is that the candidate's message is not to be completely trusted.

Fulfilling the Candidates' Imperative

To fulfill their imperative, presidential candidates must be provided with opportunities to make significant broadcasts, largely under their own control, that will be regarded by the electorate as opportunities to learn about the candidates' policy and leadership intentions.

The simplest proposal would be to give presidential candidates blocks of free time, much as many European political systems grant free broadcast time to parties and candidates. Free broadcasts, however, may be less useful to candidates than is commonly assumed. The electorate may not take these programs seriously. This is what has happened in Britain, apparently unnoticed by those who have proposed similar programs for American elections. Although the British party broadcasts have large audiences, they are neither a highly attentive nor a trustful audience:

> labelled from the start as unopposed propaganda—and standing "solitary" in that respect from the rest of election output . . . they seem almost tailor-made to put audiences on their guard and to trigger anti-party and anti-political sentiments. Although the judgment of another informant—"they tend to be counter-productive, because it's in the nature of things that party broadcasts are meant to be misleading"—may seem extreme, we all immediately recognize that point of his remark. Even politicians are sensitive to the resulting gap between principle and practice. . . .[47]

British disenchantment with party broadcasts has been progressive. When the BBC's audience research department first questioned British voters in 1959, a substantial majority indicated that they enjoyed the party broadcasts. Surveys in each succeeding election found declining satisfaction and attention. This trend was nationwide, affecting voters even when watching the broadcasts of their party. By 1974, 60 percent of the British electorate said they were dissatisfied with the programs, and a majority deliberately avoided exposure to any of the party broadcasts. The common British complaint was that the broadcasts lacked credibility; the candidates were perceived to be engaged in unrestrained efforts to sell themselves.

American presidential debates, in contrast, draw a large, interested audience. These debates provide substantial opportunities for the candidates to convey their messages to the public. Although journalists ask questions, candidates typically have not felt severely constrained by them and have used the debates primarily to stress the policy and leadership themes they have been emphasizing throughout their campaigns. If their statements are not ordered and structured exactly as they would be in the absence of participating journalists, what they say is at least a fair representation of their conception of their candidacies.

The influence of broadcasters on presidential debates comes primarily through the news coverage that precedes and follows each debate. The pattern of this coverage is that of election news generally. The 1976 Ford-Carter debates are an example. As the debates approached, reporters began to "hype" them as pivotal to the election outcome, and the news was dominated by speculations on how the candidates would perform, who would win, and how the campaign might be affected. A typical news report was the following:

> A television audience of perhaps 100 million Americans will be watching. A large percentage of them might well decide which man to support on the basis of what they see that night. Even though there will be two more debates between Carter and Ford, first impressions are difficult to shake, as the 1960 opening debate between Jack Kennedy and Richard Nixon demonstrated. It may well be that the Philadelphia showdown is a more crucial test for Carter than it is for Ford. That had not seemed true when Ford issued his debate challenge at the Republican Convention in mid-August. Then Carter was far ahead in all the opinion polls and Ford seemed to be playing a desperate catch-up game. The President still trails, but much more narrowly. Yet for better or worse, depending on the voter, he is a known quantity. By contrast, despite Carter's all-out post-convention campaigning, he remains the man on whom millions of voters are still reserving judgment. If he reassures his shaky majority, he might breeze on toward certain victory. If he fails to do so, his support could erode badly.

By the time the first debate took place, the contest theme clearly dominated news coverage, and it was largely in this context that the debates subsequently were reported. More than half of the postdebate coverage concerned the debate's competitive aspects; about a fourth of that coverage dealt directly with the question of who had won, the rest with matters of performance and the debates' effect on the candidates' chances of election. Only about a third of all news space was given to the issues that the candidates addressed.

The effect on voters of this pattern of debate reporting is substantial. On their own, viewers of a debate naturally tend to draw conclusions about who won and who lost, but this impression is thoroughly mixed with their thoughts about the substance of the candidates' remarks. Polls taken immediately after the first presidential debate of the 1984 general election indicated that a majority of viewers thought Mondale "won" the debate but a majority also said they found Reagan's answers closer to their own thinking on the issues. Studies indicate, however, that as a debate recedes in time, and people are exposed to postdebate news analyses, they become increasingly preoccupied with the candidates' styles and performances, largely apart from the substance of the candidates' remarks. The news media's question—who won?—becomes the electorate's lasting impression of the significance of a debate.[48]

These observations are an argument, not against debates and candidate programs, but against the context in which they normally occur. Their context must be altered if these broadcasts are to meet adequately the needs of candidates and voters. The rest of this essay contains a proposal for election debates and candidate programs that is designed to frame them in a way that will better serve the electorate's interest. The proposal is a specific one, but the details are less important than the underlying idea.

A Modest Proposal

A first principle for new-style television broadcasts is that they must draw attention primarily to what candidates say rather than how they say it. A candidate's performance inevitably is part of any televised appearance, but its significance should not be so exaggerated that the substance of what the candidate says becomes secondary. This is the problem of presidential debates as they are presently organized.

A second principle for these election broadcasts is that they must allow candidates to say what they want to say, yet under conditions in which they can be held accountable for their remarks. The candidates' advocacy, in short, must be coupled with immediate scrutiny.[49]

The problem with the British party broadcasts is that they do not include mechanisms of accountability. Candidates are free to say whatever they want and often make extravagant claims. Recognizing this, the electorate is both less interested and more skeptical of what they say. When their statements are subject to immediate review, however, the candidates are likely to address policies more realistically, and the electorate, in turn, is more likely to regard what they say as important and interesting.

A proposal that meets these conditions would combine presidential debates with broadcasts that are mainly, but not solely, opportunities for the candidates to present themselves as they choose. Specifically:

Four weeks before election day. In the fourth week preceding the general election, there would be a national broadcast in which each major party candidate would have the opportunity to present a lengthy (say, twenty minutes) prepared statement on domestic policy, followed immediately by a period (perhaps ten minutes) in which journalists, acting as public trustees, would respond as they saw fit (including questions of the candidate).

Three weeks before election day. In the third week before the general election a candidate debate on domestic issues would be broadcast. This debate could be similar in format to those of recent elections, although alternative formats that allow for a more free-wheeling give-and-take between the candidates should be considered. The debate, in part, would provide an opportunity for candidates and their questioners to explore further the policy discussion of the previous week's broadcast. However, neither the candidates nor the participating journalists would be confined to topics that were raised in the previous broadcast.

Two weeks before election day. A broadcast similar to the one in the fourth week, except on foreign policy.

One week before election day. A debate similar to the one in the third week, except on foreign policy.

This proposal would provide an entirely different setting for election broadcasts than either debates or candidate programs alone. The first major broadcast event of the general election would be the candidates' domestic policy presentations. This advocacy broadcast would have none of the qualities of a debate. Its main feature would be the uninterrupted period it provides candidates to present their domestic policy agendas. Unlike a debate, in which the discussion moves quickly from one candidate to the other, the candidates' presentations would be concentrated and entirely within their control. Each statement, however, would be subject to immediate scrutiny by participating journalists, who could present questions to the candidate and observations of their own choosing. (Presumably, however, their attention would be concentrated on critical evaluations and follow-up questions to the candidates' remarks.)

The press buildup to the advocacy broadcasts might concentrate on the question of which candidate was likely to "win." It is unlikely, however, that this concern would dominate to the extent that it presently does in predebate news. The broadcast would direct journalists' projections partly to speculation about what the candidates would say, and how this would clarify their candidacies. The postbroadcast reporting also could be expected to treat the domestic policy differences between the candidates. To be sure, journalists would be concerned about the candidates' performances, but it is unlikely that this concern would be as consuming as it has been in recent postdebate coverage.

The advocacy broadcast likely would influence news about the debate on domestic policy that would follow in the next week. There would be speculation about how the debate might clarify some of the policy positions taken during the broadcasts. After the debate the news emphasis undoubtedly would shift to the question of who won and who lost. Nevertheless, this concern would be tempered by the news media's build-up of the next week's broadcast, which would feature the candidates' foreign policy statements.

Correspondingly, the public's attention would be affected by the nature of these broadcasts and the attending news coverage. Although the debates probably would draw larger audiences, the advocacy broadcasts would have a substantial following. People would be attracted by the advance news coverage; by the link between each broadcast and the debate that follows; and by the coupling of candidate advocacy with journalistic scrutiny.

The series of four broadcasts would help to fulfill the candidates' imperative,[50] while providing journalists with additional opportunities to meet theirs. Each broadcast would give the candidates a significant opportunity to present themselves on their own terms, subject to review by journalists in their role as public trustee. The benefits to the voters would be substantial. Relative to present arrangements, the four broadcasts would direct voters' attention to the candidates' policies and leadership abilities.

The four broadcasts, or another arrangement based on the same considerations, could be organized by the networks or a group such as the League of Women Voters. The advocacy broadcasts may or may not conform to the FCC's conception of bona fide news events, but they do contain the essential elements—joint appearance of the candidates and journalistic scrutiny—that governed the FCC's recent exemption of debates from the section 315 requirement. If the FCC should decide against the advocacy broadcasts, which seems unlikely given its increasingly laissez-faire position on broadcasting, congressional action would be necessary.

In theory a similar series of broadcasts would seem advisable during the presidential campaign's nominating phase. The establishment of a set policy for this period, however, is confounded by questions of timing and participation. From one perspective the ideal period would be before the first of the state contests so that interested voters around the nation would have the opportunity to assess the full field of contenders. But recent contested nominations have attracted a half dozen or more candidates, which can result in unwieldy forums. Furthermore, once the state contests begin, the candidates' standing in the race can change suddenly and dramatically. Also, when an incumbent president is seeking renomination, there may or may not be justification for broadcasts of that party's contest.

For such reasons a flexible broadcasting policy—one responsive to existing situations—would seem desirable. There will be times, such as the Ford-Reagan race of 1976, when a series of national broadcasts like that proposed for the general election would be sensible at the earliest stage of the nominating contest. In other situations, like the Mondale-Hart-Jackson race of 1984, the series could come later in the nominating campaign. When the field is so large as to be unmanageable (as in the Republican race at its early stage in 1980), consists only of the incumbent (the Republican race in 1984), or is winnowed to a single nonincumbent at an early stage (the Democratic race in 1976), broadcasters could reasonably decide that the public interest would not be served by a series of national telecasts. In any case, the uncertainty that attends the present nominating system requires judgment about the merits of special broadcasts. These are essentially news judgments and unless the nominating system is altered significantly, would appear to be best left to the discretion of broadcasters.

Above all, the commercial networks should be encouraged to be more responsive to broadcast opportunities during the nominating phase. When national broadcasts are clearly needed, there is no effective alternative to network involvement. Noncommercial television and statewide broadcasts have played an important role in recent presidential nominating campaigns and should continue to make this contribution. Only network telecasts, however, attract large national audiences and thereby can serve the legitimate needs of the full electorate. The networks' public service obligations are not fulfilled by leaving their noncommercial counterpart or local stations to carry the burden of candidate-centered broadcasts during the nominating phase.

This observation can be extended to network telecasts of the national party conventions. Conventions clearly do not have extraordinary audience appeal, and it obviously is tempting for a network to curtail convention broadcasting in favor of entertainment programming. A national party convention, however, is a time of extraordinary importance to the polity, regardless of whether it contains the built-in drama of an uncertain outcome. A convention is a socializing and galvanizing event for the electorate, and a legitimate opportunity for the major party nominees to clarify and establish their agendas. Broadcasting decisions about these events based on their entertainment value are totally inconsistent with the broadcasters' role as public trustee. This is not an argument for gavel-to-gavel coverage or for broadcasters to act solely as common carriers during their convention broadcasts. It is to argue, however, that broadcasters must realize that the airwaves they dominate must serve the broader interests of the political system as well as the narrower needs of the licensees.

A Concluding Note

This chapter began by positing two imperatives of presidential election television: that candidates must have significant opportunities to present themselves to the electorate as they wish, and that broadcasters must have significant opportunities, as the voters' trustee, to assess the candidates. It concluded that the existing system of election television enables broadcasters to fulfill their imperative, but does not allow candidates to meet theirs. Along with a few minor proposals for reform, the essay presented a major one: a series of broadcasts during the general election campaign that combines candidate advocacy with journalistic scrutiny.

Such a series is almost a necessity if today's television-based presidential campaigns are to serve the voters' needs for information. The proposed broadcasts also would help create a more constructive relationship between candidates and broadcasters. Television has become so important in the selection of presidents that neither candidates nor broadcasters are willing to respect and recognize fully the proper function of the other. Candidates constantly try to manipulate the news agenda, which is one reason for their uneasy and often tense relationship with broadcasters. For their part, broadcasters have placed themselves more and more in the way of candidate advocacy. To describe presidential conventions, debates, and news interviews as "candidates' time" is to ignore the great influence that broadcasters have over the content of these telecasts.

The proposal for a series of broadcasts in the general election is premised on a different relationship between candidates and broadcasters. It accepts neither the fiction that broadcasters can organize public opinion nor the opposite fiction that unfettered candidate advocacy meets the needs of today's sophisticated electorate. Yet it asks neither candidates nor broadcasters to compromise their respective advocacy and scrutiny functions. Instead, it combines these functions in a complementary way that would enable candidates to present their agendas and broadcasters to assess them. This arrangement not only respects the roles of candidates and broadcasters, but would enable America's voters to understand more clearly the momentous choice they face in the election of their next president.

13 Presidential Selection and Succession in Special Situations

ALLAN P. SINDLER

When the customary selection process works without hitch, a presidential and vice presidential candidate win a majority of electoral votes, take office, and complete the four-year term without interruption. The unexpected may occur, however, as in the case of a deadlocked election or the death or disability of a victorious candidate or officeholder. Unusual circumstances like these call for tailored modes of presidential selection.

The selection procedures that have been adopted to take care of such special situations are the subject of this essay. The initial, critical choice of procedures is between special presidential elections and presidential successorship by a stated sequence of public officials. In American practice, special elections have been consistently rejected and, within the context of successorship, the vice president has been accorded first place. Much of this essay, accordingly, deals with succession and the vice presidency in its description and evaluation of selection methods for special situations.

Several terms concerning presidential successorship that are used frequently in this essay should be defined at the outset. "Direct," "first," or "immediate" successorship refers to the elected vice president. A "double vacancy" is said to exist when both the president and vice president who initially were elected are unable to complete their terms of office. (Prior to ratification of the Twenty-fifth Amendment in 1967, a vacated vice presidency remained unfilled and a double vacancy meant that the two top offices were unoccupied. For the period since 1967 the presidency and vice presidency each could be occupied by a person who originally was nominated by a president and confirmed by Congress as a successor vice president. "Double vacancy" as used here also includes this situation.) "Contingent" successorship refers to the line of succession that comes into play when a double vacancy exists, that is, the list of persons designated to succeed to the presidency in the event that the originally elected vice president is unable to do so, including anyone appointed to fill a vacated vice presidency.

Basic Practices

When an American president is unable to finish the four-year term of office, the arrangements for what follows differ from those of other major and mature democracies. In other nations, the dominant party or party coalition promptly designates a new governmental leader or an interim head makes do temporarily until a special election can produce a new leader. In the United States, by contrast, specific public officials, beginning with the vice president, are authorized to succeed to a vacated presidency and to complete the balance of the interrupted term. These basic American practices—an avoidance of special presidential elections and a reliance on the vice president as the first successor and on other officials as contingent successors to a vacated presidency—warrant further discussion.

Avoidance of Special Presidential Elections

Proponents of special presidential elections advance at least three arguments.[1] The first and most fundamental claim is that in a democracy based on popular sovereignty the only acceptable president is one who has been elected as president, not someone who was chosen to be something else and then succeeds to the presidency upon its vacancy. From this perspective, no other public official can properly serve as a full presidential successor. Many advocates of this view note, as a second line of argument, that the original Constitution required the president to "be elected," and commend this as a sound concept. The third argument, made either in conjunction with the others or independently, is that the only way to ensure a presidential-quality successor is by special presidential election.

However theoretically meritorious the special presidential election may be, it fails on practical grounds. Its opponents observe that for the United States, as elsewhere, political succession arrangements lie close to the heart of the political system, are often fragile, and require continuing care. Many other countries have been plagued by persistent and severe problems of political succession, contributing at times to chronic instability in the basic regime. In contrast, the American experience has been one of rapid and legitimate succession, even under such trying circumstances as assassination or incipient impeachment of the president. Stability is seen as no small virtue of the present system and it should not be taken for granted as a guaranteed outcome no matter what succession arrangements are in force.

Since the need for a presidential successor may occur under conditions of high social stress, the prevailing judgment is that succession by means of special election is too risky. It would involve, on the one side, a constricted caretaker government for a significant period of time and, on the other, an intense, competitive and perhaps divisive campaign. In 1974, for example, would it have been advantageous to have followed President Richard Nixon's resignation with a special election rather than the automatic succession of the vice president? Moreover, what of the possible dangers to the country in having to operate with a mark-time government pending the running of the presidential campaign and the outcome of the election?[2]

Although American practice on presidential succession has consistently rejected special elections, the intent of the original Constitution is less clear. Article II, Section 1 required that both the president and the vice president "be elected," and provided (in clause 6) for succession as follows:

> In Case of the Removal of the President from Office, or of his Death, Resignation, or Inability to discharge the Powers and Duties of the said Office, the Same shall devolve on the Vice President, and the Congress may by Law provide for the Case of Removal, Death, Resignation or Inability, both of the President and Vice President, declaring what Officer shall then act as President, and such Officer shall act accordingly, until the Disability be removed, or a President shall be elected.

The ambiguity of two phrases left the interpretation of this clause open to disagreement. Did "the Same shall devolve on the Vice President" refer to the presidency itself or merely to the powers and duties of the office? And did "until . . . a President shall be elected" imply that a special election could or should be held?

Some have urged that the phrases in question should be read as limiting the vice president (or any other successor) to only a brief stint as acting president, pending the outcome of a special election.[3] A provision of the Twelfth Amendment arguably lends support to that view. When the House is obligated to choose a president, but is unable to do so by inauguration day, the amendment states: "The Vice President shall act as President, as in the case of the death or other constitutional disability of the President."

Others have maintained, however, that Congress lacks authority under Article II, Section 1, to provide by statute for a special election to fill a vacated presidency; to do so would require, in their view, a constitutional amendment.[4] Helpful to this position, at least with respect to the original Constitution, was the Framers' provision for awarding the vice presidency to the runner-up presidential candidate.

Successorship to the vice presidency, unlike that to the presidency, was dealt with unambiguously in the Constitution. The matter was left entirely to congressional determination, including the possibility of not providing for any successor to that office. Indeed, to leave a vacant vice presidency unfilled made excellent sense in view of the original award of the vice presidency to the major losing presidential contestant, for whom there could be no successor.[5] Once arrangements were made to handle the situation of a double vacancy, the absence of a vice presidential incumbent would raise no grave problems.

Acting under its constitutional authority (clause 6), Congress set a contingent succession line in the event of a double vacancy, with the successor serving until "a President shall be elected." The first presidential succession law, enacted by the Second Congress in 1792, provided that if a double vacancy occurred when more than six months of the presidential term remained, the contingent successor would act as president only until a new president (and vice president) were chosen in a special election, conducted under the electoral college method used for regular elections. The scheduling of the special election depended on the time of year that the double vacancy occurred; the maximum period a contingent successor could serve was seventeen months. Although the 1792 law was not explicit on the length of term for a specially elected president and vice president, it probably intended a new and full four-year period of service.

In the judgment of the Second Congress, then, the Constitution required or at least permitted a provisional successorship under conditions of a double vacancy. Confirmation of this judgment by later events cannot be had, of course, because the first instance of a double vacancy was not until 1974, by which time the Twenty-fifth Amendment had altered the Constitution's original provisions on succession.

Whatever the Framers' intentions with regard to presidential succession, and whatever the theoretical arguments for and against full or provisional successorship, history has settled the matter. The first opportunity to apply clause 6 came in 1841, when President William Henry Harrison died shortly after his inauguration. Amid debate that revealed confusion and disagreement over what the Constitution required, Vice President John Tyler successfully asserted a right —aptly symbolized by his taking the presidential oath of office—of full successorship for the remainder of the uncompleted term. Successor presidents have held to that practice ever since.

In explicitly endorsing the practice of full successorship in the present presidential succession law (passed in 1947), Congress also rejected the recommendation of President Harry S. Truman concerning succession to a double vacancy. As a successor president himself, Truman felt strongly that in a situation of double vacancy the contingent successor should serve only until a new president and vice president could be chosen in a special election to complete the existing term. Congress disagreed, on the grounds that requiring a special election would produce an excessive discontinuity of leadership within a period of less than four years. Instead, Congress placed the House Speaker and the Senate president pro tempore first and second, respectively, in the line of contingent succession after the vice president and, for the first time, directed the contingent successor to serve "until the expiration of the then current presidential term."

Final rejection of the special election device took place when the Twenty-fifth Amendment was adopted in 1967. Section 1 flatly states that "in case of the removal of the President from office or of his death or resignation, the Vice President shall become President." The amendment also provides, for the first time, for the filling of a vacant vice presidency; the designated method is by presidential nomination and congressional confirmation. Even under conditions of a double vacancy, then, the present constitutional arrangement is for succession by an appointed vice president rather than by the victor of a special presidential election.

The Vice President as First Successor

In both its constitutional design and practice the United States has always placed the vice president at the head of the line of presidential succession. This decision originally was made by the Framers, and it raised for them—as it has for later generations—a paradoxical and vexing question. On the one side, the role as first successor calls for a vice president of presidential quality, someone who by record and reputation has earned national standing as, in effect, an alternate president. On the other side, the formal powers assigned to the vice president are meager, indeed trivial: to preside over the Senate, except in the conduct of an impeachment trial of the president, and to cast a vote to break a tie in that body. The contrast between what the vice president would become after succeeding to a vacated presidency and the official, day-to-day authority of the vice presidency scarcely could be more marked. The troubling problem thus emerged from the outset: How could persons of acknowledged presidential quality be persuaded to become vice president?

The Framers' solution. The Framers imbedded an ingenious and effective solution to the vice presidential problem in the new Constitution, but it proved to be short-lived. Their central insight was to rely solely on presidential elections to produce vice presidents of presidential quality. Thus, although the mode of presidential election was essentially intended to shape the character of the president, it also set that of the vice president.

In the original Constitution, presidential electors were required to vote for two persons for president, "of whom one at least shall not be an inhabitant of the same state with themselves," and without being able to indicate a preference between them. By means of this double vote device each state's electors were encouraged to go beyond parochial support for local leaders and to vote also for prominent leaders in other states. The winning presidential candidate, therefore, usually would have significant backing from enough states to approximate, in total, a national consensus. Since the vice presidency was awarded to the presidential candidate with the second highest number of electoral votes, his pattern of support was also expected to be more national than local in character. In terms of both the size and qualitative meaning of his voting support, then, the vice president could be appropriately viewed as an alternate president.

To succeed, the Framers' election arrangements for the vice presidency depended on two conditions being met. The first was that electors, when casting their two votes, would confine their preferences to genuine presidential candidates. If, instead, electors informally differentiated in their double vote between presidential and vice presidential contestants, the vice presidency would be awarded not to the runner-up presidential contender but to the leading vice presidential candidate. The second condition, implicit in the Framers' design, was that political parties either would not exist or would be willing to have the leader of an electorally defeated party succeed to a vacated presidency. These two conditions reflected the Framers' hope that electors would function as an enlightened elite, free from ties of party or faction, in selecting a president and, as a by-product of that process, in designating a vice president as well.

Both conditions soon proved unrealistic. The beginnings of political parties were evident during George Washington's tenure, and as parties developed they quickly rejected the idea that the vice presidency should be assigned to the major losing presidential aspirant. Instead, each party insisted on sharply distinguishing between its presidential and vice presidential candidates and on controlling both offices.

This basic change in the political environment not only made the original design of vice presidential selection infeasible but also opened the presidential election process to partisan exploitation and abuse. Both major parties distinguished between their presidential and vice presidential candidates and sought to capture both offices. In 1796, Federalist electors deliberately gave John Adams (their presidential candidate) more votes than Charles Pinckney (their vice presidential candidate) to assure Adams's election, but that enabled Thomas Jefferson (the opposition's presidential candidate) to come in second and win the vice presidency. In 1800 the Republicans gave Jefferson and Aaron Burr the same majority of electoral votes, thus requiring the House of Representatives to choose between them for president. Although the Republicans clearly intended Jefferson to be president, the lame-duck House was controlled by a Federalist majority, and for two months and thirty-five ballots no House majority was produced for either Jefferson or Burr. The stalemate finally was broken when Alexander Hamilton decided to back Jefferson, who was then chosen with the support of ten of the sixteen state delegations.

Prior to the 1804 election, the Federalists (by then the minority party) threatened to manipulate the election process to the Republicans' disadvantage unless they were, in effect, guaranteed the vice presidency for their presidential candidate. If some Federalist electors were to cast their votes for the Republicans' vice presidential candidate, they could make him the presidential winner in place of the Republicans' presidential candidate. To be sure, the Republicans thus would capture both offices, but only at the cost of reversing their intended order of candidates: their presidential candidate would become vice president and their vice presidential candidate would become president. In exchange for not allocating their votes in this fashion, the Federalists demanded that the Republicans hold back on voting for their vice presidential candidate so that the Federalist presidential contestant would have the second highest number of electoral votes and become vice president. Faced with this blackmail strategy, the Republicans threatened to retaliate by reversing the Federalists' order of candidates. By allocating votes to the opposition's vice presidential candidate, the Republicans could ensure that he, rather than the Federalists' presidential candidate, came in second and won the vice presidency.

If both parties had executed their threats, the result would have upended the constitutional design: candidates of vice presidential (not of presidential) quality would have been president and vice president. These maneuverings provoked bitter quarreling; each party castigated the other for subverting the intent of the Constitution. In truth, the breakdown of the Framers' plan was unavoidable because it was premised on partyless competition. Recognizing the transformation that had been caused by the durable reality of party rivalry, the Republicans quickly secured congressional approval of the Twelfth Amendment, which was ratified promptly by the states to take effect before the 1804 election. This formal revision of the Constitution marked the official end of the Framers' clever attempt to ensure that vice presidents would be of presidential quality.

The Twelfth Amendment and recurrence of the problem. The

Twelfth Amendment reserved the presidential race solely for presidential candidates and set a separate competition for the vice presidency. The double voting device was eliminated; each elector now had a single vote to cast for president and another single vote for vice president. The winning vice presidential candidate, like the victorious presidential contender, had to receive a majority of electoral votes. Should that condition not be met the Senate was empowered to choose between the two vice presidential candidates with the largest number of electoral votes.[6] Finally, the eligibility of vice presidents was stated explicitly: "no person constitutionally ineligible to the office of President shall be eligible to that of the Vice President. . . ."

The Twelfth Amendment thus guaranteed that the presidential election would be won by a presidential and not a vice presidential candidate, but at the cost of institutionalizing the separation of vice presidential from presidential choice. Once this separation was built into the election process, the basic paradox of the vice presidency reappeared: How could an office that was "nothing" in itself nonetheless attract persons worthy to be the initial successor to a vacated presidency? In truth, the American experience has been that vice presidential candidates are not ordinarily selected for their qualifications to become president through succession.

The running mates of presidential nominees typically have been chosen to satisfy the needs of the upcoming campaign, not the postelection needs of governance or successorship. The predominant concerns in the designation of vice presidential candidates have been their anticipated contribution to unifying the party, enlarging its electoral appeal, and meeting other election-related objectives—that is, to ticket balancing. Not surprisingly, then, many vice presidential nominees have been relatively obscure political leaders and the vice presidency generally has remained a thoroughly subordinate office.

To be sure, well-known leaders occasionally have been selected to complete the ticket, as in the recent examples of Lyndon B. Johnson under John F. Kennedy (1960), Hubert H. Humphrey under Johnson (1964), Walter Mondale under Jimmy Carter (1976) and George Bush under Ronald Reagan (1980). Even in these instances, however, the relative influence of ticket balancing and first successorship criteria remains open to argument.

The thin and irregular provision of vice presidents of presidential quality has provoked considerable criticism and many reform proposals over the years. These suggestions typically seek to strengthen the standing, authority, and independence of vice presidential candidates and vice presidents, at the nominating, electing, or governing stages. Although varied in their particulars, the proposals broadly share the critical flaw of pursuing an illusory quest. The dynamics of the American political system allow no viable role for an "alternate president" in addition to the president. This is the systemic reason why, despite the acknowledged need for highly qualified presidential successors, vice presidents have not ordinarily been chosen with that consideration much in mind.[7]

This systemic explanation applies not simply to the vice presidency but to any office whose primary purpose would be to supply presidential-quality successors to a vacated presidency. Relatively few posts merit consideration: on the elective side, the House Speaker and Senate president and, on the appointive side, the cabinet heads and the chief justice of the Supreme Court. (Except for the chief justice, those are the persons who have been designated as contingent successors in the event of a double vacancy.) Whichever post might be picked to replace the vice presidency as first in presidential succession, there is little likelihood that its occupant would be chosen with that function uppermost in mind. And, in truth, when the roster of recent incumbents of these offices is reviewed, not many of them would have been considered at the time of their selection to be of presidential caliber. In sum, placing some office other than the vice presidency at the head of the line of presidential succession would not enhance the prospects for providing leaders of presumed presidential status on a regular and routine basis.

A modern transformation of the vice presidency? In recent years the political standing of the vice presidency appears to be on the increase. The Twenty-fifth Amendment provides for the first time that a vacant vice presidency will be filled, that the vice president has a significant role in the determination of presidential disability, and that a successor vice president (one nominated by the president and confirmed by Congress) has the same status and authority as the initially elected vice president. The vice president's formal authority has been expanded in recent years to include membership on the National Security Council, the National Aeronautics and Space Administration, and the board of the Smithsonian Institution. By

custom and the acquiescence of successive presidents, the vice president has become a member of the cabinet and has an official residence and a sizable staff. Recent presidents have chosen to make
more effective use of their running mates as political and policy
advisers after the election, as in the case of Carter and Mondale and
of Reagan and Bush.

Additional evidence of the enlarging role of vice presidents is provided by changes in the patterns of renomination, consideration for
presidential nomination, and victory in the presidential race. A much
higher proportion of vice presidents have sought and gained renomination in this century than in the nineteenth century. All four elected
vice presidents who have succeeded to the presidency since 1900
easily won presidential nomination in their own right and then went
on to election victory. (This record may say more, however, about the
expanding role of the presidency than of the vice presidency.) In
sharp contrast to the 1800s, nearly all twentieth-century vice presidents seriously pursued and were considered for presidential nomination, the most recent examples being Richard Nixon in 1960 (lost
the election) and in 1968 (won), Humphrey in 1968 (lost), and Mondale
in 1984 (lost). From the start, George Bush was widely considered to
be a major contender for his party's presidential nomination in 1988.

The rising perception of the vice presidency as a base from which
to launch a serious presidential candidacy has contributed significantly to the political attractiveness of the office. Ours is an age
when political careers may be greatly affected by media attention
and name recognition among the public. In this setting, a surefooted
incumbent can use the vice presidency to promote his visibility and
image as a major candidate for presidential nomination. Through
party organizational activities, moreover, the vice president can effectively connect with party and interest group leaders around the country and develop political loyalties and debts from candidates whose
campaigns he has assisted. Heightened public visibility, together with
a national network of friends and potential backers, are valuable
assets to anyone contemplating a run for a party's presidential nomination. The change in the vice presidency from career dead end to
springboard to presidential candidacy is reflected in the greater willingness of major political leaders to accept the second place on the
ticket. Examples include Henry Cabot Lodge and Johnson in 1960,
Edmund Muskie in 1968, and Bush in 1980.

Although these developments plainly have enhanced the standing of the vice president, do they add up to or necessarily presage a transformation of the office, as some commentators have urged? Such a judgment is both overstated and premature because there is no guarantee that these positive developments will last. After all, the fundamental characteristics of the anomalous office of vice president have remained essentially the same, which greatly inhibits the extent to which that office can be transformed.

The fate of the vice presidency remains as firmly as ever in the hands of presidential nominees. Their commitment to balance the ticket in order to win the election continues to thrive. Presidential successorship criteria presumably played a modest role at best in the following instances of recent vice presidential nominations: Truman (1944), John Bricker (1944), Alben Barkley (1948), Nixon (1952), John Sparkman (1952), William Miller (1964), Spiro Agnew (1968), Thomas Eagleton and his replacement Sargent Shriver (1972), Robert Dole (1976), and Geraldine Ferraro (1984).

The striking example of traditional ticket balancing by Ronald Reagan in 1976 merits special mention. As the principal challenger to President Ford's nomination, Reagan estimated shortly before the Republican national convention that he needed only a small number of additional delegate votes to win. In an effort to secure those votes, Reagan announced that his running mate would be Richard Schweiker, a little-known senator from Pennsylvania who was far more liberal than Reagan. He then called on Ford to follow suit by naming his own intended nominee in advance of the convention. Ford declined to do so and went on to defeat Reagan for the nomination.

Although some major leaders have accepted second place on the ticket, others have remained uninterested. Senator Edward Kennedy indicated his lack of interest in the position to Humphrey in 1968 and to McGovern in 1972; Rockefeller did the same to Nixon in 1960, as did Reagan to Ford in 1976. This disinclination to take on the vice presidency reflects generic as well as idiosyncratic considerations. One is that even if the vice presidency now is viewed more positively as a launching pad for a presidential bid, it is but one of several such offices, including senator and governor. Another consideration is that the prominence that comes from being associated in the public mind with a particular president and his administration is a two-edged sword. A vice president who seeks to become the party's standard-bearer cannot readily reject current policies or espouse new policies that are at marked variance from those of the president without inviting party disunity, charges of disloyalty, and adverse public perceptions of his credibility, competence, and trustworthiness. Thus Vice President Humphrey paid a high price for his identification with President Johnson's position on America's war in Vietnam, and for his inability or unwillingness during most of his 1968 presidential campaign to disassociate himself from the president on that issue. In 1984, Mondale had a comparable problem because of the unpopularity of the Carter administration. As one commentator shrewdly observed: "Carter's 1980 defeat is a disaster Mondale must distance himself from, yet he must do so without seeming to be disloyal or denying his own history. Indeed, Mondale wants his vice presidency remembered as much as he wants Jimmy Carter forgotten. It is a tricky balancing act."[8]

Even a vice president in a popular administration may find the greater visibility of the office to be as much a liability as an asset when competing for the presidential nomination. This is a problem Bush had to contend with in preparing for the 1988 election. Chosen as running mate in 1980 because he had been Reagan's leading rival for nomination and a leader of the moderate wing of the Republican party, Bush as vice president demonstrated thorough loyalty to the president and unequivocal support of his policies. As a result, Bush's own ideological identity became blurred and confused, which undermined his standing within the party. Many conservatives, unpersuaded of the genuineness of his seeming change in policy outlook, continued to regard Bush as an outsider while some moderates ceased to view him as a reliable member of their group.

Fundamentally, then, the vice president's dependency on and subordinacy to the president—from nomination to election campaign to the activities of office—have undergone no real change. The increase in the formal authority of the vice presidency has been slight, and in no way alters the president's continued control of the role of the vice president in the administration. President Carter's greater reliance on Mondale and President Reagan's on Bush provide a model that later presidents may or may not choose to emulate. The relationship during the four-year term will continue to turn on the extent to which the president personally trusts the vice president, respects his talents, values his advice, and wants to put him to good use; the operating style of the president and his staff; and how well particular roles and assignments for the vice president fit the administration's political circumstances and needs.

The meaning of the modern vice presidency's increased standing relates more, therefore, to heightened prominence and publicity than to durably expanded power. It remains the case that for a vice president to function significantly in office, the president must desire that to happen and the vice president must take care to operate in the carefully circumscribed role of agent for the president, avoiding any appearance of being an independent political actor. In addition, the practice continues of selecting vice presidential nominees for reasons other than their abilities to be first-rate presidents should succession be required. Without substantial revision of these core characteristics of the office, no transformation of the vice presidency is likely to occur.

Contingent Succession

Over the course of American history nine presidents have failed to complete their term; seven of them departed with more than half the term remaining. In this century there have been fifteen elected presidents covering twenty-two terms of office (four terms for Franklin D. Roosevelt, two terms for Woodrow Wilson, Dwight D. Eisenhower, Nixon, and Reagan, and one term for the others). Five of these presidents were unable to serve their full term: two were assassinated (William McKinley in 1901 and Kennedy in 1963), two died from natural causes (Warren G. Harding in 1923 and Roosevelt in 1945), and one resigned (Nixon in 1974). Since a vacant vice presidency was left unfilled before the adoption of the Twenty-fifth Amendment, that office has been unoccupied a significant portion of the time. Prior to 1967 there was no vice president during part of eight administrations for reasons other than succession (seven died in office and one, John C. Calhoun, resigned) and during part of eight other administrations because of succession. Overall, the office was unoccupied for thirty-seven years, more than 20 percent of the time.

As these data on presidential succession and vice presidential vacancy make clear, luck accounts for the fact that in every instance of an interrupted presidency a vice president was available to succeed to the office for the balance of the four-year term. Every time the elected president was unable to finish his term, it happened that the vice president was available as first successor; and every time the vice presidency was vacant, it happened that the elected or successor president was able to complete the term. Contingent succession extending beyond the vice presidency has never had to be used to fill a vacated presidency and, since the Twenty-fifth Amendment now provides for an appointed successor to a vacant vice presidency, there is little chance that contingent succession will need to be used in the future.

Implementing its constitutional authority under clause 6 of Article II, Section 1, Congress legislated on contingent succession in 1792, 1886, and 1947. Because the 1792 act provided for provisional service and a special election, a contingent successor was not required to give up his regular office to serve temporarily as president. A short successor list was set, consisting of the two formal leaders of Congress: first the Senate president pro tempore, then the House Speaker. This arrangement was completely overturned in 1886, when a cabinet line of succession was established and ordered according to the dates the departments were created, starting with State and Treasury. The two congressional leaders were omitted altogether. The 1886 law also abandoned the requirement of a special presidential election, and instead gave to Congress discretionary power to decide whether and when to call a special election.

The present contingency succession law, enacted in 1947, reinstated the two legislative leaders at the head of the line, but reversed the 1792 sequence by placing the Speaker before the Senate president pro tempore. The cabinet department heads completed the list. Provisional successorship and a special election were rejected. The contingent successor was explicitly directed to serve "until the expiration of the then current presidential term." In such a case, therefore, the Speaker or Senate president pro tempore would be required to resign both his legislative leadership post and his seat in the chamber as a condition of assuming the presidency.

The interplay of politics and principle explains the changes in succession in the three statutes. In 1792, Jefferson was secretary of state and his forces were most powerful in the House; Hamilton was secretary of the treasury and his Federalist party controlled the Senate. The House voted for a cabinet line of succession, beginning with the secretary of state; the Senate chose the two congressional leaders, starting with the Senate head. The 1792 arrangements reflected the victory of the Federalist view.

The revamping of contingent succession in 1886 was sparked by the happenstance that there was neither a Senate president nor a House Speaker when Vice President Chester A. Arthur succeeded to the presidency on President James Garfield's assassination or when Vice President Thomas Hendricks died less than a year after taking office. Once the issue of succession was reopened, considerable opposition to the composition of the 1792 list, not just its brevity, became apparent.

One concern was that, although the Constitution confined Congress in its determination of contingent successors to persons who were "Officers" of the United States (clause 6), it was arguable that a congressional leader was not a national officer within the constitutional meaning of that term. Another principled concern was that the service of a congressional leader as president or as acting president, especially while retaining his legislative post, did not square with the separation of powers doctrine, or with Article I, Section 6, which stated that "No Person holding any Office under the United States shall be a Member of either House during his continuance in Office." A third worry was that when a Senate president pro tempore (or House Speaker) was serving as acting president, the Senate (or House) could replace him by selecting another legislative leader in his place. Furthermore, there was a potential conflict of interest, revealed in the impeachment of President Andrew Johnson in 1868, in having a contingent successor preside over the body whose judgment would determine whether the president would be impeached. Finally, and by no means least, there was concern that the 1792 arrangements could result in the party that was defeated in the last presidential election gaining control of the White House through succession.

The deficiencies that were attributed to the 1792 act led Congress to abandon its succession provisions: the two congressional leaders were excluded and the cabinet heads assigned in their place. This arrangement held until the strong beliefs of a successor president, Truman, led him to propose its revision in 1947. Reflecting his personal view of what American democratic values required, Truman urged that a contingent successor should be an elected rather than an appointed official and, most especially, that it should not be an official who had been nominated to an appointive post by the president. Congress went along with this recommendation, thus reintroducing the top legislative leaders (this time with the Speaker ahead of the Senate president) as the initial contingent successors, followed by the cabinet department heads.[9]

The unexpected and unprecedented events of 1973 and 1974—when in the year following the resignation of Vice President Agnew, President Nixon also resigned—produced the first and only instance of a double vacancy in American history. Had the successorship in that situation been determined by the 1947 act, the House Speaker, Democrat Carl Albert, would have become President.[10] This did not occur because the Twenty-fifth Amendment, adopted only seven years earlier and primarily to settle the question of presidential disability, had a provision bearing on contingent succession. Reversing the practice followed since the Constitution was adopted, the amendment required that a vacated vice presidency be filled by presidential nomination and congressional confirmation, and gave to a successor vice president the same authority as that of an elected vice president, including the status of first successorship to a vacated presidency. Hence, when President Nixon resigned in 1974, the appointed vice president, Gerald Ford, was already in place and ready to assume the presidential office for the balance of the term.

By ensuring that the vice presidency would seldom be unoccupied, the Twenty-fifth Amendment made it almost certain that a vice president would be available to succeed to a vacated presidency.[11] Its practical effect, therefore, was to substitute the new position it created—an appointed vice president—for the House Speaker as first contingent successor. This substitution completed the hold of the vice president, whether elected or appointed, on presidential succession, whether direct or contingent.

Basic Criteria and Their Application

If the basic practices discussed in the preceding section are considered acceptable and not open to serious revision, what criteria should be used to judge the merits of proposed modifications? Several criteria are proposed in this section, then applied to identify defects in current arrangements and to suggest corrective changes.

Same-Party Control in Succession

Presidential succession arrangements should satisfy the criterion of same-party control: a president who is unable to finish the four-year term to which he was elected should be succeeded only by someone of the same party. The emergence and growing appeal of this criterion, it will be recalled, undercut the Framers' original design of the vice president as presidential successor and brought about the institutional changes that are embodied in the Twelfth Amendment. In modern times this criterion has become so well entrenched as to make unthinkable any serious effort to re-create the Framers' plan to secure a successor of presidential quality by awarding the vice presidency to the major defeated presidential candidate.

Same-party control should be maintained in any succession arrangement because of the important connection between governance and popular sovereignty. The American party system, however loose it may be compared to its European counterparts, still serves as the major institution that links the public and the government, structures governance, and subjects the administration of the day to review and criticism. Turning over a vacated presidency to the opposition party not only would violate the integrity of the party system, but also would betray popular sovereignty by overturning the electorate's decision.

In spite of this criterion's importance and widespread support, it has not been incorporated as a required condition in either the constitutional or legislative provisions for successorship. Depending on circumstances, the possibility has always existed that a succession could take place that contradicts the principle of same-party control. This undesirable happening could occur under direct or contingent succession, although it is more likely in the latter case.

The criterion of same-party control is disregarded when first contingent successorship is assigned to the two highest legislative leaders, as Congress did from 1792 to 1885 (Senate president and House Speaker, in that order) and from 1947 to the present (House Speaker, then Senate president). For the period 1821 to 1985, the party of either or both of the legislative leaders differed from that of the president in fifty-eight of the 164 years. (The out party controlled both chambers for thirty years, the House for twenty-four years, and the Senate only for four years.) From 1821 to 1886, the president pro tempore and the president were from different parties for ten years

(15 percent of the time); the vice presidency was vacant in one instance, while Millard Fillmore served as successor president. During the period from the enactment of the current succession statute (1947) to the adoption of the Twenty-fifth Amendment (1967), the Speaker and the president came from different parties for eight of twenty years; the vice presidency was unoccupied in two instances, while Truman completed the balance of Roosevelt's fourth term and Johnson completed Kennedy's term.

The Twenty-fifth Amendment's designation of an appointed vice president as first contingent successor greatly reduces but does not wholly eliminate the possibility of the Speaker succeeding to a vacated presidency. No successor vice president can take office until his nomination has been confirmed by Congress, so the president cannot fill the office temporarily with an acting, interim, or recess appointment. The amendment sets no time limit, once the vice presidency is vacated, for either the president to submit a nominee or for Congress to decide on confirmation. In 1973, Congress took 57 days after receiving the nomination to confirm Ford and, in 1974, 121 days to confirm Rockefeller. Throughout both these periods the Speaker was first in the line of presidential succession.

In working out the terms of the Twenty-fifth Amendment, the Senate considered but rejected a proposal to set a thirty-day limit to fill a vice presidential vacancy or to require that Congress complete its confirmation review and come to a decision immediately. Specifying time limits for action was unwise, it was felt, because nominations would require varying amounts of review, including the need to conduct a thorough investigation of the nominee's background, activities, and record. Any inclination of Congress to exploit an open-ended time period for political advantage would be curbed, it was believed, by the public's expectation that Congress was obligated to finish its confirmation process expeditiously and responsibly.

Although this argument for no time limit has merit, the sounder solution is to specify a generous time limit. An excessively long confirmation process could discredit the integrity of Congress's performance and the legitimacy of its decision. Rather than run the risk of delayed action on confirmation, presidents might choose to confine their nominations to "politically safe" persons who would be expected to arouse little congressional opposition. Similarly, the absence of a time limit provides Congress with an incentive to use the threat of confirmation delay as leverage for influencing the president in the selection of the nominee. (Note, in this regard, the persistent rumors in 1974 that some Democratic legislators wanted to hold off Rockefeller's confirmation beyond early November so that Republican candidates in the midterm elections would be deprived of his campaign efforts on their behalf.) On balance, then, it seems sensible to set an adequate time limit—say, ninety days from the date of the president's nomination—for congressional completion of the review process.[12] If Congress failed to act within that time, the nominee would be considered confirmed and would become vice president.[13]

To be faithful to the standard of same-party control, anyone not of the president's party should be ineligible to succeed to a vacated presidency. Congress should revise the existing succession statute accordingly: the category of legislative leaders should be omitted (as in the 1886 succession law) or, if retained, it should be broadened to include the leader of the minority party in each chamber. Under the latter arrangement, the Speaker and the House minority leader would have equal successorship standing, with eligibility assigned to the one who belonged to the president's party. While a cabinet line of succession is simpler and probably more appealing politically, it could violate the criterion of same-party control if the president had chosen an opposition-party member to be secretary of state. Hence even if contingent succession was confined solely to the heads of cabinet departments, eligibility should still be explicitly conditioned on the successor being of the same party as the president.

Departures from the principle of same-party control also remain at least theoretically possible with respect to the vice president as the direct or as the first contingent successor. A presidential candidate could nominate, subject to the approval of the party convention, a vice presidential nominee from outside the party.[14] Similarly, a president could choose or could be pressured by Congress to fill a vacated vice presidency with someone not of his party.[15] More worrisome, perhaps, are the procedures mandated by the Constitution to resolve an election in which no candidate has secured a majority of electoral votes. Because the House chooses the president and the Senate the vice president, the possibility arises that the two national officials might be from different parties. Admittedly, such situations are unlikely to occur, but prudence suggests the wisdom of planning for the unexpected. (What odds would have been given on the possibility that an appointed president and vice president would be in office during the same term?) The troubling examples noted above can be dealt with by requiring that presidential succession by the vice president take place only when it also satisfies the principle of same-party control.

Presidential Control of Succession

Succession arrangements in the modern era not only have concentrated initial successorship in the vice presidency but also have greatly expanded the president's role in selecting the vice president. In the beginning an incumbent president had no say on successorship because the runner-up presidential candidate was awarded the vice presidency and the contingent successors were legislative leaders. Even after the Twelfth Amendment, which formalized the changed character of the vice presidency, the presidential nominee was only one of many party leaders who participated in the process of designating the second member of the ticket. In recent decades, however, the party's candidate for president has come to play a major, often decisive, role in the selection of the vice presidential nominee. Reflecting and reinforcing this practice, the Twenty-fifth Amendment provides for a presidentially nominated successor vice president.

Congress's decision to empower the president to name a successor vice president recognized the unsoundness of imposing on a president a vice president he neither prefers nor perhaps even wants. As a practical matter, it was acknowledged that the president defined the vice president's role in office and, therefore, that the initiative in selection should come from the president, subject to congressional review. Moreover, if presidential successorship were to occur, the chances of having policy continuity and a smooth transition would be strengthened if the successor president had been the choice of the president.

Assigning the president the major role in designating his successor is desirable because of its fit with the principle of popular sovereignty as well as with the workings of the political system. Succession should be understood as filling not a vacant but a vacated office, not as beginning a new, abbreviated term of office but as completing an interrupted term. The departed president represents the most recent popular verdict on the presidency and his successor, therefore, should be acceptable to him and sensitive to the policy preferences of his administration. In this sense the best way to approximate a special presidential election is to structure succession in a way that makes more probable the successor's continuation of the president's programs. Assuring the president a dominant role in naming his successor promotes that objective, although it plainly cannot guarantee its achievement.

Applying the presidential choice criterion, succession by a congressional leader (whether or not from the president's party) would be disallowed. So, too, would the selection of a vice president by popular election if that process were not dominated by the presidential nominee. As it is, a major party's vice presidential candidate is a junior partner of the standard-bearer, and in effect takes a piggyback ride to victory or defeat in an election that is dominated almost entirely by the presidential race. Requiring the vice presidency to be voted on would set constraints, to be sure, for the presidential nominee in choosing a running mate, but the office is not a genuinely elective one in the customary meaning of that term. This criterion also necessitates the rejection of most of the numerous reforms that have been proposed to strengthen the vice presidency. Although their particulars differ, they share the general objective of promoting the independence and authority of the office by reducing its subordinancy to and dependency on the president.

One proposal to change the way vice presidents are selected is consistent with the criterion of presidential control and, therefore, merits consideration. Building on the innovation introduced by the Twenty-fifth Amendment and its subsequent application in 1973 and 1974, the proposal would amend the Constitution to convert the vice presidency from an elective to an appointive office, to be filled by the same procedure now used to designate a successor vice president. Presidents thus could choose as vice president someone to help meet their postelection governance needs rather than, as at present, someone to promote the chances of election victory. As a consequence, it is likely, although far from certain, that the prior record and standing of appointed vice presidents would be superior, on the average, to that of elected vice presidents.

The proposal's political feasibility, unfortunately, is much lower than its substantive merits. Its chief political vulnerabilities reflect mistaken notions but because these notions are widely held and resistant to change they constitute formidable barriers to adoption of the proposal. One notion (emphasized by Truman in his recommendation to Congress to revise the succession statute) is that for a president to control successorship is repugnant to a democracy. The other (also stressed by Truman) is that presidential successorship offices should be elective, not appointive. If these criticisms were valid, they would dispose of the proposal promptly and negatively.

When these two notions are applied to the presidential successorship role of the vice president, they support succession by a vice president who was elected but not by one who was appointed. The root error in this judgment is to mistake form for substance. In both cases presidential control is predominant but must be exercised in awareness of the confirmatory role of others. For the elective vice president, the presidential nominee's choice must not offend the convention, fellow partisans, or the voting public. For the appointive vice president, the president's choice must not offend Congress, fellow partisans, or the public. Most fundamentally, the special claim that is made for an elected vice president is hollow because, as indicated earlier, the election is more nominal than real. From the standpoint of popular sovereignty, neither the elected nor the appointed vice president is linked directly to the voters. Both are linked, instead, indirectly through the president who selected them and whom the voters elected. It follows that the successorship standing of an appointed vice president should not be sharply distinguished and downgraded from that of an elected vice president. Whether these arguments could counter the opposition's theme that the vice presidency should not be removed from popular selection and control is, however, very doubtful.[16]

Although the criterion of presidential control ordinarily is buttressed by the principle of popular sovereignty, they conflict on one important matter that is easier to resolve in theory than in practice. The Twenty-fifth Amendment sets no closure, other than the time limit of a fixed four-year term of office, on the possibility of a repetitive cycle of appointed vice presidents and presidents. Should such a cycle of appointed vice presidents succeeding to a vacated presidency be limited and, if so, in accordance with what principle? Popular sovereignty, expressed through the election of the president, is the appropriate touchstone for sorting out this issue.

Anyone whom the elected president has picked to be vice president

—whether the elected vice president or a subsequently appointed one—is entitled to succeed to a vacated presidency. The situation is theoretically quite different, however, for a successor president and the successor vice president(s) he appoints. Their relationship to the originally elected president is too distant and attenuated for the successor vice president to claim a right to presidential succession on grounds of popular sovereignty. Applied to the events of 1973–74, this position countenances Ford's succession to the presidency but not Rockefeller's right to succeed Ford.

The rule, then, should be that multiple successions to a vacated vice presidency, but only one succession to a vacated presidency, would be permitted. The cycle of successor vice presidents—or indeed, of any other officials—serving as president would be stopped at the point when the initial successor president was unable to finish the term. A special presidential election at this point would be required to satisfy the logic of the popular sovereignty position. But the authors of the Twenty-fifth Amendment subordinated popular sovereignty to other concerns when they stipulated that multiple succession was preferable to a special election. Their decision for a successor vice president is thoroughly supportable, and accounts for the absence of limits on a possible continuing cycle of appointive presidents and vice presidents.

A Deadlocked Presidential Election

The constitutional provisions for resolving a deadlocked election —one in which no presidential or vice presidential candidate has a majority of electoral votes—raise several problems. Two relate to basic characteristics of the process; the other problems involve smaller or more technical matters.[17]

The main actors in resolving an electoral vote deadlock are national legislators: the House selects the president and the Senate the vice president. One major defect of the procedure is the purely federal basis of House voting—each state delegation has one vote—that resulted from a political compromise at the Constitutional Convention. The obvious remedy is to give greater emphasis to the populistic principle of representation. The House voting base should be changed to "one legislator, one vote" or, if the interests of the smaller states or of senators must be accommodated to secure Senate support for revision, the Senate could be included, with both chambers operating by one vote per legislator.

Another large problem stems from the absence of agreed-upon decision rules to guide legislators in choosing the president. Should a representative vote for the presidential candidate of his party, or for the candidate with the most popular votes in his district, his state, or in the nation? What role should a legislator's political ambitions, conscience, and policy preferences play in deciding how to vote? However the respective merits of these diverse guidelines are assessed, what is disturbing about the current process is that individual legislators remain free to base their votes on whatever considerations they wish. This is not an acceptable context for making a critical choice that, in the eyes of the public, must meet high standards of legitimacy in both appearance and substance. It would be better for Congress to operate by an imperfect but uniform decision rule than by no rule at all.

It is the newly elected House that selects the president from among the three candidates with the highest electoral votes.[18] Voting is by state delegations, with each state having one vote; an evenly decided delegation casts no vote. A secret ballot is required, and the backing of an absolute majority of the delegations (twenty-six of fifty) is needed for a candidate to win.[19] The Senate, including senators who have not completed their six-year term and those, about one-third of the body, who were just elected, chooses one of the two candidates with the most electoral votes as vice president. Each senator has one vote, and a majority vote (fifty-one of one hundred) is required for election.[20]

The initial deadline for House action is January 20, the date of inauguration for the new president and vice president. This leaves about two weeks after Congress officially counts the electoral vote and announces that no presidential or vice presidential candidate has secured the requisite majority of electoral votes. In the event the House is unable to make a presidential choice by January 20, the Twentieth Amendment specifies that the vice president-elect "shall act as President until a President shall have qualified." If the House is able to select a president by the March 4 deadline set by the Twelfth Amendment, he would assume the presidency immediately and the acting president would become vice president.

The separation of presidential and vice presidential selection is troubling for obvious reasons. The electorate's choice is between paired tickets, which is the appropriate basis, one consistent with the criterion of same-party control. The Constitution's arrangements allow divided party control of the presidency and the first succession post and, if no president is selected, require the Senate to choose a vice president without knowing who the president will be. Consideration should be given to correcting this defect by requiring the president and vice president to be designated as a team, by majority vote of both the House and the Senate.

If neither the House nor the Senate makes its selection by inauguration day, the provisions of the 1947 succession act take effect. To become acting president, however, the House Speaker (or the Senate president pro tempore) must relinquish not only his legislative leadership post but his seat in the chamber. Should he not be willing to take on a temporary presidency at that cost, the cabinet line of succession would be used. Note, though, that the only cabinet heads available to become acting president would be the carryovers from the previous administration. Once the Senate selected a vice president, he would immediately displace, of course, any of these contingent successors as acting president.

There needs to be a consistent sequence of subsequent contingent succession whenever the Speaker or someone further down the succession line becomes acting president. With but one exception, this has been accomplished. If the Speaker resigns his House seat and becomes acting president, his replacement as Speaker becomes the new contingent successor next in line. If the president pro tempore becomes acting president because the Speaker declined or failed to qualify for that post, he cannot be supplanted by a new Speaker. If the former president pro tempore dies in office as acting president, contingent successorship goes first to the Speaker, if different from the Speaker at the time the president pro tempore became acting president, and then next to the new president pro tempore. However, whenever a cabinet department head becomes acting president because of the absence of a Speaker and president pro tempore, he may be displaced by a subsequently elected Speaker or president pro tempore. This latter "bumping" provision, unlike the others, is inappropriate and should be eliminated.[21]

The Twenty-fifth Amendment's provision for filling a vacant vice presidency does not apply if an acting president is in office; otherwise, an impossible situation would result. If the vice president-elect was acting president, his designation of anyone but himself as the vice presidential nominee would lead to his transfer of that office to a replacement. If the Speaker (or anyone else further down the contingent succession sequence) was acting president, he would be displaced in the latter role by any newly appointed vice president. And who would the new appointee be? On the one side, congressional confirmation of one of the two candidates who led in the deadlocked popular election would be unlikely because the Senate already had been unable to muster majority support for either of them. On the other, both the acting president and Congress would be reluctant to designate as vice president someone other than the chief rival in the last election. Plainly, then, a temporarily unoccupied vice presidency would be treated as occupied—as in the instance of a vice president serving as acting president during a period of presidential disability—under the conditions of resolving an electoral vote deadlock.

Presidential Inability

The main purpose of the Twenty-fifth Amendment was to handle the problem of presidential inability in office, which had been poorly dealt with in the original Constitution and had remained ever since as a defect in institutional design that required correction. Article II included inability along with other causes of presidential vacancy and stated: "In Case of . . . Inability to discharge the Powers and Duties of the said Office, the Same shall devolve on the Vice President . . ." Whether "the Same" meant just the powers of the presidency or the office itself was a critical ambiguity that could be, and was, interpreted either way.

Acting President, Not President

As earlier discussed, there are good grounds for believing that the Framers intended the vice president's role to be that of an acting president. In the case of the removal, death or resignation of the president, the vice president would serve as president until a special election could be held to choose a new president. In the case of the president's disability, the acting president would return to the vice presidency when the disability ended and the president resumed the presidency. When Vice President Tyler succeeded to the vacated presidency in 1841, however, he established an enduring precedent by claiming the office, with all of its powers, for the remainder of the uncompleted term. Successor presidents followed the Tyler example, and it was explicitly approved by Congress in the 1947 succession law.

Since the first part of clause 6 lumped "inability" in with "removal, death or resignation," rather than differentiating that situation from the others, the Tyler precedent could be held to apply in part to presidential inability as well—that is, a vice president would become president, not acting president, for the period that the original president was unable to perform the powers and duties of his office. No vice president was to put this constitutional question to the test, for fear of appearing to be a usurper of the presidency. (Vice President Thomas Marshall, for example, made no effort to assume leadership during the lengthy period of President Wilson's disability.) In the 1950s and 1960s, prompted initially by the three occasions of President Eisenhower's disability, the president and vice president worked out an agreement providing that the latter would serve as acting president during any period of presidential disability. Entered into between Eisenhower and Nixon, then Kennedy and Johnson, and Johnson and Speaker John McCormack, these agreements had, of course, neither constitutional nor legal standing.

Seen against this background, the Twenty-fifth Amendment provides a clear resolution of the matter. Presidential inability is properly distinguished from the removal, death, or resignation of a president, and the vice president's role is differentiated accordingly. In the case of inability the vice president serves as acting president, and the president returns to office when the period of inability has ended (Sections 3 and 4). When the president has permanently vacated the office, however, "the Vice President shall become President" (Section 1). It is no small accomplishment of the Twenty-fifth Amendment to have put this long-standing problem to rest.

The Pivotal Role of the Vice President

Section 4 of the Twenty-fifth Amendment treats the most difficult category of disability, which is when the president is unwilling or unable to declare inability on his own and, therefore, others must make the determination and the declaration. The vice president and a majority of cabinet department heads, taken together, are authorized to make that declaration, after which the vice president would become acting president. When the president later submits a declaration that his inability has been removed, the same bodies—the vice president (now acting president) and a cabinet majority—may challenge that declaration. If they do, the challenge is referred to Congress, which has twenty-one days to act. Unless more than two-thirds of those present and voting in both chambers vote against the president, he reassumes the presidency and the vice president ceases to be acting president.

Section 4 empowers Congress to set up a body in place of the cabinet, and gives the legislators wide latitude in devising whatever substitute they wish. That is not the case, however, with respect to the vice president's role, which is fixed and not subject to congressional alteration. Without the agreement of the vice president (even if the cabinet was unanimous), no Section 4 declaration of presidential inability can be made and no Section 4 challenge to a president's declaration that the disability is ended can be successful. In sum, the vice president is the most important official in the arrangements set by Section 4.

The vice president's pivotal role in a Section 4 disability is consistent with and provides a partial explanation of Congress's decision to require, for the first time, that a vice presidential vacancy be filled (Section 2). Congress thus approved the power of an appointed vice president, like that of an elected vice president, to serve as acting president or as a successor president (Section 1). This gives added weight to the recommendation made earlier that a time limit be set for congressional action on an appointed vice presidential nomination submitted by the president. In addition, the wisdom of not providing for the disability of a vice president or an acting president should be reconsidered.

The Need to Accustom the Public to Disability Situations

When considering what to do about presidential inability, the traditional worry is how to avoid or contain an aggressively ambitious vice president in collusion with cabinet allies. This is a legitimate concern, but to emphasize it too strongly misdirects attention. Realistically, the major problem is not the possible misuse of the disability procedures but rather the failure to use them when appropriate. The chief difficulty to be dealt with is a reluctance to act, not an eagerness to aggrandize.

Sections 3 and 4 of the Twenty-fifth Amendment increase the likelihood of inaction because they assign the critical roles in disputed disability situations to officials who were selected by the president, who are close to him, and who would be the highest government officers during the takeover period. Anxious to protect the president and to avoid any appearance of usurpation, these officials would be intensely disinclined to push for a declaration of inability that the president was unwilling to make on his own. From this perspective, an outside body would be less disposed to inaction and, therefore, would be a more suitable mechanism. This external body also might be relied on, in place of Congress, to determine whether the president should be supported or opposed if his declaration ending the inability period was challenged.

At bottom, however, the resolution of the disability problem depends less on devising apt mechanisms than on ridding the concept of presidential inability of its profoundly negative connotations. Unless that is accomplished, it is unlikely that either Section 3 or 4 will be used except when there is absolutely no way to escape invoking it. Consider, in support of that judgment, certain events in the Reagan presidency.[22] On March 20, 1981, President Reagan underwent lung surgery to remove a bullet fired by an assassin. Four days later, he had a high fever requiring an examination by bronchoscope, a procedure that necessitated heavy sedation or anesthesia. The leaders of the White House staff—"the president's men"—considered whether the question of presidential inability should be raised for cabinet discussion and decided against it. They reasoned that disclosure of the cabinet's attention to that subject would heighten media and public concern about the president's capacities and health. They also feared that a review of the situation by the cabinet and the vice president might result in their urging the president to declare his temporary inability under Section 3 or, if he was unwilling to do that, in their having to consider whether they were obligated by Section 4 to make such a declaration themselves. In sum, no serious discussion by any officials other than the White House staff took place on the question of Reagan's temporary incapacity.

Neither the thinking of President Reagan's staffers nor their "thwarting" of Sections 3 and 4 should surprise anyone. As long as an announcement of presidential inability is seen primarily as a threat to the stability and strength of the administration and the nation itself, it will be invoked only when such action literally cannot be avoided. It follows that if presidential inability is to be used for anything other than the most extreme situations, efforts to revise its present connotations must be undertaken.

As part of such efforts, presidents should try to routinize the perception of inability by using Section 3 to declare their own disability for short periods of time when they are temporarily ill. To be sure, this strategy runs the risk of trivializing the concept of inability, and hence must be used advisedly. It would promote the understanding, however, that brief periods of presidential inability, in which the vice president serves as acting president, are normal occurrences that pose no threat to the stability of the government. As a side benefit, the stature of the vice president would be enhanced by his highly visible service as acting president.

Admittedly, there is little reason to suppose that future presidents would be willing to follow the strategy here proposed. It seems clear, nonetheless, that the disability arrangements established by the Twenty-fifth Amendment will remain paper solutions for the most part until the idea of disability is defanged.

Death of the Winning Presidential Candidate

Since the presidential and vice presidential candidates who win the November election are not inaugurated until more than two months later, succession provisions are needed in the event either dies during that period. Congress was empowered by the Twentieth Amendment (1933) to set succession arrangements to cover that situation, but it has taken no action to date. As a consequence, some problems exist that deserve solution.

Suppose, to illustrate one such problem, that the November presidential election victor died before the members of the electoral college were able to cast their votes in December. Under the rules of the major parties, the national committee would select a replacement; the Republican rules also allow the committee to call a new convention for that purpose.[23] In making its choice, the party body would be under no legal obligation to make its vice presidential winner the successor; it would be free to choose whom it wants. Since the electors are constitutionally authorized to vote as they wish, no legal problem would be raised by their voting for the person named by the party's national committee.[24]

This arrangement does obvious violence to the norm of popular sovereignty. In theory, a new presidential election should be held, but this would require a lengthy period for the nominating and campaign stages that would extend well beyond the scheduled start of the four-year term in January. The most practical solution, therefore, is to mandate that the vice presidential winner be designated. After his inauguration as president he would fill the vacant vice presidency as directed by the Twenty-fifth Amendment. Congress could accomplish this change by statute, implementing its authority under the Twentieth Amendment. Indeed, even if the present arrangement is left intact, Congress should give it the standing of a law rather than letting it remain merely a party rule.

To take another category of special situations, suppose that the November presidential winner died during the period after the electoral college cast its vote and before Congress officially counted that vote. There are two positions on the question of whether Congress should count electoral votes for a dead candidate.[25] These positions produce very different results and, paradoxically, it is the seemingly weaker one—that Congress should count such votes—that leads to the outcome that is greatly to be preferred.

Consider what follows from the proposition that Congress should refuse or is forbidden to count the electoral votes cast for the deceased presidential winner. The presidential election is deadlocked because no live candidate can have a majority of electoral votes, and, under the Twelfth Amendment, it is then referred to the House for resolution. The House's choice is confined to the three candidates with the most electoral votes. However, since it is almost inconceivable that someone from the deceased candidate's party would place within the ranks of the remaining three contestants, the House's selection could not help but contradict the voters' election decision and violate the standard of same-party control. It would be better, therefore, that the House not choose the president at all. This would allow the vice president-elect to become acting president on January 20 and president on March 4, after which he would submit his nominee for congressional confirmation as vice president.

In contrast, the succession consequences of the alternative position are simple and direct, and they accomplish the desired objective
without the risk of serious pitfalls along the way. If Congress counts
the electoral votes cast for the dead victorious candidate, he would
be declared president-elect and the provisions of the Twentieth
Amendment would become immediately applicable. The vice
president-elect would become president on January 20 and then, in
accordance with the Twenty-fifth Amendment, would designate his
vice president, subject to congressional review and confirmation.
Congress, accordingly, should put an end to the possible confusion
by embodying this position in appropriate legislation.

The third category of special situations arises with the death of
the president-elect after Congress has counted the electoral vote in
early January but before inauguration on January 20. The succession
arrangements that apply in this case are clear, straightforward, and
present no problems. The Twentieth Amendment comes into play,
and the vice president-elect becomes president on inauguration day.
In the event that there is no vice president-elect, the line of succession set by the 1947 act is activated. Once in office, the president
would fulfill the requirement of the Twenty-fifth Amendment by
nominating a successor vice president.

Political Feasibility

Securing revision of the modes of presidential selection that cover
the various special situations will be no easy job. The issue's salience
to Congress is low, and that body's attention to such matters generally has been fitful and brief. Neither the public nor the media has
exhibited much concern and even good-government groups that seek
to improve the political process have not shown interest in the problems in this area. Given the predisposition of the political system to
produce reactive rather than preventive policy, the chances of moving these matters to the front burner appear low.

The relatively few changes that require amending the Constitution are especially handicapped in the effort to gain adoption because
of the difficulty of that process and the disinclination of legislators
to go the amendment route unless the issue is of major importance
and urgent to resolve. Thus, for example, even if Congress were to
agree that the Twenty-fifth Amendment would be improved by set-

ting a time limit for congressional confirmation of a successor vice president, the change would likely not be seen as significant or pressing enough in its own right to warrant a constitutional amendment. This same constraint partially explains Congress's failure to adopt two changes in presidential election procedures that, taken by themselves, do enjoy widespread backing. One change would end the possibility of electors voting for someone other than their party's candidates by legally obligating them to do so or by eliminating the post of elector (while retaining the electoral vote system). The other change would repeal the provision for state voting equality in the House when it must select a president because of a deadlocked election, and substitute a one-vote-per-legislator standard. Since few electors have been "faithless" and no deadlocked election has occurred since 1824, neither problem has been considered sufficiently grave or compelling to merit a constitutional amendment.

There is a deeper reason for congressional inaction on these two changes, aptly stated in the perceptive political maxim that lesser change is the enemy of greater change. Disagreement on the larger issue of what presidential election method is most appropriate has prevented Congress from cleaning up widely recognized deficiencies in the present system. In considering whether to correct those defects, legislators plausibly assume that no more than one constitutional amendment on the subject will be enacted and that its terms will fix the method of presidential election for the indefinite future. In such circumstances, to enact the two moderate changes under discussion would be an implicit rejection of major change, such as direct national election. These constitutional amendments will be ripe for congressional adoption, then, only when two-thirds of each chamber is satisfied that a more extensive revision or replacement of the electoral college system is not called for.

Changes that can be accomplished by statute face, of course, less formidable barriers to enactment. Most of the recommendations advanced in this essay are adoptable by Congress as legislation. For example, Congress has the authority to reconfigure the line of contingent succession to make it fully consistent with the criterion of same-party control. Congress also can mandate that the victorious vice presidential candidate take the place of the presidential winner who dies before the electoral college meets. The difficulty in securing these laws is, as earlier noted, the lack of interest that customarily characterizes this kind of issue.

Recent history suggests how such indifference might, on occasion, be countered. It was Truman's status as a successor president that led him to recommend the alteration of contingent succession, to which Congress responded favorably in part. New interest in the old problem of presidential disability was initially provoked by Eisenhower's several periods of illness, and Senator Birch Bayh later provided the leadership that led to congressional adoption of the Twenty-fifth Amendment. Attention to electoral reform was rekindled by the close elections of 1960, 1968, and 1976, and by the deliberate attempt of third-party candidate George Wallace to deadlock the 1968 election. Again supplying the requisite legislative leadership, Senator Bayh twice led an unsuccessful drive to adopt direct national election of the president, first in 1969–70 and later in 1977–79.

These examples indicate that a triggering event, in combination with committed leaders who propose solutions to what has suddenly become recognized as a genuine and important problem, can overcome inattention and bring about serious congressional consideration of proposals to improve the political process. The same combination could occur with respect to the problems discussed in this chapter.

Notes

3 Changing International Stakes in Presidential Selection

1 *The Economist* 257, November 1, 1980, 19.
2 Quoted in *Time* 60, November 10, 1952, 32–33.
3 *New York Times*, October 26, 1980, pt. 4, p. 5.
4 Ibid., October 31, 1984, A21.
5 Sanford J. Ungar, "The Presidency: Views from Abroad," *TWA Ambassador* 17 (October 1984):75–81. Reporting recent surveys of Japanese public opinion, William Watts comments on the large quantity of media coverage given to American affairs: "Television news programs give such material top billing almost as a matter of course. Radio does the same. The major dailies feature massive coverage of the American scene." *The United States and Japan, A Troubled Partnership* (Cambridge, Mass.: Ballinger, 1984), 97. See, more generally, Barry Rubin, *How Others Report Us*, The Washington Papers, vol. 1, no. 8 (Beverly Hills, Calif.: Sage Publications, 1979).
6 James W. Markham, "Foreign News in the United States and South American Press," *Public Opinion Quarterly* 25 (Summer 1961):249–62.
7 L. J. Martin, "Analysis of Newspaper Coverage of the United States in the Near East, North Africa and South Asia," United States Information Agency, Report R 2-76, January 22, 1976.
8 *Wall Street Journal*, October 31, 1984, 30.
9 Peter Temin, *The Jacksonian Economy* (New York: W. W. Norton, 1969).
10 I argue this point at considerable length in *American Imperialism, A Speculative Essay* (New York: Atheneum, 1968). See also Robert Kelley, *The Transatlantic Persuasion* (New York: Alfred A. Knopf, 1969).
11 See Durand Echeverria, *Mirage in the West, A History of the French Image of American Society to 1815* (Princeton, N.J.: Princeton University Press, 1957); Horst Dippel, *Germany and the American Revolution* (Chapel Hill: University of North Carolina Press, 1977); and David Paul Crook, *American Democracy in English Politics, 1815–1850* (Oxford: Clarendon Press, 1965).

12 See Frederick Merk, *The Oregon Question* (Cambridge, Mass.: Harvard University Press, 1967); Wilbur D. Jones, *The American Problem in British Diplomacy, 1841–1861* (Athens: University of Georgia Press, 1974); Alan Dowty, *The Limits of American Isolation: The United States and the Crimean War* (New York: New York University Press, 1971); David Paul Crook, *The North, the South, and the Powers, 1861–1865* (New York: John Wiley and Sons, 1974); Otto, Graf zu Stolberg-Wernigerode, *Germany and the United States of America during the Era of Bismarck* (Philadelphia: Henry Janssen Foundation, 1937); and Ernest R. May, *Imperial Democracy, The Emergence of the United States as a Great Power* (New York: Harcourt Brace, 1961).

13 See David Fewtrell, *The Soviet Economic Crisis* (London: International Institute for Strategic Studies, 1983).

14 James Bryce, *The American Commonwealth*, 3d ed., vol. 1 (New York: Macmillan, 1907), ch. 8; Aron in *Il Giornale*, quoted in *Christian Science Monitor*, September 15, 1983, 23.

15 *Christian Science Monitor*, July 11, 1980, 3.

16 Ibid., January 31, 1984, 7.

17 Russell W. Howe and Sarah H. Trott, *The Power Peddlers: How Lobbyists Mold America's Foreign Policy* (Garden City, N.Y.: Doubleday, 1977), 6.

18 James N. Rosenau, *National Leadership and Foreign Policy* (Princeton, N.J.: Princeton University Press, 1963) is the basic analytic work. Joan S. Black, "Opinion Leaders: Is Anyone Following?," *Public Opinion Quarterly* (Summer 1982):169–76; and Robert W. Oldeneck and Barbara Ann Bardes, "Mass and Elite Foreign Policy Opinion," *Public Opinion Quarterly* (Fall 1982):368–82, offer amendments and updated guidance to the literature.

19 Ungar, "The Presidency," 76.

20 *Newsweek* 40, November 17, 1952, 44–46.

21 When the government began tracking immigrants in 1908, it found that about one-third did not stay. The available data appear in House Committee on the Judiciary, *Study of Population and Immigration Problems*, 88th Cong., 1st sess., pt. 1–17.

22 The Foreign Agents Registration Act of 1938 made illegal any contributions by or on behalf of "foreign principals" if "the principal purpose . . . is aiding to influence legislation by direct communication with members of Congress." Its applicability to presidential campaign contributions was never raised or tested. On September 30, 1974, in the second session of the 93d Congress, Representative Holtzman proposed HR 16946, forbidding U.S. citizens to contribute to foreign elections. On January 14, 1975, in the first session of the 94th Congress, the Judiciary Committee reported out the bill that ultimately passed. Meanwhile, the Foreign Agents Registration Act had been amended to substitute "foreign national" for "agents of foreign principals." In addition to the *Congressional Record*, see U.S. Department of Justice, *The Foreign Agents Registration Act of 1938 as Amended*, and the *Rules and Regulations* prescribed by the attorney general.

4 Learning to Govern or Learning to Campaign?

1 See Paul Taylor, "Kemp and Gephardt: Image-Building in Iowa," *Washington Post*, March 17, 1986, National Weekly Edition, 6.

2 For convenience, the political head of government in a European parliamentary system is described as the prime minister, although constitutional as well as linguistic differences inevitably produce a variety of titles. For differences between different national political leaders in Europe, see Richard Rose and Ezra Suleiman, eds., *Presidents and Prime Ministers* (Washington, D.C.: American Enterprise Institute, 1980) and Richard Rose, *The Presidency in Comparative Perspective*, University of Strathclyde, Studies in Public Policy, no. 130 (Glasgow, 1984).

3 Richard E. Neustadt, *Presidential Power* (New York: John Wiley, 1960); George C. Edwards III, *Presidential Influence in Congress* (San Francisco: W. H. Freeman, 1980).

4 Jean-Claude Colliard, *Les Régimes Parlementaires Contemporains* (Paris: Presses de la Fondation Nationale des Sciences Politiques, 1978).

5 Richard Rose, "British Government: The Job at the Top," in Rose and Suleiman, *Presidents and Prime Ministers*, table 1.2.

6 See, for example, Martin P. Wattenberg, *The Decline of American Political Parties 1952–1980* (Cambridge, Mass.: Harvard University Press, 1984).

7 Cesare Merlini, ed., *Economic Summits and Western Decision-Making* (New York: St. Martin's Press, 1984); Robert D. Putnam and Nicholas Bayne, *Hanging Together: The Seven-Power Summits* (London: Heinemann, 1984).

8 See Richard Rose, "Can the President Steer the American Economy?" *Journal of Public Policy* 5 no. 2 (1985):267–80, and the books reviewed therein, such as James Pfiffner, ed., *The President and Economic Policy* (Philadelphia: Institute for the Study of Human Issues, 1986).

9 Richard Rose, "The Making of Cabinet Ministers," *British Journal of Political Science* 1 no. 4 (1971):393–414. Experience of ministries does not depoliticize politicians; they continue to practice the arts of political management; see Richard Rose, *Ministers and Ministries: A Functional Analysis* (Oxford, Clarendon Press, forthcoming).

10 Nevil Johnson, *Government in the Federal Republic of Germany: The Executive at Work* (Oxford: Pergamon Press, 1973); Renate Mayntz and Fritz Scharpf, *Policymaking in the German Federal Bureaucracy* (Amsterdam: Elsevier, 1975).

11 Ezra Suleiman, *Politics, Power and Bureaucracy in France* (Princeton, N.J.: Princeton University Press, 1974); J.-L. Bodiguel and J.-L. Quermonne, *La Haute Fonction Publique sous la Ve Republique* (Paris: Presses Universitaires de France, 1983).

12 For an attempt to link popular support with policymaking, see Dennis Simon and Charles Ostrom, "The President and Public Support: A Strategic Perspective," in G. C. Edwards III, S. A. Shull, and N. C. Thomas, eds., *The Presidency and Public Policy Making* (Pittsburgh: University of Pittsburgh Press, 1985), 50–70.

13 George P. Shultz and Kenneth W. Dam, *Economic Policy Beyond the Headlines* (New York: W. W. Norton, 1978), 2.

14 Kristen R. Monroe, *Presidential Popularity and the Economy* (New York: Praeger, 1984).

15 Cf. Nelson Polsby, *Consequences of Party Reform* (New York: Oxford University Press, 1983), and Austin Ranney, "The President and his Party," in A. S. King, ed., *Both Ends of the Avenue* (Washington, D.C.: American Enterprise Institute), 148ff.

16 Carl Baar and Ellen Baar, "Party and Convention Organization and Leadership Selection in Canada and the United States," In D. R. Matthews, ed., *Perspectives on Presidential Selection* (Washington, D.C.: Brookings Institution, 1973), 49–84.

17 Cf. Richard Rose and T. T. Mackie, "Do Parties Persist or Disappear? The Big Trade-off Facing Organizations," in Kay Lawson and Peter Merkl, eds., *When Parties Fail* (Princeton, N.J.: Princeton University Press, forthcoming).

18 That reform was concerned more with the social representativeness of delegates (that is, by race or gender) rather than with the electoral representativeness of the electorate; Austin Ranney, *Curing the Cause of Faction: Party Reform in America* (Berkeley: University of California Press, 1975).

5 The Linkage of Policy to Participation

1 Seymour Martin Lipset cites increased participation in Germany during the 1930s as an example of high voter turnout signaling a breakdown of democratic procedures; Lipset, *Political Man: The Social Bases of Politics* (Garden City, N.Y.: Doubleday, 1960), 32. Similarly, Samuel Huntington views the "democratic surge" that occurred in the United States during the 1960s and 1970s—mass-based, non-voting activities in particular—as a symptom of social conflict that created problems of governance, in "The Democratic Distemper," in Nathan Glazer and Irving Kristol, eds., *The American Commonwealth 1976* (New York: Basic Books, 1976), especially pp. 15 and 37. Others who have argued that political apathy contributes to the political stability of a democratic system include Bernard Berelson, Paul Lazarsfeld, and William McPhee, *Voting* (Chicago: University of Chicago Press, 1954), ch. 14; Henry B. Mayo, *An Introduction to Democratic Theory* (New York: Oxford University Press, 1960), 124; and Gabriel A. Almond and Sidney Verba, *The Civic Culture: Political Attitudes and Democracy in Five Nations* (Princeton, N.J.: Princeton University Press, 1963), 343.

2 Austin Ranney speaks most eloquently for this point of view. See "Nonvoting Is Not a Social Disease," *Public Opinion* 6 (October/November 1983):16–19.

3 Election surveys reveal that the participation of nonvoters would not have reversed final election results because nonvoters, being most susceptible to immediate tides of opinion, favor winning candidates even more than actual voters do. If they were to vote, they would exaggerate the choices of the regular electorate, increasing the winning candidates' majority. This pattern holds for every presidential election since 1952 except 1980. See John R. Petrocik, "Voter Turnout and Electoral Preference: The Anomalous Reagan Elections" (Paper presented at the Thomas P. O'Neill, Jr., Symposium in American Politics, Boston College, Chestnut Hill, Mass., October 3–5, 1985). The size of the active electorate probably exerts a more powerful effect on the final outcomes of sub-presidential elections and presidential primaries.

4   Benjamin Barber, *Strong Democracy: Participatory Politics for a New Age* (Berkeley: University of California Press, 1984).

5   "Agenda for Action" (Summary report of the Harvard-ABC Symposium on American Voter Participation, Washington, D.C., October 1, 1983), 1.

6   George Will, "In Defense of Nonvoting," *Newsweek*, October 10, 1983, 96.

7   Lipset, *Political Man*, 181.

8   One study argues that the views of politically active and inactive citizens are quite different; another questions that conclusion. See Sidney Verba and Norman H. Nie, *Participation in America* (New York: Harper and Row, 1972), ch. 15; Raymond E. Wolfinger and Stephen J. Rosenstone, *Who Votes?* (New Haven: Yale University Press, 1980), 108–14. However murky the evidence, there is less inconsistency between these seemingly contradictory conclusions than may first appear. Neither voters nor nonvoters are homogeneous groups. Because each group contains a diverse collection of individuals, it is difficult to discover a distinctive set of policy views for either group as a whole. Further, since the greatest difference between voters and nonvoters is their social status, the two groups tend to hold different views on policy questions most closely related to social status, and more similar views on other kinds of issues.

9   Verba and Nie, *Participation in America*, ch. 17–19.

10 The material presented here on voter turnout is a revised version of Gary R. Orren and Sidney Verba, "American Voter Participation: The Shape of the Problem" (Paper delivered at the Harvard-ABC Symposium on American Voter Participation, Washington, D.C., September 10–October 2, 1983).

11 Determining the proportion of Americans who vote is not as straightforward as one may expect. Voter turnout estimates differ from source to source depending on whether aliens, overseas military personnel, and institutionalized persons are included in the voting age population. The turnout estimates reported in figure 5.1 were calculated by Walter Dean Burnham. Unlike conventional estimates, which divide by the total voting age population (since 1972, those age eighteen and over), these estimates are based on the voting age citizen population, which excludes aliens and the institutionalized population. Such adjustments yield slightly higher turnout rates. For example, as a percentage of the total voting age population, voter turnout was 52.6 in 1980 and 53.3 in 1984, an increase of 0.7 percent. By comparison, the turnout for the citizen voting age population was 54.3 in 1980 and 55.2 in 1984, a rise of 0.9 percent. I am grateful to Professor Burnham for generously providing his estimates.

12 See Paul Kleppner, *Who Voted? The Dynamics of Voter Turnout, 1870–1980* (New York: Praeger, 1982), 17–19.

13 This decline in voter turnout in presidential elections was mirrored in nonpresidential contests. With the exception of the 1942 wartime vote, turnout in midterm congressional elections steadily increased from 1926 to 1962. It declined from 1966 until 1982, which showed the first increase in sixteen years. Turnout in gubernatorial elections also has declined in these years, as has turnout in municipal elections.

14 According to Burnham's calculations, the lowest turnout in non-Southern states was recorded in 1980 (56.6 percent). The next lowest turnouts came in the two

elections that followed the enfranchisement of women, 1920 (57.3 percent) and
1924 (57.5), and then in the 1984 election (57.8).

15   Most of the data reported in the following pages for population subgroups (blacks,
     whites, women, etc.) were compiled from the Census Bureau's *Current Popula-
     tion Surveys*. Like all surveys, these report an inflated turnout rate. The inflation
     is fairly uniform from year to year: 6.1 percentage points in 1964, 5.5 in 1968, 7.0
     in 1972, 4.2 in 1976, 6.6 in 1980, and 6.6 in 1984. Despite this discrepancy
     between reported and actual votes cast, the census data yield useful comparisons
     among subgroups of the population.

16   The racial gap in voter registration also narrowed in 1984. According to the
     Census Bureau, white registration increased only one percentage point between
     1980 and 1984, while the rate for blacks climbed 6 percent. For young blacks
     (between eighteen and thirty-four) there was a 10 percent increase in registration.

17   Verba and Nie, *Participation in America*, 157; Wolfinger and Rosenstone, *Who
     Votes?*, 90.

18   If persons identified as noncitizens are excluded, the Hispanic turnout rate is 48
     percent, according to the Census Bureau.

19   In fact, except for Alaska, the only states to show an increase in turnout between
     1960 and 1984 were Southern states. This contrast between the South and the
     rest of the nation also is seen in midterm congressional elections since 1962.

20   Harold W. Stanley, "The Political Impact of Electoral Mobilization: The South
     and Universal Suffrage, 1952–1980" (Paper delivered at the annual meeting of
     the American Political Science Association, New York, 1981), 3.

21   The internal dynamics of this shift are interesting. While women age fifty-five
     and over continue to vote at a rate lower than men of that age, women below age
     fifty-five have a higher turnout rate than their male counterparts. Older women
     are typically less educated than women in younger cohorts and were politically
     socialized at a time when politics was considered the province of men. Wolfinger
     and Rosenstone have concluded that "nearly all the difference in turnout between
     older men and women is due to other demographic variables" and "generational
     differences in political socialization." Presumably, as this older cohort of women
     moves out of the population, turnout differences between men and women over
     fifty-five will diminish if not disappear altogether. See Wolfinger and Rosenstone,
     Who Votes?, 42–43.

22   Richard W. Boyd, "Decline of U.S. Voter Turnout: Structural Explanations," *Amer-
     ican Politics Quarterly* 9 (April 1981):133; and Stephen D. Schaffer, "A Multivari-
     ate Explanation of Decreasing Turnout in Presidential Elections, 1960–76," *Amer-
     ican Journal of Political Science* 25 (February 1981):79.

23   David Glass, Peverill Squire, and Raymond Wolfinger, "Voter Turnout: An Inter-
     national Comparison," *Public Opinion* 6 (December/January 1984):49–55.

24   Sidney Verba, Norman Nie and Jae-on Kim, *Participation and Political Equality:
     A Seven-Nation Comparison* (Cambridge: Cambridge University Press, 1978), 75.
     A recent study based on survey data from twenty democracies adds support to
     this conclusion. It reports that socioeconomic status has far greater predictive
     value. G. Bingham Powell, Jr., "American Voter Turnout in Comparative Per-
     spective" (Paper presented at a conference on "Where Have All the Voters Gone?,"

University of Chicago, April 26–28, 1984), 23–27.

25 Verba and Nie, *Participation in America*, 79–80. The remaining 7 percent were unclassifiable according to their typology.

26 Angus Campbell, Philip Converse, Warren Miller, and Donald Stokes, *The American Voter* (New York: John Wiley and Sons, 1964), 50.

27 Samuel Barnes, et al., *Political Action* (Beverly Hills, Calif.: Sage Publications, 1979); Verba, Nie, and Kim, *Participation and Political Equality*, 58–59; and Powell, "American Voter Turnout," 4–5.

28 See Richard Brody, "The Puzzle of Political Participation in America," in Anthony King, ed., *The New Political System* (Washington, D.C.: American Enterprise Institute, 1978), 318.

29 Rosita Maria Thomas, "Public Funding Through the Federal Income Tax Check-Off Option," in Campaign Finance Study Group, *Financing Presidential Campaigns: An Examination of the Ongoing Effects of the Federal Campaign Laws Upon the Conduct of Presidential Campaigns* (Institute of Politics, Kennedy School of Government, Harvard University, January, 1982); Internal Revenue Service, Department of the Treasury, *Annual Report of the Commissioner and Chief Counsel*, September 30, 1984.

30 The number of adults writing letters to public officials increased from 17 percent (1964), to 20 percent (1968), to 27 percent (1972), to 28 percent (1976). Warren E. Miller, Arthur H. Miller, and Edward J. Schneider, *American National Election Studies Data Sourcebook, 1952–1978* (Cambridge, Mass.: Harvard University Press, 1980), 305.

31 Figures from committee reports of the House of Representatives quoted in Michael J. Robinson and Margaret A. Sheehan, *Over the Wire and on TV: CBS and UPI in Campaign '80* (New York: Russell Sage Foundation, 1983), 267.

32 Alexis de Tocqueville, *Democracy in America*, vol. 1 (New York: Alfred A. Knopf, 1945), 198.

33 Allan J. Cigler and Burdett A. Loomis, "The Changing Nature of Interest Group Politics," in Allan J. Cigler and Burdett A. Loomis, eds., *Interest Group Politics* (Washington, D.C.: Congressional Quarterly Press, 1983), 11.

34 Most groups report having used grass roots lobbying efforts and letter writing campaigns—methods that involve the direct participation of individual citizens —more than in previous years. See Ronald J. Hrebenar and Ruth K. Scott, *Interest Group Politics in America* (Englewood Cliffs, N.J.: Prentice-Hall, 1982), 9; Jack L. Walker, "The Origins and Maintenance of Interest Groups in America," *American Political Science Review* 77 (June 1983):390–406; Kay Schlozman and John Tierney, "More of the Same: Washington Pressure Group Activity in a Decade of Change," *Journal of Politics* 45 (May 1983):351–77; Michael Hays, "Interest Groups: Pluralism or Mass Society?," in Cigler and Loomis, *Interest Group Politics*, 113; Public Affairs Research Group, *Public Affairs Offices and Their Functions* (Boston University School of Management, 1981); "PACs: Vital Force in Politics," in *Dollar Politics*, 3d ed. (Washington, D.C.: Congressional Quarterly Press, 1982), 43; 1985 data on PACs from the Federal Election Commission.

35 Verba and Nie, *Participation in America*, 132; Verba, Nie, and Kim, *Political Equality*, ch. 7. One mode of political activity, individual contacting, is not corre-

lated with social status. Higher-status citizens are not more inclined to write letters to public officials than lower-status citizens.

36 Kay L. Schlozman, "What Accent the Heavenly Chorus? Political Equality and the American Pressure System," *Journal of Politics* 46 (November 1984):1006–32.

37 James Q. Wilson, *Political Organizations* (New York: Basic Books, 1973); and David Truman, *The Governmental Process* (New York: Alfred A. Knopf, 1971).

38 Cigler and Loomis, *Interest Group Politics*, 11–20; Schlozman and Tierney, "More of the Same," 368–71; and Walker, "Interest Groups in America," 29–31.

39 A book-length review of the political science literature on the determinants of voter turnout is Lester W. Milbrath and M. L. Goel, *Political Participation: How and Why People Get Involved in Politics* (Chicago: Rand McNally, 1977). A brief summary of that literature appears in Orren and Verba, "American Voter Participation," 13–16.

40 Turnout actually "bottomed out" in 1924, but reached a "normal" level of 60 percent in 1936.

41 Walter Dean Burnham attributes the turnout decline to changes in the party system, in particular to the political realignment of 1894–96, which diffused partisan competition and eroded the links between political parties and social groups. Philip Converse and Jerrold Rusk trace the decline to changes in the way elections were conducted—the introduction of the Australian (secret) ballot, rigid new registration requirements, and deliberately discriminatory barriers such as literacy tests imposed in the South. While it is difficult to say which set of factors was more important, it is clear that both contributed to the decline. Walter Dean Burnham, "The Changing Shape of the American Political Universe," *American Political Science Review* 59 (March 1965):7–28; Philip E. Converse, "Change in the American Electorate," in Angus Campbell and Philip Converse, eds., *The Human Meaning of Social Change* (New York: Russell Sage, 1972); Jerrold G. Rusk, "The Effect of the Australian Ballot on Split-Ticket Voting: 1876–1908," *American Political Science Review* 64 (December 1970):1220–38; and Jerrold G. Rusk, "Comment: The American Electoral Universe: Speculation and Evidence," *American Political Science Review* 68 (September 1974):1028–49.

42 On age see Wolfinger and Rosenstone, *Who Votes?*, 37–60; Richard Boyd, "Decline of Voter Turnout," 133; Schaffer, "Decreasing Turnout," 68–95, especially pp. 79, 90, 92. On civic attitudes see Almond and Verba, *Civic Culture*; Paul R. Abramson and John H. Aldrich, "The Decline of Electoral Participation in America," *American Political Science Review* 76 (September 1982):502–21. On partisanship see Campbell, Converse, Miller, and Stokes, *American Voter*, 5–55; Verba and Nie, *Participation in America*, ch. 12; Abramson and Aldrich; and Verba, Nie, and Kim, *Political Equality*, ch. 8.

43 Compared with other democracies, the American attitudinal environment is quite favorable to citizen participation. It should facilitate, not impair voting. Powell, "American Voter Turnout," 4–5. Glass, Squire, and Wolfinger cite such comparative evidence to show that attitudes cannot be a major explanation for Americans' lower turnout. Glass et al., "Voter Turnout," 49–51.

44 For example, Powell finds in his cross-national study that although American political attitudes and demographic characteristics (with the exception of the age

structure) lead one to expect higher levels of voting in the United States compared to other democracies, institutional factors—the legal context, partisanship, and party organization—inhibit voting here. Powell, "American Voter Turnout," 2–15.

45 There are signs that the nearly two decade decline in public confidence may be
turning up. Arthur Miller, "Is Confidence Rebounding?," *Public Opinion* 6 (June/
July 1983): 16–20.

46 See Nelson W. Polsby, *Consequences of Party Reform* (New York: Oxford University Press, 1983).

47 Wolfinger and Rosenstone, *Who Votes?*, 103.

48 Harvard-ABC "White Paper," 51.

49 Richard Smolka, "Can Sunday Voting Make a Difference?" (Paper presented at
the Harvard-ABC Symposium on American Voter Participation, Washington, D.C.,
September 30–October 2, 1983), 1.

50 "King Holiday Cost Estimated at $7.5b," *Boston Globe*.

51 Two other changes have been proposed to make it easier to vote on election day.
The sheer frequency of elections doubtless depresses turnout. Increasingly, elections for different offices are held on different election days. Therefore, some have
suggested that elections be consolidated on fewer days. Such a reform would
require state-by-state action, and adoption would be difficult. In most states
elections for different offices have been deliberately separated for political reasons, and an effort to reverse this trend would meet stiff resistance. The second
change is voting by mail. A few states, particularly Oregon, have experimented
with this technique in local elections, mostly for school bond issues. Again, such
a reform must be adopted state by state. At least for now, this is not an answer to
the problem of nonvoting in presidential elections.

52 See Paul Weaver, "Captives of Melodrama," *New York Times Sunday Magazine*,
August 29, 1976, 98, 107–11; and Robinson and Sheehan, *Over the Wire*.

53 Michael J. Robinson, "Improving Election Information in the Media" (Presented
at the Harvard-ABC Symposium on American Voter Participation, Washington,
D.C., September 30–October 2, 1983), 1–3. Also see his "Television and American
Politics: 1956–1976," *The Public Interest* (Summer 1977):3–39, which develops
the argument that television has fostered public cynicism and alienation.

54 After the 1960 election, Barry Goldwater introduced legislation to prohibit the
broadcast of presidential returns until midnight. Ironically, four years later one
network declared Lyndon Johnson the victor over Goldwater long before the
California polls closed. In 1972, West Coast polls were open several hours after
two networks projected Nixon the winner. Again legislation was introduced to
curb the early forecasting but none was enacted.

55 Paul Wilson, "Election Night 1980 and the Controversy Over Early Projection,"
in William C. Adams, ed., *Television Coverage of the 1980 Presidential Campaign*
(Norwood, N.J.: Ablex Publishing, 1983), 148–57; Jonathan Friendly, "Exit Polls
of Voters Pose Question of News vs. Effect on Elections," *New York Times*,
December 20, 1983, A22.

56 For example, on the NBC seven o'clock news on Tuesday, April 3: "In New York,
where the polls are still open, Mondale appears to be winning by a decisive

margin. Interviews with voters leaving the polling places indicate that Mondale is the first choice of most groups." Quoted in "Democracy Enlarged; Also Polluted," *New York Times*, April 5, 1984, A22.

57   John E. Jackson, "Election Night Reporting and Voter Turnout," *American Journal of Political Science* 27 (November 1983):615–35. Other studies have found evidence of declines in turnout attributable to network television broadcasts, including: Phillip L. Dubois, "Election Night Projections and Voter Turnout in the West: A Note on the Hazards of Aggregate Data Analysis," *American Politics Quarterly* 11 (July 1983):349–63; Raymond Wolfinger and Peter Linquiti, "Tuning In and Turning Out," *Public Opinion* 4 (February/March 1981):56–60; and Michael X. Delli Carpini, "Scooping the Voters? The Consequences of the Networks' Early Call of the 1980 Presidential Race," *Journal of Politics* 46 (August 1984):866–85. The three latter studies estimate smaller effects than Jackson does, generally in the 2 to 3 percent range.

58   Wilson, "Election Night 1980," 152. Those who have argued that an association between early projections and voter turnout has not yet been clearly established include Laurily Epstein and Gerald Strom, "Election Night Projections and West Coast Turnout," *American Politics Quarterly* 9 (April 1981):479–91, and "Survey Research and Election Night Projections," *Public Opinion* 7 (February/March 1984):48–50; and Percy H. Tannenbaum and Leslie J. Kostrich, *Turned-On TV/Turned-Off Voters* (Beverly Hills, Calif.: Sage Publications, 1983), especially pp. 82–84.

59   The chance that an individual's single vote will affect the final results is miniscule, yet individual citizens receive the benefits of an electoral verdict whether or not they vote. See Anthony Downs, *An Economic Theory of Democracy* (New York: Harper and Row, 1957).

60   Quoted in Albert Cantril, "Election Projections: The Unanswered Question," letter to editor, *New York Times*, December 28, 1983, A22.

61   Federal District Judge Jack Tanner found the Washington state law unconstitutional since exit polling "is not disruptive to peace, order, and decorum and therefore is not subject to regulation" (*Daily Herald v. Munroe*). The state of Washington appealed the ruling to the Ninth Circuit Court of Appeals.

62   There is no evidence yet that early projections have affected the outcomes of presidential elections, although that would be possible, of course, in a close contest. There are signs, however, that turnout depressed by television projections has altered the outcomes of several lower level races, especially in the West. See Delli Carpini, "Scooping the Voters?," 879–80.

63   The material presented here on voter registration is a revised version of Garry R. Orren, "Registration Reform" (Paper delivered at the Harvard-ABC Symposium on American Voter Participation, Washington, D.C., September 30–October 2, 1983).

64   See Orren, "Registration Reform," p. 2 for a categorization of the fifty states according to the length of time between registration deadlines and election day, the availability of absentee registration, and the convenience of registration office hours. Beyond statutory differences, local officials exercise considerable discretion in administering rules, as people who move from one part of a state to another often discover. A study of 251 communities conducted by the League of

Women Voters in 1972 found, for example, that only 29 percent of the communities that could legally employ deputy registrars actually did so. William J. Crotty, "The Franchise: Registration Changes and Voter Registration," in William J. Crotty, ed., *Paths to Political Reform* (Lexington, Mass.: Lexington Books, 1980), 91.

65 In countries with "compulsory" voting systems citizens are bound by law to vote, although in fact, the penalties for shirking on election day are often rather mild. Australia levies a two dollar fine on nonvoters without sound excuses, while Belgium assesses one to three francs for a first offense. In countries with "automatic" systems, the government takes the initiative in compiling voter lists, generally based on existing official records. The West Germans, for example, use police files of names and addresses, and in Sweden voting lists are generated from computerized files the government maintains for other purposes. The "canvassing" systems are less centralized and call for some kind of interaction between voters and officials. Town clerks in the United Kingdom deliver registration forms—by mail and in person—to every household while government-paid "enumerators" in Canada go door-to-door registering eligible voters.

66 See, for example, David Osborne, "Registration Boomerang," *New Republic*, February 25, 1985, 14–16.

67 Campbell, Converse, Miller, and Stokes, *American Voter*, 110–15; Angus Campbell, "Surge and Decline: A Study of Electoral Change," in Angus Campbell, Philip E. Converse, Warren E. Miller, and Donald E. Stokes, eds., *Elections and The Political Order* (New York: John Wiley and Sons, 1966); and Petrocik, "Voter Turnout and Electoral Preference," 6–8.

68 Stanley Kelley, Richard E. Ayres, and William G. Bowen, "Registration and Voting: Putting First Things First," *American Political Science Review* 61 (June 1967):359–79; Jae-On Kim, John R. Petrocik, and Stephen N. Enokson, "Voter Turnout Among the American States: Systemic and Individual Components," *American Political Science Review* 69 (March 1975):107–31; Steven J. Rosenstone and Raymond E. Wolfinger, "The Effects of Registration Laws on Voter Turnout," *American Political Science Review* 72 (March 1978):22–45; John P. Katosh and Michael W. Traugott, "Costs and Values in the Calculus of Voting," *American Journal of Political Science* 26 (May 1982):361–76; and Powell, "American Voter Turnout," 38–43.

69 Richard G. Smolka, *Registering Voters By Mail: The Maryland and New Jersey Experience* (Washington, D.C.: American Enterprise Institute, 1975), 84. Safeguards against fraud exist in each state that permits voters to register by mail, but in practice they are not always scrupulously enforced.

70 Collectively, the eighteen states that adopted mail registration prior to 1976 experienced downturns in voting in the first two presidential elections under the plan. In 1976, these states suffered a 2.1 percentage point decline while the national dropoff was only 1.2 points. In 1980, the figures were 1.4 and 0.4, respectively. Individually, six of the states had increases of more than a percentage point in 1976 while only four did in 1980. Moreover, average turnout from 1972 through 1980 for states with mail registration was only two points higher than states without a mail provision. See *Election Administration Reports*, vol. 7, no. 1, January 5, 1977.

71 After reviewing the available evidence, Robert Erikson concluded that easing registration rules does increase turnout, but that holding registration on election day provides little additional boost to turnout. Robert S. Erikson, "Why Do People Vote? Because They Are Registered," *American Politics Quarterly* 9 (July 1981):259–76.

72 In Canada enrollment costs were about seventy cents per voter for parliamentary elections in the early 1970s. This works out to more than $100 million for the American electorate. See Crotty, *Paths to Political Reform*, 104. On the other hand, the costs of our current registration system are rarely considered in the debate over the cost of changing to universal enrollment. The expense of operating the more than 6,500 current registration offices across the United States obviously must be incorporated into any appraisal of the cost of adopting the new reform.

73 An important question is whether Congress can pass such reforms by statute, or whether a constitutional amendment is required. The Constitution grants to the states the authority to determine who can vote (Article I, Section 2). Consequently, extending the franchise to blacks, women, and youths has required amendments to the Constitution. Authority to determine how voting will be conducted —the "times, places, and manner of holding elections"—is also delegated to the states. However, the Constitution is quite explicit that "Congress may at any time by law make or alter such regulations" (Article I, Section 4). Therefore, Congress has the authority to change registration procedures for federal elections by statute, rather than through the more arduous process of constitutional amendment. This greatly simplifies the adoption of nationwide registration reforms, like those included in the "hybrid" plan.

74 Wolfinger and Rosenstone, *Who Votes?*, 78.

75 Glass, Squire, and Wolfinger, "Voter Turnout," 54.

76 The idea of transferring registration in this way was first suggested by Raymond Wolfinger. For a more detailed discussion of this procedure, see Peverill Squire, Raymond E. Wolfinger, and David P. Glass, "Residential Mobility and Voter Turnout" (Paper presented at the Annual Meeting of the American Political Science Association, New Orleans, August 28–September 1, 1985).

6 Who Vies for President?

1 James Bryce, *The American Commonwealth*, vol. 1 (New York: Macmillan, 1924), 77. (Originally published in 1888.)

2 Alexis de Tocqueville, *Democracy in America*, vol. 1 (New York: Vintage, 1945), 183. (Originally published in 1835.)

3 Steven V. Roberts, "Is It Too Late for a Man of Honesty, High Purpose, and Intelligence to Be Elected President of the United States?" *Esquire* (October 1967), 89ff.

4 Joseph E. Kallenbach, *The American Chief Executive* (New York: Harper and Row, 1966), 156–58.

5 James Madison, *Notes of Debates in the Federal Convention of 1787* (Athens: Ohio University Press, 1966), 425–27.

6 Ibid., 561.

7   This is the version that appears in the Constitution, after "copy editing" by the Committee of Style. The motion of the Committee on Postponed Matters actually read: "No person except a natural born citizen or a citizen of the U.S. at the time of the adoption of this Constitution shall be eligible to the office of President; nor shall any person be elected to that office, who shall be under the age of thirty five years, and who has not been in the whole, at least fourteen years a resident within the U.S." Ibid., 575.

8   Quoted in Charles C. Thach, Jr., *The Creation of the Presidency* (Baltimore: Johns Hopkins University Press, 1969), 137.

9   Ibid.

10   Cyril C. Means, Jr., "Is Presidency Barred to Americans Born Abroad?" *U.S. News and World Report*, December 23, 1955, 28.

11   Ibid.

12   Edward S. Corwin, *The President: Office and Powers*, 4th ed. (New York: New York University Press, 1957), 32.

13   Max Farrand, *The Framing of the Constitution of the United States* (New Haven: Yale University Press, 1913), 78.

14   John P. Roche, "The Electoral College: A Note on American Political Mythology," *Dissent* (Spring 1961):198.

15   For a fuller discussion of the creation of the electoral college and vice presidency, see Erwin C. Hargrove and Michael Nelson, *Presidents, Politics and Policy* (Baltimore: Johns Hopkins University Press, 1984), ch. 2.

16   Clinton Rossiter, ed., *The Federalist Papers* (New York: New American Library, 1961), 391.

17   Quoted in Means, "Is Presidency Barred?," 28.

18   Ibid. The three were Hamilton, McHenry of Maryland, and Butler of South Carolina.

19   Rossiter, *Federalist*, 396, 437–38.

20   The amendment states that "no person constitutionally ineligible to the office of President shall be eligible to that of Vice President of the United States."

21   Corwin, *President*, 32.

22   Ibid., 330.

23   Charles Gordon, "Who Can Be President of the United States: The Unresolved Enigma," *Maryland Law Review* (Winter 1968):1–32.

24   Corwin, *President*, 33.

25   Means, "Is Presidency Barred?," 30.

26   For a discussion of the politics of the Twenty-second Amendment, see Clinton Rossiter, *The American Presidency*, rev. ed. (New York: New American Library, 1960), 221–27.

27   "Who May Run for President: A Proposed Change," *New York Times*, June 30, 1983, 10.

28   Calculated from data in the U.S. Department of Commerce, Bureau of the Census, *Detailed Population Characteristics, Part I: United States Summary*, 1–7.

29   William R. Keech and Donald R. Matthews, *The Party's Choice* (Washington, D.C.: Brookings Institution, 1976), 2.

30   Thomas E. Cronin, *The State of the Presidency*, 2d ed. (Boston: Little, Brown, 1980), 28.

31 Keech and Matthews, *Party's Choice*, ch. 1. My reading of the Gallup records for 1944, 1956, and 1964 led me to revise their figures upward. Polls have been compiled in George H. Gallup, *The Gallup Poll, 1935–1971*, 3 vols. (New York: Random House, 1972); *The Gallup Poll, 1972–1977*, 2 vols. (Wilmington, Del.: Scholarly Resources, 1978); and *The Gallup Poll* annuals (Wilmington, Del.: Scholarly Resources, 1979–1986).

32 Compiled from Vanderbilt Television News Archive, *Television News Index and Abstracts*, a monthly publication of the Vanderbilt University Library (November 1968–August 1980).

33 Of the eighteenth- and nineteenth-century presidents, only James Buchanan, a bachelor, was an exception. All twentieth-century major party nominees were white male Christians. All but Adlai Stevenson were married, and his divorce seems to have hurt him at the polls.

34 Benjamin I. Page and Mark P. Petracca, *The American Presidency* (New York: McGraw-Hill, 1983), 90; Richard Watson and Norman Thomas, *The Politics of the Presidency* (New York: John Wiley, 1983), 115–16. Another possibility for such a list is a small-state residence. Three of the biggest electoral losers of the century were small-staters—Alfred Landon (1936), Barry Goldwater (1964), and George McGovern (1972). Still, no known prejudice against small-state politicians exists (certainly none that is not outweighed by the favored place of Vermonters, Kansans, and the like in popular culture), and the recent nationalization of American politics and media makes the need for a large-state electoral base less compelling than it used to be. Unitarians are included as Christians.

35 Governor Jerry Brown and singer Linda Ronstadt earned the cover of *Newsweek*. See "Ballad of Jerry and Linda" (April 23, 1979), 26. A 1978 Gallup poll discovered that by a margin of 66 percent to 26 percent, Americans would not consider voting for a homosexual for president. (Gallup, *Gallup Poll*, 1978.) Voter tolerance registered 29 percent in 1983—not a statistically significant increase. William G. Blair, "Voters Found Growing More Tolerant in U.S.," *New York Times*, September 1, 1983, 11.

36 Rossiter, *American Presidency*, 193–94.

37 Watson and Thomas, *Politics of Presidency*, 110.

38 Robert L. Peabody, Norman J. Ornstein, and David W. Rohde, "The United States as a Presidential Incubator," *Political Science Quarterly* (Summer 1976):242–43. They define a "contender" as one who receives 10 percent or more of the votes on any national nominating convention ballot.

39 A fuller discussion of these issues can be found in Keech and Matthews, *Party's Choice*, ch. 1.

40 Eve Lubalin and Robert Peabody, "The Making of Presidential Candidates," in Charles W. Dunn, *The Future of the American Presidency* (Morristown, N.J.: General Learning Press, 1975), 27.

41 Ibid., 46–47.

42 Quoted in James Doyle, "Is There a Better Way?," *Newsweek*, June 16, 1980, 24.

43 Joel K. Goldstein, *The Modern American Vice Presidency* (Princeton, N.J.: Princeton University Press, 1982); Paul C. Light, *Vice Presidential Power* (Baltimore: Johns Hopkins University Press, 1983).

44 Gallup data in this paragraph and the next are reported in Blair, "Voters Found

Growing More Tolerant."
45 A confidential random survey of eighty representatives and senators found that 95 percent believed in God (however defined) and 71 percent believed in the divinity of Jesus Christ. Peter L. Benson, "Religion on Capitol Hill," *Psychology Today* (December 1981):47–57.
46 Quoted in Theodore H. White, *The Making of a President 1960* (New York: Pocket Books, 1961), 128–29.
47 White, *Making of a President 1960*, 65.
48 Public opinion surveys on candidate preference also aid in this process, according to Keech and Matthews, *Party's Choice*, 7–9.
49 The federal election law of 1974 limited an individual's contributions to any candidate to $1,000. In the 1976 case of *Buckley* v. *Valeo* the Supreme Court removed the limit on contributions to one's own campaign.
50 Watson and Thomas, *Politics of Presidency*, 103.
51 Joseph A. Schlesinger, *Ambition and Politics* (Chicago: Rand McNally, 1966), 178.
52 William C. Mitchell, "The Ambivalent Social Status of the American Politician," *Western Political Quarterly* (September 1959):683–98.
53 John H. Aldrich, *Before the Convention* (Chicago: University of Chicago Press, 1980), 43–48.
54 Woodrow Wilson, *Constitutional Government in the United States* (New York: Columbia University Press, 1908), 79–80.
55 Aldrich, *Before the Convention*, ch. 2. Aldrich acknowledges that his definition and operationalization of "risk taker" are borrowed from David W. Rohde, "Risk Taking and Progressive Ambition," *American Journal of Political Science* (February 1979):1–26.
56 Harold P. Lasswell, *Power and Personality* (New York: W. W. Norton, 1948); James David Barber, *The Presidential Character* (Englewood Cliffs, N.J.: Prentice-Hall, 1972, 1977), ch. 1.
57 Cronin, *State of Presidency*, 28.
58 Steve Neal, "Our Best and Worst Presidents," *Chicago Tribune Magazine*, January 10, 1982, 9–18.
59 Jeffrey Tulis, "The Two Constitutional Presidencies," in Michael Nelson, ed., *The Presidency and the Political System* (Washington, D.C.: Congressional Quarterly Press, 1984), 59–86.
60 Quoted in John Charles Daly, ed., *Choosing Presidential Candidates: How Good Is the New Way?* (Washington, D.C.: American Enterprise Institute, 1980), 2–3.
61 Quoted in Allen J. Mayer, "Is This Any Way to Pick a President?," *Newsweek*, October 15, 1979, 69.
62 Austin Ranney, *The Federalization of Presidential Primaries* (Washington, D.C.: American Enterprise Institute, 1978), 34.
63 Quoted in "Primaries '80: Once Again the System Worked—Sort of," *New York Times*, June 6, 1980.
64 Bryce, *American Commonwealth*, 79.
65 Michael Nelson, "The Presidential Nominating System: Problems and Prescriptions," in Richard Zeckhauser and Derek Leebaert, eds., *What Role for Govern-*

ment? (Durham, N.C.: Duke University Press, 1983), 34–51.

66 Hargrove and Nelson, *Presidents, Politics, and Policy,* ch. 4.

7 Methods and Actors

1 Nelson Polsby, *Consequences of Party Reform* (New York: Oxford University Press, 1983).

2 Mark J. Wattier, "The Simple Act of Voting in 1980 Democratic Presidential Primaries," *American Politics Quarterly* 11 (July 1983):267–92. The original citation is Stanley Kelley, Jr. and Thad W. Mirer, "The Simple Act of Voting," *American Political Science Review* 68 (June 1974):572–91.

3 Scott Keeter and Cliff Zukin, *Uninformed Choice: The Failure of the New Presidential Nominating System* (New York: Praeger, 1983).

4 J. David Gopoian, "Issue Preferences and Candidate Choice in Presidential Primaries," *American Journal of Political Science* 26 (August 1982):523–46; Keeter and Zukin, *Uninformed Choice.* But, see Paul R. Abramson, John H. Aldrich, and David W. Rohde, *Change and Continuity in the 1984 Elections* (Washington, D.C.: Congressional Quarterly Press, 1986).

5 Walter J. Stone and Alan I. Abramowitz, "Winning May Not Be Everything, But It's More Than We Thought," *American Political Science Review* 77 (December 1983):945–56.

6 John H. Aldrich, *Before the Convention: Strategies and Choices in Presidential Nomination Campaigns* (Chicago: University of Chicago Press, 1980). "Momentum" is taken to mean the "spiral" of success (or of failure). That is, it captures the dynamic of electoral success leading to increased media attention and monetary and related contributions, leading to greater popular support and, in turn, greater electoral success (or its opposite counterpart).

7 Stone and Abramowitz, "Winning May Not Be Everything."

8 Aldrich, *Before the Convention.*

9 Paul T. David, Ralph M. Goldman, and Richard C. Bain, *The Politics of National Party Conventions* (Washington, D.C.: Brookings Institution, 1960).

10 Ibid., 137.

11 Joseph Schlesinger, *Ambition and Politics: Political Careers in the United States* (Chicago: Rand McNally, 1966).

12 Ibid.

13 See for instance, Robert L. Peabody, Norman J. Ornstein, and David W. Rohde, "The United States Senate as a Presidential Incubator: Many Are Called but Few Are Chosen," *Political Science Quarterly* 91 (Summer 1976):237–58; Robert L. Peabody and Eve Lubalin, "The Making of Presidential Candidates," reprinted in Lengle and Shafer, eds., *Presidential Politics* (New York: St. Martin's Press, 1980); Aldrich, *Before the Convention;* Abramson, Aldrich, and Rohde, *Change and Continuity.*

14 Schlesinger, *Ambition and Politics.*

15 Gordon Black, "A Theory of Political Ambition: Career Choices and the Role of Structural Incentives," *American Political Science Review* 66 (March 1972): 144–59; David W. Rohde, "Risk-Bearing and Progressive Ambition: The Case of

Members of the United States House of Representatives," *American Journal of Political Science* 23 (February 1979):1–26; Abramson, Aldrich, and Rohde, *Change and Continuity.*

16 See, in particular, Peabody, Ornstein, and Rohde, "The Senate as Presidential Incubator." See also Barbara Hinckley, Richard Hofstetter, and John Kessel, "Information and the Vote: A Comparative Election Study," *American Politics Quarterly* 2 (April 1974):131–58.

17 Aldrich, *Before the Convention*; James W. Davis, *National Conventions in an Age of Party Reform* (Westport, Conn.: Greenwood Press, 1983); Abramson, Aldrich, and Rohde, *Change and Continuity.*

18 James Beniger, "Winning the Presidential Nomination: National Polls and State Primary Elections, 1936–1972," *Public Opinion Quarterly* 40 (Spring 1976):22–38.

19 David, *National Conventions.*

20 Donald S. Collat, Stanley Kelly, Jr., and Ronald Rogowski, "The End Game in Presidential Nominations," *American Political Science Review* 75 (June 1981): 427–35.

21 These arguments are made more generally in Gerald Pomper, *Nominating the President* (Evanston, Ill.: Northwestern University Press, 1963); William G. Carleton, "The Revolution in the Presidential Nominating Convention," *Political Science Quarterly* 72 (June 1957):224–40.

22 See Aldrich, *Before the Convention.*

23 Theodore H. White, *America in Search of Itself: The Making of the President, 1956–1980* (New York: Harper and Row, 1982).

24 John Rhodes, for example, would pass the David, et al. test for inclusion in the 1968 Republican list. David, Goldman, and Bain, *The Politics of National Party Conventions.*

25 These data come from Mark J. Wattier, "The Simple Act of Voting in 1980 Democratic Presidential Primaries," *American Political Quarterly* 11 (July 1983):267–92.

26 These involved some judgments based on the short biographies in *Dictionary of American Biography* (New York: Charles Scribner's Sons, 1972, 1980), various issues; *Current Biography Yearbook* (New York: H. W. Wilson), various years, 1940–present.

27 See, for example, David, Goldman, and Bain, *The Politics of National Party Conventions.*

28 The terminology comes from Peabody, Ornstein, and Rohde, "The Senate as Presidential Incubator."

29 Walter Dean Burnham, *Critical Elections and the Mainsprings of American Politics* (New York: W. W. Norton, 1970).

30 This table is adapted from David, *National Conventions.*

31 Robert E. DiClerico and Eric M. Uslaner. *Few are Chosen: Problems in Presidential Selection* (New York: McGraw-Hill, 1984), 179–84.

32 Polsby, *Consequences of Party Reform.*

8 Public Opinion Polling

1   David Burnham, "Reagan's Campaign Adds Strategy Role to Use of Computer," *New York Times*, April 23, 1984, B7.
2   Larry J. Sabato, *The Rise of Political Consultants: New Ways of Winning Elections* (New York: Basic Books, 1981), 81.
3   Charles W. Roll, Jr. and Albert H. Cantril, *Polls: Their Use and Misuse in Politics* (New York: Basic Books, 1972), 10.
4   Ibid., 11.
5   Sabato, *The Rise of Political Consultants*, 112–13.
6   Stanley Kelley, Jr., *Professional Public Relations and Political Power* (Baltimore: Johns Hopkins University Press, 1956), 160–69, 189–201.
7   Louis Harris, "Polls and Politics in the United States," *Public Opinion Quarterly* 27, no. 1 (Spring 1963):3.
8   Theodore H. White, *The Making of the President 1960* (New York: Atheneum, 1961), 101.
9   Ibid., 51.
10 Thomas W. Benham, "Polling for a Presidential Candidate: Some Observations on the 1964 Campaign," *Public Opinion Quarterly* 29, no. 2 (Summer 1965):189.
11 Bruce E. Altschuler, *Keeping a Finger on the Public Pulse: Private Polling and Presidential Elections* (Westport, Conn.: Greenwood, 1982), 30.
12 Joe McGinniss, *The Selling of the President 1968* (New York: Trident, 1969).
13 Ibid., 76–78.
14 Gary Hart, *Right from the Start: A Chronicle of the McGovern Campaign* (New York: Quadrangle, 1973), 91.
15 Altschuler, *Keeping a Finger on the Public Pulse*, 119–20.
16 Sabato, *The Rise of Political Consultants*, 91.
17 Everett C. Ladd and G. Donald Ferree, "Were the Pollsters Really Wrong?" *Public Opinion* 3, no. 6 (December/January 1981):13.
18 Richard Wirthlin, Vincent Breglio, and Richard Beal, "Campaign Chronicle," *Public Opinion* 4, no. 1 (February/March 1981):43–44.
19 David Rosenbaum, "Mondale is Using New Polling Method," *New York Times*, April 4, 1984, B7.
20 Robert J. Giuffra, Jr., *The Best Campaign Money Could Buy: The 1982 New York Governor's Race* (Unpublished undergraduate thesis, Woodrow Wilson School, Princeton University, 1983), pp. 263–67.
21 Burnham, "Reagan's Campaign Adds Strategy Role to Use of Computer," B7.
22 Ibid.
23 Sabato, *The Rise of Political Consultants*, 91.
24 Ibid., 77.
25 Ibid., 83.
26 William J. Vanden Heuvel and Milton Gwirtzman, *On His Own: Robert F. Kennedy, 1964–1968* (Garden City, N.Y.: Doubleday, 1970), 291.
27 Altschuler, *Keeping a Finger on the Public Pulse*, 91.
28 Eugene McCarthy, *The Year of the People* (Garden City, N.Y.: Doubleday, 1969), 63.
29 David Chagall, *The New Kingmakers* (New York: Harcourt Brace Jovanovich,

1981), 135, 142.

30 Robert Lindsey, "Dark Horse from California," *New York Times Magazine*, December 4, 1983, 3.

31 Roll and Cantril, *Polls*, 23.

32 Altschuler, *Keeping a Finger on the Public Pulse*, 44.

33 Sabato, *The Rise of Political Consultants*, 83.

34 Roll and Cantril, *Polls*, 23–24.

35 Harris, "Polls and Politics in the United States," 5.

36 Robert Agranoff, *The Management of Election Campaigns* (Boston: Holbrook, 1976), 34.

37 Ibid.

38 Benham, "Polling for a Presidential Candidate," 189–91.

39 Sabato, *The Rise of Political Consultants*, 89.

40 Jeff Greenfield, *Playing to Win: An Insider's Guide to Politics* (New York: Simon and Schuster, 1980), 103.

41 Ibid.

42 Elmer E. Schattschneider, *The Semisovereign People: A Realist's View of Democracy in America* (Hinsdale, Ill.: Dryden, 1975), 66.

43 Altschuler, *Keeping a Finger on the Public Pulse*, 171.

44 Harris, "Polls and Politics in the United States," 5.

45 Altschuler, *Keeping a Finger on the Public Pulse*, 95.

46 Ibid., 127.

47 Sabato, *The Rise of Political Consultants*, 91.

48 Altschuler, *Keeping a Finger on the Public Pulse*, 174.

49 Ibid., 172.

50 Sabato, *The Rise of Political Consultants*, 92.

51 Roll and Cantril, *Polls*, 61.

52 Sabato, *The Rise of Political Consultants*, 173.

53 Ibid.

54 Kelley, *Professional Public Relations and Political Power*, 188.

55 Chagall, *The New Kingmakers*, 171.

56 Ibid., 217.

57 Harris, "Polls and Politics in the United States," 3.

58 Hart, *Right from the Start*, 169–70.

59 Theodore H. White, *The Making of the President 1972* (New York: Atheneum, 1973), 146.

60 Altschuler, *Keeping a Finger on the Public Pulse*, 175.

61 Chagall, *The New Kingmakers*, 183–84.

62 Wirthlin, Breglio, and Beal, "Campaign Chronicle," 44–45.

63 Ibid., 47.

64 Stephen J. Wayne, *The Road to the White House: The Politics of Presidential Elections*, 2d ed. (New York: St. Martin's Press, 1983), 110.

65 Altschuler, *Keeping a Finger on the Public Pulse*, 73–74.

66 Kurt Andersen, "A Wild Ride to the End," *Time*, May 28, 1984, 35.

67 Altschuler, *Keeping a Finger on the Public Pulse*, 128.

68 Chagall, *The New Kingmakers*, 192.

69 Ibid., 171–72.
70 Altschuler, *Keeping a Finger on the Public Pulse*, 178.
71 Chagall, *The New Kingmakers*, 90.
72 Ibid., 101.
73 Wirthlin, Breglio, and Beal, "Campaign Chronicle," 48.
74 Chagall, *The New Kingmakers*, 244.
75 Ibid., 244–45.
76 Roll and Cantril, *Polls*, xxv.
77 White, *The Making of the President 1960*, 51.
78 Altschuler, *Keeping a Finger on the Public Pulse*; Chagall, *The New Kingmakers*; Sabato, *The Rise of Political Consultants*.
79 Sabato, *The Rise of Political Consultants*, 320.
80 Roll and Cantril, *Polls*, 152–53.
81 Sabato, *The Rise of Political Consultants*, 321.
82 Roll and Cantril, *Polls*, 136.

9 The Three Campaigns for President

1   Martin Schram, "A Memo to Someone Who Isn't Running Helped Hart Take Off," *Washington Post*, March 19, 1984, National Weekly edition, 10–11.
2   Brian Usher, "The Undoing of Glenn," *Akron Beacon Journal*, March 25, 1984, A1, A8.
3   Schram, "A Memo to Someone," 10–11.
4   FEC *Record* (March 1985), 6.
5   Nelson W. Polsby, *Consequences of Party Reform* (Oxford: Oxford University Press, 1983).
6   James Lengle, *Representation and Presidential Primaries* (Westport, Conn.: Greenwood Press, 1981). Austin Ranney, *Curing the Mischief of Faction* (Berkeley: University of California Press, 1975). Commission on Presidential Nomination and Party Structure (Morley Winograd, chair), *Openness, Participation, and Party Building: Reforms for a Stronger Democratic Party* (Washington, D.C.: Democratic National Committee, January 25, 1978).
7   Herbert B. Asher, *Presidential Elections and American Politics*, 3d ed. (Homewood, Ill.: Dorsey Press, 1984), 233–53.
8   Maxwell Glen, "The FEC Celebrates Its 10th Birthday Quietly," *National Journal*, March 16, 1985, 582.
9   Asher, *Presidential Elections*, 190.
10 Herbert E. Alexander, *Financing the 1980 Election* (Lexington, Mass.: D. C. Heath, 1983).
11 Ibid., 329–30.
12 Ibid., 305–6.
13 Herbert E. Alexander, *Financing Politics*, 3d ed. (Washington, D.C.: Congressional Quarterly Press, 1984), 117–18.
14 Alexander, *Financing the 1980 Election*, 146–47.
15 Ibid., 446.
16 Alexander, *Financing Politics*, 118.

17 Maxwell Glen, "Starting a PAC May be Candidates' First Step Down Long Road to 1988," *National Journal*, February 16, 1985, 374–77.

18 Ibid., 375.

19 Elizabeth Drew, *Politics and Money* (New York: Macmillan, 1983), 126.

20 Angelia Herrin, "Presidential Candidates Stretch Spending Ethics," *Akron Beacon Journal*, March 30, 1986, D1, D4.

21 Thomas B. Edsall, "FEC Staff Challenges Bush PAC Plans in Michigan," *Washington Post*, March 5, 1986, A7.

22 FEC *Record* (May 1983), 6.

23 Alexander, *Financing the 1980 Election*, 308.

24 Ibid., 304.

25 Ibid., 310.

26 Ibid., 125–26.

27 FEC *Record* (February 1984), 11.

28 Thomas B. Edsall, "Closing the Money Gap," *Washington Post*, May 20, 1985, National Weekly edition, 14.

29 Thomas B. Edsall, "Democrats Will Use the Hard Sell to Pull in the Soft Money," *Washington Post*, July 23, 1984, National Weekly edition, 13.

30 Herbert E. Alexander, "Making Sense About Dollars in the 1980 Presidential Campaigns," in Michael Malbin, ed., *Money and Politics in the United States* (Chatham, N.J.: Chatham House, 1984), 22.

31 Drew, *Politics and Money*, 126.

32 Ibid., 16.

33 Ibid., 104.

34 Ibid., 104.

35 Ibid., 107.

36 John F. Noble, "PAC Counsel: Soft Money," *Campaigns and Elections* 5 (Summer 1984):44–45.

37 Ibid., 44.

38 Federal Election Commission, *Campaign Guide for Political Party Committees*, 15.

39 Thomas B. Edsall, "A Hard Run at Soft Money," *Washington Post*, December 5, 1983a, National Weekly edition, 13; Thomas B. Edsall, "The Quest for 'Soft Money,'" *Washington Post*, September 10, 1984, National Weekly edition, 15.

40 Edsall, "The Quest for 'Soft Money'," 15.

41 Edsall, "A Hard Run at Soft Money," 13.

42 Edsall, "The Quest for 'Soft Money'," 15.

43 Russ Hodge (Ohio Republican Finance Committee), interview by Herbert B. Asher, 1984.

44 Ronald Brownstein and Maxwell Glen, "Money in the Shadows," *National Journal*, March 15, 1986, 632–37.

45 Federal Election Commission, "The FEC and the Federal Campaign Finance Law," (Washington, D.C.: U.S. Government Printing Office).

46 Ibid., p. 4.

47 Jo Freeman, "Political Party Expenditures Under the Federal Election Campaign Act: Anomalies and Unfinished Business" (Paper presented at the Annual Meet-

ing of The American Political Science Association, Chicago, September 1–4, 1983).

48 Drew, *Politics and Money.*
49 Ibid.
50 Ibid., 186.
51 Ibid., 138.
52 Alexander, *Financing the 1980 Election*, 145.
53 Ibid., 144–45.
54 Ibid., 168.
55 Ibid., 168.
56 David Hoffman, "Mondale Slow to Realize Political Danger Delegate Panels Posed," *Washington Post*, May 1, 1984, A6.
57 George Lardner, Jr. and David Hoffman, "Mondale Groups Show Pattern of Coordination," *Washington Post*, April 25, 1984, A1.
58 Ibid., A1.
59 Thomas B. Edsall, "'Delegate Committees' Boost Mondale Funds," *Washington Post*, March 29, 1985, A1.
60 Robert Pear, "Delegate Groups Continue Despite Mondale's Pledge," *New York Times*, May 28, 1984, 1.
61 Herbert E. Alexander, "FEC Update: When Should the Watchdog Bite?" *Campaigns & Elections* 5 (Winter 1985):33.
62 Ibid., 34.
63 Alexander, *Financing Politics*, 129.

10 Regulating Campaign Finances

1 In 1907 the Tillman Act prohibited corporate contributions following the 1904 election of Theodore Roosevelt when the Republican party raised millions of dollars by systematically assessing corporations around the country. In 1910, Congress passed a "Publicity Bill" that required public disclosure of contributions in reports filed by campaign treasurers to the clerk of the House of Representatives. In 1911 both senators and representatives were required to file reports, although a major loophole in the law required the reports only of campaign committees, thereby allowing any number of separate committees to spring up and spend without filing. The 1911 legislation also set limits on contributions and expenditures, and extended the period of coverage to preelection publicity, primaries and conventions. George Thayer, *Who Shakes the Money Tree?* (New York: Simon and Schuster, 1973), 54.
2 Herbert Alexander, *Financing Politics* 2d ed. (Washington, D.C.: Congressional Quarterly Press, 1980), 28.
3 Ibid.
4 Ibid., 29–30.
5 Michael J. Malbin, *Parties, Interests Groups and Campaign Finance Laws* (Washington, D.C.: American Enterprise Institute, 1980), 4.
6 Alexander, *Financing Politics*, 31.
7 Ibid., 35; See also Gary C. Jacobson, *Money in Congressional Elections* (New

Haven: Yale University Press, 1980) for a comprehensive analysis of the benefit a financial floor from public financing would give to challengers compared to the marginally less effective role of money for incumbents.

8   Ibid., 35–36.

9   Ibid.

10 Richard Smolka, "The Campaign Law and the Courts," in Michael J. Malbin, ed., *Money and Politics in the United States: Financing Elections in the 1980s* (Chatham, N.J.: Chatham House, 1984), 214–15.

11 Ibid.

12 Drawn from Malbin, *Parties, Interest Groups and Campaign Finance Law*, 5, and Edwin M. Epstein, "Business and Labor Under the Federal Election Campaign Act of 1971," in Malbin, *Money and Politics*, 114.

13 The most controversial decision made by the FEC, known as the SunPac decision, concerned the Sun Oil Company and its right to solicit employees. Against labor's wishes, the FEC allowed a solicitation twice a year through the mails. Jerald S. Howe, Jr., "The Federal Election Commission: The Regulation of Politics and the Politics of Regulation" (unpublished thesis, Woodrow Wilson School of Public and International Affairs, Princeton University, April 12, 1978), 46.

14 Milton Shapp's presidential campaign was found to have received $300,000 in matching funds under fraudulent circumstances. He repaid the FEC out of personal funds after the election. Howe, "The FEC," 56.

15 Federal Election Commission, *Annual Report*, 1982, 47.

16 Susan B. King, Campaign Finance Study Group Report, 1982, 5–22; Gary Orren, "The Nomination Process: Vicissitudes of Candidate Selection," in Michael Nelson, ed., *The Elections of 1984* (Washington, D.C.: Congressional Quarterly Press, 1985), 46–49.

17 FECA, Sec. 441 (b) (A) and (C), Amendments of 1979, Pub. L. No. 96–187.

18 "Financing Presidential Campaigns: An Examination of the Ongoing Effects of the Federal Election Campaign Laws upon the Conduct of Presidential Campaigns" (Research report by the Campaign Finance Study Group to the Committee on Rules and Administration of the United States Senate) (The Institute of Politics, John F. Kennedy School of Government, Harvard University, 1982), F. Christopher Arterton, 3–10.

19 Ibid., 3–16.

20 FECA, 9033 (c) (1) (B).

21 Arterton, Campaign Finance Study Group Report, 1982, pp. 3–14.

22 Susan B. King, "Living with the Act: The View from the Campaigns," Campaign Finance Study Group Report, 1982, 5–17.

23 Kayden, "Report on Campaign Finance: Based on the Experience of the 1976 Presidential Election," 40–41.

24 "FEC Index of Independent Expenditures, 1979–80," November 1981.

25 Kayden, Campaign Finance Study Group Report, 1982, 7-5; "Independent Expenditure Index by Committee/Person Expending," Federal Election Commission, March 1985.

26 "Independent Expenditure Index."

27 "Excerpts From Ruling on Political Spending Curb," *New York Times*, March 19, 1985, A18.

28 Ibid.

29 There is an argument to be made that the rules changes have helped the Democrats in party building by increasing participation, but it is not germaine to this
chapter.

30 The lists are drawn from reports filed by the national committees with the
Federal Election Commission.

31 Elizabeth Drew's book, *Politics and Money: The New Road to Corruption* (New
York: Macmillan, 1983), is the most often cited and broadest statement of the
position that things are bad and getting worse, a view the media is quite consistent in repeating according to Michael Malbin, who cites major stories in *Time*,
Newsweek, *U.S. News and World Report*, the *New Republic*, *Business Week*, the
Washington Post, the *Baltimore Sun*, the *Wall Street Journal*, and the *New Yorker*.
According to Malbin, "It takes a large set of blinders to miss the fact that the
emergence of PACs represents an improvement over what went on before." "Looking Back at the Future of Campaign Finance Reform: Interest Groups and American Elections," in Malbin, *Money and Politics*, 247.

32 Report from The Television Bureau of Advertising, April 1985.

33 Drew, *Politics and Money*, 4–5.

34 "FEC-Releases 18-Month PAC Study," Federal Election Commission, October 26,
1984.

35 Margaret Lawton, Paul Risley, Lorri Staal and Lisa Peterson, "PAC Contributions
to 1984 House and Senate Candidates: January 1, 1983 through November 22,
1984," Congress Watch, January 3, 1985, xerox.

36 "House Incumbents Get 44 Cents of Every Campaign Dollar from PACs in 1984
Election," Common Cause Report, April 12, 1985.

37 Ralph K. Winter, *Campaign Financing and Political Freedom* (Washington, D.C.:
American Enterprise Institute, 1973).

38 Alexander, "Making Sense About Dollars," in Malbin, ed., *Money and Politics*,
31–32.

39 Campaign Finance Study Group Report, 1982.

40 Ibid., 11–14.

41 "FEC Approves Matching Funds for 1984 Presidential Candidates," Press Release,
Federal Election Commission, March 21, 1985.

42 Marver Bernstein, *Regulating Business by Independent Commission* (Princeton,
N.J.: Princeton University Press, 1955), 153.

43 "FEC 1983–84 Independent Expenditure Index."

44 Alexander Heard, *The Costs of Democracy* (Chapel Hill: University of North
Carolina Press, 1960), 471.

45 Carole Pateman, *Participation and Democratic Theory* (Cambridge: Cambridge
University Press, 1970), 1.

11 Presidential Politics and the Myth of Conciliation

1 James D. Barber, *The Pulse of Politics: Electing Presidents in the Media Age*
(New York: W. W. Norton, 1980).

2 Kathleen A. Frankovic, "Public Opinion Trends," in Gerald Pomper et al., *The
Election of 1980: Reports and Interpretations* (Chatham, N.J.: Chatham House,

1981), 113, 115.

3   See James D. Barber, *The Presidential Character: Predicting Performance in the White House*, 3d ed. (Englewood Cliffs, N.J.: Prentice-Hall, 1985).

4   Cf. *The Presidential Character*, ch. 16.

5   See Gerald Pomper et al., *The Election of 1984: Reports and Interpretations* (Chatham, N.J.: Chatham House, 1985).

12   Television and Presidential Politics

1   The imperatives are suggested by the study of the British system by Jay G. Blumler, Michael Gurevitch, and Julian Ives, "The Challenge of Election Broadcasting" (unpublished paper, July 25, 1977).

2   Gerald Pomper, *Elections in America* (New York: Dodd, Mead, 1968), 194.

3   *Letter to Citizens for Reagan* (WCKY-TV), 58 FCC 2d 925, 927 (1976).

4   FCC, *The Law of Political Broadcasting and Cablecasting*, p. 38.

5   *Socialist Labor Party*, 7 FCC 2d 857 (1967).

6   *FCC Letter to Theodore Pearson*, December 8, 1976, which cited as precedents: *Martin Dworkis*, 40 FCC 361 (1962); *Honorable Terry Sanford*, 35 FCC 2d 938 (1972); *Honorable Sam Yorty*, 35 FCC 2d 572 (1972).

7   *Richard B. Kay*, 26 FCC 2d 235 (1970).

8   *DeBerry-Shaw Campaign Committee*, 40 FCC 394 (1964); *Letter to Lester Gold, Esq.*, August 12, 1976.

9   *Aspen Institute*, 55 FCC 2d 697 (1975).

10 *Chisholm v. FCC*, 538 F. 2d 349 (D.C. Cir., 1976).

11 *American Independent Party and Eugene McCarthy*, 62 FCC 2d 4 (1976).

12 *Station KFDX-TV*, 40 FCC 374 (1962).

13 There is a modest amendment to section 315 that would give broadcasters greater flexibility in fulfilling their trustee role. This amendment would increase the number of states in which a presidential candidate would have to be ballot qualified in order to be eligible for "equal opportunities" on national television. At present a candidate must qualify in ten or more states to be considered ballot-qualified in all states. If the minimum was raised to two-thirds of the states, the number of qualified candidates would be lower and, within a party, even smaller. The networks could then arrange programs without much worry about having to include "insignificant" candidates.

14 *Federal Register* 39, no. 139 (July 18, 1974), p. 26387.

15 FCC, *The Law of Political Broadcasting and Cablecasting*, 87–88.

16 Ibid., 8.

17 *In the Matter of Amendment of Part 73 of the Rules*, 8 FCC 2d 721 (1967).

18 *Allen C. Phelps*, 21 FCC 2d 12 (1969).

19 Information on application of Fairness Doctrine was provided the author by an FCC staff attorney, April 1986.

20 Carl Leubsdorf, "The Reporter and the Presidential Candidate," *Annals* (September 1976):6.

21 Timothy Crouse, *The Boys on the Bus* (New York: Ballantine, 1973), 323–24.

22 Walter Lippmann, *Public Opinion* (New York: Free Press, 1965), 221, 226. (First published in 1922.)

23 Paul Weaver, "Is Television News Biased?" *Public Interest* 26 (Winter 1976):69.

24 Paul Lazarsfeld, Bernard Berelson, and Hazel Gaudet, *The People's Choice* (New York: Columbia University Press, 1968), 115–19. (Published originally by Duell, Sloan, and Pearce in 1944.)

25 Thomas Patterson, *Mass Media Election* (New York: Praeger, 1980), 24; for data on 1972 and 1980, respectively, see Thomas E. Patterson and Robert D. McClure, *The Unseeing Eye* (New York: Putnam, 1976), and Michael Robinson and Margaret Sheehan, *Over the Wire and On TV* (New York: Russell Sage Foundation, 1983).

26 Weaver, "Is Television News Biased?," 67–68.

27 Robinson and Sheehan, *Over the Wire and On TV*, 7.

28 Blumler, Gurevitch, and Ives, "The Challenge," 13; Patterson and McClure, *Unseeing Eye*, ch. 8.

29 Pomper, *Elections in America*, 194.

30 Michael Robinson, "The Media in Campaign '84, Part I," in Michael Robinson and Austin Ranney, eds., *The Mass Media in Campaign '84* (Washington, D.C.: American Enterprise Institute, 1985), 17.

31 Benjamin I. Page, *Choices and Echoes in Presidential Elections* (Chicago: University of Chicago Press, 1978), ch. 6.

32 Patterson, *Mass Media Election*, 35.

33 Lippmann, *Public Opinion*, 220.

34 Robinson and Sheehan, *Over the Wire and On TV*, 302.

35 Michael Robinson, "Improving Election Information in the Media" (Paper presented at Voting for Democracy Forum, Washington, D.C., September 1983), 2.

36 Ibid., 3, 7.

37 Patterson, *Mass Media Election*, ch. 8–13.

38 Robinson and Sheehan, *Over the Wire and On TV*, 302.

39 Patterson, *Mass Media Election*, ch. 12; Patterson and McClure, *Unseeing Eye*, ch. 2.

40 There is only one "news" situation for which a change seems warranted, and this requires the action of the FCC or Congress rather than broadcasters. Section 315 does not apply to bona fide news programs, including live and complete coverage of press conferences that deal with significant public issues. The press conferences of presidential candidates seldom deal with significant controversies and consequently do not qualify for the exemption. An exception is a press conference called by an incumbent president running for reelection in order to discuss an important national development. Since these forums often are discretionary, a president could use a press conference primarily to advance his campaign. The exact motives of the president would be impossible to determine and, to discourage abuses, it may be useful in the sixty-day period before the general election to provide the nominee of the other major party with equal time for a response. This policy would be unlikely to discourage a president from calling a press conference when it seemed in the national interest. The situations that call for such broadcasts usually boost a president's standing and would do so even if the major opposing candidate had the right of response.

41 Larry Sabato, *The Rise of Political Consultants*, (New York: Basic Books, 1981), 241.

42 Patterson and McClure, *Unseeing Eye*, 103.

43 Patterson, *Mass Media Election*, 35.

44 Ibid.

45 Other critics have proposed not that televised advertising be banned, but that candidates be provided equal access to it. One proposal is to apply the Fairness Doctrine to provide free time to candidates who could not afford to buy as much time as an opponent. This idea, however, would be difficult to apply in practice because mechanisms for determining whether a candidate could afford to buy time would have to be established. Another proposed solution to equalizing candidates' access to televised political advertising is to make it free. Each of the major party candidates would receive free advertising time, just as they now receive federal funds. However, if it is felt that presidential nominees do not have sufficient resources for their campaigns, the idea of giving them free time seems inherently inferior to a policy of giving them more federal funds. This would allow each candidate to decide whether additional televised advertising or other communication would be the best way to reach voters. Candidates already are assured "reasonable access" and "the lowest unit rate" for their time buys. Within the framework established by these favorable conditions, candidates should be left to decide for themselves what proportion of their campaign resources will be allocated for televised advertising.

46 Patterson and McClure, *Unseeing Eye*, chs. 4, 5.

47 Blumler, Gurevitch, and Ives, "The Challenge of Election Broadcasting," 10.

48 Patterson, *Mass Media Election*, 39–41, 123–24.

49 This principle is suggested by Blumler, Gurevitch, and Ives, "Challenge of Election Broadcasting."

50 A related issue that should be addressed in this process is the matter of participation by candidates other than the two major party nominees. In Europe, broadcast participation is determined by either a party's showing in the previous election or its representation in the national legislature. This criterion is not useful in the United States. Most major independent or third-party candidates in the United States have strength in one election only. A suitable method of determining whether such a candidate would be allowed to participate is a scientific survey of the presidential preferences of a large sample (perhaps ten thousand) of America's potential voters. The survey could be conducted by the Census Bureau in the late summer, after the nominating conventions had concluded.

Any candidate with substantial public support (say, 5 percent or more of the sample) would be eligible to join the major party nominees in the broadcasts. Such candidates would receive time proportionate to their public support, except that no participating candidate would receive less than half the broadcasting time given to a major party nominee. On all broadcasts the major party nominees would appear first. These arrangements largely parallel those in Europe. Only Italy and the Netherlands provide equal time to all qualifying parties; West Germany, Great Britain, France, and Belgium are among those having proportional allocations based on electoral strength.

13 Presidential Selection and Succession in Special Situations

1 For a vigorous exposition of the argument of special presidential elections (and of the abolition of the vice presidency), see Arthur M. Schlesinger, Jr., "On the Presidential Succession," *Political Science Quarterly* 89, no. 3 (Fall 1974).

2 If the device of special presidential elections was adopted, some difficult practical problems would have to be resolved. One problem is how soon to hold the election after the presidential vacancy occurs: a short period reduces the time of public uncertainty and of governance by a transitory caretaker, but a lengthier period is fairer to the political parties and potential candidates. Another severe problem relates to the role of provisional successor. Who should it be? Should he have full authority as acting president? Should he be allowed to run in the special election? If so, how might that affect the conduct of his provisional presidency and the unity of his party? Should the elected successor president serve only for the balance of the vacated term or for a new four-year term? Should the vice president be the provisional successor? If not, should that post be retained, abolished or altered?

3 See, for example, E. S. Corwin, *The President: Office and Powers 1787–1957*, 4th rev. ed. (New York: New York University Press, 1957); Ruth Silva, *Presidential Succession* (Ann Arbor: University of Michigan Press, 1951); and Schlesinger, "On the Presidential Succession."

4 John D. Feerick, *The Twenty-fifth Amendment* (New York: Fordham University Press, 1976), 225, accurately notes that constitutional scholars and members of Congress have disagreed on whether the Constitution empowers Congress to enact a statute that calls for a special presidential election to fill a vacancy. If Congress does have such authority, repeal of parts of the Twenty-fifth Amendment would be required.

5 By the same reasoning, the Twelfth Amendment's formal transformation of the vice presidency should have led to a reconsideration of whether to provide successorship to a vacated vice presidency. It was not until the Twenty-fifth Amendment, however, that such a basic reexamination took place, which resulted in a strongly affirmative decision.

6 The Twelfth Amendment also changed some of the procedures for House selection of the president in the event that no presidential candidate secured an electoral vote majority. The number of leading candidates from whom the House could choose was reduced from five to three, and provision was made for the new vice president to become president if the House had not selected the president by March 4. (The Twentieth Amendment added the earlier deadline of January 20, at which date the vice president would become acting president if the House had not chosen a president.)

7 For a full analysis of the inhospitability of the American political system to "president-like" vice presidents, see my *Unchosen Presidents: The Vice President and Other Frustrations of Presidential Succession* (Berkeley: University of California Press, 1976).

8 David Harris, "Understanding Mondale," *New York Times Magazine*, June 19, 1983, 32.

9   As indicated earlier, Congress turned down President Truman's recommendation for provisional successorship and a special presidential election.

10 It is arguable, however, that Nixon might not have chosen to resign had his successor actually been the House Speaker, rather than the appointed vice president, fellow Republican Gerald Ford. Had he not resigned, Nixon's ability to complete his presidential term would have turned on the willingness of the House to impeach him and of the Senate to convict him of the impeachment charges.

11 The vice presidency will still be unoccupied for the period from the date of vacancy until the postconfirmation date of the appointee's assumption of office.

12 Consideration also should be given to fixing a time limit (perhaps thirty days) for the president to submit a nominee, and to establish comparable procedures to cover the situation of congressional rejection of a nominee and the need for the president to submit another nomination.

13 A technical question would arise if a nomination were submitted close to the midterm elections and both houses of Congress were unable to complete the confirmation process by early January, when the newly elected Congress began its session. Would a nomination approved by the previous House or Senate hold for the new House or Senate?

14 The Whigs in 1840 and the Republicans in 1864 named a Democrat as vice presidential nominee in an effort to increase their voting strength. In the latter instance the Republicans even abandoned their name temporarily—during the Civil War—and became the Union party. In both cases the party won but the president died and the vice president, a member of the opposition party, succeeded to the office. Since then, parties have avoided such strategic risks and have kept their vice presidential nominations within the party.

15 In the only two instances to date of a vice presidential nomination-and-confirmation process (1973 and 1974), neither presidential nor congressional behavior provided grounds for such concerns. One can reasonably expect that a president will nominate a member of his party and that Congress, even when controlled by the opposition party, will honor his right to do so.

16 For a fuller analysis of the proposal for an appointive vice presidency, from which the discussion here has been adapted, see my *Unchosen Presidents*, 90–110.

17 The present essay is not the appropriate place to consider alternative modes of presidential election. For analysis of that subject, see my "Basic Change Aborted: The Failure to Secure Direct Popular Election of the President, 1969–70," in A. P. Sindler, ed., *Policy and Politics in America* (Boston: Little, Brown, 1973), 31–80; and my "Should Direct National Election Replace the Electoral College System?" in A. P. Sindler ed., *American Politics and Public Policy* (Washington, D.C.: Congressional Quarterly Press, 1982), 3–41.

18 The original Constitution provided for House selection of the president (and the vice president) from the five candidates with the most electoral votes. The Twelfth Amendment confined the House to choosing the president from the leading three candidates and the Senate to designating the vice president from the leading two candidates.

19 A quorum requires two-thirds of the state delegations (thirty-four of fifty), but the

presence in the House of just one member of a state's delegation is sufficient to qualify that delegation.

20 Two-thirds of the total number of senators (sixty-seven of one hundred) constitutes a quorum.

21 Feerick, *The Twenty-fifth Amendment*, 26, strongly urges this change.

22 This account is drawn from William Safire, "Ignoring Section 4," *New York Times*, June 6, 1983; Safire's source, acknowledged in his column, is Laurence Barrett, *Gambling with History: Ronald Reagan in the White House* (Garden City, N.Y.: Doubleday, 1983).

23 Each major party would also name a replacement if its presidential nominee died before the November election.

24 The unsettled constitutional question runs in the opposite direction, namely, can electors be bound by statutes, like those adopted in almost half the states, to vote for the national candidates of their party.

25 I am indebted to the following two sources for calling attention to this problem and the opposing arguments: Stephen Fuzesi, Jr., "A Gap in the Succession Laws," *Wall Street Journal*, November 16, 1976; and Walter Berns et al., "After the People Vote: Steps in Choosing the President," American Enterprise Institute, Washington, D.C., 1980, 18–21.

Index

Editors and Contributors

Alexander Heard served as chancellor of Vanderbilt University from 1963 until 1982 and as professor of political science until 1985. He was chairman of President Kennedy's Commission on Campaign Costs in 1961–62 and held several appointments under Presidents Johnson and Nixon. He has been a member of the board of trustees of the Ford Foundation since 1967 and its chairman since 1972, and was a director of TIME Incorporated from 1968 to 1987. He assisted V. O. Key in the writing of *Southern Politics in State and Nation* (Alfred A. Knopf, 1949) and is the author of *The Costs of Democracy* (University of North Carolina Press, 1960), *A Two-Party South?* (University of North Carolina Press, 1952), and other writings.

Michael Nelson is associate professor of political science at Vanderbilt University. A former editor of *The Washington Monthly*, his articles have appeared in the *Journal of Politics, The Public Interest, Saturday Review, The Virginia Quarterly Review, Harvard Business Review, Newsweek,* and *Congress and the Presidency,* among others, and he has won writing awards for his articles on classical music and baseball, including the ASCAP-Deems Taylor Award. He is the author of *The Culture of Bureaucracy* (with Charles Peters, Holt, Rinehart and Winston, 1979), *Presidents, Politics, and Policy* (with Erwin C. Hargrove, Johns Hopkins University Press and Alfred A. Knopf, 1984), *The Presidency and the Political System* (Congressional Quarterly Press, 1984), and *The Elections of 1984* (Congressional Quarterly Press, 1985).

John H. Aldrich is professor of political science at Duke University and the author of *Before the Convention: Strategies and Choices in Presidential Nomination Campaigns* (University of Chicago Press, 1982) and *Change and Continuity in the 1980 Elections* (with Paul R. Abramson and David W. Rohde, Congressional Quarterly Press, 1982).

Herbert Asher is professor of political science at The Ohio State University. He is the author of *Presidential Elections and American Politics: Voters, Candidates, and Campaigns Since 1952* (Dorsey Press, 1976), *Freshman Representatives and the Learning of Voting Cues* (Sage Publications, 1973), and *Theory-Building and Data Analysis in the Social Sciences* (University of Tennessee Press, 1984), among others.

James David Barber is James B. Duke Professor of Political Science at Duke University. He is the author of several books, including *The Lawmakers: Recruitment and Adaptation to Legislative Life* (Yale University Press, 1965), *The Presidential Character: Predicting Performance in the White House* (Prentice-Hall, 1972), and *The Pulse of Politics: Electing Presidents in the Media Age* (W. W. Norton, 1980).

James R. Beniger, assistant professor of sociology at Princeton University, is the author of *Trafficking in Drug Users: Professional Exchange Networks in the Control of Deviance* (Cambridge University Press, 1983) and of several dozen articles in academic books and journals, including the *American Sociological Review*, the *Journal of Social Issues*, and the *Public Opinion Quarterly*. Robert J. Giuffra, Jr., also of Princeton University, shared in the research and writing of this chapter.

Ralf Dahrendorf, formerly director of the London School of Economics and Political Science, is professor at Universitat Konstanz. Among his many books are *Class and Class Conflict in Industrial Society* (Stanford University Press, 1959), *Essays in the Theory of Society* (Stanford University Press, 1968), *Life Chances: Approaches to Social and Political Theory* (University of Chicago Press, 1979), and *On Britain* (University of Chicago Press, 1982).

Xandra Kayden, a writer whose doctorate is in political science, is a member of the Campaign Finance Study Group at Harvard University's Kennedy School of Government. She is the author of *The Party Goes On* (with Eddie Mahe, Jr., Basic Books, 1985).

Ernest May is professor of history at Harvard University and the former dean of Harvard College. He is the author of numerous books, including *Ultimate Reason: The President as Commander-in-Chief* (Brazilier, 1960), *From Imperialism to Isolationism* (Macmillan, 1963), *Lessons of the Past: Use and Misuse of History in American Foreign Policy* (Oxford University Press, 1973), and *The Making of the Monroe Doctrine* (Harvard University Press, 1976).

Gary Orren is associate professor in Harvard University's Kennedy School of Government and a member of its Institute of Politics. Widely experienced in presidential election politics and a contributor to numerous academic books and journals, he is the author of *Democrats vs. Democrats: Party Factions in the 1972 Presidential Primaries* (with William Schneider, Kennedy School, 1977), *Economic and Political Equality: The Attitudes of American Leaders* (Kennedy School, 1983), and *Equality in America: The View From the Top* (with Sidney Verba, Harvard University Press, 1985).

Thomas E. Patterson is professor and chair of political science at the Maxwell School of Citizenship and Public Affairs of Syracuse University. His books include *The Unseeing Eye: The Myth of Television Power in National Politics* (with Robert D. McClure, Putnam, 1976) and *The Mass Media Election: How Americans Choose Their President* (Praeger, 1980).

Richard Rose is director of the Center for the Study of Public Policy at the University of Strathclyde. Among his many books are *Managing Presidential Objectives* (Free

Press, 1976), *Presidents and Prime Ministers* (with Ezra Suleiman, American Enterprise Institute, 1980), *Politics in England: An Interpretation for the 1980s* (Little, Brown, 1980), *Understanding Big Government* (Sage Publications, 1984), and *Public Employment in Western Nations* (Cambridge University Press, forthcoming).

Allan P. Sindler is professor and dean of the Graduate School of Public Policy at the University of California at Berkeley. His books include *American Politics and Public Policy* (Congressional Quarterly Press, 1982) and *Unchosen Presidents: The Vice President and Other Frustrations of Presidential Succession* (University of California Press, 1976), among others.